'DEAR MRS. GRIGGS'

Genevieve G. McBride
&
Stephen R. Byers

'DEAR MRS. GRIGGS'
WOMEN READERS POUR OUT THEIR HEARTS
FROM THE HEARTLAND

MARQUETTE
UNIVERSITY
PRESS

DIEDERICH STUDIES IN MEDIA AND COMMUNICATION

No. 4

BONNIE BRENNEN, SERIES EDITOR

LIBRARY OF CONGRESS CATALOGING-IN-PUBLICATION DATA

McBride, Genevieve G.
'Dear Mrs. Griggs' : women readers pour out their hearts from the heartland / Genevieve G. McBride & Stephen R. Byers.
pages cm. — (Diederich studies in media and communication ; no. 4)
Includes bibliographical references and index.
ISBN 978-0-87462-038-2 (pbk. : alk. paper) — ISBN 0-87462-038-4 (pbk. : alk. paper)
1. Women—Middle West—Social conditions—20th century. 2. Women—Middle West—Social life and customs—20th century. 3. Advice columns—Wisconsin—Milwaukee. 4. Griggs, Ione Quinby. 5. Advice columnists—United States—Biography. I. Byers, Stephen R., 1943- II. Title.
HQ1438.M53M43 2014
305.40977—dc23

2013048692

∞The paper used in this publication meets the minimum requirements of the American National Standard for Information Sciences— Permanence of Paper for Printed Library Materials, ANSI Z39.48-1992.

Association of American University Presses

MARQUETTE UNIVERSITY PRESS
MILWAUKEE

The Association of Jesuit University Presses

Contents

Introduction

Decades before the debut of "Ann Landers" and "Dear Abby" in the mid-1950s, millions of Milwaukeeans and others across Wisconsin and the Midwest already read and relied on an advice column, primarily written by readers, not by the columnist. But her byline on the column, Ione Quinby Griggs, became legendary among advice columnists across the country for more than half a century, six days a week, a record career in the "advice industry." When she began dispensing daily wisdom to readers in distress in the mid-1930s, in the depths of the Depression, "Ann" and "Abby" still were teenagers in small-town Iowa.[1] Indeed, they had been only toddlers when Griggs had been the talk of that "toddlin' town," Chicago, as the song goes. There, Griggs had gained unusual training for an advice columnist, from coverage of women criminals that had made her byline famous on the front page in the "Jazz Age" of Chicago journalism in the 1920s.

Yet she receives no mention in many histories of Chicago's press and merits only minor historical attention in a recent book on the "girl reporters" on the "girl-crime beat" in the city's streets and jail cells in the era.[2] She deserves better, as Ione Quinby was among better-known, bylined, front-page journalists in "bohemian circles" of Chicago writers, who met near the city's "Newspaper Row" and "Bughouse Square," and whose "literary renaissance" in the era reframed American culture in the 1920s. However, her writings differed from those of others, and for many reasons. Most remarkable was her range of reportage. She

---

1   Margalit Fox, "Ann Landers, Advice Giver to the Millions, Is Dead at 83," *New York Times*, June 23, 2002; "Eppie Lederer, 1918-2002: Ann Landers Was a Friend to Millions," *Chicago Tribune*, June 23, 2002.

2   See, for example, Wayne Klatt, *Chicago Journalism: A History* (Jefferson, N.C.: McFarland, 2009); John J. McPhaul, *Deadlines & Monkeyshines: The Fabled World of Chicago Journalism* (New York: Prentice-Hall, 1962); Douglas Perry, *The Girls of Murder City: Fame, Lust, and the Beautiful Killers Who Inspired* Chicago (New York: Viking, 2010).

made her reportorial reputation by telling lurid stories of women of lesser repute, the "murderesses" and mobsters' molls of the notorious 1920s in her city, but she also told the stories of other women then entering politics, business, and other workplaces. All told, the byline of Ione Quinby topped more than a thousand stories in and of her city, most often reportage on women, which put their names as well as hers on the front page. In a word, women made news, because she knew how to reframe their stories as news, as it then was defined— and in doing so, she and other women journalists, reporters as well as columnists, would begin to reframe the definition of news then and for decades to come.

For her readers in the 1920s, Griggs' reportage on many aspects of women's lives served as advice on coping with many changes in urban culture, and nowhere more so than in Chicago, for experience that presaged her next career in a far different city for the next half-century. As a colleague at the *Milwaukee Journal* would recall, after all that Griggs had witnessed in reporting on the crime "beat" and in retelling the tales of homicidal women in her book, *Murder for Love,* "there was no way a former Chicago 'sob sister' could be astonished at anything that happened in Milwaukee."[3] We suspect that she also would not have been surprised by this study of her career, of her advice column, and especially of her readers. We also suspect that their "Dear Mrs. Griggs" would not mind historical attention that this book may bring, not only to her own story but also to her readers' stories, in their own words, of their lives—the lives of women and girls, who comprised most of her column's readers, and to whom she devoted most of her long life.

As with her Chicago years, her Milwaukee years and her advice column for—and, we argue, by and with—her millions of readers for more than five decades also rarely merit mention in many histories of Milwaukee, of media, and of women, nor in the few histories of the "advice industry." In his analysis of the work of "Ann" and "Abby," media historian David Gudelunas argues that "advice columns as a site of research have been largely ignored by journalism scholars interested in 'objective' hard news and media theorists focused on 'texts.'" He calls for treatment of "the actual text of the newspaper advice column

---

3   Robert W. Wells, *The Milwaukee Journal: An Informal Chronicle of Its First 100 Years* (Milwaukee, Wis.: Milwaukee Journal, 1981), 262.

as a serious topic of study."[4] In this study of the "Dear Mrs. Griggs" column, we argue that our rereading of her readers' letters may further historical understanding of their everyday lives, especially the lives of women in a working-class city in the Midwest. They also have been too often neglected by scholars since, owing to their gender, class, and region, and despite their significance in a momentous era in women's history, in media history, and in Midwestern history—indeed, in American history.

In researching and teaching American social history, we determined that we need to know more about her readers, women in a working-class city as well as many others from small towns and farms across the Midwest. In women's history, with work still to be done to tell the stories of famous foremothers, who finally won the right to vote for all women in the country only as Griggs began her career, we need to know more not only about its impact but also about many other matters in the lives of our mothers, grandmothers, and others in the era. Many went into new workplaces for women in the era, as well as to other places to which her workplace in the 1920s sent Griggs "out on assignment" and into the streets, police stations, and jail cells of the major metropolis of the Midwest to report the stories of other, far more infamous women.

We also need to know more about how she and other women coped as the world of work collapsed in the 1930s, in the depths of the Depression, when she created a new career with her column that welcomed their stories of their lives in times of desperation. We need to know more about their lives in wartime in the 1940s, when her women readers went from their homes into new workplaces on the homefront, especially the defense plants and farm fields of the Midwest. We need to know more about the women who then went back home in the postwar "baby boom" of the 1950s—and also about the women who remained in the workplace or soon returned to it to afford their sizeable families, including in new suburbs of Milwaukee, where some wrote letters that reported to Griggs and her readers on sagas of "spiked *kaffeeklatsches*" and other means by which the daughters of the city's "*hausfraus*" adapted to the reality of a new "American dream."

---

4   David Gudelunas, *Confidential to America: Newspaper Advice Columns and Sexual Education* (New Brunswick, N.J.: Transaction Press, 2008), 3-4.

Research also remains to be done to tell the stories in the 1960s of the Midwestern founders of the modern women's movement, many of them from Milwaukee and environs, and the milieu from which others came to feminism by the millions from similar working-class cities. We also need to know more about the next, massive movement of women in the 1970s, onto campuses and into new career fields for women. And we also need to know about many women who were not part of movements and perhaps were resistant to such changes but faced other challenges, owing in part to the impact of another Midwestern woman, who followed in Griggs' footsteps from Illinois to Wisconsin—but Phyllis Schlafly did so to defeat the Equal Rights Amendment, in a harbinger of the "conservative revolution" to come in the country in the 1980s. Then, after more than half a century, the country's longest-lasting advice column came to an end.

All of these women and their stories are part of Griggs' story, and of this study, as their thousands of stories told in their letters to the column live on as her legacy and theirs. We know that in women's history, we learn by looking not only at the conflicts but also at the continuities in their lives, and we especially learn by listening to women speak to us from the past in their own words—as we can do, with their letters to "Dear Mrs. Griggs." Just as the continuities in their lives still resonate for us in reading their letters today, so also do her replies—her "common sense" that still makes sense today. Decades before other advice columnists from the Midwest, "Ann" and "Abby," became known for their "straight talk" from their debut in the 1950s, Griggs had conveyed that regional sensibility in her column. One of her admirers recently wrote of that regionalism. He grew up reading her column in Milwaukee, before he also became a nationally syndicated newspaper columnist, and recalls the influence in her region of "a woman with the unlikely name of Ione Quinby Griggs" who "gave no-nonsense Midwestern counsel."[5] She gave her readers what they wanted, not nonsensical romanticism nor sanctimonious "sermonettes" too typical of previous advice columns by her predecessors in other regions of the country.

Griggs also realized that her readers sought not only "straight talk" from her but also a form of community forum to talk with each

---

5   John Allen Paulos, *A Mathematician Reads the Newspaper* (New York: Anchor Books, 1995), 1.

other—a sort of "sociable media" that, we argue, she created many decades before modern "social media," even before computers. New technologies now make possible instantaneous communication, but the interactivity of "social media" is not new, as evidenced by reader interaction encouraged by Griggs, not only with her but also with other readers. The column became an intriguing collaboration between a columnist and her readers, because she gave a voice to many women rarely heard in media—or in history. The "letters to the editor" pages provided forums for discussion but often of politics or other issues of importance, as long defined by male editors and publishers, and were not the place for women to talk of "love problems," as Griggs termed the topic—nor of neighbors or children, and certainly not husbands, lest "letters to the editor" hit too close to home in the lives of the male editors.

In a catchphrase of the modern women's movement to come, "all politics are personal," and Griggs realized that "love problems" were not the only issues in readers' letters and lives. We also argue, from reviewing hundreds of her columns and reading thousands of letters from her readers, as told in their own words, that their concerns included many other topics on societal issues in their discussions in the column, which soon ranged far beyond the stereotypical "love stories" or "sob sister stuff." This analysis, then, tracks their topics of discussion for more than half a century to attempt to track changes in the lives of her readers, in their times and in their place—and especially as they experienced changes in "women's place" in the twentieth century.

In sum, in giving over her authoritative and authorial voice, Griggs gave empowerment to her readers to turn her column into their column, a community forum for discussion of the issues that mattered most in their lives; in turn, the column thus gives us a glimpse into women's issues across five significant decades, from the mid-1930s to the mid-1980s, in their history and ours—but not only "women's issues." In addition to gendered issues that they experienced as women, they discussed other issues that generations of women experienced as members of a larger community, coping with momentous changes for themselves, their families, and their neighbors.

We also argue that, within readers' own words on the issues in their lives, as voiced in Ione Quinby Griggs' column, lie stories of larger significance that were ignored by newspapers' male-dominated management ranks of editors and others, who determined the news agenda.

For example, well before introduction of "the Pill" in 1960 and debates on the local laws limiting its availability, widespread support for wider access to the new form of birth control became evident among women writing to Griggs, as did other discussions that presaged the rise of the modern women's movement to come, which would not make front-page news for another decade. Similarly, signs of rebellion to come in the 1960s against societal norms and parental control were evident in earlier decades in thousands of letters from teenagers—long among the largest groups of contributors to the column—on their attempts to assert their independence in their communities, in Milwaukee and across the Midwest, famed for resistance to change. These continuities and conflicts that emerged early in their letters on the back page of the newspaper offer insight into issues that often went unreported in the "news pages" until decades later.

First, we start with the story of Ione Quinby Griggs, and of her unique collaboration with her readers, in an opening chapter on her first career, which provided an unusual prologue to her career-to-come as an advice columnist. As a "girl reporter" on the "girl-crime beat" in Chicago, she won front-page bylines for many of the more than a thousand stories that she told of that city's gangsters, mobsters, gun molls, "murderesses," and other girls done wrong or women who went wrong in the 1920s. However, she also reported on other women, in other workplaces, who also were winning progress in new professions for women. In remaining chapters on her career as an advice columnist, from the 1930s through the 1980s, we also follow the guidance of "Dear Mrs. Griggs" in focusing on the stories of her readers, as told in their own words, by hundreds of her correspondents among her millions of followers, mainly women and girls, who turned to her column, their column, to pour out their hearts to her, and to each other, from the Heartland.

Genevieve G. McBride and Stephen R. Byers
Milwaukee, Wisconsin

1

Prologue: From the 'Gilded Age' to the 'Jazz Age' and the Front Page, 1891-1933

"The discovery has been made as to why I wear a hat," confessed Ione Quinby, writing to her readers of the *Chicago Evening Post* from the newsroom, where she wrote that her male colleagues had "never quite figured out" the foibles of the first newswoman in their midst in the 1920s. Famed as the *Post's* "girl reporter," although she was in her thirties, Quinby wrote that the men "were never sure about my age." They also were baffled by her habit of never removing her hat, whether at her desk in the newsroom or out on assignment in the city's streets. As her "unmarcelled bob" customarily was "crowned with a $5 turban," she wrote, the men "didn't know whether my bangs were sewed to my hat or annexed to my scalp." Quinby's behaviors so bemused her editor that he sent her out on a "stunt story" for free psychoanalysis offered by the faculty "alienists" at nearby Northwestern University. Typically, Quinby took the assignment in good humor, turning in a light-hearted, self-deprecating story that won her one of more than a thousand bylines earned by a phenomenon of the era: a woman journalist on the front page in the "Jazz Age" in Chicago.[1]

---

1 Ione Quinby, "This Tells Why Wearing a Hat Gives You Nerve/Girl Reporter Undergoes Psych[o]analysis Test at College," *Chicago Evening Post*, January 21, 1926. Hereafter, Ione Quinby's byline is cited as IQ, and the *Chicago Evening Post*, as a source, is cited as *CEP*.

Typically, too, Quinby had persevered to get the story, after the psychology professor initially rejected her request. He "looked at me kindly but said they were only taking subjects who had something wrong
with them," she wrote, such as "children who misbehave in school" or
"persons sent by the police department" for disorderly conduct. The
Post photographer helpfully protested to the professor on behalf of
the men in the newsroom, stating that "you'd better take her," as "there's
something radically wrong with her." The reporter readily agreed, offering two trappings of her job as a journalist—her trademark hats
and her desk's placement in the newsroom—that had become her to-
tems. "I've got a lot more nerve when I've got a hat on" in "encounters
with people I interview ... from those who treat me to sodas to those
who try to throw me out the door. I always have on a hat," she admitted. "And it upsets me terribly to have my desk moved" from the site
where she made her most "important decisions" amid constant deadlines in the competition among the city's press for headlines—and for
front-page bylines.[2]

The professor, apparently intrigued by a "girl reporter" well known
for covering the so-called "girl-crime beat" of murders and other mayhem in Chicago in the 1920s, agreed to give a glimpse into her psyche.
She regaled her readers with his assessment of her attachment to her
ever-present headwear, writing that "subconsciously, I have made myself believe" that a hat also helped her to "reach big decisions," especially "in desperate situations." Indeed, compared to the physical risks of
"stunts" and stories that sent women reporters into the worst of their
cities' streets, an assignment that took her to a campus and risked only
a look into her mind may have been a relief. She shared her wariness,
however, that her sources now would be "mean enough to take advantage of this discovery" about the quirky Quinby. Her newsroom colleagues also now would know of the significance that she placed upon
the placement of her desk. "You don't like to have your desk moved,"
the "alienist" advised, as "it satisfies your ego as the only little girl reporter" among men on the "news side," not off to the side with the
distaff staff of "women's pages." Her story gave a rare glimpse behind
the studied persona that Quinby had so carefully constructed. Owing
to her unusual place in the press, Quinby apparently so intrigued the
professor that he pressured her to participate in his study "to promote

---

2   Ibid.

Ione Quinby with trappings of her job as a journalist—her trademark hat, and at her desk—at the *Chicago Evening Post*. She explained to her readers that she "got a lot more nerve" when she "got a hat on" for interviews with newsmakers. She also explained the significance of her desk's locale in the newsroom as the site of her most "important decisions" amid constant deadlines and competitors for headlines and bylines in a cutthroat era in the city's press. (Courtesy of Western Springs Historical Society)

social adjustment." The "girl reporter" retreated, however, upon realizing that participation required filing a form that would reveal her best-kept secret: her age.[3] Only after her retirement, six decades later—in her mid-nineties—and as she neared her death, at a hundred years old, would co-workers discover that she had been a decade older than she had claimed.

---

3   Ibid.; Karen Herzog, "Ione Quinby Griggs Dies; Advised Lovelorn," *Milwaukee Sentinel*, August 19, 1991; Jackie Loohauis, "'Dear Mrs. Griggs': A Legend Dies," *Milwaukee Journal*, August 19, 1991. Hereafter, the *Milwaukee Sentinel*, the *Milwaukee Journal*, and the *Milwaukee Journal Sentinel*, as sources, are cited, respectively, as *MS*, *MJ*, and *MSJ*.

By then, despite her fame in the 1920s, Quinby's remarkable career would be forgotten in her city. She is noted in only one of many histories of the Chicago press in the era, and only is noted to mischaracterize her as solely a "sob sister," a "girl reporter" on the "girl-crime beat," covering sordid lives of other women also deemed better forgotten from the city's crime-ridden streets and Cook County jail cells. Instead, as a colleague later would describe her colorful Chicago career, Quinby was a memorably risk-taking reporter. He wrote that "she had seen a man murdered, watched bodies of twenty women and children removed from an excursion boat hit by a lake storm, attended a gangster wedding, shared a candy bar with Al Capone," and had "lent her compact to a woman who wanted to freshen up a bit after killing her husband with an axe." A colleague at the time also called her the city's foremost "sob sister," if in admiration of her status among her cohort of women reporters. However, writes historian Alice Fahs, "sob sister" became a "false and derogatory term," too often "used to stigmatize and stereotype *all* newspaper women's writings" as merely "emotive writing." A means of subtly attacking women reporters for their "accrued power" and "perceived 'invasion' of public spaces" that previously had been the purview of men, the term was a form of "hidden politics" by men of the press, who denigrated women journalists' work as "sob stuff," she writes. Decades later, the "sob sister" term remains part of newsroom parlance. Chicago newsman and historian Wayne Klatt writes in his recent chronicle of Chicago's press that "nearly every paper in the nation had a 'sob sister,'" needed to "introduce emotion to the once-dry news" of "old-fashioned political sheets," if the "newsmen may have mocked them" then—as have some historians of media since. Although the work of women journalists long has been "hiding in plain sight" in newspaper archives, so-called "sob stuff" has been "little studied by historians," Fahs writes. As a result, women journalists then famed nationwide among their millions of readers "might have been surprised by their invisibility today," she writes, in scholarship on women, media, mass culture, and their cities.[4]

---

4   Wells, *Milwaukee Journal*, 262; Robert St. John, *This Was My World* (Garden City, N.Y.: Country Life Press, 1953), 36, 158; Alice Fahs, *Out on Assignment: Newspaper Women and the Making of Modern Public Space* (Chapel Hill: University of North Carolina Press, 2011), 2-9, 13-15, 91, 102, emphasis in the original; Klatt, *Chicago Journalism*, 109. On origins of the term "sob sister," most sources attribute its first use for women

Quinby made women her wide-ranging "beat," with coverage of not only "girl criminals" but also of many women emerging in the era in politics, business, and other sectors of urban life in the metropolis of the Midwest. This study argues that the result of lack of recognition of the range of her reportage—first in Chicago and throughout her remarkable career—is that more than her own story has been missed. Also lost from scholarly literature and public memory have been her stories of the women of Chicago, in more than a thousand contemporary accounts that comprise a social history of their lives—as well as their misguided loves—in an era when they and their city had significant roles in a larger societal transition. Recovering her body of work adds to recent research on women journalists in urban media, who reached millions of readers in the era, toward a fuller understanding of "a lost world of women's writings that placed women at the heart of a new public life," as Fahs writes. "Out on assignment," they were "urban explorers who crisscrossed cities in search of their 'stories,'" the stories of other women still unexplored in scholarship in urban studies, and especially in the era's "emerging world of working women"—other women making news for more than murder and mayhem. "Precisely because most newspaper women were hired" to write for women readers, as Fahs writes, their work proved "vital in shaping and disseminating ideas regarding women's changing lives" and in creating "public conversations about the cultural politics of modern life." In the case of Quinby, her versatility as well as her ability accounted for her success, which provided her with a platform to advance opportunities for other women, not only in newsrooms but also in many workplaces. Her coverage also acted as means of "social control," at times countering other messages from media regarding gender roles, and served as advice for women in coping with momentous societal change in the 1920s, nowhere more than in the Midwestern metropolis of Chicago.[5]

This examination of Ione Quinby's work in her Chicago career, an unusual training for her next career as an advice columnist, includes quantitative content analysis of all of her bylined stories in the *Evening*

---

journalists at a New York City trial in 1907, notably the Wisconsin-born former Chicagoan Winifred "Annie Laurie" Black Bonfils. For earlier use of the term for her, see Robert E. Park, "The Natural History of the Newspaper," *American Journal of Sociology* 29:3 (November 1923), 287.

5   Fahs, *Out on Assignment*, 2-9.

Post, more than a thousand stories in a dozen years, to recapture the range of her reportage on many women who made news in the era.[6] To suggest the range of her work into other media as well, also noted are some of hundreds of stories that she retold—and sold—for national syndication in other newspapers and in crime magazines such as *Master Detective,* as her byline became known well beyond Chicago. Much of that body of work, like her later book *Murder for Love,* capitalized on the country's fascination with her city in the era, especially her coverage of gangsters' girlfriends, mobsters' gun molls, and other women gone wrong or done wrong in Chicago. However, by also covering women from politicians to circus workers to celebrities, she was among women journalists of the era who expanded "women's place" in the news as well as in newsrooms—and, again, nowhere more than in the newsrooms of Chicago.

Reportage of Chicago journalists then, in the city's "literary renaissance," is recognized as significant in reframing perceptions of their city and redefining popular culture in the era. As Klatt writes, they penned their prose in "a peculiarly American voice." However, he and many media historians argue for a peculiarly masculine voice by focusing on the brethren of the press. Although Chicago's metropolitan media had made the city a mecca for women journalists, few are noted in histories of its press, and none notes Quinby. She does merit mention by journalist Douglas Perry in *The Girls of Murder City,* but he focuses only on the "girl-crime beat" of the 1920s in Chicago.[7] However, Quinby also had a reputation for a remarkable range of reportage.

In her day in the 1920s, the heyday of "Jazz Age" journalism, Quinby was among the few journalists—women or men—whose work consistently won front-page bylines in metropolitan newspapers for coverage

---

6 On methodology for quantitative content analysis for this chapter, the authors analyzed the *Chicago Evening Post* from January 1, 1920, to October 31, 1932, examining each daily edition and coding each bylined story on front pages and all stories on all pages with the byline of "Ione Quinby," for a total of 1,086 stories, then coded for content in ten categories: business, celebrities, courts, education, fashion, general features, government, health, police, and politics.

7 Klatt, *Chicago Journalism,* 106; Perry, *Girls of Murder City,* passim; see also Michael Lesy, *Murder City: The Bloody History of Chicago in the Twenties* (New York: Norton, 2007), which relies on newspapers as sources but not her newspaper and thus neglects her coverage.

of crime and courts, the focus of the country for "trials of the century" that both chronicled and contributed to major shifts in American popular culture. However, in a city where the press was king, front-page reporters were local royalty, who literally danced with visiting European royalty—as she did—or hobnobbed with Hollywood stars—as she also did—and redefined "news" in the 1920s. Quinby's byline became known for reportage that reframed women *as* news, not only in police stations and courtrooms but also in politics and commerce—and in the new popular culture of stage and screen. She regularly regaled her readers with heartfelt, hilarious, or racy human-interest stories on the doings of touring celebrities and other indigenous celebrities in her city, from a Congresswoman to mob molls and "murderesses." All gave her "exclusives" that put their names—and hers—on the front page.

The impact on popular culture of her city's journalism in the era is evident in fictional accounts, from books to plays to films penned by her contemporaries in the city's press, such as *Chicago* and *Front Page*. The latter later was remade as *His Girl Friday* and, writes historian Jean Marie Lutes, featured "the most famous film image of a newspaperwoman," an intrepid "girl reporter," for whom Quinby could have been the inspiration. She prized her independence and frequented Chicago's famed "bohemian" writers' circles at Emil's Café and the Dil Pickle Club, flouting convention and flaunting "flapper" fashions of the era—except when she allegedly shed the latter in an infamous if probably apocryphal incident at a "society" outing on Lake Michigan. Allegedly bored by the assignment, she was said to have abandoned not only the ship but also her apparel, scandalizing the city's elite at the event by stripping to swim back to shore.[8]

---

8   Perry, *Girls of Murder City*, 229; Jean Marie Lutes, *Front-Page Girls: Women Journalists in American Culture and Fiction, 1880-1930* (Ithaca, N.Y.: Cornell University Press, 2006), 162. Maurine Watkins of the *Tribune* authored *Chicago*, on Broadway in 1926 or 1927 (sources vary), adapted for film and for a musical among the longest-running shows in Broadway history. Her success encouraged Ben Hecht and Charles MacArthur of the *Daily News* to pen *Front Page* for Broadway in 1928, later adapted for stage, screen, radio, and television. Bartlett McCormack of the *Daily News* authored *The Racket* for Edward G. Robinson on Broadway in 1927, as John Bright, a colleague of Quinby at the *Evening Post*, was penning the screenplay for the film *Public Enemy* for former office boy James Cagney in 1931. As for nonfiction works, Maureen McKernan of the *Tribune* authored *The*

Neither that incident nor some of Quinby's other, later stories of her life in Chicago are verified by records on a "girl reporter" who had not been a girl for decades. In her era, writes Fahs, "shaving a few years" from their ages was "common practice among newspaper women."[9] That Quinby would continue the practice, as it became uncommon later in her career—and even afterward, in her later years in retirement—is indicative of repeatedly remaking herself, her reportorial persona, and then reveling for the rest of her long life in mysteries of her early years. However, she revealed little about her personal and professional setbacks that would end her Chicago career, after only a dozen years, and lead her to have to leave the city that she had called home for most of her first forty years, her own "sob story" that needed no embellishment.

Ione Quinby was born in the West and spent her infancy in the South, but she lived most of her first forty years in Chicago, after her footloose father finally settled in the Midwest. For William Paine Quinby, transiency was a family trait. He had been born on the eve of the Civil War in 1859 in the South, in Memphis, Tennessee, to two displaced Northerners: Mary Paine Quinby of Indiana and William Thomas Quinby of Pennsylvania, the prosperous founder and president of Quinby & Robinson Company, then one of the South's largest ironworks. Ione Quinby's paternal grandparents and their young family survived the Civil War on their Georgia plantation, although their home and holdings suffered. After the war, the family fled for refuge with relatives in Warren, Ohio, in the "Western Reserve," ceded to the

---

Amazing Crime and Trial of Leopold and Loeb (Chicago: Plymouth Court Press, 1924), later adapted for plays and films; and Lloyd Wendt and Herman Kogan of the Tribune authored Lords of the Levee: The Story of Bathhouse John and Hinky Dink (1943; rep. Evanston, Ill.: Northwestern University Press, 2005). On the city's writers' circles, Quinby came to disdain the milieu of the Dil (variously, Dill) Pickle Club; see IQ, "Vagabonds and Half-Baked Creeds," 134-135, in Franklin Rosemont, ed., The Rise & Fall of the Dil Pickle: Jazz Age Chicago's Wildest and Most Outrageously Creative Hobohemian Nightspot (Chicago: Kerr, 2003). A colleague concurred that only "poseurs" met there, near "Bughouse Square," but "real bohemians" met at Emil's, near the "newspaper row;" see Robert St. John, This Was My World (Garden City, N.Y.: Country Life Press, 1953), 158-159.

9   Fahs, Out on Assignment, 299.

then-young country after the Revolutionary War. Accounts vary as to
whether a Revolutionary War veteran from the East Coast, Ephraim
Quinby, had been awarded the "bonus land" for his service or had purchased his holding, where he had founded Warren in 1798. He was
Ione Quinby's great-great-grandfather.[10]

---

10   Ione Quinby Griggs to Maude, November 20, 1972; "William P.
Quinby, Resident in 1880, Is Called by Death," November [n.d.], 1933,
unidentified newspaper, Quinby Papers, Western Springs Historical
Society, Western Springs, Ill.; Henry Cole Quinby, *Genealogical History
of the Quinby (Quimby) Family in England and America* (Salem, Mass.:
Higginston, 1993, rep. of Tuttle, 1915), 174-175, 435. On her name, some
sources incorrectly transcribe it from census records as "Jane;" she is listed as Ione in the 1915 family history and in the *Chicago City Directory*
(Chicago: Chicago Directory Co., 1911), 1118. On her age, the family history lists her birth as in 1891 but errs on the date; see Quinby, *Genealogical
History*, 435. She altered her age to census takers as early as 1920, listing age 27 when her age was 28, and in 1930, listing age 35—aging only
eight years in a decade—when she was 39 years old. By the mid-1930s, she
claimed to colleagues to be younger by a decade and listed only her date
of birth but no year of birth on records; see personnel forms, Milwaukee
Journal Sentinel Library, Milwaukee, Wis., February 1, 1961, August 20,
1969, and November 16, 1979, in the authors' possession.
     On her family history and newspapering, the Warren, Ohio, founder
Ephraim Quinby's half-brother Samuel Quinby published the *Western
Reserve Chronicle*, one of Ohio's oldest newspapers, predecessor of the
current *Warren Tribune Chronicle*. (Their mother was the much-married
Elizabeth Hall Halliday Quinby Quick Quick, an Episcopalian bishop's
daughter who unknowingly wed a bigamist in the East before marrying
and burying a Quinby and then one Quick after another—but at least,
if not quickly, she wed them in succession.) Another ancestor in Ohio,
Joseph Bailey Quinby, also was an "oldtime newspaper man" and an "old ab-
olitionist" as editor or publisher of several newspapers, including the *Times*
and *National Banner*, a Union paper in the Civil War in Cincinnati, a city
with a sizeable Southern populace on the border between slave and free
states. He co-published a post-Civil War newspaper with his wife, Annie
Haven Quinby, who also published a pioneering women's rights newspaper, the *Cincinnati Aegis*. Their son wrote that his parents "dared to think
for themselves and far in advance of their time," as his mother also had
carried him "as an infant in arms to one of the first, if not the first, women's
rights conventions in the United States," perhaps referencing conventions
for women's rights held in Ohio from 1850 forward, following soon after

In Ohio, the Quinbys long had been a newspapering family, including the founder of one of the first newspapers in the North-West
Territory. Another ancestor, a foremother, had founded and published
a pioneering newspaper for women's rights, and other Quinbys had
become editors and publishers in every region of the country. In every locale, they often also had become local characters with the "family characteristics," as an Ohio observer wrote, which Ione Quinby
would share: "black eyes, quick motions," and a "pleasing manner" but
"brusque and determined in speech," from a determination to succeed
that would help her to achieve her ambition in newspapering. "Nothing
is too difficult to accomplish if once undertaken" by a Quinby, as the
Ohio observer wrote, although the family also had faced many "trials,"
a trait that Ione Quinby also would share. Despite her tragedies, however, as the observer had said of others in the colorful clan, she would
rise "by sheer industry" to "the front rank" of the field of journalism.[11]

Family fortunes recovered by the 1870s, as did Chicago after the
Great Fire of 1871, when family connections among the city's elite had
brought her father to the reborn metropolis. A schoolteacher while
studying law, he resided with relatives, early settlers in the city whose
State Street "mercantile business" had "burned in the big Chicago fire,"
as his daughter would recall. But they had not rebuilt. Instead, as she
would write with understatement, sale of prime real estate and other
properties allowed the family to live on "a very nice residential avenue,"

---

the first women's rights convention in the world, in 1848 in Seneca Falls,
New York. Half a century later, into Ione Quinby's time, family traditions
of newspapering and newsmaking continued. Near her childhood home,
a relative published and edited a newspaper in Georgia, and an Ohioan,
Margaret Quinby, wrote a family historian, made news when "American
papers were full of her pictures and rumors of her engagement to a no-
bleman" in Germany; she was presented to the court "and found favor in
the Saxon King's eyes." Among family with a variant surname spelling, actress Gertrude Quimby was called "the prettiest girl in America" by the
New York City press. Even better known in the news, and in the newspaper business, was William E. Quimby of Michigan, longtime *Detroit Free
Press* publisher and U.S. ambassador to the Netherlands in the 1890s. See
Quinby, *Genealogical History*, 124-125, 175, 256-257, 328-335, 378-379.

11   Griggs to Maude, November 20, 1972, "William T. Quinby," biograph-
ical forms, Quinby Papers; Quinby, *Genealogical History*, 124-125, 175,
256-257, 328-335, 378-379.

Prairie Avenue, among the city's first millionaires. By then, another locale had lured Chicago banker Walter L. Newberry and other investors to buy land for a train line for commuters from "the Queen of the Western Suburbs," as the settlement of Western Springs advertised itself in 1880 in a promotional campaign that had attracted the Quinbys. The family moved to the site, first settled with farms in the 1830s and a quiet "temperance town" of Quakers by the 1870s. The Quinbys were descended from New England Quakers and first worshipped at the Friends' meetinghouse with other newcomers, who incorporated the village of Western Springs in 1886.[12]

By then, her restless father had moved again. In 1885, in Salina, Kansas, he opened a law office, ran for office, lost, and was left "feeling pretty low," his daughter would recall, because the loss of a political livelihood also left him with low prospects to wed a local girl, Laura Peck. However, as their daughter would recall, her "mama must have been willing to take the chance" and hectic years ahead: They wed in 1888, had a son in 1889, and moved in 1890 to Memphis, before her mother went home to Kansas for the birth of Ione Marie Quinby on April 22, 1891.[13]

Her earliest memories apparently came with the family's return to Western Springs, where the Quinbys would be prominent for decades. Their first return to the town coincided with the World's Fair in 1893

---

12 Griggs to Maude, November 20, 1972, and July 18, 1976, "William P. Quinby," Quinby Papers; Jacquelyn Heard, "A 'Queen' of a Town Springs Up," *Chicago Tribune*, November 2, 1988. On family in the city, Griggs' letters state that an aunt nee Quinby and uncle lived on Prairie Avenue, among the street's early elite; they later are listed on Wabash Avenue; see *Full Reversed Directory of the Elite of Chicago, 1883-4: Giving the Names of Prominent Residents on the Most Fashionable Streets of the City and Principal Suburbs* (Chicago: Elite Publishing Co., 1884), 125, in the Lawrence J. Gutter Collection, University of Illinois at Chicago, accessed September 22, 2011, at www.archive.org/details/reverseddirector00lawr.

13 Herzog, "Ione Quinby Griggs Dies;" "WS Settler Leaves Gift," unidentified newspaper, January [n.d.], 1992, Quinby Papers. Laura Peck Quinby was born in Watertown, N.Y., in 1868 to Eliot J. and Persis Peck; see "Mrs. Laura Quinby Is Called by Death," unidentified newspaper, September 10, 1937, Quinby Papers. Some sources state incorrectly that Griggs' father was village marshal; see "Resolutions on the Death of W.T. Quinby," November 8, 1898, Quinby Papers.

in Chicago, where her father opened a law office and seemed settled. He also achieved political office, at last, in 1894, if not at the polls but by appointment as village attorney in Western Springs, where his father served as village marshal until his death in 1898. Their son moved his mother into the city of Chicago and again moved his growing family to their plantation in the South and then to his wife's family home in the West, for a few years. William and Laura Quinby returned to Western Springs in 1907—by then, with six children—and, amid the many moves, their eldest daughter would recall amassing "little formal schooling," listing her education vaguely and variously. At times claiming to have a high school diploma, she also wrote of having been home-schooled by her mother, for "a thorough education," with parental encouragement to pursue a precocious ambition for a writing career. Ione Quinby earned her first byline at the age of ten years old. The name of the periodical is unknown, but decades later, she would share a faded clipping with a *Saturday Evening Post* writer, conducting an interview of Quinby on her career. The writer would pan both the "baldly propagandistic share-the-wealth piece" and Quinby's fledgling attempt at fiction, a novel about a girl who spoke only in rhyme. "Happily," as the *Saturday Evening Post* put it, the manuscript had "created no stir in publishing circles" when the young Quinby had handed it to a family friend, a publisher, who "read it, or said he did," according to the magazine. He had "advised Ione to keep on writing."[14]

Another aspiring writer could have heard sarcasm in the publisher's advice, but Quinby's ambition for a newspaper career was as unquenchable as it was unusual for women in her era. Her family's return to Chicago, however, provided proximity to more role models than in most cities, although most often on "women's pages," which the *Chicago Tribune* had helped to pioneer nationwide in 1852 with its "Home Department," bylined only as "Edited by a Lady." The rarity of bylines in the era, even for men, meant an anonymity that may have enabled some women to succeed in the field by the 1870s, when Frances Willard was editor of the *Chicago Daily Post*, prior to her rise to fame as a reformer,

14   "William P. Quinby," Quinby Papers; personnel forms, Journal Sentinel Library, Milwaukee, Wis.; IQ, *Murder for Love* (Chicago: Covici, Friede, 1931), jacket; Jackie Loohauis, "A Love Story of Long Ago," *MJ*, February 14, 1983; "What to Do With Ropes," *Saturday Evening Post*, December 9, 1944, 4; "Wisconsin's Voice of Conscience: I.Q.G.," Milwaukee (May 1971), 23-25.

and Margaret Buchanan Sullivan wrote for the *Post*, then the *Herald*, then the *Tribune*. Although not known by a byline, Sullivan was known for her high hemlines that freed her to "chase after stories of murders, fires, and suicides" with her brethren of the press, writes Chicago press historian Klatt of the woman called "the best man on the paper" at her newspapers, a mistaken gender identity that resulted from her refusal of a byline then and when she became an even greater rarity, a woman editorial writer, in the 1880s. Other women progressed from anonymity to pseudonyms on columns on urban "bachelor girls" like themselves, "unmarried working women" who "strained behavioral norms" by refusing "to marry, stay home, and have children," writes historian Daphne Spain in *How Women Saved the City*. Others used pen names as "stunt girls" on stories such as exposés of factory conditions for women and girls. Few women worked fulltime in newsrooms; more submitted their copy by correspondence to be paid per inch in a journalistic equivalent of piecework pay, "space rates."[15]

Other women were unpaid contributors. Jane Addams, founder of the city's famed Hull-House and the settlement-house movement nationwide, collaborated with *Chicago Tribune* reporter Winifred "Annie Laurie" Black—later dismissed as the first of the "sob sisters"—in an expose of juveniles' incarceration that led to founding of the first children's court in the country, after a campaign by Addams' cohort of clubwomen, including Ellen Martin Henrotin, president of clubwomen nationwide in the 1890s. Clubwomen of color, Mary Church Terrell and Fannie Barrier Williams, also promoted their causes in African American newspapers in the city, where the "princess of the black press," publisher Ida B. Wells-Barnett, editorially rallied for a defining moment for their race in demanding inclusion in the city's showpiece, the Columbian Exposition of 1893. A "defining moment for women journalists" also came at the Chicago World's Fair, writes Fahs, as they

15 Fahs, *Out on Assignment*, 32, 79, 137; Lutes, *Front-Page Girls*, 39-64; Klatt, *Chicago Journalism*, 39; McPhaul, *Deadlines & Monkeyshines*, 132; Kathleen S. Cummings, *New Women of the Old Faith: Gender and American Catholicism in the Progressive Era* (Chapel Hill: University of North Carolina Press, 2009), 21-22; Eric W. Liguori, "Nell Nelson and the *Chicago Times'* 'City Slave Girls' Series: Beginning a National Crusade for Labor Reform in the Late 1800s," *Journal of Management History* 18:1 (2012), 61-81; Daphne Spain, *How Women Saved the City* (Minneapolis: University of Minnesota Press, 2001), 25.

came from across the country for a Women's Press Congress. For the rest of the decade, however, the ladies of the clubs were likelier to be found in newsrooms than were working women journalists, with the spread of fundraising stunts or "silk editions" by society women welcomed into newsrooms, if only for a day. In Chicago, Polish American clubwomen published a "*Wydanie dla Kobiet*" in the *Zgoda*, for a week, while women students also published an edition of their own of the University of Chicago's weekly campus newspaper.[16]

By the turn of the century, in Quinby's formative years, many women had written, edited, and published small-town newspapers for more than a century, although most of a few thousand women in the metropolitan press nationwide remained far from male bastions of newsrooms. Chicago, however, boasted higher numbers of women journalists than in other cities. By the turn of the century, the *Tribune* alone employed sixteen women, although most were relegated to "women's pages." Resented by some women journalists, the sections also were exploited by others as opportunities for renegade reporting, possible because many male editors who created "women's pages" for advertising purposes rarely read them, according to historian Alice Fahs. Few women won front-page bylines in major media, although exceptions included a distant relative of Quinby's in a distant state. Her generation also witnessed headlines heralding the new century's "New Women" with education, careers, even the right to vote in many states prior to 1920, including Illinois. In his history of Chicago crime coverage

---

16   Fahs, *Out on Assignment*, 79, 137; Lutes, *Front-Page Girls*, 39-64; Klatt, *Chicago Journalism*, 63, 71; Ruth Bordin, *Frances Willard: A Biography* (Chapel Hill: University of North Carolina Press, 1986), 3-23; Victoria Bissell Brown, *The Education of Jane Addams* (Philadelphia: University of Pennsylvania Press, 2004), 4; Juliet E.K. Walker, "The Promised Land: The *Chicago Defender* and the Black Press in Illinois, 1862-1970," 20-23, in H. Lewis Suggs, ed., *The Black Press of the Middle West, 1865-1985* (Westport, Conn.: Greenwood, 1996); Paula J. Giddings, *Ida: A Sword Among Lions* (New York: Harper Collins, 2008), 244-245, 268-282, 345-346; Ann Colbert, "Philanthropy in the Newsroom: Women's Editions of Newspapers, 1894-1896," *Journalism History* 22:3 (Autumn 1996), 90-99; William J. Galush, "Purity and Power: Chicago Polonian Feminists, 1880-1914," *Journal of Polish American Studies* 47:1 (Spring 1990), 20; *University of Chicago Weekly*, March 14, 1901, University of Chicago Archives, Chicago, Ill.

in the era, Douglas Perry credits the Eighteenth Amendment for creating opportunities for women journalists, arguing that Prohibition gave rise to a "girl-crime beat" in the 1920s. Women in Chicago covered crime prior to 1920, however, in hiring that more likely correlated with the campaign for the Nineteenth Amendment, which was won in 1920 after a decade of state-level victories, especially in Illinois, the first state east of the Mississippi River where its women won suffrage in presidential elections. The campaign correlated with media-created fear of women, writes historian Jessie Ramey, as "too independent, too free, losing their dependence on men and their commitment to their families," as they "won the right to vote, and even were pushing for an equal rights amendment." Indeed, headlines nationwide in 1921, when Quinby first would crack the front page of the *Chicago Evening Post*, would herald news of enactment of the first state Equal Rights Amendment, billed as "the first bill of rights for women," won nearby in Wisconsin.[17]

Illinois women's political prowess already had empowered more women to win entré into more newsrooms prior to 1920. The *Chicago Tribune* promoted its "suffrage column" and also promoted future media icon Fanny Butcher from "women's pages" and "society news" to crime coverage. Like politicians' awkward attempts to attract the

---

17 Alice Fahs, "Newspaper Women and the Making of the Modern, 1885-1910," *Prospects* 27 (2002), 303-339; Perry, *Girls of Murder City*, 33, 69; Eleanor Flexner, *Century of Struggle: The Woman's Rights Movement in the United States*, rev. ed. (Cambridge, Mass.: Harvard University Press, 1975), 269-270; Jessie Ramey, "The Bloody Blonde and the Marble Woman: Gender and Power in the Case of Ruth Snyder," *Journal of Social History* 37:3 (Spring 2004), 632; Genevieve G. McBride, *On Wisconsin Women: Working for Their Rights from Settlement to Suffrage* (Madison: University of Wisconsin Press, 1994), 268; Genevieve G. McBride, "'Forward' Women: Winning the Wisconsin Campaign for the Country's First ERA, 1921," 79-136, in Peter G. Watson Boone, ed., *Quest for Social Justice III: Morris Fromkin Memorial Lectures, 1992-2002* (Milwaukee: University of Wisconsin-Milwaukee, 2005). On the famed family journalist, Harriet Quimby of Michigan and then California also was among the clan's "acroplanists" with a variant surname spelling, including W.F. Quimby, who held "flying apparatus" patents in the 1860s. She became the first woman in the U.S. and second in the world with a pilot's license in 1911, a year prior to her death in a fall from a plane at age thirty-seven—although she also had claimed to be younger; see Quinby, *Genealogical History*, 435, 399-500, 513, 541.

new, long-neglected women voters, however, the *Tribune* publicized columns for both woman suffrage and "household hints" in the same "house ads." Other publishers only belatedly began attempts to appeal to women readers, with new definitions of "women's news" to include politics and aspects of women readers' lives other than only housewifery. Many male editors and underlings remained resistant to changing their reportorial ways, unwilling to forgo their reputations as hardboiled "newspapermen," who had witnessed humanity at its worst—as if women had not witnessed the worst from Chicago men's infamous attacks on them in a 1916 suffrage parade. A former Midwestern journalist and national suffrage leader, Carrie Chapman Catt, wrote knowingly then of Chicago that "some dead men vote, as do some who never have been born, and yet the women are not let in with the boys" in backrooms of politics. Not that all women "let in" newsrooms would remain; for example, Butcher's stint in covering Cook County "morals courts" was brief, because she disliked the work so returned to "women's pages" and the "literary beat." Other women also endured for only a few years in "hard news," owing not to the hard work—as it was—but to other factors. As a journalism textbook at the time warned, the work would "rub the bloom off a woman" facing low pay, lack of advancement, and men's "prejudices." By 1920, although the Chicago press provided more opportunities than in most major cities, no women were city editors or managing editors on any major newspapers there or elsewhere, nationwide.[18]

In 1920, Chicago editors sought women with the skills and the will to withstand demands of journalism in the city, where decades of violence in circulation wars had caused dozens of deaths in the streets and reduced the number of daily newspapers from ten at the turn of the century to six. Then, competition became even more heated, in the mode that Klatt calls "the hellbent style of Chicago journalism." Breaking news stories hit the streets almost hourly, in multiple

---

18 Fahs, *Out on Assignment*, 9, 89-90, 176, 272, 294; Fanny Butcher, *Many Lives, One Love* (New York: Harper and Row, 1972), 40, 205-207; Louise R. Noun, *Strong-Minded Women: The Emergence of the Woman-Suffrage Movement in Iowa* (Ames: Iowa State University Press, 1969), 227-257. On woman journalists as career-oriented "professional women" but often reporting on working-class women also amid gendered transitions, see Phyllis Leslie Abramson, *Sob Sister Journalism* (Westport, Conn.: Greenwood Press, 1990), 2-3.

editions, "replates," "chasers," and "special bulletins," before becoming superfluous because of then-emerging media technologies. An early center of the film industry, Chicago produced a fifth of the country's motion pictures, or "movies" as immigrants called them, and "newsreels," increasing in popularity with the new technology of sound in the 1920s, when the lurid melodramas with "fake actualities" were witnessed weekly by forty million moviegoers, among them many members of murderers' "fan clubs." Sensationalist entertainment increased with newly commercial radio as well, although the *Chicago Tribune* fortunately abandoned plans for broadcasting on its station, WGN— call letters immodestly denoting the "World's Greatest Newspaper"— from Cook County courts, where newsreel crews' cables already snaked across the courtroom floors, and harsh camera lighting overheated already-overcrowded courtrooms.[19]

If newsrooms were somewhat safer than the courts or streets, competitive pressures had made for brief careers for her few female predecessors at Quinby's future employer, the *Chicago Evening Post*, and none had won front-page bylines. The newspaper had been high-minded from its founding almost four decades before, writes Klatt, and despite circulation wars between the *Tribune* and Hearst newspapers, "the *Evening Post* snubbed the trend toward playing up sordid crimes and called itself the paper for 'the man with only three minutes for murder.'" In aiming for a male audience, the *Evening Post* had not hired women journalists as readily as had the Hearst papers and the leading newspaper in the city, the *Tribune*—and at its new *Daily News*, where a former woman journalist held power as the publisher's wife. "No one thought her influence unusual" by then, he writes, "because the period after the war saw women kicking up their heels at college dances, opening speakeasies, and joining newspapers in larger numbers," if

19 Klatt, *Chicago Journalism*, 83, 94, 102, 139; McPhaul, *Deadlines & Monkeyshines*, 14; Raymond Fielding, *The American Newsreel, 1911-1967* (Norman: University of Oklahoma Press, 1972), 3-5, 153; Arnie Bernstein, *Hollywood on Lake Michigan: 100 Years of Chicago and the Movies* (Chicago: Lake Claremont Press, 1998), 1-11. On the city's daily newspapers in 1920 and their (generally agreed) dates of founding: the *Daily Journal* (1844), *Tribune* (1847), *Daily News* (1876), *Evening Post* (1886), *American* (1900), and *Herald and Examiner* (1918). The *Evening Post* founded in 1886 was unrelated to an earlier *Daily Post*, founded in 1865 and merged into the *Daily Post and Mail* in 1874; see Klatt, *Chicago Journalism*, 35-38, 66.

only to work in "women's pages." As Perry writes, in retrospect, "'girl reporters' almost never made it to the front page," because the best assignments went to "the best reporters, and that meant men" to male editors. According to a Quinby contemporary, journalist Ishbel Ross, "even the most experienced men" found front-page pressure problematic. However, as she memorably wrote in her classic history of her sisterhood, *Ladies of the Press*, male editors believed women to be unreliable, owing to "the variable feminine mechanism." As a result, writes historian Jean Marie Lutes, front pages had few bylines of "front-page girls"—"and rarely were they 'girls.'"[20]

————   ————   ————

For the *Chicago Evening Post*, city editor Walter A. Washburne was fortuitously placed to find his "front-page girl," Ione Quinby. She had begun working as an office clerk in the city almost a decade before, in 1911, one of the "bachelor girls," as they had been called, who had moved into the urban workforce by the turn of the century. By 1911, they were so numerous in Chicago that the *Tribune* had accorded them a column and new nomenclature in "For and By Business Girls." Quinby progressed to a position as a writer in advertising and promotion for a manufacturing firm, at a salary of thirty-five dollars per week, and already may have freelanced for news services. Her income went far; unlike single women in the city's boardinghouses, she did not need to go far to commute from home in Western Springs, well-served by mass transit from its founding. Late-night trains enabled her to enroll in "night school" in the Loop, where Northwestern University's new Medill School of Journalism offered classes in 1921, including one taught by Washburne. Although Quinby would recall that her first course with Washburne helped her to "worm her way" into a journalism job by first working for the *Post* for free, she also would recall that Washburne hired her in 1921 at fifteen dollars per week, less than half of her previous pay. Her salary improved after a second course from Washburne, who told his prize pupil "to quit the class," she would claim, "as she already knew all the answers and would only embarrass him by further attendance." She again knew the answer and agreed to do so, "if he would give her a raise." He did. Whether owing

20   Perry, *Girls of Murder City*, 33, 176-177; Ishbel Ross, *Ladies of the Press: The Story of Women in Journalism by an Insider* (New York: Arno, 1974; rep. 1936), 6; Lutes, *Front-Page Girls*, 1.

Ione Quinby in her Chicago years, about 1920, with her hair shorn in an "un-marcelled bob," as she would write in the *Chicago Evening Post*—but without her customary hat, requisite for women journalists in the era to go "out on assignment" into streets of the cities. (Courtesy of Western Springs Historical Society)

to high rents or familial affection, however, she would remain living at home in the suburbs, despite her reputation in the city as a risk-taking reporter frequenting "bohemian" clubs and flirting with male colleagues on "newspaper row."[21]

21   What to Do," 4; Wade H. Mosby, "The Heart of Milwaukee," *American Mercury* (July 1957), 54; *Chicago City Directory* (Chicago: Chicago Directory Company, 1911), 1118. On her higher education, she variously

That she failed to charm her way past a guard without paying admission fees at the Field Museum of Natural History led to a first-person "stunt story" and her first byline in the *Evening Post*, in 1921, the first of more than a thousand to come—and a front-page byline in one of its two daily editions, where a front-page byline, even for men, remained rare. But the first-person voice of experiential "stunt stories" required bylines and became a bonus for women journalists, because men rarely were willing to do "stunt stuff." In 1920, only three *Post* staffers had front-page bylines: One was the *Post*'s man on the political beat, and the others covered sports.[22]

Quinby's brethren of the press in the newspaper's promotional department promptly dubbed her "the *Post*'s little girl reporter" in its "house ads," an appellation that she apparently relished, although—or perhaps because—she was thirty years old when she began her career. In addition to claiming to be a decade younger, she also claimed to be five-foot-one, adding half an inch to her height as easily as she subtracted years from her age. Framing her youthful face with a fashionably shorn "bob" and "bangs," Quinby also flaunted "flapper"-style short skirts, still shocking to a more sedate set. So, quitting her Northwestern University studies proved wise, in an era when the *Chicago Evening American* reported that its faculty denounced the attire and "decided that for a pretty coed to display a pretty knee in a picture is unfavorable publicity."[23] Had she continued as a "coed," her alma mater may have had to convene even more campus committees to debate further resolutions regarding publicity won by its alumna,

---

stated her college work at Northwestern University as two years, two semesters, or only two classes. On her pre-1920 career, Perry states that she "definitively" freelanced for syndicated news services but cites stories in 1920 without bylines that he labels as "unquestionably" by Quinby, owing to "her unique prose style;" see Perry, *Girls of Murder City*, 277; "Sued Wife Keeps Detective Guard," *Waterloo* (Ia.) *Evening Courier* April 10, 1920; "Finds Liberty as Taxi Driver," *Waterloo* (Ia.) *Evening Courier* August 4, 1920. The authors also suspect that Quinby freelanced prior to 1920 but, finding no bylined stories before 1921 and that her style reflected the genre in general, find cause only for conjecture and not for conclusions.

22   "What to Do," 4; IQ, "Flip Smiles No Passport for Field Museum," *CEP*, April 9, 1921.

23   Perry, *Girls of Murder City*, 77-78.

who soon showed Chicago far more than her knees for one of her most memorable "stunt stories."

Quinby donned a colorful but skimpy costume in the role of the "Queen of Sheba" to ride the lead elephant in the grand march of a circus entering her city and, while women in unusual workplaces were standard topics for often-superficial "stunt stories," she reported her respect for circus women, who carried a weighty workload, quite literally. She later recalled that her "head and headdress with 12 pounds of beads and features were almost taken off" in her stint for the stunt. However, she had "kept the headdress on" and kept her seat, and she had "made a good Queen of Sheba, if I do say so myself." To shadow another working woman under the big top, a big-cat trainer, she was outfitted to work with a tiger and lived to tell the tale. "In those days I wasn't afraid of anything," Quinby would recall of the exploits, first popularized by pioneering journalist Elizabeth "Nellie Bly" Cochran and her emulators in the late nineteenth century. "If there was a woman on a newspaper who didn't write on fashion and food, she was the paper's 'stunt girl,'" historian Kay Mills writes. Even if she had been "hired as an 'all round' reporter or as a 'stunt' reporter," writes Fahs, a woman journalist rarely could "avoid the woman's page … over the course of her newspaper career." The *Post's* new "girl reporter" expanded her resume by also taking on tamer tasks, filling in on formulaic "Four F's" stories—food, fashion, family, and furnishings—on "women's pages" staffed by the only other woman reporter at the *Post*, at least when Quinby started.[24] However, she wanted more, in a time of transition in journalism.

---

24 Alicia Armstrong, "'Dear Mrs. Griggs': A Pioneer Among 'Sob Sisters,' I.Q.G. Has Helped Thousands," *MJ*, March 3, 1980; Alicia Armstrong, "'Dear Mrs. Griggs': In Chicago, Mrs. Griggs Met the Famous and Infamous," *MJ*, March 4, 1980; Alicia Armstrong, "'Dear Mrs. Griggs': Can You Imagine I.Q.G. Riding Atop an Elephant," *MJ*, March 5, 1980; Alicia Armstrong, "'Dear Mrs. Griggs': Mrs. Griggs Really Cares for Those Asking Her Help," *MJ*, March 6, 1980; Alicia Armstrong, "'Dear Mrs. Griggs': Issue on Teenage Morals Brought 7,000 Letters," *MJ*, March 7, 1980; Angela Borden, "Local Personalities Have Fond Memories of Circus," *MJ*, July 7, 1985; Fahs, *Out on Assignment*, 4-5; Kay Mills, *A Place in the News: From the Women's Pages to the Front Pages* (New York: Columbia University Press, 1988), 24. On other women at the *Post*, she long carried and showed to later colleagues a photograph with one other

As the only woman on the "news side" of her newsroom, Quinby quickly rose from a limited role as a "stunt girl" to a versatile position as a feature writer on the wide range of stories that reflected a wider world for women, ranging from politics to commerce to a "girl-crime beat" of gangsters and gun molls in wide-open Chicago. The term "feature writer" was fairly new and often dismissed in the field with the same disdain as for "stunt girls" and "sob sisters;" one of the city's new sociologists sniffed that "the sob sister is often known in newspaper parlance as a 'feature writer,'" who contributed "chiefly cheap sentimentality and specious moralizing." Her features gained the respect of colleagues, however, and a following of readers for her reportage from the "women's angle" on news that crossed over from "women's pages," events of the sort for which she was better suited than "society reporters" to identify the unusual social strata of her city. Quinby covered the wedding of the sister of Al Capone and provided readers with standard stuff of wedding stories, from the length of the bridal train to the number of bridesmaids—six—as well as the colorful guest list. She would recall many memorable rites of "gangster weddings, like gangster funerals ... done with a big splash," such as a "wedding cake twelve feet high."[25]

In her encounters with the notable and quotable, or those refusing comment, her attention to details revealing of the high and mighty both regaled and vicariously represented Quinby's readers. As a carry-over from her stint on stunts, she continued to interject herself—and thus, her readers—into stories of celebrities, which increased in media in the 1920s. For example, another encounter with the portly Capone came in covering his trial for income tax evasion, where he offered her

woman, a staffer on *Post* "women's pages;" see Jackie Loohauis, "'Dear Mrs. Griggs'...," *MJ*, March 31, 1995. On her work for "women's pages," however, the authors' analysis of bylined stories counters her later colleague's claim that Quinby did not cover such stories.

25   Armstrong, "In Chicago, Mrs. Griggs." On use—and abuse—of the term "feature writer" in the era, a Chicago contemporary editorialized *sans* evidence in a scholarly journal that "the sob sister is often known in newspaper parlance as a 'feature writer'" of "chiefly cheap sentimentality and specious moralizing;" see Joseph L. Holmes, "Crime and the Press," *Journal of the American Institute of Criminal Law and Criminology* 20:2 (August 1928), 282. On the gendering of early feature writing as from the "hen coop," see Fahs, *Out on Assignment*, 91.

half of a candy bar, telling her that he had to lose weight, while she "couldn't weigh more than 100 pounds." His estimate was close, she informed readers; she weighed one hundred and four. The petite reporter wrote about meeting a towering giant and other sizeable celebrities, heavyweight boxers Gene Tunney and Jack Dempsey, the latter for an exclusive parlayed from an interview with his wife and picked up nationwide. She interviewed willowy flyer Amelia Earhart on tour home to the Midwest and Hollywood royalty, from Mary Pickford to Fanny Brice to local girl Jean Harlow, who enjoyed Quinby and would call for dinner when in town. The city was a stop for European royalty, who found her prone to mishaps in meeting nobility; she almost fell under the Prince of Wales' horse and lost a shoe in hopping a train to interview Queen Marie of Romania. The great were gracious, as Quinby reported to readers: The prince reined his horse, expressing concern, and the queen showed her how to manufacture makeshift footwear. Cadging a regal invitation to a ball held for the Romanian royalty, Quinby regaled her readers by reporting that she received an invitation from the queen's son for a dance, for which the commoner now was shod in "gold pumps" complementing "an emerald-green chiffon gown." As for the attire of the queen, whose luggage was lost, royalty carried off life's little problems with aplomb: Quinby reported that the queen resorted to a wearing a negligee to the ball.[26]

In sum, in the first three years of her bylined work, from 1921 through 1923, Quinby exhibited both her ability and versatility on a range of "beats" well beyond the limited focus of women journalists' work product—"sob stuff"—as portrayed by many media then and historians since. In 1921, she earned 21 bylines for coverage of politics,

---

26 Armstrong, "In Chicago, Mrs. Griggs;" Armstrong, "Pioneer Among 'Sob Sisters;'" Loohauis, "'Dear Mrs. Griggs;'" IQ, "Mary Pickford's Cut her 'Famous Curls,'" *CEP,* June 23, 1928; IQ, "Fanny Brice Here on Way to Coast for Screen Test," *CEP,* June 26, 1928; IQ, "Jean Harlow, Chicago Film Star, Dazzles Admirers Here," *CEP,* November 18, 1930; IQ, "Wee Girl Reporter, 5 Feet 1, Busses Mr. Earle, 8 Foot 3," *CEP,* November 21, 1930; IQ, "I'll Never Quit the Ring/Dempsey, in an Exclusive Interview, Declares He'll 'Fight Forever,'" *Portsmouth* (N.H.) *Herald,* August 30, 1927; IQ, "I'll Fight 'Til I Drop, Declares Tunney," *Lancaster* (Ohio) *Daily Eagle,* September 28, 1927; Florence Morony, "Meeting Queen Marie, Lunching with Film Stars All in Day's Work," unidentified newspaper, n.d., Quinby Papers.

education, and government as well as fashion and general feature topics; she quadrupled that tally in 1922 to 82 bylines for coverage of
those "beats" as well as crime and courts, celebrities, and health. In
1923, Quinby earned 134 bylines, her third-highest tally in the doz-
en years of her career in Chicago, for stories on previous "beats" but
adding the business "beat" with a story on women working in the city's
commercial sector. Overall, 83.2 percent of her stories in the three-
year period covered women newly in the news of the city as well as the
sorts of stories traditionally targeted to women readers.

Quinby's byline increasingly appeared for "beats" that long had been
male bastions, such as her series on women in politics that comprised
more than a third of her bylined stories in 1923 and established a new
"beat" for the rest of her Chicago career.[27] In 1923, her second-highest
tally of bylined stories came in coverage of courts, a "beat" that would
become her claim to fame—and to the front page—in the following
year. Steadily increasing coverage of courts from no bylined stories in
1921 to more than a dozen in 1922 to triple that number in 1923, she
had a total of almost 40 bylined courts stories accounting for almost
30 percent of her bylines that year.

With 237 bylines in the first three years of her *Post* career, in more
than a fourth—27.4 percent—of all editions, Quinby's record progressed from "cub reporter" status to position her as a "star reporter" in
1924, a banner year for "banner" headlines on women and crime. She
would continue to display her versatility with bylines on almost every
"beat," but the burgeoning "girl-crime beat" would build her reputation
nationwide, not for her wide-ranging reportage but for her writing in
the tradition of another Chicagoan, Winifred "Annie Laurie" Black.
Her coverage of a notorious New York City murder trial early in the
century first had earned the sobriquet of "sob sister." If the term was
comparatively new, however, the form was not; her city's highly competitive press long had employed overwrought writing to evoke emotions—and sell papers.[28]

---

27   On Quinby's series on women in politics, see *CEP*, January 23 through
      April 25, 1923.

28   Armstrong, "In Chicago, Mrs. Griggs;" Armstrong, "Pioneer Among
      'Sob Sisters;'" Loohauis, "'Dear Mrs. Griggs;'" Morony, "Meeting Queen
      Marie."

Quinby's description of the execution of infamous New York State "murderess" Ruth Snyder in 1924 typified the form in florid adjectives, exclamatory punctuation, and muddled imagery, from satanic figures to trench warfare to window hardware.

> They had assembled to see a woman killed, and centuries of man's chivalry to women seemed to rise up at that moment in a desperate urge to save the woman now crouched before them.... Ruth whimpered again as she gazed straight toward them.
>
> The silence!... A crunching sound as the grim executioner rammed down a lever! A sinister, crackling whine, and a sputtering noise.... The eerie sound of ships sinking at night!
>
> Fascinated, unable to move, the twenty-four men were like creatures in some diabolical nightmare. As they watched, blue darts of electricity emerged from Ruth's body in sinister spurts like small pale devils dancing about....
>
> Then came a weird silence that strained at their ears and bore down upon their minds as if weighted by sash weights....
>
> Seconds crawling slowly like wounded soldiers dragging themselves back to the trenches.... Finally the guards reassembled about the chair, picked up Ruth's inert body, and wheeled it out of the room.[29]

Her coverage also could display wit, as when Quinby sniffed that a "murderess" who had opted for "a corset salesman" instead of an artist had "burned for her bad taste" in men. Sentimentality for sensationalism, however, was the forte of the "sob sisters" hired to cover crime and courts. As Ishbel Ross wrote in *Ladies of the Press*, "trials brought out women reporters in force" for stories of how women fared in the courts—and trials brought out women spectators as well.[30]

A 1924 divorce trial brought Quinby a front-page byline for a standard girl-done-wrong story, although her take took a skeptical turn at the tale told in court by the lawyer for the wife, portrayed as a "child victim of a millionaire," a Chicago manufacturer. He was "painted in

---

29 IQ, *Murder for Love*, 47.

30 IQ, *Murder for Love*, jacket; Ross, *Ladies of the Press*, 65-66; McPhaul, *Deadlines & Monkeyshines*, 132; Klatt, *Chicago Journalism*, 121. On the 1924 trial in New York City, the Ruth Snyder case inspired a novel and play by journalist James M. Cain, *Double Indemnity*, later adapted for film by Raymond Chandler; see Landis MacKellar, *The 'Double Indemnity' Murder: Ruth Snyder, Judd Gray, and New York's Crime of the Century* (Syracuse, N.Y.: Syracuse University Press, 2006).

no uncertain terms" by the wife's lawyer "as a man of the world, who unwittingly led a young girl, one-third his age, into wrongdoing"—his, not hers. Quinby quoted the lawyer as claiming that the husband had put a prenuptial contract, "as he saw fit to word it," before his bride on the night before their wedding, the very "eve of their marriage." Yet she also reported that alimony of more than a thousand dollars monthly allowed the wife to afford adorning herself for court in "different cos-tumes" daily, accessorized by a sizeable diamond ring. In other stories, Quinby also questioned sincerity of "victims" concerned more about their appearances than their crimes.[31]

Despite her departures to witty wisdom on the ways of women—and men—her stories generally subscribed to the social-control role of media in conveying gendered warnings to women on crime and pun-ishment, especially in times of societal transition, such as the 1920s. On the front page with Quinby's divorce story, other stories from the Cook County courts on that day alone included coverage of anoth-er divorcee, a matricide, a "wild auto chase"—the new "devil wagons" often were "wild" in the era—and Prohibition-era reports of men "nabbed" with a "carload of whisky" and an "ex-deputy" held for boot-legging, as were hundreds of Chicago's finest on the public payroll and working for Capone. Historians document a rise during the decade in such cautionary tales that communicated disapproval of an alleged decline in middle-class morality, as media coverage of disgraced divor-cees, "fallen women," and other types of transgressive females occurred at a rate far higher than their actual incidence in the culture. In the context of the array of social-control stories, Quinby's coverage of a divorce case suggests a dichotomous role for women reporters, if their role in social control conflicted with their "sob sister" role of sympathy for victims. Quinby reported, instead, on the "intense interest" in trial proceedings by the "child-victim" wife, who remained dry-eyed. Her story contrasted with the "sob sisters' function," wrote Ishbel Ross, "to watch for the tear-filled eye ... the widow's veil, the quavering lip, the

---

lump in the throat, the trembling hand. They did it very well," she wrote.[32]

In Chicago, the so-called "sobber set" included a growing sisterhood, beset by sibling rivalry, as Quinby was not alone on the "girl-crime beat" that came to dominate the city's press and captivate the country in 1924. The Hearst-owned *Herald and Examiner* and *Daily American* had a "sob squad" of Sonia Lee and Patricia "Princess Pat" Dougherty, who embellished prose as befitted Hearst papers. But on any "beat" in the city, the major competition came from the newspaper with the largest circulation, the *Tribune*, where reporter Maureen McKernan would become a "commanding presence" in both courtrooms and her newsroom, joining experienced reporter Genevieve Forbes and a newcomer to newsrooms, Maurine Watkins. They wrote and dressed conservatively to suit an employer claiming to disdain "sob sister" styling. The *Tribune* had editorialized against those in the press sympathetic to suspects in "sob stories," after the Cook County courts had freed dozens of women in a row in the first three years of the decade. The streak of acquittals, if deemed as news by the *Tribune*, was not new. Historian Jeffrey S. Adler finds in his study of Chicago crime records that its homicide rate had increased more than 400 percent in four decades prior to 1920. Most were spousal murders, most often by men, in a "slaughter [of] their wives in explosions of rage" for "threatening their patriarchal authority."[33]

32　IQ, "Paints Mrs. Saal;" John D. Stevens, "Social Utility of Sensational News: Murder and Divorce in the 1920s," *Journalism Quarterly* 62:1 (Spring 1985), 53-58; Ross, *Ladies of the Press*, 65-66.

33　Klatt, *Chicago Journalism*, 102, 130; Linda Steiner and Susanne Gray, "Genevieve Forbes Herrick: A Front-Page Reporter 'Pleased to Write About Women,'" *Journalism History* 11:1 (Spring 1985), 8-16; Jeffrey S. Adler, *First in Violence, Deepest in Dirt: Homicide in Chicago, 1875-1920* (Cambridge, Mass.: Harvard University Press, 2006), 46, 274-275. On the *Tribune* campaign against gendered leniency in the courts, beginning in the 1890s and continuing into the 1970s, see L. Mara Dodge, *'Whores and Thieves of the Worst Kind': Women, Crime, and Punishment in Illinois, 1835-1973* (DeKalb: Northern Illinois University Press, 2002), 284, 289. On gendered staffing in the era in other newsrooms with higher proportions of women than in the daily press, African American newspapers that published weekly included the *Chicago Bee*, where women comprised the entire reportorial staff; see Walker, "Promised Land," 24-39.

Even prior to 1924, Chicagoans who more often were the victims of domestic violence—women—increasingly had retaliated in murderous ways. Many also were immigrants, at a time that the *Tribune* endorsed restrictive quotas soon to come from Congress. The *Tribune* conflated the factors, as nativism and misogyny both factored into its editorial call for no leniency in the next murder case to arise after its claim of favoritism to women in the courts. In the case of an Italian immigrant woman held for homicide of her husband, the *Tribune* clearly decreed that Forbes be freed to employ flagrant ethnic stereotyping, despite its stated claim of distaste for sensationalism—and despite her own claim to fame. She had finally moved into reportorial ranks at the *Tribune* in 1921 with a "stunt story," for which she had disguised herself as an immigrant for an exposé of Ellis Island and a series of front-page bylines that instigated federal reforms. However, Forbes' coverage of the case of the immigrant woman held for homicide contributed to the result that, for only the second time in Illinois history, a woman was sentenced to execution.[34]

Public discourse on women and crime proved crucial as a context of coverage by Quinby and her peers, although she often employed a healthy skepticism rather than nativism or sexism often seen in others' coverage. For example, as the case of the condemned woman, Sabella Nitti, came up for appeal in 1924, other women prisoners—"Comrades of Mrs. Nitti," as they signed a letter to the *Tribune* to protest its prejudicial coverage—and her lawyer, a woman, prepared the immigrant for the trial-by-media by tutoring her not only in the English language but also with beauty tips. Quinby, aware of the importance of "image creation" from coverage of fashion and of celebrities, reported the result as "one of the few cases on record" in which "long confinement behind bars did a prisoner any good.... It takes clothes to make the woman," she wrote, "but it took more than clothes to make this one as she is today." The court took a new look at the case of the newly

---

34   "Let Immigration Law Alone," *Chicago Tribune*, November 23, 1924. On sympathetic coverage in the *Tribune* on immigration, see Genevieve Forbes, "Tribune Woman Runs Gantlet of Ellis Island," *Chicago Tribune*, October 14, 1921, and subsequent stories in the series. On her nativist coverage, see Genevieve Forbes, "Ladies in Crime," *Chicago Tribune*, April 10, 1923; Genevieve Forbes, "Death for 2 Women Slayers," *Chicago Tribune*, July 10, 1923; Genevieve Forbes, "Dialect Jargon Makes 'Em Dizzy at Nitti Trial," *Chicago Tribune*, July 7, 1923.

fashionable-looking "Mrs. Nitti," released her, and ordered a retrial, never held.[35]

Quinby continued to counter too-typical "sob stuff." In coverage for an audience of women on outcomes in courts for "outlaw" women, historian Claire Bond Potter argues, women journalists' tales of beauty tips or "costumes" of divorcees may have subtly communicated more than societal norms to subvert social-control messages by covering transgressive women flouting societal convention. Such stories romanticized "ambitious and independent choices," she writes, over "domestic security." In another 1924 case, writes historian Jessie Ramey, the fashionable dress of the first woman to be executed in New York State in decades "absolutely dominated the press coverage," as her beauty captivated the press but for one reporter: Quinby. The *Chicago Post* reporter alone questioned media portrayals of the accused as maternal, instead depicting the murderer as not "a mother-woman, who feels that she has fulfilled her destiny in giving birth."[36] Under the guise of a message that only seemed to convey social control, the childless Quinby may have covertly communicated a different message that could have been read quite differently to resonate with her readers who also were not determined or destined to be "mother-women."

Her *Tribune* competitor, Forbes, also departed from the "sob sister" norm, although for other reasons, as she felt forced to cover the "girl-crime beat." She and her newspaper claimed to be for the higher-minded reader and preferred covering women in politics—as if women could escape the seamy politics of the city—with an insider's advantage on the political beat, owing to *Tribune* ties to an influential source: Ruth Hanna McCormick. Married into the clan that owned the *Tribune*, she ran Republican women's national committee and would run for Congress, after Forbes first advanced the candidacies of McCormick and other women in 1922 by reporting on their odds against the Cook County machine. The *Tribune* coverage goaded competitors, such as the *Post*, with Quinby's series that followed with almost four dozen stories on women in politics in the next year

---

35   IQ, "Prison Life Is Civilizing Upon Woman Slayer," *LaCrosse* (Wis.) *Tribune and Leader-Press*, March 23, 1924.

36   Claire Bond Potter, "'I'll Go the Limit and Then Some': Gun Molls, Desire, and Danger in the 1930s," *Feminist Studies* 21:1 (Spring 1995), 44; Ramey, "Bloody Blonde," 640.

alone. Both reporters remained best-known for the "girl-crime beat," however, although Quinby soon was almost alone among women journalists on that job in her city after 1924, when Forbes would feel "her status as the top 'girl reporter' at the *Tribune* slipping away," writes Perry. Weary of covering criminals and other celebrities, Forbes eventually left Chicago for Washington to cover the politics of presidential spouses. First, she still had to cover other sorts of celebrities, if with an increasingly wry eye, as when penning a tale of Hollywood agents' telegrams to alert the press to meet at train stations, where starlets expressed surprise at the press presence and inevitably repeated a scripted line that "Chicago, there is really nothing like it."[37]

For Quinby, there would be nothing again like Chicago in 1924. Other competitors also soon fled the field or entirely fled the city within months of their hiring. Maureen McKernan, hired in 1923, left journalism in 1924 to turn to a literary effort, writing a book on a notorious trial in 1924. Also in 1924, within months of her hiring but owing to her unhappiness on the "girl-crime beat," Maurine Watkins left the city. She had taken a different path to Chicago and to journalism and would take a different path away. A small-town Indiana minister's daughter with a degree from Radcliffe College, she disliked urban life and its impact on lives of women whom she covered in courts, so Watkins would return to academe to study playwriting. If her brief time on the "girl-crime beat" had not been enjoyable, it proved unforgettable. She penned a play that first debuted on Broadway as *The Brave Little Woman* but would be retitled *Chicago*. According to Perry, the play was her form of revenge as a former reporter in recounting the confluence of events in 1924 that sent women journalists into Cook County jail cells and courts and reflected the "churning change" of the era and challenges that, in contrast, "so thrilled" her *Post* competitor, Quinby.[38]

Fear never stopped Quinby from a story, and in an unusual feat in Chicago journalism, she outlasted many *Tribune* competitors and

---

37 Steiner and Gray, "Genevieve Forbes Herrick," 8-16; Ross, *Ladies of the Press*, 539, 543; Kristie Miller, *Ruth Hanna McCormick: A Life in Politics* (Albuquerque: University of New Mexico Press, 1992), 201; Perry, *Girls of Murder City*, 261; Genevieve Forbes, "Hollywood Admires Chicago's Sky-Line," *Chicago Tribune*, June 12, 1927.

38 Perry, *Girls of Murder City*, 19-20, 53, 76-78, 222.

bested them on the "girl-crime beat," the grist for coverage that made her city a major story as "murder city," with the leading murder rate among major cities in the 1920s. *Tribune* reporter Robert St. John, who had risked his life and lost his newspaper in Cicero in the "mob wars" for investigating its infamous citizen Al Capone and would become famed as an NBC broadcaster covering other wars around the world, recalled that "Ione Quinby, if not the first, was at least the foremost of a new phenomenon in journalism called, for lack of a more subtle name, the sob sister." Perry also calls her "Chicago's foremost chronicler" on the "girl-crime beat," in part because both her sources and competitors discovered that the youthful appearance of "the *Post's* little bob-haired reporter" could prove deceptive, as "she reveled in police sergeants and competing reporters underestimating her." A colleague who saw her competitive side described "a certain little toss of her head when she talks and a tiny little compression of her lips that denote a strength that one might not suspect in one so small."[39]

To be taken seriously in the newsroom and the streets, she had to counter her diminutive size and girlish demeanor with courage, which earned respect from colleagues as well as bylines for the best stories, which often were found in the least inviting streets of the city, an area called "the Levee." Nationally noted crime reporter Herbert Asbury, the author of *Gangs of New York*, called the Levee the largest "red-light district" in the country. As historians Alice Fahs and Jean Marie Lutes assert, women denigrated as "sob sisters" for seeking stories of the streets were not weak but were bold, risk-taking reporters. Even in the district's "hundreds of brothels, saloons, and opium dens," Perry writes, Quinby "had no qualms about getting out on the street," where a "young woman walking in the Levee always had to worry. But Quinby did it anyway." Curiosity, indefatigability, and a sense of humor took

---

39   St. John, *This Was My World*, 36, 158; Douglas Martin, "Robert St. John, 100, Globe-Trotting Reporter and Author," *New York Times*, February 8, 2003; Perry, *Girls of Murder City*, 76-77. On Quinby's closeness to St. John, despite being competitors, a later *Milwaukee Journal* colleague noted that after decades in her career as an advice columnist, she would name St. John as the only man, other than her husband, to whom she personally had given advice; see Arville Schaleben, "Remarks at Theta Sigma Phi Dinner Honoring I.Q.G. as 'Newswoman of the Year,' 1970," Wisconsin Historical Society Archives, Golda Meir Library, University of Wisconsin-Milwaukee, Milwaukee, Wis.

her beyond the crime beat to even riskier endeavors in her wintry, windy city. Sent to allegedly safer but icy streets to test pedestrian safety, as the *Post* put it, "Miss Quinby was given good opportunity to study human nature in its most pleasant and unpleasant attitudes" of "rushing Chicagoans" on a "cold corner at Randolph and LaSalle."[40]

More dangerous than a mob of freezing Chicago pedestrians was "the mob" in the 1920s, when even an apparently innocuous floral shop proved to be a front operation, as Quinby found in tracing the whereabouts of a much-widowed gangster's moll about to marry again. A bouquet sent to the bride—the widow of "Big Tim" Murphy, she would be widowed again within a year of wedding a partner in bootlegging, John "Dingbat" Oberta—led Quinby to the shop, where she stated that she was a reporter on a story. A worker said he had "seen that girl somewhere" and warned the manager, who wielded a gun at Quinby. To his disappointment, she did not flinch. Impressed, he proudly displayed a weapons cache stashed amid floral supplies and chivalrously supplied a ride through the Loop to file her story. When told of the story, her mother more than flinched; she advised her daughter "never to ride with gangsters again." More often, her daughter would recall decades later, Laura Peck Quinby was "the most cooperative and interested mother of any newspaperwoman I know." But she had given birth to a born reporter, for whom everyone in the city offered potential for a human-interest story—and for a front-page byline. "The upside was too big," as Perry writes, for a big-city crime reporter to be beat on the "mob" beat.[41]

Another "upside" to the "girl-crime beat" came in side income, as Quinby increasingly lined up lucrative syndication of her stories. The common practice to augment low reportorial pay also augmented her reputation well beyond Chicago, and as Perry writes, a Quinby story

---

40   Herbert Asbury, *Chicago: Gem of the Prairie* (Garden City, N.Y.: Garden City Publishing, 1942), 37; Perry, *Girls of Murder City*, 76-77; Jean Marie Lutes, "Sob Sisterhood Revisited," *American Literary History* 15:3 (Fall 2003), 510, 516; Fahs, *Out on Assignment*, 6-8, 45-48, 175-176; "Girl Reporter Writes Story of Tagging Monday," *CEP*, October 23, 1925. On high crime levels in the Levee, despite a "white slavery" crusade and crackdown, see Karen Abbott, *Sin in the Second City: Madams, Ministers, Playboys, and the Battle for America's Soul* (New York: Random House, 2007), 282-293.

41   McPhaul, *Deadlines & Monkeyshines*, 128-129; "What to Do," 4.

was "always a cracker" and easily sold to syndicated news services and
national magazines, such as *Master Detective* and *True Confessions*.
She "embraced the entrepreneurial spirit of the Levee," writes Perry,
with contracts in her purse for suspects to sign and assign rights to
their stories that she first penned for the *Post* and then adapted for an
audience nationwide.[42] Her readers liked lurid details, although sensationalism fueled public discourse and fuming from pulpits regarding
the increasing crime reportage as signs of an alleged decline in middle-class morality. Of course, each such sermon served only to prove
that everyone, even men of God, read the papers.

The press responded to readers' yen for evidence of societal decline,
which elevated some reporters, including Quinby, to becoming part of
their stories. John J. McPhaul of the *Times*, in his history of Chicago
journalism in the "bizarre 1920s," recalls that the Chicago press found
that to provide "a balanced presentation of the news, it was as necessary
to have contact with Capone as it was to have a White House correspondent." Coverage of "gangsters and dance marathons and spicy divorces and all the other flotsam and jetsam of the big city were of more
interest" than news of "the nation's capital or faraway countries" in "a
wacky and engrossing time, a fine time, a time worth reading about,"
recalled Robert Cromie of the *Tribune*. William T. Moore of the
Tribune also fondly recalled a "fabulous era for the news," as "murder
mysteries most fascinated readers." Readers also were intrigued by the
press hierarchy and followed the work of "the highest-paid reporters
... who could steal diaries from love nests," and "next came those who
professed familiarity with Al Capone," including Quinby. Her press
competitors soon reported when "the inimitable Ione Quinby" came
to a crime scene to "give a story her special touch," as St. John of the
Tribune recalled. Quinby had risen to "star reporter" status, described
by a media historian as one "whose presence at an event became an
integral part of the news."[43]

---

42   Perry, *Girls of Murder City*, 76. On her freelancing, Perry's assertion that
      her practices of contracting for syndication and magazine stories first re-
      ported in the *Post* were "unknown to her employer," however, seems unlike-
      ly, as her numerous bylines in national media hardly could have eluded her
      editors' notice, nor was the practice unusual in newsrooms then (or since).

43   McPhaul, *Deadlines & Monkeyshines*, 182; William T. Moore, *Dateline
      Chicago: A Veteran Newsman Recalls Its Heyday* (New York: Taplinger,

The "murder capital" of Chicago captivated readers nationwide in 1924, when police captured more than a dozen suspected "murderesses," including five who came into court on one memorable day, and Quinby would obtain their stories—her stories—by befriending the women. In a "vintage decade for female sharpshooters," writes McPhaul of the *Times*, a series of women "knocked off husbands, boyfriends and, occasionally, the other woman," and several became publicity-seekers who "went from the courtroom to the vaudeville stage." Quinby shared his cynicism about some of the accused but saw cause for sympathy for others, such as one who was only a teenager, sought as an accessory to a murder by her husband. Police released a portrait of Katherine "Kitty" Baluk's "twinkly-eyed" toddler, Tootsie, to "lure the mother out of hiding," Perry writes. The ploy succeeded. Quinby was present, in the police station, for the surrender, and returned often to the jail. She brought the toddler for visits, Perry writes, and "talked police into letting mother and daughter have Thanksgiving dinner together," establishing a bond with Baluk that continued through trial, conviction, and a life sentence at the state Penitentiary for Women in Joliet. "I would pick up Tootsie, telling her that we were going to see her mother in a hospital," Quinby recalled. "The first time we drove up in a cab, Tootsie cried, 'What a beautiful hospital!'" The prison, in reality, was a "gray, stone, fortress-like place," although a matron allowed an inmate to "serve Tootsie milk and cookies," Quinby recalled. She even took Tootsie to Western Springs for a weekend, and the girl's grateful mother sent gifts stitched in prison.[44]

Such womanly arts eluded Quinby in her so-called jail "school," in which she conducted classes in reading and writing to assist in their cases for the "more illiterate" among murder suspects, who reciprocated for the reporter with instruction in knitting and crocheting—and with exclusives. "She had a way of prying the details of unhappy

---

1973), 17-18; Robert Cromie, "Foreword," in Moore, *Dateline Chicago*, 7; St. John, *This Was My World*, 36, 158; Lutes, *Front-Page Girls*, 7.

44   IQ, "Five Women Are in Court Today," *CEP*, April 21, 1924; McPhaul, *Deadlines & Monkeyshines*, 264; Armstrong, "In Chicago, Mrs. Griggs." On the case of the teenaged mother, Quinby continued for years to call for her release, as in a nationally syndicated story; see IQ, "May Free Convict," *Charleston* (S.C.) *Gazette*, July 19, 1931. Decades later, she had lost contact and told a colleague, "I would like to know what became of Tootsie."

marriages, unrequited love, and secret sex experiences out of the most non-communicative murderesses; they would confide facts to her which they had withheld even from their own attorneys," according to St. John.[45]

Not that all murders made headlines in Chicago, where a woman journalist may have had a gendered advantage for access to incarcerated women in the era, while many other women were at a disadvantage. The number of women arrested, convicted, and imprisoned in Illinois soared in the 1920s. For most of the century from the 1830s through the 1930s, women had comprised little more than two percent of more than seventy thousand inmates in Illinois, writes historian L. Mara Dodge. Most were "abortionists, bigamists, burglars, con artists, drug addicts, embezzlers, forgers, grand larcenists," or "domestic servants who stole from their employers; prostitutes who robbed their clients; impoverished women who forged checks out of economic necessity," not only "habitual shoplifters" but also others who had stolen items valued at under a dollar. Women "selected for prosecution and punishment were typically the most socially and economically marginal," the "poor, working-class, immigrant, or minority women" with abusive spouses or lovers and lack of opportunity, which "combined with the even greater burdens of race and class," Dodge writes. Women of color comprised almost half of women inmates, who were approximately only two percent of the state's population. But all had traversed "bounds of proper femininity," she writes, so their perceived character, and social class, determined their punishment, not their crimes. For example, among many "murderesses" in Cook County jail cells in 1924, some went free—fodder for more fuming editorials from the *Tribune*—although most were convicted. Some faced execution. Most were incarcerated for life or for long sentences.[46]

Progressive Era reforms based on alleged psychological factors in female criminality meant that women were more likely to be convicted than were men for similar offenses, and with harsher sentences for women in every category of crime. "Alienists" as witnesses fascinated readers and reporters, although Quinby's limning of women's lives focused less on psyches and more on societal causes, such as ethnic and racial prejudice. That many "murderesses" in 1924 were white—and

---

45   St. John, *This Was My World*, 36, 158.

46   Dodge, '*Whores and Thieves*,' 3-4, 76-77, 260, 286, 290-292.

that there were so many—made news, even when "murder was so
common in the era" and in Cook County, as St. John recalled, that homicide no longer guaranteed headlines. Murder required an "unusual
twist to receive much newspaper space" or needed suspects with "social
position."[47] Both criteria were met by the case that received the most
coverage in 1924, with added attractions of "alienists" as witnesses as
well as legendary Chicago defense lawyer Clarence Darrow and well-
known women reporters from as far as New York City. That the suspects were male did not deter the "sob squad," as sexuality was a crucial
factor in the case.

The murder trial of Nathan Leopold and Richard Loeb reframed
media's boundaries for women reporters. Even those hired by editors,
who had hired women to send them into the city's streets to provide
coverage beyond bounds of past constraints, for coverage of heterosex-
ually motivated murders, now coped with editors who refused to send
women into a courtroom for testimony on a topic that remained un-
printable: homosexuality. Media scholars still debate the influence of
a prejudicial press on the prosecutorial call for capital punishment for
the suspects, including the involvement in the investigation by sleuthing reporters that would win the *Chicago Daily News* a Pulitzer Prize
for journalism. Also debated is whether the defendants would have
benefitted from sympathetic "sob sister" treatment, had the *Tribune*
assigned the likes of Watkins to cover the trial. However, only court
reporters, not newspaper reporters, heard psychologists' testimony on
the defendants' sexuality, after the judge—to "protect" women reporters—ordered the press removed from the courtroom and had witnesses whisper testimony before the bench.[48]

---

47   St. John, *This Was My World*, 36, 158.

48   Paula S. Fass, "Making and Remaking an Event: The Leopold and Loeb
      Case in American Culture," *Journal of American History* 80:3 (December
      1993), 919- 951. On age as a factor, Fass finds that the defendants' youth
      was a focus of coverage in Cook County, site of the country's first juvenile
      court; see also L. Mara Dodge, "'Our Juvenile Court Has Become More
      like a Criminal Court': A Century of Reform at the Cook County Juvenile
      Court," *Michigan Historical Review* 26:2 (Fall 2000), 51-89. On gender as a
      factor, a jury trial would not have altered the judge's action, as Illinois juries
      were all-male; see "Women to Start Serving on Juries," *Chicago Tribune*,
      July 9, 1939. On women journalists, Perry is incorrect in stating that no
      "prominent female police reporters" covered the trial and that Quinby's

Some women journalists overcame media constraints and covered the Leopold and Loeb trial, including Quinby. Not one to miss an opportunity for competition with male colleagues, who were assigned to the main story, nor was she one to miss a major murder case—especially the one that became "more than just another 1920s murder case," writes historian Paula S. Fass. Showcasing her ability to find a fresh angle on a story, even on an event that evoked thousands of inches of repetitive coverage by other reporters, Quinby found a different story for "sidebars." As St. John wrote of her enterprise, "Quinby made a discovery which, in the worlds of business and industry, had already turned small profits into great fortunes: the by-product" guaranteed to win bylines. If she "sensed that a story was worth only a paragraph or two in the papers," he wrote, she "would still work on the case as if it were going to be a front-page sensation."[49]

Amid sensationalism that reached new levels in coverage of the Leopold and Loeb trial, and amid several stories on the trial that day, an example of her enterprise for "sidebar" that topped page two offers evidence of her ability, not only in reporting news but also in newsroom battles for bylines. Quinby's "by-product" focused on the victim, often forgotten or neglected in the news, as she reframed the story as "the Franks trial" for the murdered boy, Bobby Franks, rather than award more notoriety to the names of the thrill-seeking Leopold or Loeb. A favorable photograph of the victim, not a standard half-column "head shot" but a two-column portrait, also dominated the top of page two, which was placement second only to the coveted front page.[50]

Her content also differed from coverage of the usual suspects in a trial—the suspects, lawyers, and officials of the court—and focused instead on "the usual number of court fans." Subtly countering judicial and editorial decisions to shield women from testimony, she counted the courtroom audience daily and analyzed the gender balance—or imbalance—to report that women regularly comprised the majority of a "hundred-odd representatives of a curious or interested public."

---

editors "likely" saw "the subject matter [as] too rough and perverse for a woman," Perry, *Girls of Murder City*, 229.

49   St. John, *This Was My World*, 36.

50   IQ, "Men Crowd Court Today for Franks Slaying Trial," *CEP*, July 26, 1924.

She found fewer women in the courtroom only on the day of the week that, she literally exclaimed, was "cleaning day!" for housewives. Their absence afforded "a few masculine court fans a chance" to attend and to be interviewed by Quinby, who found that all were fathers with sons of the age of the victim. She also found lesser courthouse figures for interviews, from a "kindly bailiff" who saved "good seats for the short women," such as Quinby, to a "burly policeman making his rounds" who offered observations on regulars in the rows, such as an elderly woman called the "crumpled lace court fan" for her outdated fashions. Quinby even counted the number of attendees in court with fashionable tortoise-shell glasses to suggest their ubiquity, as similar spectacles at the crime scene became crucial evidence. Only at the end did she note a name that often led other stories, the name of the prosecutor, whom she nicknamed as a "Beau Brummel" for sporting a different necktie every day—evidence again that she attended daily, despite the distaste of some editors against sending women reporters to cover the trial.[51]

Yet even Chicago could not offer a "crime of the century" on a daily basis, as murders in the city became everyday matters after the Leopold and Loeb trial. Quinby continued to cover courts but also other "beats," even society news, although the local elite proved less entertaining than her "murderesses." The former "stunt girl" enjoyed telling of the alleged stunt of her own at the sailing party, where she was said to have become bored so had stripped and swam to shore, shocking Chicago socialites. Decades later, in another lakeshore city, an editor would hear of the legendary tale and ask the then-elderly former reporter for verification. "Oh yes, I did that," she would reply, offering incontrovertible evidence for any editor on the Great Lakes: "The water was very cold." At other times, however, she would relate a story of her alleged rescue after a fall from a ship—fully dressed, including her hat—because, she claimed, she could not swim.[52]

---

51   Ibid. On women at the trial, see also Fass, "Making," 922. The case inspired the play *Rope* by Patrick Hamilton and the book and play *Compulsion* by Meyer Levin, all later also adapted for film.

52   Perry, *Girls of Murder City*, 229; Armstrong, "Issue on Teenage Morals." On the story of the swim to shore, Perry suggests that she abandoned the ship and a story owing to anger at not being assigned to the Leopold and

Perhaps in part owing to her own notoriety, the notorious year of 1924 in Chicago contributed to a considerable increase in Quinby's bylines in the second three-year period of her career. The period, for a fourth of her Chicago years, accounted for almost a third of her bylines in the entirety of her *Post* career. From 1924 through 1926, she earned 341 bylines, an increase of 44 percent from her tally from her first three years. Coverage of courts accounted for more than a third of her bylined stories in the second period, comprising the largest category, owing to the many cases of murder in 1924 that came to trial in the next year. The increase in coverage of courts also occurred for divorce cases, perhaps owing in turn to increased reader interest, also a likely reason for increased coverage of celebrities in more than fifty stories from 1924 through 1926, compared to a dozen in the previous three-year period. Her coverage of politics declined, however, without a series similar to the one in 1923, but her bylines in other categories remained stable by comparison with the previous three-year period subjected to content analysis.

Her record was indicative of a reporter of versatility and value to the desk, even on slow news days—if few slow news days existed in Chicago in the era, when she earned more than a dozen bylines on the front page in the second three-year period of her career. In coming years, she would continue to earn more bylines than would most colleagues, and for stories on an array of issues from mayhem to more mundane matters. Less than 5 percent of local stories in the *Post* would earn bylines from 1927 through 1932, but hers would appear in almost a third of editions. After earning bylines for a total of 578 stories in the first half of her Chicago career, however, Quinby would not quite match that record in her remaining years ahead in the city and its press.

The heyday of "Jazz Age" journalism had passed for Quinby, her city, her newspaper, and others in her industry, as all were headed toward hard times. "The zesty period of police reporting was starting to fade," writes Klatt, as the coming economic crash would cause the *Post* to start reducing staff and to require remaining reporters to increase output, at a cost to content that earned bylines. Yet, if not in the numbers attained in better times, Quinby continued to earn bylines with

---

Loeb trial—or owing to inebriation. As she covered the trial, he also has no basis and no evidence—or source cited—for stating that she was "drunk."

consistency, every month of every year of the last half of her Chicago career. More than 60 percent of her bylines would come for coverage on women, from a news story on a court case brought by beauty-school students for return of fees to stories for "women's pages," from features on bridal fashions to a hilarious report of a beauty expert's pronouncement on women's "props," or legs. Quinby quoted the expert on the local prevalence of "prop" types: "20 percent of Chicago's women have sacks legs; 14 percent baby grand piano legs; 18 percent knock knees; 9 percent bow legs, and 29 percent spike legs." The expert did not describe the remaining one in ten legs of Chicago women, generally provided with two "props" apiece.[53]

To the end of her Chicago career, Quinby continued to cover more traditionally male territory, as in her exclusive interview in 1927 with prizefighter Jack Dempsey, the sports story picked up nationwide. More often, almost 20 percent of her 508 bylined stories in the years to come concerned crime, courts, or politics—or all combined, in stories such as her coverage of a rally in Chicago, part of nationwide protests of nativism in the murder trial of Ferdinando Sacco and Bartolomeo Vanzetti. In Quinby's final three-year period at the *Post*, almost 9 percent of her bylined stories won front-page placement: 35.7 percent on crime, 29.3 on courts, and 23.4 percent on politics. Her rate of front-page placement, at almost 9 percent of her bylined stories, scored significantly higher than the 6.6 percent rate for front-page placement for all bylined stories by all reporters in her final three years at the *Post*, from 1929 through 1932—the final three years of the *Post*, among many newspapers doomed to die during the Depression to come.

Quinby still filled pages with pathos for readers seeking sensation in maudlin accounts of murder, as in her "sob story" telling of another tragic case of little boys lost in Chicago in 1928.

> "Aw, gee, we wish we were going to see our grandma, too." Just a little more than a month ago, a dozen dressed up tads with their faces smeared with lollipops stood about two of their schoolboy friends ... on the eve of departure ... to visit their "grandma."

---

53   Klatt, *Chicago Journalism*, 116; IQ, "Tooth Infection 'Kills Pep,' Says Dental Director," *CEP*, March 16, 1927; IQ, "4 Out of 5 Pairs of Legs Homely, Expert Declares," *CEP*, January 25, 1928; IQ, "Stylish Brides to Be Shrouded in Clouds of Veils," *CEP*, April 2, 1928; IQ, "Beauty Students Revolt and Court Orders Cash Returned," *CEP*, December 16, 1931.

It was a "farewell party" given by classmates and teacher for [the boys], who two days later were to be lured to a watery grave with a fictitious 'grandmother' story more melodramatic than the famous story told Little Red Riding Hood by the wolf.

The "party," so gala in its intent but seeming so dreadful now in light of events that followed swiftly when the boys' father ... lured them to their death in the drainage canal, was brought to light today by classmates and teacher....

[They were] full of congratulations for the youngsters lucky enough to get to visit their grandma.... Then, manfully shaking the hands of "teacher," the guests of honor at the farewell "party" went home—to be taken from the river only a few weeks later.[54]

She also continued to freelance crime stories far from her city for national magazines and in newspaper syndication, including a "Chicago Chatter" column that she created in 1928.[55]

Also in 1928, Quinby increased her coverage of women in politics, as a presidential-election year provided opportunities ranging from a "peace fair" to the national convention in Chicago of the League of Women Voters. As the successor to the largest suffragist association, under its new name since 1920, the League continued to debate a campaign for an Equal Rights Amendment proposed by the National Woman's Party, which had led the campaign that had won the first state ERA in the nation in nearby Wisconsin. Other issues arose in campaigns for repeal of restrictive birth control laws and for repeal of Prohibition, amid repercussions such as crime and violence in the very city where the League convened in 1928—and, Quinby reported, where members split into "Wet Women" and "Dry Women." They also debated the peace movement, the focus of an annual "Woman's World's Fair" in Chicago in the era of increasing American isolationism. Quinby, not an isolationist, praised internationalist women as "modernly feminine" for "striving to equip an unstable world with a

---

54   IQ, "Children Gave Farewell Party to Drowned Boys," *CEP*, March 7, 1928.

55   Newspaper databases yield hundreds of bylined stories by Quinby nationwide in the 1920s and early 1930s, syndicated by the Central Press Association and then the Consolidated Press Association, the forerunners of one of the largest syndicated services, King Features, even today; see also IQ, "The Strange Death of Jake Harmon, Oklahoma's Political Czar," *Master Detective*, August 1930, n.p., Quinby Papers.

new equilibrium" and applauded local leaders who invited an "alliance of women of foreign countries" for the purpose of promoting "women's progress" as well as peace. She approved of actions more than words, alluding to the gender not featured at the fair, from men on the world court to President Calvin Coolidge for "joining the hands of nations in mutual endeavor and governmental sympathies." However, the focus of her story, like that of the fair, was on fostering the "co-operation of all women who 'do things."'[56]

Quinby scored a "scoop" in 1928 as a result of cultivation and coverage of her political sources, such as caucuses and conventions of women delegates to political parties and a powerful constituency of state clubwomen. Their "schools for mothers" exhorted that "women can turn elections" and turned out in 1928 for Ruth Hanna McCormick, elected to Congress from Illinois. In turn, she credited state clubwomen for her victory, as quoted in her first post-election press interview—a coup that could have been expected for her family's *Tribune*. Instead, Quinby won the interview for the *Post*. In a stellar year in her career, her political coverage accounted for almost 20 percent of her bylines in 1928 alone. She continued to cover politics in ensuing years, especially when both major parties would hold their national conventions in her city in the next presidential election year, 1932—the last year of her newspaper and of her Chicago career.[57]

In 1929, as the first of her final three years at the *Post* began, Quinby scored her highest number of bylined stories in any year, and all ran on news pages, which suggests her success in reframing women's news *as* news. Indeed, all but two of her 508 bylined stories in the latter half of her career at the *Post* ran in news sections. An atypical story ran in sports pages, her interview of heavyweight champion prizefighter Gene Tunney. Another exception, a play review, ran on the

---

56   IQ, "Women's Victories Are Acclaimed at Great Fair," *CEP*, May 19, 1928; IQ, "Women's World's Fair Seen as New Bond for Peace," *CEP*, May 21, 1928.

57   IQ, "Mrs. McCormick Says Women of Nation Share Her Victory," *CEP*, April 9, 1928. For convention coverage, see IQ, "Wives of Cabinet Officials, Mrs. Sabin Head G.O.P. Influx," *CEP*, June 11, 1928; IQ, "Wet Women and Drys Flock Here for Conventions," *CEP*, June 13, 1932; IQ, "G.O.P. Woman Leader Finds Democrats' Session Thrilling," *CEP*, June 20, 1932.

entertainment page. Intriguingly, her byline was not found in "women's pages" in the last half of her *Post* career, but she may have penned stories for the section that ran without bylines.

By late 1929, however, the number of her bylines and those of other *Post* reporters began to decline with the onset of the Depression. Advertisers' cutbacks reduced the number of pages per edition, limiting the "news hole." Staff layoffs followed, although the "star reporter" at the *Post* stayed to the end. Quinby had income from increasing her freelancing for crime magazines and syndicated news services and now also had royalties from *Murder for Love*, published in 1931 to national notice, although not always favorable. *The Saturday Review of Literature* sniffed at the product from the "Second City" that had provided the "ever-increasing stream of female murderers who have their little day in our headlines." The author, Quinby, "hobnobbed with murderesses as a newspaper reporter in Chicago, and conducted a school in jail for them and had them teach her how to crochet," so she could only have lost any sensible woman's "feeling of strangeness" in profiling a "sorry group," a "grisly procession" of women murderers. The reviewer panned the work as "padded, florid," and recommended "reticence" rather than "a pedestrian account" akin to a "chamber of horrors." Even the catchy title came in for criticism as "a misnomer" to "give a romantic twist to the murderous doings," as only two women profiled in the book had been "perhaps goaded to their deed by the pangs of love," while others "poisoned and hacked and shot their way to their ends goaded by nothing more romantic than a passion for money." In sum, the literary magazine supposed that "if you enjoyed that sort of thing, you will enjoy *Murder for Love*" but admitted that only "the genius of a Poe" would persuade the appalled reviewer to recommend the book. The reviewer did appreciate the author's argument that the "perpetrators" had "carefully premeditated" their crimes, which "Miss Quinby points out, is a distinguishing trait of the female killer, the male being more apt to act on impulse."[58]

More favorable commentary came in Quinby's hometown, including from academia, for years to come. Soon after publication, she was in good company in a scholarly journal, *American Literature*, in which a Northwestern University professor panned another book

---

58   Leila Taylor, "Chamber of Horrors," *Saturday Review of Literature*, May 2, 1931.

on "Bohemias" for "slighting" Chicago's "literary renaissance" and suggested that the omission could have been rectified by resort to recent
books by Hamlin Garland, a Pulitzer Prize-winner who had achieved
success before the turn of
the century—and by Ione
Quinby. More than a quarter
of a century later, another academic would cite her book
in a sociological study of
"pre-murderous kindness and
post-murder grief." More typical of popular-press reaction
at the time of publication was
a front-page puff piece in the
Post, hailing its "Little Miss
Quinby" for "having kept
faith with social outcasts" in
the Cook County jail, "just
as she would with women
she meets in club or political
or church circles." By then,
however, the Depression had
expanded her "circles." In the
reverse of first-person, standard "stunt stories" on women
in workplaces, she now stood
with women jobseekers on
unemployment lines and long
lines at "soup kitchens," one

The book jacket—in the original, in
eye-catching hues of orange and char-
treuse on a black background—of
Murder for Love, published in 1931, by
Chicago Evening Post "girl-crime beat" reporter Ione Quinby.

provided by Capone. She stayed in shelters with free beds to find the
stories of jobless, homeless women, and she accompanied census takers attempting to count unemployed women living on city streets.[59]

59   William H. Riback, *American Literature* 5:2 (May 1933), 197; Hans
von Hentig, "Pre-Murderous Kindness and Post-Murder Grief," *Journal of
Criminal Law, Criminology, and Police Science* 48:4 (November-December
1957), 371; Loren Carroll, "Ione Quinby Lays Bare 7 Souls in Exciting
Murder Tales," *CEP*, February 18, 1931; "Miss Quinby Presents Seven
Lady Slayers," *CEP*, March 20, 1931; IQ, "Girls Have Hard Time in
Hunting Jobs These Days/Girl Reporter Tries Her Hand in Jobless Role,"

The year 1932 brought her lowest number of stories in years, with only 42 bearing the byline of Ione Quinby, before she joined the jobless, as hard times hit harder for journalists. The times had been tumultuous in the Chicago media market since introduction of the *Times*, the city's first tabloid, which had joined the journalistic fray just weeks before "Black Tuesday" and the stock-market crash in 1929. The Depression led first to the demise of the *Journal*, the city's oldest newspaper. Then, the *Daily News* had endured the death of its owner and the sale in 1931 of the newspaper to a new owner, seeking new subscribers and encroaching on others' readers. The *Evening Post* could not long endure both the Depression and the increased competition, and its circulation declined to fewer than forty thousand. Finally, on October 29, 1932, after more than four decades in print and three years to the day since "Black Tuesday" had signaled the onset of the Depression, Quinby's newspaper issued a "Special Night Extra" edition. To follow journalistic tradition, black rules were turned to border a box "above the fold" on the front page, enclosing the terse announcement that the new publisher of the *Daily News* had purchased the *Evening Post*. With little warning, the last edition of Quinby's newspaper came two days later.[60]

The former "*Post's* little girl reporter," by then in her forties, never had been happier.

Quinby was engaged to Bruce E. Griggs, previously a reporter for the *Milwaukee Journal* and other newspapers across the country, and by then a successful freelance writer. He sold both syndicated news stories and serial fiction, such as a saga with sixty episodes in 1932. A

CEP, January 20, 1931; IQ, "800 Enumerators Begin Counting of Jobless in Chicago," *CEP*, March 15, 1931.

60   Frank Knox and K.L. Ames, Jr., "An Announcement," *CEP*, October 29, 1932; Klatt, *Chicago Journalism*, 147, 164, 179; McPhaul, *Deadlines & Monkeyshines*, 6, 281, 286. Ames was publisher of the *Post*. On Knox, born William Franklin Knox, the new publisher of the *News* had been general manager of the Hearst chain and, in 1936, would be the Republican nominee for vice-president; however, he was thrown out of the party at the behest of the *Tribune* on the eve of World War II for throwing his support to President Franklin D. Roosevelt, who named Knox, a veteran, as Secretary of the Navy in 1940. By then, of six daily newspapers in the city in 1920, four had folded, if another arose. The *Daily News* would survive for decades to the 1970s.

paean to his fiancée, its cast of characters included an intrepid Chicago
reporter named Ione, introduced as her "paper's official 'sob sister'" to
his readers. "Every big paper has one," he informed them, because publishers believed "that a woman can write a better human interest yarn
than a man," although "a smart sob story is the most difficult of all
newspaper yarns to write." His fictional Ione, at least, was "an understanding sort of person," an "office pet," and as much of "a fixture on
the paper" as its printing presses. Dozens of newspapers in the United
States and Canada carried the series. Despite the demise of her newspaper, his lucrative contract combined with her freelancing income
and royalties convinced the couple to move up their wedding plans.[61]

Ten days after the end of the *Post*, Ione Quinby became Mrs. Griggs,
a name that also would become famed in her next career. The wedding
was a quiet rite, as they wed so quickly that even his parents, overseas
as missionaries, could not attend. The couple had hoped to honeymoon by writing their way around the world but had to delay their
trip, when her father became ill. Then, the banking system collapsed.
The couple struggled for income, freelancing and traveling together
across the country for stories to sell and then for work in Washington,
D.C. Yet despite the Depression, job loss, family illness, and a deferred
honeymoon that never would happen, she would recall her newlywed
days as an "idyllic" time, when "material things" did not matter. "We
had the kind of fun that goes with being able to enjoy a sandwich
together on the road more than dinners at expensive hotels if we were
apart," she said. They had "packed twenty years of fun, happiness and
good living into thirteen months, which was all we had." At the end of
1933, her father had died, and she stayed home from a story, sending
her brother on the road as a traveling companion for her husband. On
icy roads on the way to the story in wintry Wisconsin, her husband
died in a car crash, her brother was hospitalized, and their car was

61   Bruce E. Griggs, "The Sacred Eye," *Winnipeg Free Press*, November 26,
      1932; "Funeral of Bruce Griggs," unidentified newspaper, n.d., Quinby
      Papers; Herzog, "Ione Quinby Griggs;" Mosby, "Heart of Milwaukee," 55.
      Bruce Griggs was the son of missionaries and educators at Seventh Day
      Adventist schools in Michigan and Nebraska; his father, Frederick Griggs,
      had served as president of Union College in Nebraska.

ransacked, robbing the heartbroken—and broke—widow of a hundred hard-earned dollars.[62]

—⁓— —⁓— —⁓—

Ione Quinby Griggs never would remarry nor return to her colorful
career in Chicago. At times, she would talk of missing her "brassy
days" in the city. In time, however, few co-workers in her next newsroom would recall that "Mrs. Griggs," by then a grandmotherly font
of innate folk wisdom known for ladylike reserve in her later years,
once had been known in the wicked city to the south as a worldly
woman and the foremost of the "girl reporters" on the "girl-crime beat."
Her impact would be immeasurable on millions of readers in her new
newsroom and new city, and she already had altered the future for
women in journalism in her former city as well as farther afield. That
she and other women in her field had succeeded in Chicago in the
heyday of "Jazz Age" journalism had significance beyond the "second
city," because the metropolis of the Midwest was the center of a region
with a third of the country's population in the period.[63]

Women had won front-page bylines under headlines that they had
engendered in the era, and despite their gender—or perhaps because
of it. Women journalists had redefined the news and reframed wom-
en's place, not only in newsrooms but also in their city and nationwide.
They had lowered many barriers in male bastions to tell the stories,
often of other women, that they had found in the city's streets, courtrooms, and jail cells. Her own tragic story had taken the byline of Ione
Quinby off the front page, but because of her stories, other women
would follow with front-page stories on women making progress in
politics, professions, and other sectors of society, owing to coverage of
women in the 1920s as they never had been covered before.

Women in the field of journalism and in the city would incur setbacks; Chicago newsman and historian Wayne Klatt writes that not
for another decade would a "war gal," hired to fill in for men overseas,
become the first fulltime woman police reporter in Chicago. Then, in

---

62 "What to Do," 4; Mosby, "Heart of Milwaukee," 55; "Bruce Griggs
   Dies in Crash," *MJ*, December 19, 1933; "Bruce Griggs Killed in Auto
   Crash/Elliott Quinby Recovering from Injuries," unidentified newspaper,
   December 22, 1933, Quinby Papers.

63 U.S. Census Office, *Compendium of the Fifteenth Census, 1930*, I:
   Population (Washington, D.C.: Government Printing Office, 1931), 10.

postwar years, women again would "encounter difficulties getting into the news business," as returning servicemen would "replace their sisters and aunts." By the 1950s, writes Chicago journalist John J. McPhaul, "modern news girls pursuing, as virtually all of them are, the bland beats of religion, education, and cornerstone dedications," would "envy their predecessors of the 1920s."[64]

The enviable impact of women journalists in the "Jazz Age" was as immense as their city and went even beyond the city and their medium. Just as had more acclaimed male colleagues, "girl reporters" reached millions of readers nationwide. Women also authored or inspired works of significance in the city's "literary renaissance" in fiction, theater, and film. The full range of their reportage remains a literal mother lode for further research to explore the urban past as they did, so widely and well, in an era when what happened in Chicago had not stayed in Chicago but also forever had altered popular culture, owing in part to stories of women in her city, as told to her city and retold nationwide by Ione Quinby.

She would not stay in Chicago and would miss her "brassy days" there but would bring her familiar habits—and her hats—that became part of local lore in her new life in a new locale, where she would win an even larger following, for more than half a century ahead. She would be deskbound, but her desk would remain in the newsroom, amid front-page reporters competing against the clock to meet deadlines and against each other for bylines. Her byline was different now, no longer on the front page, but "Mrs. Griggs" would be a daily byline and would become a draw to bring readers to the most popular page of the most popular newspaper in her next city.

And, for more than fifty years yet to come in her next career, she would continue to wear a hat every day—missing only a day's work in decades, which would land her name in headlines again. She would return regularly to Chicago, taking the train and having her hair done, only to reappear in her new newsroom wearing a hat over her unchanging hairdo. Curious colleagues would be told that her hat was "a holdover" from her "earlier days as a newspaperwoman in Chicago,"

---

64   Ross, *Ladies of the Press*, 6; Mills, *A Place in the News*, 22; Lutes, *Front-Page Girls*, 119-165; Klatt, *Chicago Journalism*, 176, 193; McPhaul, *Deadlines & Monkeyshines*, 128; see also "Patricia Leeds, Tribune Reporter, Covered Police Beat for 25 Years," *Chicago Tribune*, January 23, 1985.

an era when women wore hats in the city, and "girl reporters" had to be ready to go "out on assignment" to gain the experience that would take some to the top of their profession—to take their readers along for their experiences, as well. As Fahs writes, if newswomen of the 1920s rarely moved upward into management, they expanded women's place "outward"—"out into the world they 'covered,' out into new experiences in cities."[65]

For Ione Quinby Griggs, a new city, new experiences, and millions of new readers—and their stories—awaited. She hardly was alone among the unemployed in the depths of the Great Depression, nor among middle-aged, lonely widows and other women readers of her advice column to come. After the demise of her newspaper in Chicago and the death of her husband, her life's tragic lessons would serve her readers in her next career, because the byline of the front-page "girl reporter" had been known nationwide for stories of "murderesses" but also of the jobless, whose lives also had taken unlikely downturns in the era. If many another journalist out of a job also had a hard-luck story and had to start over, few would so remake themselves—yet again, in her case—to prove their ability and versatility to a new employer. In her new career and with a new byline in her new city of Milwaukee, she now would become beloved as "Mrs. Griggs."

---

65   Dan Chabot, "From All of Us, Goodby Mrs. Griggs," *MJ*, September 23, 1985; Jackie Loohauis, "Update: Looking in on a Green Sheet Legend," *MJ*, March 15, 1988; Jackie Loohauis, "'Dear Mrs. Griggs,'" "IQG Wrote a Legend of Compassion," *MJ*, August 20, 1991; Dan Chabot, "A Tribute to Mrs. Griggs," *MJ*, August 20, 1991; "Wisconsin's Voice," 23-24; Fahs, *Out on Assignment*, 121-134, 273.

2

'Dear Mrs. Griggs' and the Great Depression, 1934-1940

I one Quinby Griggs' move less than a hundred miles north on Lake Michigan's shore from Chicago to Milwaukee meant a far different milieu in many ways, including in its local media industry and in its newspaper readers. She also moved up to the major newspaper in her new city and state, the *Milwaukee Journal*, the most popular newspaper in Wisconsin by the mid-1930s, little more than half a century since its founding, and she landed work on one of the most popular sections in the newspaper. Readers had made the "Green Sheet" a regular part of their day since the section's brief debut before the first world war, when the "Green Sheet" had begun as only one "sheet," two pages, on trademark pale-green newsprint selected by the founder and publisher of the *Journal*, just because he liked the hue—and any color only could have enlivened a newspaper deemed as drab. Aimed at men then, the section had been filled by late-breaking news and sports scores. Revived in the 1920s to compete with racier stories in the city's sensationalist Hearst papers, the "Green Sheet" again was available in street sales downtown for businessmen but decidedly not for home delivery. In the 1930s, the *Milwaukee Journal* returned to its senses and its respectability as a "family newspaper," seeing need for a section "eminently suited to go into Milwaukee homes," according to Will Conrad and Kathleen and Dale Wilson in their history of the newspaper. Under a new section editor, Larry Lawrence, the "Green Sheet" doubled to four pages, now with new features to lure a larger and more female readership. Logically, then, the new editor would have been a woman, but at least

Lawrence would have the wisdom to hire the unemployed widow of a former colleague and longtime friend from Chicago.[1]

That the name of "Mrs. Griggs" on a newspaper column would become so identified with Milwaukee, and soon after her arrival, was evidence of the ability and curiosity that the lifelong Chicagoan had shown in her reportorial career. She needed to learn much about her new locale and new readers. Griggs later would recall that she "didn't know the city at all" upon her arrival in mid-1934, although Milwaukee was the twelfth-largest city in the country. However, its almost six hundred thousand residents of the city comprised less than one-sixth of the population of her former hometown. Both were working-class cities, as manufacturing centers with massive factories, but Milwaukee prided itself on its differences from Chicago and remained more rural. Even by the mid-1930s, many farms remained within Milwaukee's borders. For farmers growing hops for beer and for other peripheral industries, from bottle factories to *biergartens*—but especially breweries that had made Milwaukee famous—Prohibition had hit hard in the 1920s. Fortunately, the city's industrial mix had made Milwaukee almost immune to immediate effects of the stock-market crash of 1929. "Even a year later, the *Milwaukee Journal* could afford to look on the sunny side," writes local historian John Gurda of the editorial boast that "Milwaukee was one of the few bright spots on the nation's business map. Here is a market immune from peaks and panics."[2] The newspaper's prideful boosterism had proved woefully wrong, however, as joblessness brought an array of new concerns among the audiences for the *Milwaukee Journal*.

The newspaper's circulation, its city, and its metropolitan area would continue to grow slowly in the 1930s, although population increases would owe less to newcomers like Griggs, who came to the *Journal* with a promise of employment, than to former farm families coming to Milwaukee in hope of finding work. The newspaper would expand circulation in the city and its surrounding area, including

---

1   Wells, *Milwaukee Journal*, 87.

2   Robert C. Nesbit, *Wisconsin* (Madison: University of Wisconsin Press, 1989), 476-490; John Gurda, *The Making of Milwaukee* (Milwaukee: Milwaukee County Historical Society, 2000), 276; Ione Quinby Griggs, "Dear Mrs. Griggs...," *Once a Year* (1984), 35. Hereafter, Griggs, as a source, is cited as IQG.

working-class suburbs such as West Allis, soon the second-largest city in the state, with a population increase of almost 80 percent during the decade. However, 80 percent of all Milwaukee County residents lived in the city, whose population would increase, in part owing to the end of Prohibition. Through the peculiar lens of its locale, the local press hailed the event in 1933, not as a loss for reformers, nor as a victory for lobbyists for "liquor interests." Instead, Prohibition's demise was a win for democracy, as defined by the city's citizens, who were "interested solely in obtaining liquor in decent quantities at reasonable prices," editorialized the *Journal* on the return of residents to taverns and the return of jobs to breweries and related industries. However, that did not mean employment for many newcomers to the city.[3]

More than forty thousand farmers, farm workers, and their families were leaving the land in Wisconsin, as the state's farm population peaked at mid-decade in the 1930s to decline forever afterward. Many farm families had been hard-hit by a Midwestern drought at its most severe in 1934, when wind storms from the west dropped soil from the Dust Bowl onto Milwaukee. Fully a fifth of all families in the county lived on the dole at mid-decade, when New Deal programs were newly underway. A "Hooverville" of homeless families lived in shacks in a park on the site of the city's original center, Cathedral Square, but a few blocks from the newspaper plant. The name of the site signified the centrality of religion in local culture, especially Catholicism, from the city's founding a century before by both French Canadians and *Métis*, the descendants of fur traders who had intermarried with Native Americans. More than half of all of the residents of Milwaukee and Wisconsin professed Catholicism even in the mid-1930s, when Griggs arrived.[4]

Reporters new to the city—and, certainly, an advice columnist—were wise to recognize need for sensitivity to religious sensibilities of readers, more churchgoing than in most regions of the country. After the French Canadians had come sizeable influxes of more immigrants, from the first Irish Catholics to others of the faith among Germans

---

3   Nesbit, *Wisconsin*, 476-490; Gurda, *Making of Milwaukee*, 277, 284; Will Conrad, Kathleen Wilson, and Dale Wilson, *The Milwaukee Journal: The First Eighty Years* (Madison: University of Wisconsin Press, 1964), 142-143.

4   Nesbit, *Wisconsin*, 476-490; Gurda, *Making of Milwaukee*, 277, 284.

and then Poles and Italians, much like the ethnic mix of Griggs' former hometown. However, as Chicago had attracted more Irish than
any city, Milwaukee had become best known as the home of German
immigrants with more religious diversity, many of them Lutherans—
of many synods—as well as German Jews and German "freethinkers"
of no religious affiliation, fewer in numbers but influential for founding many major institutions in the city. Despite religious differences,
German immigrants had made Milwaukee famous for *gemuetlichkeit*,
the "good life," and Griggs' column-to-come at times would seem a sort
of *kaffeeklatsch* in print form for local *hausfrauen* to meet on matters
of love, marriage, family—the concerns that initially would dominate
the column—and more issues that reflected the region's past, while
readers also were amid changes soon to come in Milwaukee.[5]

Milwaukee also remained remarkably homogenous in the mid-
1930s. In both Milwaukee and Chicago, African Americans working
on the Great Lakes and in the fur trade had been among the first settlers, more than a century before. Unlike Chicago, however, Milwaukee
had not seen sizeable numbers since from the Great Migration and
was home to a miniscule African American community, among the
smallest in the urban North. The first Mexican American migrants, or
primeros, also remained few, after their earlier *barrio* had disappeared
early in the Depression. Instead, almost one in five Milwaukeeans was
foreign-born, far more than in most cities in the country then, and
they held firmly to their faiths. Indeed, in the 1930s, as Wisconsin
historian William F. Thompson writes, "church affiliation was perhaps the single most powerful institutional force" in the city and state,
where residents "remained loyal to the church of their ancestors" and
to "inherited attitudes about marriage and the role of men and women,
about children and education, about indebtedness and home ownership"—all among contested issues to come from future contributors
to Griggs' column. As a newsroom colleague would recall, "people believed in God and Mrs. Griggs then. But Ione Quinby Griggs received
more mail."[6]

---

5   Ibid.; Kathleen Neils Conzen, *Immigrant Milwaukee: Accommodation
    and Community in a Frontier City* (Cambridge, Mass.: Harvard University
    Press, 1976), 15-21.

6   Joe William Trotter, Jr., *Black Milwaukee: The Making of an Urban
    Proletariat, 1915-1945* (Urbana: University of Illinois Press, 1985), 8;

Ethnic enclaving meant that residents prayed in many languages still spoken in the state and the streets as well as in the pews, many languages in which they also read the news in the era. Among dailies in the city, her newspaper competed for circulation with Hearst papers that, combined, matched that of the *Milwaukee Journal*: the sensationalist *Wisconsin News* that also published in afternoons and the conservative *Milwaukee Sentinel* in mornings. All also competed across the state for loyal readers of local alternatives, such as the *Wisconsin State Journal* and *Capital Times* in the state capital of Madison and daily newspapers in more than a dozen smaller cities. Loyal readers also supported more than a hundred weeklies in Wisconsin, including more than a dozen foreign-language and English-language ethnic weeklies. Even in Milwaukee, where most newspapers long had been published in German, the *Journal* contended with at least three daily foreign-language newspapers as well as a weekly African American newspaper.[7]

In the era, the news in every newspaper reached readers of every ethnicity in soup kitchens and on bread lines. Despite boastful editorials, the Depression hit hard in Milwaukee and across Wisconsin. After the stock-market crash, despite initially minimal impact in the state, Wisconsinites witnessed 116 bank failures, 1,500 business closings, and hundreds of farm foreclosures. As farm prices fell, and farm income dropped 14 percent, dairy farmers waged "milk strikes" across the state and region. However, farm workers had been only a fourth of the state workforce. Employment fell 33 percent statewide and more than 44 percent in Milwaukee County, where wages had dropped more than 64 percent in a few years. For women, the situation could be worse. Often "first fired" owing to federal policies, few had the protection of unions, which long had made women unwelcome, with major

---

Genevieve G. McBride, "The Progress of 'Race Men' and 'Colored Women' in the Black Press in Wisconsin, 1892-1985," in Suggs, ed., *Black Press in the Middle West*, 336-339; Joseph Rodriguez, Sarah Filzen, Susan Hunter, Dana Nix, and Marc Rodriguez, *Nuestro Milwaukee: The Making of the United Community Center* (Milwaukee: UCC, 2000), 8-10; William F. Thompson, *History of Wisconsin, Vol. VI: Continuity and Change, 1940-1965* (Madison: State Historical Society of Wisconsin, 1988), 35-38; William Janz, "Phil Osofer Says He's Feeling Blue About Passing of the Green," *MS*, March 18, 1994.

7   Thompson, *History of Wisconsin*, 31-32, 36.

impact in the labor mecca of Milwaukee. Women had lost work at an
even greater rate than had men, who were rescued by state work programs set up by one La Follette in Wisconsin, the governor, and then by
federal work programs lobbied by another La Follette in Washington,
in the Senate. An exception to New Deal programs, primarily providing relief for men, would come with the Milwaukee Handicraft
Program, created under the Works Progress Administration of 1934.
The Milwaukee program trained women for work in textile factories.
Other women, its founders, first would open the doors in 1935, only
to find a long line of hundreds, a "careworn, and harassed group of
women," weak from malnutrition and looking for work, writes historian Leslie Bellais. More than 60 percent of the city's jobless women
willing to seek welfare in the 1930s had been self-supporting in past,
reported the *Journal*, which just had hired Griggs for the staff of the
"Green Sheet."[8]

The new editor of the "Green Sheet" and his new assistant would
fashion a formula for the section that not only would succeed in competing for readers in the 1930s but also would be followed faithfully
for more than five decades to become a folksy fixture of the city, featuring oddities in the news that fit nowhere else in the *Milwaukee Journal*.
If unique in the newspaper industry, the section provided a place for
many newspaper mainstays, with a motley collection of comic strips,
cartoons, crossword puzzles, and local features of a sentimental sort
to supplement syndicated material from around the world and from
maudlin to weird. The newly "wholesome" section, writes *Journal*
reporter and historian Robert W. Wells, now "no longer specialized
in Manhattan love nests and Chicago trunk murders." Yet a former
Chicago reporter, famed for front-page coverage of its murders and
"murderesses," soon would create a community forum with her readers

8   Paul J. Glad, *History of Wisconsin, Vol. V: War, a New Era, and Depression,
1914-1940* (Madison: State Historical Society of Wisconsin, 1990),
356, 380-382, 396-397, 467-479, 492-494; Nesbit, *Wisconsin*, 476-490;
Gurda, *Making of Milwaukee*, 278; Henry J. Schmandt, John C. Goldbach,
and Donald B. Vogel, *Milwaukee: A Contemporary Urban Profile* (New
York: Praeger, 1971), 14-16; Herbert Austin Jacobs, "The Wisconsin Milk
Strikes," *Wisconsin Magazine of History* 35:1 (Autumn 1951), 30-35;
Leslie Bellais, "'No Idle Hands': A Milwaukee WPA Handicraft Project,"
Wisconsin Magazine of History 84:2 (Winter 2000-2001), 48-56; "Jobless
Unattached Women Are Studied by Labor Board," *MJ*, July 26, 1938.

in her new and seemingly more sedate city, penning the most popular feature in the newspaper's most popular section—a column that would realize the aim of reaching women readers by the millions in Milwaukee, in Wisconsin, and eventually even beyond its borders.[9]

Ione Quinby Griggs would create a forum for community discussion from a woman's perspective of topics, such as sex, that were unimaginable to the men in the newsroom then—but abetting her male editor's aim to make the "Green Sheet" a means for media social control in the city and state. He already had introduced a regular feature, photographs of Milwaukee elders marking golden wedding anniversaries, with a flippant comment to his news-side colleagues that running the sentimental "pictures in the paper" was fully justified in the *Journal*, "if two people put up with each other for fifty years." Actually, his motive was social control, according to the historians Conrad and the Wilsons, if not in so many words. They write that he saw the feature as "a reassuring antidote to divorce stories" in the headlines of the news section. Then came the new editor's next conception to improve his readers, which made even more evident the agenda to promote marital stability in the city and beyond, to the newspaper's entire circulation area.[10]

The advice column, also a prime example of media social control, could impart implicit or even explicit messages about community norms. As scholar David Gudelunas writes, advice columns perform the function of a "public discourse" between readers and the columnist, with immense impact in popular culture. Historically, he writes, the "primary function" of an advice columnist has been to serve as "a cultural benchmark" and as a "moral barometer" that "both identifies and helps to shift social norms." Even "readers who never actually mail a letter to the columnist" use advice columns as a means "to gauge their own behavior" and values, he argues—and for entertainment value, from "eavesdropping" on friends and neighbors. Eventually, the "modern advice column" would evolve with a participatory function for readers to also serve as writers, especially women. "Just as anxious to weigh in with their own advice as they are to seek it from the columnist,"

9   Wells, *Milwaukee Journal*, 133-134, 204, 261.

10   Ibid.; Chris Chan, "Milwaukee's Local Color: The *Journal*, the Green Sheet, and Its Readers," *Wisconsin Magazine of History* 94:4 (Summer 2011), 16; Conrad, Wilson, and Wilson, *Milwaukee Journal*, 116-117.

he writes, women were welcome in advice columns to engage in "public discourse" by contributing to their corner of the newspapers that otherwise allowed only men to do so in letters-to-the-editor columns, long a gendered and "contested journalistic terrain" in a "largely masculine press" dominated by male values and voices. Advice columnists' "uniquely feminized voice" instead invited women readers to discuss a wide range of issues dismissed by mainly male editors, Gudelunas writes—just as "advice columns never have been taken terribly seriously" by scholars, according to his analysis of media history and of the "advice industry."[11]

At first, the "Green Sheet" editor would conceive of an "advice to the lovelorn" column, typical of the time, when "Dear Mrs. Griggs" would debut late in 1934 with a promise to resolve "love problems"—but not for long would her readers accept so restrictive an agenda. They soon would reframe the feature as their own, while her willingness to accede to collaborating with her readers would contribute to the immediate success of the column. "Dear Mrs. Griggs" also, almost immediately, became an early example of the "modern advice column," as defined by Gudelunas. Although his study samples columns that came later, and that came elsewhere in the country, his analysis provides useful context for understanding the significance of Griggs' work as ahead of its time in the "advice industry." He finds that advice columns fall into three periods of development in "topics and tones," with an initial period into the 1930s with a focus only on women and "courting practices"—also initially the topic of Griggs' column, and one that would continue throughout following periods. Not until the mid-1940s and even into the 1950s does the analysis discover a next phase, with topics of and by teenagers and "frazzled parents." Finally, from the mid-1950s forward, came columns with a focus on "explicit discussion of sexuality and more general societal concerns" of serious and controversial import, such as domestic violence—if leavened by lighthearted letters about spouses, such as "husbands who hog blankets in bed."[12]

---

11   Gudelunas, *Confidential to America*, 4-5. Similar findings of a range of topics in an advice column from the mid-1950s forward that were "innovative" even then also are evident in an earlier study; see David I. Grossvogel, *Dear Ann Landers: Our Intimate and Changing Dialogue with America's Best-Loved Confidante* (New York: McGraw-Hill, 1989).

12   Gudelunas, *Confidential to America*, 3-6.

The modern, mediative role of the columnist-as-moderator and the range of topics in a "modern advice column" already were evident in "Dear Mrs. Griggs" almost from its inception, as she willingly adapted to allowing her readers, primarily women, to set the agenda for their page of the newspaper then and for more than half a century to come. If she was prescient in her column, her ability and its popularity were not foreseen by *Milwaukee Journal* management. In a memoir marking her fiftieth anniversary with the company, she would recall that the managing editor would not put her on the regular payroll, at first. Instead, "until he was sure that I would do," and that "the *Journal* could afford another employee" in the uncertain economic times, she went on the journalistic equivalent of piecework or "space rates" per inch of copy. Fortunately, her "Green Sheet" editor gave Griggs sufficient piecework to pay for a room in a residential hotel, although only "a tiny, bathless room," where she "had to subsist for five days on bread and peanut butter" for the first lonely weeks in her new locale, as Griggs would recall, even long decades later. "But I was so glad to be working, that didn't faze me," Griggs would write.[13]

She soon would find a welcome in the city, as both the first resort for millions of lonely readers seeking solace or as the "final say," as they said in Milwaukee, on many an issue. Her newcomer status at the start may have been a reason for her willingness to welcome readers' guidance that would make Griggs' column ahead of its time. She became recognizable to readers because of other decisions, as well, about her new byline in her new hometown and about where she would call home. A columnist could become a "warm presence in an otherwise impersonal, ostensibly objective newspaper," as Gudelunas writes, although most advice columnists hid behind their "stylized and constructed personalities" and pseudonyms, which achieved only a "presumed authenticity." In contrast, Griggs would have an unusual "authenticity" in having her own name in the column and, indeed, as the name of the "Dear Mrs. Griggs" column, which would help to make her recognizable to readers at a time when other columnists continued to privilege a pseudonymous "journalistic authority," as Gudelunas writes. More important for Milwaukee women may have been that they were given a more participatory role in public discourse, and that they trusted a recognizable columnist giving her own name—but more important for Griggs, her

---

13   Ibid.; IQG, "Dear Mrs. Griggs," 35.

column's success would put her on the regular payroll, not a moment
too soon for her to be able to afford better meals and housing in her
new hometown.[14]

Like many newcomers, Griggs had few guides, other than her late
husband's friends in the newsroom and her daily reading of the newspaper, not only to learn about her new locale but also to find housing,
and her choice of lodging and its locale also would help to make her
more recognizable. A new experience for a newly widowed woman
far from family, "it was the first time I ever had lived alone," she later
would recall. Like millions of displaced widows and other single wom-
en, almost invisible in the Depression but determined to remain visi-
bly "respectable," Griggs first could afford lodging only at a somewhat
rundown hotel downtown. Even after she went on the regular payroll
and for most of the rest of her life, however, she would make her home
in downtown residential hotels, but a few blocks' daily walk—she did
not drive—from work. Decades later, a hotel that would be her last
home would enshrine photographs of Griggs in its lobby to enlighten
tourists to its most famous resident. From her first decade in the city,
locals would delight in sightings of the behatted and beloved "Mrs.
Griggs," strolling the streets, stopping and shopping at downtown department stores, and dining in the downtown diners and eateries that
she never would abandon for suburban malls that later would arise
around the city.[15]

A fast learner, Griggs again proved her versatility to pen the range
of stories needed to fill the newly expanded "Green Sheet." That she
went off piecework pay so swiftly was a feat at a time when lines of
jobless were seen daily at the state employment office near her newspaper plant. A colleague and the newspaper's historian, Robert W. Wells,
would recall a reason for her swift promotion with cynicism, writing
that Griggs proved so prolific on piecework pay "that management decided it would be cheaper to put her on the regular payroll." But Griggs
always would be grateful, recalling that "a full-time job on the *Journal*
… meant security at a time when it was almost impossible to get a
job." So insecure was Griggs about her finances, having seen her first

---

14   Gudelunas, *Confidential to America*, 3-6.

15   IQG, "Dear Mrs. Griggs," 35; Elaine S. Abelson, "'Women Who Have
     No Men to Work for Them': Gender and Homelessness in the Great
     Depression, 1930-1934," *Feminist Studies* 29:1 (Spring 2003), 104-127.

journalism job disappear in a matter of days during the Depression, that she would continue to write features for the "Green Sheet" and to freelance nationally syndicated stories for years, getting out of the office and "out on assignment." Her continued fascination with circuses took her hours north of Milwaukee to Manitowoc to report on a "circus school" run by a retiree from the "big top." Another feature on a large family in the small town of Allenton, "Seventeen Wisconsin Brothers And Sisters Vote on Name for Number Eighteen," was picked up by press in the East. She even sold serial fiction to the "Green Sheet" and other outlets, such as "Daughters Grow Up," subtitled as a "True to Life Novel With Milwaukee Setting Full of Human Interest."[16]

Her next career, however, would become a sinecure and make her indispensable to her new employer. The "origin story" of Griggs' advice column, like all good myths, continues to be contested by colleagues. Some accounts suggest that editors were dissatisfied with nationally syndicated advice columns available, before a letter came that would launch her new career, if the origins of the letter and identity of the writer are disputed. Some sources state that the letter, allegedly from a reader, actually had been "hammered out" by her editor, not only looking for a local advice column but also inspired by local police reports in the Depression of increasing calls for "family trouble," a euphemism for domestic violence. Other accounts suggest that the letter had been sent by a reader to the city desk, which then had routed it to the feature editor. In sum, "origin stories" vary according to sources vying for credit for the creation of "Dear Mrs. Griggs." Whatever its authorship, the letter portrayed the plight of a woman pleading for help with an alcoholic, adulterous husband, with the potential for domestic violence that had led to headlines in the "murder city" of Chicago and front-page bylines for former police reporter Ione Quinby. Accounts generally agree that, when handed the letter, she handled the reply so well that her editor offered the advice column that again would bring her bylines, but now as "Mrs. Griggs."[17]

---

16   IQG, "Dear Mrs. Griggs," 35; IQG, "Seventeen Wisconsin Brothers And Sisters Vote On Name For Number Eighteen," *Baltimore* (Md.) *Sun*, May 15, 1938; IQG, "Circus School in Manitowoc," *MJ*, September 1, 1936; IQG, "Daughters Grow Up," *MJ*, April 22, 1936; Wells, *Milwaukee Journal*, 262.

17   Ibid.; Chan, "Milwaukee's Local Color," 16.

Griggs agreed to the advice column with "misgivings," she would recall, but needed the work—a guarantee for a onetime "girl reporter" who
had covered murders and mayhem. Griggs' misgivings arose from her
lack of training for the task, although her predecessors had not shared
any standard preparation. They had come from a range of careers to
pen advice columns as early as the eighteenth century in England, according to historian Margaret Beetham, who notes that women columnists in British "ladies' magazines" were belittled as "agony aunts;"
no nickname was bestowed on male counterparts in men's magazines.
In America, advice columns arose in the nineteenth century on the
"four F's" of women's magazines: food, fashion, furnishings, and especially family to foreshadow a new form near the end of the century
from "America's first personal advice columnist." Historians Madelon
Golden Schilpp, Sharon M. Murphy, and Maurine S. Beasley agree
that the first was Elizabeth Meriwether Gilmer. A fiction writer before
her column had debuted in 1896 in the *New Orleans Picayune*, she
established the form's norms by following Victorian-era practice for
women in the "public sphere," such as a pseudonym.[18]

As "Dorothy Dix," the "first personal-advice columnist" in the country was "a cultural force" as well as a suffragist and a social feminist to
the end of her career as one of the best-known and highly paid journalists of her era, syndicated to sixty million readers in several countries.
However, she called her columns "sermonettes," and termed her letters from readers as "confessionals," evidence of religiosity that caused
journalist and historian Ishbel Ross to call her "America's Mother
Confessor." That format causes historian Alice Fahs to argue against
Gilmer as the first advice columnist and to credit a contemporary,
Marie Manning. Also a fiction writer prior to her journalism career,
Manning began her column as "Beatrice Fairfax" in 1898 for newspa-
pers in New York, first the *World*, and then the *Journal*. Manning later
returned to writing magazine fiction before reviving her column for

---

18   Wells, *Milwaukee Journal*, 252-254; Margaret Beetham, *A Magazine of
      Her Own? Domesticity and Desire in the Women's Magazine, 1800-1914*
      (London: Routledge, 1996), 22-25; Abramson, *Sob Sister Journalism*, 38-
      40; Harnett Kane, *Dear Dorothy Dix: The Story of a Compassionate Woman*
      (Garden City, N.Y.: Doubleday, 1952), 44-50; Fahs, *Out on Assignment*,
      121-132, 299; Madelon Golden Schilpp and Sharon M. Murphy, *Great
      Women of the Press* (Carbondale: Southern Illinois University Press),
      112-120.

national syndication, which she also would continue to the mid-twentieth century. Both "Dorothy Dix" and "Beatrice Fairfax" would have many imitators of less longevity and more disparate backgrounds, such as a nurse who later would be the original advice columnist called "Ann Landers," long years later in the Midwest.[19]

None of her predecessors, however, nor any others since, would match Ione Quinby Griggs' longevity and productivity in the "advice industry" as a daily columnist for more than half a century. She also was an anomaly in using her own name and in coming from a career as a front-page crime reporter, unusual for an advice columnist, which initially caused her concern. She overcame her misgivings, however, when she realized that she could rely on her experiences under the byline of Ione Quinby to guide her work as "Dear Mrs. Griggs." Or, as she said to her editors in accepting the assignment, she could draw upon "the common sense I could muster and the knowledge of human nature" gained as a "girl reporter" covering crime and "murderesses" in Chicago as the perfect training for handling anything that might come her way in Milwaukee.[20]

---

19   Kane, *Dear Dorothy Dix*, 44-50; Ross, *Ladies of the Press*, 75-83; Fahs, *Out on Assignment*, 121-132, 299; Schilpp and Murphy, *Great Women of the Press*, 112-120; Maurine H. Beasley, "Elizabeth M. Gilmer as Dorothy Dix: A Southern Journalist Rewrites the Myth of the Southern Lady," paper presented at the Dorothy Dix Symposium, Trenton, Ky., September 27, 1991, in the Dorothy Dix Collection, F. G. Woodward Library Archives, Austin Peay State University, Clarksville, Tennessee.

20   Dan Chabot, "From All of Us, Goodby Mrs. Griggs;" "IQG Wrote a Legend of Compassion;" "Wisconsin's Voice," 23-24. On other advice columnists of longevity, others' careers spanned more years but they had a hiatus, or their columns were not daily throughout, or the columns were not conducted solely by one columnist; Griggs alone conducted her column alone, six days a week for fifty-one years. Elizabeth Meriwether "Dorothy Dix" Gilmer's career spanned fifty-five years, almost matched by Griggs' fifty-one years, although Gilmer's column did not run daily throughout her career. Marie "Beatrice Fairfax" Manning's column spanned almost as many years, although with a mid-career hiatus, for a total run of less than a quarter of a century; see Gudelunas, *Confidential to America*, 37-70, and Fahs, *Out on Assignment*, 121-134.

Later columnists of longevity, "Ann Landers" and "Dear Abby," had little journalistic training, and like "Dix" and "Fairfax," also used pseudonyms.

For her readers, in a series of promotional pieces penned in
November 1934 prior to her first column, Griggs reviewed her credentials, with rather racy highlights as well as cautionary tales from
her Chicago career. "My reportorial scrapbooks contain hundreds of
stories," she wrote, confidently claiming that the moral of the stories
was to ask for advice from a woman whose "wealth of experience"
would put readers "on the right road." In the news section, the headline on her promotional piece screamed, in inch-high type, about a
Chicago "murderess" imprisoned for life, "Because She Did Not Ask
for Advice" from Griggs. On another, unabashed bit of puffery in the
"Green Sheet"—amid tidbits on tarantulas and "Whamdoodles," a
collection of cryptic commentary on world news ranging from Irish
sweepstakes to Australian kangaroos to Siamese royalty—the headline that streamed across the section's front page promised her potential readers that, "If You Have a Love Problem Mrs. Griggs Will Help
You Solve It!"[21]

The promotion for Griggs' column reverted to the form and florid
writing style of her "sob sister" reportage in Chicago but that she soon
would abandon, fortunately, in her new city.

Ruth Crowley, a nurse and also a columnist on child care, created the "Ask
Ann Landers" column and pseudonym in 1943 for the *Chicago Sun-Times*;
she continued to 1948 and again from 1951, when the *Sun-Times* syndicated the column, to her death in 1955. Others conducted the column until
the hiring in 1956 of Esther Friedman Lederer, who switched in 1987 to
the *Chicago Tribune*; the column ended at her death in 2002. She employed
assistants, as did her twin, Pauline Friedman Phillips, who created the
pseudonym of "Abigail van Buren" and the "Dear Abby" column in 1956
and retired in 2002; her daughter continued the column. See Gudelunas,
Confidential to America, 93-134; Janice Pottker and Bob Speziale, *Dear
Ann, Dear Abby: The Unauthorized Biography of Ann Landers and Abigail
Van Buren* (New York: Dodd, Mead, 1987); "Obituary: Ann Landers,"
Chicago Tribune, June 23, 2002; Margalit Fox, "Pauline Phillips, Flinty
Advisor to Millions as 'Dear Abby,' Dies at 94," *New York Times*, January
17, 2013.

21   "If You Have a Love Problem Mrs. Griggs Will Help You Solve It!" *MJ*,
     November 6, 1934; IQG, "'Tiger Girl' Went to Prison for Life Because She
     Did Not Ask for Advice; She Sobbed Her Story to Me," *MJ*, November
     8, 1934.

> Ione Quinby Griggs, who will give advice to anyone who has a love problem, has listened to the sad stories of many women whose lives have been broken because they had no one to turn to in hours of trial…. Love problems have led to murder, many times.
>
> And most of those murders could have been prevented had the hot headed killer asked for advice. In her capacity of reporter, she has loaned her powder puff to several women who had killed for love or lack of understanding of their own love problems.[22]

They were "women in the shadow of the noose," a fate from which they could have been spared, had they but sought advice from Griggs, who "knows present day problems must be fought with modern methods." More than anyone, she wrote in words that could be interpreted as about her fame in Chicago as much as its many "murderesses," she could vouch that "ladies accepted in the best drawing rooms have achieved headline fame by the homicide route." Sadly, women's motivations for murder were many, and "the old idea that civilized ladies never think of throwing things or shooting" was passé. As an alternative, she wrote, they could write to their columnist.[23]

> Wives have poured out their hearts about unpunctual husbands, sarcastic husbands, domineering husbands, and philandering husbands.
>
> Mothers-in-law have cried on her shoulder. Daughters-in-law have slapped mothers-in-law in front of her….
>
> Girls have cried out their hearts to her in delinquent courts and police stations.[24]

She also welcomed male letter writers, as "men have given her the low-down on nagging wives, extravagant wives, untidy wives and unfaithful wives."[25] Many men would admit to reading the column for decades to come, although almost nine of every ten letter writers would be women.

Perhaps most intriguing in Griggs' promotional pieces—and most promising for research—was a line predictive of a participatory role for women readers, whom she would empower to help her to write her page as their page of the newspaper. Promotion of the column

---

22 "If You Have a Love Problem."

23 Ibid.

24 Ibid.

25 Ibid.

positioned her as the woman of experience and repeatedly had requested that readers seek her help—"write me your problems"—until
a day before the column's debut. Then, in her last line, Griggs invited
her readers to give advice as well: "If you've found a recipe for happiness, send me that, so I can pass it along to others."[26] If almost an
afterthought, her promise of so participatory a role for women readers
was new in her newspaper as well as in most major media, in an era
when most newspapers and magazines limited audience feedback to
letters to the editor. Letter writers on the editorial pages apparently
were male readers, and all letter writers responded to newspapers' reporting on news of the day, an agenda determined by the editors, most
of them also men.

Relevant research on "the way that gender informs genre," in an analysis of rural women letter writers—like many of Griggs' readers—to an
advice column in the era suggests impact of their empowerment from
the experience of a collaborative exercise as compared to that of male
letter writers to media. Their letters suggest that men were more motivated by individualistic aims to impose their perspectives on others,
while women letter writers were more likely to share autobiographical
narratives, telling personal stories to form a group identity and a supportive, collective "consciousness," according to scholar Janet Galligani
Casey. She looks at letters from farmwomen for four decades, writing
to a magazine with more than a million subscribers by the 1930s. She
argues that *The Farmer's Wife* was a forum for "a particular form of
self-narrative that assumed prominence with the proliferation of popular women's magazines" in the era, as "women weighed in on a variety
of social issues" and "shared their personal experiences" in a communal
forum that encouraged "public revelations" regarding the previously
"private domain of home and family" as well as their "specialized labor and class concerns." The rural women letter writers—like Griggs'
readers, both rural and urban but also primarily "working-class white
women with middle-class aspirations," as Casey writes—"lay outside
of the usual boundaries" of self-expression in print that limited opportunities to voice their viewpoints and concerns.[27]

---

26   IQG, "'Tiger Girl.'"

27   Janet Galligani Casey, "Farm Women, Letters to the Editor, and the
     Limits of Autobiography Theory," *Journal of Modern Literature* 28:1
     (Autumn 2004), 89-94.

The research on rural women has relevance for other, urban, work-ing-class women readers and letter writers, also "marginalized or pa-tronized" by media that favored middle-class, suburban women. From often-isolated circumstances of rural lives, Casey writes, letter writ-ers in her study had opportunity to be heard "in their own words," on their own agenda, to the point that they occasionally silenced "the larger editorial voice" of staff forced to accede to unexpected "discus-sions" that led to floods of letters. For example, readers debated a defi-nition of "success" after a letter from a cheerful farmwife led others to counter with "intimate revelations," including from childless read-ers who felt devalued by a rural focus on childrearing. In part, both rural farmwomen and urban working-class women were besieged by media social-control messages of "bourgeois versions of domesticity and demeanor." In response, readers encouraged each other with con-tributions that constructed their reality more realistically than had the overly optimistic reader and reframed the magazine's agenda, as "farm success stories" became a recurring theme and regular feature in *The Farmer's Wife*. In sum, Casey writes, the magazine offered readers "the possibility that individual farm women could contribute, through self-narrative," to "a collective narrative" of their lives, with readers rewriting the "modern concept of the farmers' wife." That prospect proved "a compelling incentive" for readers' participation, a significant reason for the unprecedented circulation and popularity of such a spe-cialized periodical, although the magazine often offered other incen-tives and prizes—cash—for the letters deemed best.[28]

Griggs' readers gladly would author their page in the newspaper for free, for no greater compensation than the opportunity to be heard, to advise and be advised, not only by the advice columnist but also by their peer group in the "Green Sheet." Her page would evolve swiftly, as she came to act less as a "mother confessor" and more as a moderator in collaboration with her readers, predominantly women, who would write most of the column. The wide-ranging discourse on their lives also would evolve in decades of societal change and challenges ahead.

And, owing to the unusual connection with her readers, the colum-nist would become a legendary icon in her city in decades to come, despite Griggs' initial "misgivings" about the changes and the chal-lenges for a onetime "girl reporter," who had covered murders and

---

28 Ibid.

mayhem "out on assignment" in the streets of a major city but now would be restricted to a desk, reading letters, in the much smaller city of Milwaukee. However, she would be in the newsroom, and although her column would be aimed at women, her desk was set not to the side in the "women's pages" section but was with the feature sections' staff, closer to the middle of the newsroom, where reporters wrote the front page amid the chaos of competing against the clock to meet deadlines and write headlines, as well as to compete with each other for bylines. Also, her byline now would be secure, six days a week—and, if not on the front page, her name would top the page to which millions of readers would turn first daily, the most popular page in the most-read newspaper in town. And they would do so for more than the next half-century.[29]

In time, her desk in the newsroom—not the nearby offices of men, the publishers and editors, whom she would outlast—would become a destination in Milwaukee, the most popular stop on daily tours of the newspaper plant for thousands of readers. Like the *Journal*, its ad-vice columnist became an institution in the city, but Griggs personified an often-impersonal media for readers. They wanted only to watch a tiny woman at her desk, and in her trademark hat, reading letters and typing her column. They needed only to know, some would say, if there really was a Mrs. Griggs—not someone using a pseudonym, such as some man adopting a female pen name, nor a staff taking turns at sorting mailbags full of letters to reply with a few platitudinous lines.[30]

Journal tour guides would be trained to reassure the groups of vis-itors that "the real Mrs. Griggs" read their letters by the hundreds weekly and really wrote the replies to readers. As the column grew in popularity, so would her workload, but she would refuse repeated of-fers of a secretary. She alone would read all letters and type all replies, published or private, often after hours of research for community

---

29   "IQG Wrote a Legend."

30   Wells, *Milwaukee Journal*, 263. On males masquerading as women col-umnists in past, Edward Bok, publisher of the *Ladies' Home Journal*, fa-mously used a female pseudonym in 1889 for his "Side Talks With Girls;" see Jennifer Scanlon, *Inarticulate Longings: The Ladies' Home Journal, Gender, and the Promises of Consumer Culture* (New York: Routledge, 1995), 50-51; on the tactic continuing today, see Gudelunas, *Confidential to America*, 1.

resources and relief available for readers who needed far more than an advice columnist could provide. At times, Griggs even would directly intervene to call, meet, and assist troubled readers, who would be forever grateful. As a result, she would receive many invitations to weddings, while readers remaining unwed would honor her in other ways. With a "considerable ... unwed mother constituency" within the first years of her column, as a colleague recalled, "she'd had seven girls named for her, and one boy was named for her late husband, Bruce. The mother of the first of the numerous newborn Iones would get the father to marry her. Mrs. Griggs attended the wedding and acted as godmother to the baby."[31]

That readers with less personal experience of her intervention also needed to know if there really was a Mrs. Griggs also was understandable—although in time, as her earlier career would recede from public memory among new co-workers as well as newspaper readers, they never would know why she would work so hard to "keep needless unhappiness out of the lives of her readers," a colleague would recall. Reasons for the end of her Chicago years and career had "scarred her life," he recalled, but "only a handful of her co-workers realized the extent of her efforts" to try to prevent heartbreak for her readers. Occasionally, she would reveal impatience with women who exploited their gender, her gender that she never had allowed to stop her from a story. More often, she would show the sense of humor that had carried her through heartbreak as well. However, she never would be "flippant, never insensitive to others' infirmities," nor would she ever employ "sarcasm or wise-cracks" with readers, as colleagues would write—and as readers knew. A reader would write, many decades later, that in a field "often occupied by superficial or smug advisors," she would be a welcome contrast with "wise-cracking latecomers Ann and Abby," syndicated columnists who would be carried in other Milwaukee newspapers in an attempt to dislodge market dominance of the *Milwaukee Journal* with "Dear Mrs. Griggs."[32]

And in time, as Griggs would become known for her ladylike reserve in the newsroom and would gain a reputation as a grandmotherly font of innate folk wisdom, she would seem far removed from the worldly woman who once had been the foremost "girl reporter" in Chicago and

---

31   Ibid.
32   Wells, *Milwaukee Journal*, 263; Mosby, "Heart of Milwaukee," 55.

now offered her experience in the wicked city to the south for her new readers in Milwaukee. However, even when her column first appeared, with her racy self-introduction to readers that promoted her as an expert on "love problems," their enthusiastic response and reframing of the column to encompass a far wider agenda suggests their need for connection, not only with the columnist but also with each other, as they formed a community of support in the newspaper.

The phenomenon argues against theories of "passive media consumers" in past, as this study provides evidence of a forerunner—utilizing only print technology—of "user-generated content" in today's terms, a "participatory journalism" or "collaborative journalism" as a form of "citizen journalism" combining contributions of the public and the professional journalists. "What began as a sympathetic ear for unhappy women," writes historian Chris Chan, "eventually evolved into an all-purpose community forum" that would continue for more than half a century.[33] From mothers to daughters and granddaughters, generations in turn would turn to "Dear Mrs. Griggs" to find constancy and continuities, the hallmarks that may differentiate women's history from more traditional history, amid many decades of societal conflict for Milwaukee and the country.

Her impact would be immeasurable on her newspaper—and theirs—and on Milwaukee, as this study affirms. This study employs quantitative methodology to attempt to measure and to map that impact in tracking the issues that mattered to many thousands of women and girls, as well as many men and boys, as evidenced in the content of their letters to "Dear Mrs. Griggs" for more than five decades. Their letters that began in the depths of the Great Depression in the mid-1930s then spanned a series of societal transitions, from another World War through the Vietnam War and beyond—from the flood of more women into the wartime workforce in a working-class city in the 1940s, through apparent retreat in the ostensibly quiescent 1950s, to social movements of the 1960s, into the era of the modern women's movement in the 1970s, into another apparent retreat with defeat of the Equal Rights Amendment in the 1980s—more than half a

---

33   Shayne Bowman and Chris Willis, "We Media: How Audiences Are Shaping the Future of News and Information" (American Press Institute Media Center, 2003), accessed at http://www.hypergene.net/wemedia/weblog.php; Chan, "Milwaukee's Local Color," 17.

century after a previous "wave" of women's history had culminated in a Constitutional amendment for woman suffrage in 1920, the same year that Griggs had begun her successful career in Chicago. That its sudden end had led her to join many jobless women, other widows and other women left alone and lonely, only added to experiences that had prepared her for a new career in Milwaukee. As Griggs arrived in the city, the Great Depression also had altered the lives of millions of

As the Depression continued, urban women factory workers—probably including readers of the then-pro-labor *Milwaukee Journal* as well as of Griggs' advice column—marched at the forefront of a labor parade downtown, past the Milwaukee Public Library on the city's main street, Wisconsin Avenue, with protest signs promoting unionization at Allis-Chalmers Company. (Wisconsin Historical Society, WHS-28324)

her future readers in industrial Milwaukee and in agricultural areas of Wisconsin also served by her new employer, the leading newspaper in the city and the state in both readership and respectability.

In sum, the column that provided a welcome recourse for her readers in past also can serve readers today, scholars and others, as a remarkable resource for research, a literal mother lode not only for insight into issues of women in a working-class city—although many were out of work during the Depression, when the column began—but also for a contemporary account of women's stories and issues, in their own words, across a momentous half-century in women's history, from the mid-1930s through the mid-1980s. The selection of Griggs' column for study also is owing to its longevity, as once again, as she had in Chicago—with the "sheer industry" of a Quinby, as an observer had written of her heritage—she would outlast competitors at the start of her column as well as others whose columns would arise in decades to come. In all, she would author—or co-author with her readers—more than fifteen thousand columns, each with several letters per column; based on sampling methodology in this study, the total number of letters may have amounted to as many as a hundred thousand letters published in more than half a century.[34]

---

34   This study employs quantitative methodology for content analysis of a scientifically randomized sampling of letters, coded in categories to track the emergence and evolution—and the increase or decline—of issues of interest to women in a working-class city in the Midwest. Relational content analysis concepts were employed to categorize concerns in readers' letters, following a pretest to identify types of issues, with direct data collection for analysis using SPSS descriptive statistics to create category totals. (With two types of information sought for analysis of the entirety of Griggs' body of work, both as a reporter and as a columnist, two means of data collection were employed for this study; for the first, on her earlier career, see note in first chapter.) For the collection of readers' letters in the "Dear Mrs. Griggs" column, six days per week for more than five decades, for a total of more than fifteen thousand columns, each with numerous letters and replies (including to letters not published), a random sampling method was employed to collect all letters and replies in five columns per year, with four selected following a formula to ensure a representative sample from varied days of the week and varied months of the year, and another selected entirely at random, for a total of 847 letters. Each letter and each reply (including to letters not published) was coded for a wide variety of data, including demographics of the writer (gender, age, locale, etc., if self-identified), categories of issue(s), information on issue(s), whether issue(s) involved the writer or others (i.e., families, friends, co-workers, etc.), type(s) of problem(s) for which advice was sought, and type of reply from the columnist (i.e., advice of a specific action or no action, referral to other individuals or agencies, or other action).

The columnist and her readers collaborated on an unparalleled legacy, a remarkable record for learning of women's lives, owing to Griggs'
unique status in the history of the "advice industry." That she surpassed
all predecessors and competitors in total number of columns during
more than half a century is sufficient in itself for study. In addition, in
comparison to advice columns conducted collectively by anonymous
staffs of assistants that altered over the days and decades in the tasks
of selecting readers' letters and authoring replies,[35] her sole authoring—or moderating—of the column, as the sole filter for selection of
letters and as the only author of replies, provides an internal control
for the study of her column—and theirs—as her readers, primarily women, would pour out their hearts from the Heartland to their
"Dear Mrs. Griggs."

"Tell me what to do. I've met a man who has been wonderful to
me."[36]

This first line in the first letter in 1934, from a reader signing herself as "M.K.C.," opened the new advice column in the *Milwaukee
Journal*—the first of many thousands of readers' letters to their "Dear
Mrs. Griggs," or I.Q.G., as Ione Quinby Griggs signed her replies for
decades to come. Not that the letter from "M.K.C." was the first to
arrive in the mail, in response to the newspaper's pre-publication publicity for the column, because not all of the letters that she received
and read would be published—or publishable. The first letter that she
received, Griggs recalled, never saw print. The memorable ten-page
screed came from a reader threatening to commit a crime: matricide. He also was atypical of letter writers to come, as a male reader,
"a thirty-four-year-old man who said he was thinking of murdering
his mother, because she had ruined every relationship he had ... and
would never let him marry," she recalled, although now "he had found

---

Microfilms of the *Milwaukee Journal* from 1934 through 1985 for analysis of the column—and in subsequent years for coverage after Griggs'
retirement—were obtained from libraries of the University of Wisconsin-
Milwaukee and Marquette University, also in Milwaukee, Wis.

35   Gudelunas, *Confidential to America*, 37-70; Fahs, *Out on Assignment*,
121-134.

36   IQG, "Should M.K.C. Accept Help from a Married Man? Mrs. Griggs
Answers," *MJ*, November 9, 1934.

a girl he really loved." Griggs could not publish a threat but replied
privately, which she would do for countless readers, according to colleagues. As for content of letters not selected for publication, she had
few hard-and-fast rules, other than not printing "letters from prisoners," she said. "They're too lonesome" and "just looking for someone to
write to them."[37]

Her personal contacts with readers, however, undoubtedly had immeasurable impact in cultivation of her faithful following and in the
column's success. In her private reply to her homicidal reader, Griggs
had told him to "live his own life" and advised that he "marry before
his mother could do anything about it." He later wrote that he had
followed her advice, marrying the woman he loved and not murdering
his mother, and others would write again in appreciation of Griggs'
guidance—far from the last given.[38] Griggs gained many grateful
readers in Milwaukee and well beyond, because her newspaper's circulation went statewide in several daily editions; one known in the
newsroom as "the WUP" for "Wisconsin and Upper Peninsula" cir-
culated into Michigan, and other editions often crossed state borders
into Minnesota, Iowa, and Illinois.

As for readership, which exceeds circulation, the column would
reach readers worldwide by the end of the decade, as evidenced by
letters from readers afar. "People of Many Lands Tell Mrs. Griggs
Their Troubles," headlined a column led by a letter from "Zealous
New Zealander," whose former "landlady's daughter" regularly sent
him copies of the column. Another reader relayed a message from a
missionary in China, writing from his living quarters above a "temple
of Buddha," where he was "enjoying the Green Sheet, especially Mrs.
Griggs' column. Even Buddha seemed to turn and shake his head at
some of the problems!" The "Green Sheets" also were "passed around
among the people near him," he wrote, then were "sent into the inte-
rior. So you see your advice goes a long way from Milwaukee." In her
reply, Griggs wrote of receiving letters from Mexico, South America,

---

37 Wells, *Milwaukee Journal*, 263; "After 50 Years, Mrs. Griggs Still Gives
    Advice," *NewsPrint*, February 1984, 2. Griggs also initially gave advice by
    telephone, until the volume of requests eventually curtailed her ability to
    do so; she stated that she did not "answer problems by telephone anymore,
    unless someone [was] asking for a certain source or social agency."

38 Wells, *Milwaukee Journal*, 263.

South Africa, and more, as many family and friends mailed sheaves of "Green Sheets" to former residents of Wisconsin, who missed their daily "Dear Mrs. Griggs."[39] She never forgot, however, that her less exotic but most faithful readers were closer to home, the stay-at-homes in the state and especially in the working-class city now her home.

Griggs knew her readers well, as reflected in an astute selection of letters for the column from the start, with the first letter from "M.K.C.": a young, single woman, and still in school. The selection proved prescient, as the writer typified the gender, marital status, and similar self-identifiers of most other writers of letters sampled throughout the first period of the column, the 1930s, to determine the demographics of Griggs' correspondents. Not that the columnist selected letters for publication based on gender, age, education, or such factors, as Griggs later explained in giving her "guidelines" to an interviewer, curious as to reasons for the column's success.

Griggs relied on her readers to guide her selection, setting the agenda of the column in their collaboration to come. "I try to print those letters that are timely and attract attention or are on a subject that's mentioned in quite a few letters," she said. Although some subjects would recur for weeks, even months, in the years to come, she would encourage the ongoing debates among readers repeatedly writing replies to others but claimed, "I try not to carry on about the same subject too long." On verifying the veracity of her correspondents, she required that they sign their letters, even if they requested that their names not be printed. Then, in preparing their letters for publication, Griggs stated that she would "edit out certain things that would identify a person too much," printing names with permission, which she often requested from contributors seeking publicity for their societal causes or agencies providing information on social services.[40]

Her roster of social agencies and other sources of support for readers would become a hallmark of the column in its function as a "community clearinghouse." Agencies actually would train the columnist as a quasi-social worker, and in years to come, she and her newspaper would receive numerous awards for serving as a source of resources

---

39 IQG, "Dear Mrs. Griggs," *Once a Year*, 36; Wells, *Milwaukee Journal*, 263; IQG, "People of Many Lands Tell Mrs. Griggs Their Troubles," *MJ*, September 11, 1940.

40 "After 50 Years, Mrs. Griggs," 2.

for readers. However, learning to turn to local agencies for assistance and research local options prior to publishing referrals had come only after an early error that could have ended her column and new career. As a newcomer, she lacked the local resources that reporters amass on a "beat"—but as an experienced reporter, Griggs made a "rookie mistake" in Milwaukee, as well she would recall, decades later.

> I made a mistake in my early months as a columnist that taught me an important lesson. A pregnant girl asked me to find her a home for unwed mothers…. At the time, I didn't know that Wisconsin social agencies objected to sending girls like this out of the state. I made arrangements for the girl to go to such a home in a Chicago suburb….
>
> When a Milwaukee social worker tried to send the girl to a facility here, the girl shocked her by saying, "Oh, Mrs. Griggs of the Journal is sending me to Illinois."[41]

The social worker had called the managing editor, Marvin Creager—the editor who initially had been unsure of Griggs' ability. He called her into his office. "By that time, Mr. Creager liked my work and didn't banish my column," she wrote. "Instead, he made a truce," assuring the social worker that the newspaper would not again contravene agency practices, while his columnist "learned to consult agencies when necessary or when in doubt," Griggs would recall. "Since then, authorized agencies have been among my staunchest supporters."[42]

Admitting her limitations as an advisor, Griggs often recommended that readers seek professional expertise, giving carefully researched referrals. She also would recall, however, an "expert" who "complained" about an amateur giving advice and asked "how can people like you handle problems?" By then, the columnist would accrue "a sizeable collection of testimonials from social agencies and churches complimenting me on my work," Griggs responded, and "if these agencies approve of me, they must like my answers. They have faith in me…. I never considered myself a social worker, yet I take an interest in what people are doing and feeling," as Griggs recalled in giving the signal "guideline" for her success, the curiosity and empathy that had characterized

---

41   IQG, "Dear Mrs. Griggs," *Once a Year*, 35.

42   Ibid.

her career as a reporter on "human-interest features"—her other and highly unusual training as an advice columnist.[43]

The first letter selected for the first column, from "M.K.C.," adroitly showed the young, female reader's naiveté regarding "love problems" to showcase Griggs' persona as an older, wiser woman. The headline bannered across the top of the back page of the "Green Sheet," although also the back page of the newspaper, was a guaranteed attention-getter that invited her readers' collaboration in the discussion, which would come to characterize the column: "Should M.K.C. Accept Help from a Married Man?" As "M.K.C." wrote, "I could fall in love with him if he wasn't a married man…. He says his wife doesn't appreciate his desire to help a girl make something of herself." In part, Griggs' first published reply to a reader typified her early work in following the format of her predecessors in the "advice industry." She penned a cautionary tale, protracted and probably fictional or based on a composite character, a "Betty," whose life had been brief, and whose last letter prior to her suicide, so the columnist claimed, had closed with "I should have known better than to love a married man." Griggs soon would adapt and find her own style, however, in abandoning the moralistic and fictional "sermonettes" of predecessors. The brief paragraph appended at the end of her cautionary tale foresaged her straightforward advice to come, asking "M.K.C.": "Do you want a more direct answer? Doesn't this story tell you clearly enough that you do not want a married man's help?" She concluded the first column with a directive, a reminder to readers to "write to Ione Quinby Griggs" with "love problems."[44]

The response suggests that readers of the *Milwaukee Journal* were remarkably lovelorn. Letters "began to arrive by the bagful" for Griggs, as a colleague would recall.[45] For the rest of the decade, during the remainder of the Depression until the onset of the next world war, the focus of more than three-fourths of letters sampled—77.4 percent— would be "love problems," whether premarital, marital, or post-marital: 57.3 percent of letters sampled that came under the category of relationships that were not marital, and another 17.1 percent of published letters sampled and categorized as about problematic marriages. As for letter writers' demographics that can be determined from self-identifi-

---

43   Ibid.

44   IQG, "Should M.K.C. Accept."

45   Wells, *Milwaukee Journal*, 263.

ers in their correspondence, seven in ten—70.3 percent—were single,
and fewer than three in ten—27.5 percent—were married; for the remainder, only a few writers of letters sampled in the first period studied were separated, divorced, or widowed.

However, Griggs and her editors, who had envisioned the advice
column as only about "love problems" would receive an education on
the range of issues faced by girls and women in their working-class
city during the Depression, as her readers began to reshape their
page in the newspaper for their purposes. In the first period studied,
the 1930s, the gender of writers could be determined from content
of more than a third of letters sampled, and 88 percent were girls or
women, a rate that would prove relatively constant throughout the run
of the column. Initially, response from younger readers was especially marked; a majority of letters sampled in which writers self-identified their ages came from teenagers or young adults. Almost half of
younger readers wrote about boyfriends or husbands; more than 30
percent about boyfriends and more than 18 percent about husbands,
whom they often had wed when only teenagers. They tended to counsel others not to do so—although not all were so inclined. The briefly wed "Blue Divorcee," for example, although only eighteen years old
and already divorced, in part owing to domestic violence, wrote of her
impatience to marry again. Griggs' reply was aptly summed up in a
column that counseled her reader to forget about finding "beaux" for
the foreseeable future.[46]

Another early letter writer apparently was not in peril of marrying
young, as her timeless problem—a perennial throughout the column's
run—resulted from seeking perfection in a mate, which merited a
sassy retort from Griggs, of a sort not often seen in previous advice
columnists' moralistic style. "Perfect Man? There Is No Such Animal,
My Dear Girl," was her headline on a letter early in 1935 from "Jane,"
whose "love problem" was a pending break-up with a "steady," whom
she had hoped to wed. Then he had acted "silly" at a party, so she "gave
him plain h____" in "just trying to change him a little for his own good."
Griggs drolly replied that, "if you want a human husband, Jane, you'll
have to quit giving men h____." Yet she readily agreed with another
reader's description of a husband as a "crybaby" and decried another

---

46   IQG, "Young Divorcee Is Advised to Forget Beaux for a Time," *MJ*,
      January 18, 1937.

husband's actions as those of a "childish adult." Griggs could be equally harsh on women readers, however, and admitted early in her column's years to "a growing belief in my mind that many husbands and wives," even if legally adults, "were like children when they can't have their own way." She added, charitably, that some of her readers perhaps were not willful but only were ill from "nerves."[47]

Readers echoed her advice then and often again, employing Griggs' column as a means to advise others. "A Happy Wife" wrote in reply to "Just Another Wife," dissatisfied with her husband's earnings and family fights about money. The former wrote that her husband hardly was perfect, as "his wages have always been small, and we have a large family." They had put food on the table but faced "bills to pay, clothes to buy and furniture and rugs that are very shabby," while he would demand "pocket money … even though the house was going to ruin." The couple's "scolding and quarreling only made things worse"—until "A Happy Wife" made clear to him that, she wrote, "I'm independent and can get along without a husband if it should come to that, rather than quarrel all the time." Her husband became "better natured than he used to be, hands over his money without complaint," and "talks to me about his work," she happily reported to other readers. By contrast, a correspondent signing herself as "Unhappy Future Ex-Wife" wrote to "Dorothy June" that she should rethink her future with a belittling boyfriend: "You are in luck that he is treating you like this now instead of later," lest she also learn more about him only after marriage, as had the writer, who was another reader unhappily heading toward divorce—and, in her case, single parenthood, as well—at the age of only eighteen years old.[48]

In welcome contrast came a letter from another rare male reader, "A Contented Family Man," married for two decades and replying to another male letter writer. Griggs readily acceded most of a column to the happy husband's response to "a man who was ashamed to push a baby buggy," because he "considered himself too much of a 'he-man'

---

47   IQG, "Perfect Man? There Is No Such Animal, My Dear Girl," *MJ*, January 8, 1935; IQG, "Complaining Hubby on Par With 8 Year Old Crybaby," *MJ*, April 12, 1940; IQG, "Childish Adults May Be Ill, May Need Doctor, Not Whip," *MJ*, March 17, 1937.

48   IQG, "She Found Why He Blew Up By Studying Boyhood Way," *MJ*, February 11, 1936.

to do anything like that. Well, let me tell him I've pushed 11 babies in buggies and still kept my dignity." A reproductive rate of almost a dozen children born over two decades was commonplace for the time and place; the dissemination of birth control information was legalized only in the mid-1930s—and even then, Milwaukee was home to more Catholics than most cities. Of course, the toll on prolific mothers homebound for decades, always either pregnant or rearing an infant and toddlers, could explain why the *pater familias* had been the one with the time to write so happily to "Mrs. Griggs."[49]

The popularity of the topic of "love problems" and many others, as well as readership for Griggs' page in the newspaper, became evident within months and affected its format, as her columns increasingly included not one letter but many from readers as well as somewhat cryptic replies to those who requested that their letters not be published. For example, a column by mid-1935, within six months of the debut of "Dear Mrs. Griggs," included two letters from married women, one wed to a "thoughtless" husband who forgot birthdays and anniversaries, and another awaiting an annulment who already was impatient to date, as she was only eighteen years old. To the latter of the letter writers, Griggs wrote that she would be wise "to wait until you are out of one scrape before getting into another!" The column also included five replies to letters that were not published, almost all about "love problems," such as a letter from the wife of a middle-aged husband who had acted "silly" with single women, and another from a soon-to-be-single woman seeking advice on whether to find a mate via matchmaking advertisements. Although advertising provided the primary source for newspapers' budgets, the *Journal* did not publish "personals," so Griggs had no dilemma in advising against the impersonal means of newspaper dating services. Nor was she willing to serve as a matchmaker, as she replied to a "Curly" regarding his letter—unpublished, unfortunately for posterity—that listed his admirable qualities, but the columnist published only her curt reply that she did not "sponsor introductions" between the sexes.[50]

---

49   IQG, "Milwaukee Man Wheeled 11 Babies and Never Quarreled," *MJ*, November 13, 1936.

50   IQG, "You Can't Cure a Husband by Returning Evil for Evil," *MJ*, July 3, 1935; IQG, "New Interest of Jilted One Must See Need of Caution," *MJ*, March 23, 1939.

Although "love problems" did dominate early columns, the same column with the reply to "Curly" included another response not about romance but about in-laws, representative of another sizeable category of concerns from readers in the period: familial conflict. Domestic disputes other than with spouses arose in 17 percent of sampled letters on generational conflict with older family members and 12 percent of sampled letters on conflict with younger family members, children, during the Depression, perhaps in part due to the Depression. Generational conflict often arose, as economic upheaval of the era meant that many young married couples were forced to move in with families, as were older women living in other women's homes, often widows who wrote to Griggs or were the subject of letters from family members. As well the widowed Griggs knew, many widows were in serious economic straits in the era, as "old age insurance," or Social Security, had begun only in the mid-1930s and, even then, excluded most working women. "More households than you may realize find it necessary to share with others who are bereaved or without funds," she wrote. Her counsel on in-laws commonly called for compromise, as "the mother-in-law problem is usually what the individuals make it."[51]

Conflict with in-laws was so common that it provided content for entire columns and for a club that used the column in monthly discussion groups, according to several young wives who wrote collectively in gratitude to Griggs for "a wonderful job of helping June brides"—a term for women married young—to "meet problems of marriage." In return, the club penned a letter to which Griggs gave most of a column, headlined "Young Women Call Widowed Mother-in-Law Enemy No. 1," which included "ten commandments" for their spouses' mothers, all widows alone. In reply, Griggs wrote that she recognized that a widowed mother-in-law might acquire a "martyr complex" from lack of companionship but asked that her readers "mix heart and judgment" and realize that "widowhood isn't easy." From her experience, which she did not note, Griggs wrote that such bereavement could be sudden and "bewildering because it follows a stunning loss, leaving heartache and emptiness. Often a woman isn't her normal self." Griggs appreciated their admiration but admonished her letter writers: "Girls, give

---

51   IQG, "You Can't Cure."

some thought to the mother-in-law's loss.... Be fair yourself! You are young and still have your husbands."[52]

Other letter writers also attested to impact on marriage partners and others in families, potentially leading to long-lasting schisms, from not resolving issues with in-laws. "Perplexed" penned an anguished letter, which filled most of a day's column, with the details of a nine-year marriage that had gone desperately wrong, even verging on potential domestic violence. The letter writer was dangerously isolated, owing to little contact with her family, as her vengeful husband had made them unwelcome. "He holds grudges about things that happened nine years ago," when they had been newlyweds living with his family, the letter writer recalled. "I'll admit I have a few grudges about the time we lived in his home, when his mother nagged me all the time, but even so, I haven't talked about it, except to you," she wrote to Griggs. Her reply was to request that the writer remain in contact—as often occurred when the columnist had concern about signs of worsening problems—and that she show the column to her husband, to whom Griggs gave the rest of her reply in counseling him to forgo grudges from long ago. He also received a request to write with his concerns, as she hoped to avert domestic violence.[53]

The category of family conflict also included complaints about parents from a younger group, especially girls chafing at chores. Griggs often offered aggregations of letters from girls aggrieved about housework or babysitting for younger siblings as well as parental restrictions, such as refusing to allow a twelve-year-old to go to the movies alone at night. "Mrs. Griggs, I can't bear it," wrote the girl of her mother, who "embarrassed her terribly" with a curfew. The columnist replied that her young readers deserved respect, "but honey, this must be on both sides." The girl also attempted to win support for a "permanent" for her "scraggly, straight hair, which won't curl by itself," which had given her an "inferiority complex." Yet her mother had refused—or perhaps could not afford—to accede. The columnist would not be drawn into the dangerous terrain between mothers and daughters: "A permanent might improve your hair. Again, honey, it might not." Noting that "no

---

52   IQG, "Young Wives Call Widowed Mother-in-Law Enemy No. 1," *MJ*, June 4, 1940.

53   IQG, "Don't Wreck Your Life by Constant Bickering at Home," *MJ*, July 18, 1938.

age is exempt from problems," as parents reading between the lines could attest regarding childrearing, Griggs recommended that the girl first prove her maturity to her mother to win approval of later hours and a fashionable "permanent."[54]

Chores expected of children proved to be a perennial cause for their protests to Griggs, to little avail, as she consistently supported parental expectations for help around the house—and especially in an era when hours of housework were increasing for women. "I receive dozens of letters from girls in their teens who wail" about having to do chores that reduced their dating time, Griggs wrote, and she replied with an outdated admonishment on housework as training for marriage, captured in the headline: "Girls, Romance Will Die if You Hate to Do Housework." However, her advice actually may have reflected that of the "modern efficiency experts" of the era in prescribing practice for girls to learn how to reduce time on housework, at a time when many housewives had to expend more hours weekly on chores than in decades before. Studies later found that then-new and widely advertised "electrical servants"—home appliances—made housework less physically demanding but more time-consuming by increasing consumption and adding new tasks. For example, twice-yearly rug-beating came to be replaced by weekly or even daily use of vacuum cleaners in urban households, more often electrified than rural homes, where manual carpet sweepers with rotator brushes remained a luxury for many farmwives.[55]

In the 1930s, three-fourths of the state's urban homes, mainly in Milwaukee, would have electrification and central heating, and most would have indoor taps and toilets—but Wisconsin had become barely more urban than rural only in 1930, a decade behind most of the country. At the start of the decade, only one in twelve rural homes in Wisconsin had indoor toilets, only one in six had indoor tap water, and only one in four had electricity. Even at the end of the 1930s, when a third of households in the country would lack electricity, fully half in Wisconsin would lack electrification. Only a fourth of farmhouses

---

54   IQG, "'Mother Can't Understand,' Girl, 12, Tells Mrs. Griggs," *MJ*, June 17, 1937.

55   IQG, "Girls, Romance Will Die if You Hate to Do Housework," *MJ*, April 2, 1935; Susan Strasser, *Never Done: A History of American Housework*, rev. ed. (New York: Henry Holt, 2000), 78-82.

in the state would have central heating, only a fifth would have indoor tap water, and only a tenth would have indoor toilets, including many in Milwaukee County, whose rural population would remain among the largest in all of the counties in the state. As a home economics professor at the University of Wisconsin in Madison stated at the time, "most farmers are more interested in better barns, new tractors,

Ione Quinby Griggs on WTMJ Radio, when her company's pioneering broadcast station celebrated its tenth anniversary on the air in Milwaukee, including the debut in 1937 of the twice-weekly "Tell Mrs. Griggs." The *Journal* columnist took to the microphone to give advice to her growing audience via the airwaves as well as in print. (Copyright 2014 Journal Sentinel, Inc., reproduced with permission)

and cars, rather than in running water or indoor toilets." Dairy barns had electricity where dwellings did not, when "most farmers' cows were better taken care of than most farmers' wives," writes historian William F. Thompson. "The farmwife had to make do with drawing water from a pump, cleaning and filling kerosene lamps, and preserving food and other perishables in iceboxes and fruit cellars" while awaiting the promise of President Franklin D. Roosevelt's New Deal Rural Electrification Administration to be able to plug in their "radio sets" to hear advertising for "electric servants."[56]

In 1937, fortunate Wisconsin farmwives with electricity for radio even would hear "Mrs. Griggs" herself, broadcasting across the airwaves twice a week from her company's WTMJ radio station. Then marking its tenth anniversary on the air with among the oldest call letters in the country, WTMJ claimed to have pioneered participatory programming with "personalities" who were "a part of the everyday life of the community." Each "Tell Mrs. Griggs" episode featured "actual letters from listeners ... dramatized by a cast," the newspaper reported, followed by the columnist taking to the microphone to give advice. Some listeners could hear the show on the popular new car radios, including one who wrote to Griggs that she had heard the program on a day when the newly on-air personality discussed another listener's letter on her pending divorce. The letter writer also had been considering divorce, she wrote, but the radio program persuaded her to drive home to "try to discover where she had failed to make her husband happy." The experiment endured for only eight episodes and actually may have been brief because of overwhelming response, as the newspaper reported that the radio show had caused Griggs' mail to grow "so much that she's burning midnight oil, answering letters." However, many of her rural readers still lacked electricity and literally had to burn oil for lighting in homes in which daily chores continued to include drawing water from outdoor wells, chopping and stacking wood for stoves, stocking and loading ice blocks in "iceboxes," and doing laundry in handwringers rather than electric or gas washing machines and then hung on clotheslines, for lack of electric dryers.[57]

---

56   Thompson, *History of Wisconsin*, 8-10, 16, 55, 87.

57   Ibid., "Hundreds of Listeners 'Tell Mrs. Griggs' on Air," *MJ*, May 23, 1937; Bill Thompson, "The Milwaukee Radio Market," *Broadcasting*, June 6, 1949, 8; "Inside Dope," *MJ*, May [?], 1937, Milwaukee Journal

Children in such households had to help not only with chores but also with more difficult challenges in the Depression, and some wrote of worry for parents whom Griggs increasingly came to serve as a liaison to community agencies. For example, the reason for contact from the reader whose signature was "Inferiority Complex" could be deduced, as Griggs' reply was to "inquire at the Marquette clinic about your teeth." She would refer many readers to the dental clinic downtown at Marquette University, where students worked for discounted fees. However, a teenaged writer, "Worried 14," whose letter was not published, received a mysterious reply that allowed readers to use their imaginations as to the reason that Griggs requested that the teenager have her mother find community resources by writing to the columnist, who would "try to help her if she will do this." Some sought Griggs' aid as a community resource of sorts as well, such as a young man named "Andy" who worried about "Frenchy," a runaway girl who had written Griggs. "I used to go with her," he wrote to Griggs, and asked that the columnist herself be a go-between: "If she reads this I would like to have her know that her mother wants her to write ... telling her that she is all right. If she won't do that, perhaps she will write you, so you can tell her mother." In reply, Griggs hoped "with all her heart" that the girl would "get in touch."[58]

Griggs' referrals of readers to community agencies increasingly would include resources for alcoholism, of course, in the drinking culture of Milwaukee, although the level of 7 percent of sampled letters on the issue in the post-Prohibition decade was low in comparison to levels to come in later eras. The letters about drinking were categorized as such for the focus of the letter writers' concern, if alcoholism often was linked to other issues, such as some "love problems" as well

Sentinel Library. On other radio programming also targeting farmwives in Wisconsin in a transitional time, discussed in two studies: on a housekeeping show for four decades, see Erika Janik, "Good Morning Homemakers!" *Wisconsin Magazine of History* 90:1 (Autumn 2006), 4-15; on a program similar to Griggs' program and column, beginning only weeks after Griggs' program began and for more than two decades, see Nancy C. Unger, "The We Say What We Think Club," *Wisconsin Magazine of History* 90:1 (Autumn 2006), 16-27.

58   IQG, "Mrs. Griggs Is Asked to Solve Telephone Problems," *MJ*, December 12, 1940; IQG, "Girls, Your 'New Freedom' Calls for Honesty, Wisdom," *MJ*, January 27, 1938.

as financial problems in relationships with family members, neighbors, and more among letters sampled. The interrelated issues also were evident in Griggs' replies with resources for readers whose letters were not published. For example, she wrote to "Worried Mother and Wife" that, if such a "situation is not any better," she should "talk to the district attorney in your town. Ask him to have a talk with your husband. You did right in regard to the bank account. You needed security for the children." Griggs added her plea that, after her worried reader would arrange for legal assistance, she also would "let me know the outcome."[59]

She also commonly recommended social workers at a specific community agency, the Family Welfare Association, as "they cooperate with me," Griggs wrote to a reader.[60] So did newsroom colleagues, as in a case in which her editor recommended his wife's gynecologist for an appointment, made by Griggs, for a bride-to-be who possibly had been raped in childhood by a relative; she had been so young and remained so unschooled about sex that she was unsure. She came from an insular ethnic community, typical in Milwaukee at the time, and discovery of her "disgrace" could end the marriage within hours of the rites, she wrote: "My father has found me a husband, as is custom, and when on my wedding night it's learned I am not a virgin, he will take me back to my parents and disgrace me." The story continued in a series of letters and took a turn when she called Griggs to report, as the columnist related to her readers, that "the wedding was off, because her prospective husband had gotten another girl into trouble." However, the father found another groom; as the girl wrote to Griggs, "there is the same problem, just a change of persons." The reader kept the appointment with the gynecologist, received reassurance that her husband would not find evidence that she was not a virgin, and Griggs attended the wedding, as did her editor and his helpful wife. All were happy to hear, years later, that their reader lived happily ever after, when she sent Griggs a photo of her children with a note: "All went well."[61]

The columnists' community contacts also were all too familiar with non-familial conflict, especially in the densely populated neighborhood

59   IQG, "New Interest of Jilted One."

60   IQG, "Complaining Hubby."

61   Ibid., 36.

enclaves that characterized the city. Conflict arose regarding childrearing in about 5 percent of letters sampled in the period, as typified by a column in which Griggs adroitly combined letters from both sides of a battle between renters and other readers who shared housing space. She led with a letter from a tenant, signed "Moving Soon," followed by one from "One of Many Disgusted Landlords"—who may have read the first letter with relief at coping only with noise complaints, compared to the saga at a duplex that had become an all-too-colorful battleground in the ongoing war between renters and landlords.[62]

> I have one of the meanest men in the world for a landlord.... I can't always watch my child. He is 5, full of life, and very imaginative. The other day he took some red paint that was left in the garage and painted pictures all over the front porch. He really has talent and you'd be surprised what a good likeness of the landlord he painted.[63]

Not surprisingly, the landlord was not impressed by the talented young portraitist and "needn't have acted like he did," wrote the parent; the landlord had said that the child needed a spanking, the parent had refused to do so, and the landlord had administered the corporal punishment. Griggs wrote with disapproval of the landlord's action but focused more of her reply on the letter writer's behavior, not only on that day but also on the next day, as her reader also reported.[64]

> I decided to teach him a lesson myself. He has a little girl 28 months old. The next day when she would play out in the yard, I put the rest of the paint where she could get hold of it and, of course, she did just what I expected. She splashed that red paint over the side of the house and all over her shoes and dress.
> When her father came out and found her, I said: "Whose child is doing things now?"[65]

That a neglectful parent also had endangered another child appalled the columnist. She deplored the writer's "ugly actions," "mean tricks," and "warlike" words with the landlord, who doubtless shared Griggs'

---

62   IQG, "Child Daubs a Porch Red and Starts Duplex Squabble," *MJ*, September 17, 1937.

63   Ibid.

64   Ibid.

65   Ibid.

relief at reading that her reader had given notice and was moving within a month. However, she asked for tolerance of tenants, too, from the "landlord and wife and mother" and author of the other letter. "Mothers may be harassed by many cares, or not in good health," she wrote, which could explain a failure to manage and "guide the lively spirits" of children.[66]

Griggs did not divulge locales or other information from her correspondents, without their permission, although columns like the one on tenants and landlords may have led to more letters from readers for information on the next destination of the writer with the artistic progeny, lest her future neighbors also be moved to move out, before their area became literally colorful. A colleague recalled that the columnist even cut off any identifying information from the rare letters retained in her files for several reasons, such as her requests to provide more information or for follow-up. The rest of her correspondence, whether published or not, was disposed of with care. Of course, identities often could be deduced, which would lead to intriguing columns—and neighbors near the duplex now splattered in red paint no doubt recognized their locale, overly colorful in many ways, so they may have shared in the landlord's relief at the renter's departure.

Indeed, in the case of a letter writer who had signed herself as "Heartbroken," she had disclosed identifying information sufficient for her husband to take the day's "Dear Mrs. Griggs" column into court as evidence in their divorce case. As the *Milwaukee Journal* reported in 1937, Griggs' correspondent, Gertrude Hein, had decided to contest her husband's divorce action, which charged her with cruelty. He also described her as "stubborn" and likely to "throw herself on the floor in quarrels," she wrote, admitting that her marriage was "going on the rocks" because of her "meanness and obstinacy." His lawyer put her on the stand, showed her the "Green Sheet," and asked: "Did you write this?" She denied it, claiming that her letter had been altered, saying that she "didn't write it just that way." The judge called for the original of the letter to the columnist to be produced, which could have brought Griggs into court, at a cost to her credibility. However, the reverse occurred. Griggs did not need to take the stand, as the *Journal* reported that "Mrs. Hein changed her testimony and admitted that the letter," as published, "was correct in all details. She said she no

---

66   Ibid.

longer desired to contest her husband's case. He was granted a decree
by default," and she "was granted a payment of $500 in lieu of alimo-
ny." In the end, the entertaining episode entered newsroom and local
lore about "Mrs. Griggs" and would resurface in many accounts of the
columnist for decades to come.[67]

Readers in more peaceful areas of the region within the reach of
the newspaper may have received comfort in reading such reports in
and about the "Dear Mrs. Griggs" column for mutual affirmation that,
even in the depths of the Depression, life could be worse on the next
block or only next door. She regularly shared letters from readers happy with their lot in life, writing not in smug self-congratulation—such
letters met with disapproval from Griggs and her readers—but in
appreciation of perspective gained from reading of others' lives. One
wrote, during the Depression decade of woeful news in the newspaper,
that "some of the letters you publish have made me realize more than
ever how happy I am," despite "these down in the dumps days!"[68]

Together, Griggs and her readers had worked through societal
changes and individual challenges of the Great Depression, and the
"greatest generation" of women as well as men again would support
each other during wartime in another difficult decade ahead. Their
page in the newspaper would continue to reflect not only the continuities in women's issues but also the new conflicts to come, regarding their societal roles on the homefront. In the first, previous period
studied, their concerns about love, marriage, and family relationships
had accounted for nine of ten letters sampled, 90.6 percent. They also
had written of concerns and conflicts with others, such as tenants and
landlords. Of almost three hundred columns and many more hundreds of letters sampled during the decade, however, only two had
raised issues of women in their workplaces—if understandably so,
with so many women out of work during the Depression.

Now, as the country prepared to again send men away to war, their
government prepared women to go into the workforce, in greater
numbers than ever before, including in workplaces where women never before had been welcome. Nor would women find a welcome even

---

67   "Letter to Paper Pops Up—to Change Tune of Wife," *MJ*, March 30,
1937; Wells, *Milwaukee Journal*, 266.

68   IQG, "Say 'No' to the Man Who Let the Engagement Lapse," *MJ*, April
22, 1938.

in many workplaces where they would work for the war, in many factories in the manufacturing center of Milwaukee that would become weapons and munitions plants or textile plants turned to other needs of millions of men in the military. Women would have their own battles ahead on the homefront, where the following for "Dear Mrs. Griggs" would reach record numbers in the next decade. They would read all about it, and they would write much of their colorful story to come, in the newspaper—not on the front page but on the back page of the "Green Sheet" that, in only the first few years of their advice column, her women readers already had made their own.

3

Women Readers, the War, and the Recovery, 1941-1948

The war effort on the homefront in Milwaukee and across Wisconsin in the 1940s would send more women out of their homes and into the workforce in the four years of World War II than ever before, as the war sent thousands of Wisconsin men—and hundreds of Wisconsin women—overseas. Women would lose their brief wartime progress in the workplace and see prosperity disappear in postwar years, when military demobilization and other factors would bring financial and personal adjustments for homefront workers and others in "housewives' strikes" or boycotts in protest of inflationary prices. However, at first, many women as well as men not called up in the war would prosper on the homefront in the major manufacturing center of Milwaukee and nearby cities, as real "Rosies" were riveters and performed other roles new for women in defense plants manufacturing military needs, from munitions to tanks to textiles. The city of Milwaukee also would witness the impact of its proximity to the Great Lakes naval base, which would bring "sailor boys" to a USO, where local women volunteers aided transient troops. The lure of the thousands of bell-bottomed "boys" on the loose would draw local girls downtown, where their flirtatious ways would cause a contretemps with "city fathers"—and many Milwaukee mothers—that, in turn, would cause teenaged angst for girls, who would flood "Mrs. Griggs" with letters. The issue finally would be resolved only when their columnist literally would march on City Hall.

Media also performed a crucial wartime role through radio, newsreels, and newspapers, despite a newsprint shortage, when everyone wanted breaking news of battles by any mode of communication but also needed the sense of community that media could provide. High demand for news and low supply of newsprint caused *Milwaukee*

Journal newsboys to run out of copies on city streets, and the newspaper asked subscribers to share copies. As the shortage worsened, advertising became another of many rationed commodities in wartime. The *Journal* reduced the number of editions daily, even reducing advertising to make room for news, and then resorted to a "Victory Edition" without a "Green Sheet." The resulting "outcry" would force the section's return within a week, according to *Journal* reporter and historian Robert W. Wells. Management moved more cautiously after the misjudgment that Milwaukeeans would accept their comics, crosswords, and advice column on plain newsprint. The "Green Sheet" would be reduced to two pages for the duration of the war, if with little reduction in space allotted to "Dear Mrs. Griggs."[1]

Everyone wanted the war news, but they also wanted the section and the column that had become a fixture in the daily lives of *Journal* readers. Griggs' success as an advice columnist would garner attention well beyond the city and *Journal* circulation area, with coverage in the most popular magazine in the country, the *Saturday Evening Post,* and other national media. As *Coronet* magazine noted, "most of us like to get things off our chest by writing 'all' to someone we can trust," in citing Griggs among half a dozen advice columnists in the country who reached a total of eighty-four million readers in the war years. Griggs alone would receive thousands of letters a week during the war—as many as seven thousand in one memorable week—that would reflect not only readers' loneliness and worry but also their rewards that came in the camaraderie of the homefront effort for women, whether in new workplaces or working as volunteers. As historian David Gudelunas writes in an analysis of advice columns in the era, elsewhere in the country, "women readers who were left at home" on the homefront faced "fragmented social networks caused by boyfriends, fiancés, and husbands missing from the domestic sphere."[2]

The *Milwaukee Journal* would remain the state's dominant media voice in circulation and influence, giving Griggs' women readers a voice and a venue to record their range of wartime experiences and even

---

1   Wells, *Milwaukee Journal,* 336-337.

2   Larry Lawrence, "Forward," n.p., in IQG, *Growing Up with Jim and Jean…. Reprinted from the Columns of Ione Quinby Griggs* (Milwaukee, Wis.: Milwaukee Journal, 1947), in the co-authors' possession; Gudelunas, *Confidential to America,* 53, 81.

Ione Quinby Griggs at her newsroom desk, covered with correspondence that came from continents around the world during World War II, when readers' letters to their advice columnist in the *Milwaukee Journal* reportedly reached record numbers of as many as seven thousand in a single week, many of them letters with petitions to local politicians that literally sent her marching on City Hall on behalf of readers opposed to a wartime curfew. (Copyright 2014 Journal Sentinel, Inc., reproduced with permission)

---

an influence in events. Her readers also would include soldiers, sailors, and other men overseas, who were sent her column as a comfort from home. An editor would recall that, "during World War II, she received letters from all over the world. Thousands of families sent the

Green Sheet to sons, husbands, brothers," and others, who "wrote Mrs. Griggs about their troubles.... One man fighting in Europe asked her to act as his proxy at the hospital while their first baby was being born." Griggs did so, and the grateful "parents named their daughter Ione," among as many as a dozen other future readers named for the columnist. Some young readers did not wait long to write to the column; her editor recalled a seven-year-old correspondent and that "boys and girls" wrote more often than other age groups. Griggs also would have a one-hundred-and-three-year-old correspondent, who had witnessed too many wars. Some older residents could not read the *Journal* but relied on others to translate not only war news, as a Milwaukee woman would recall, but also letters in English from first-generation soldier sons to immigrant parents on the homefront, among almost a third of state residents in 1940 who spoke primarily or only their native languages. However, foreign-language newspapers, many published in Milwaukee, would decline in numbers and circulation in the 1940s, as Griggs' newspaper gained readership.[3]

Servicemen and women would come home to a homefront that also would be changed by the war in a Wisconsin where, as the decade began, the governor was a German immigrant—the last immigrant to serve as governor in state history. Historian William F. Thompson writes that a "gridwork of ethnic identities and traditions had been one of the most important determinants of the state's history," and immigrant and first-generation residents continued to comprise almost 40 percent of the population in 1940 in Wisconsin. However, as he writes, the war would "test Wisconsin's ethnicity" with "a new mobility" in a "massive movement of men and women into the armed forces and industrial wartime jobs in new locations," with a "dramatic impact on old ethnic communities," which would "undermine residential stability of ethnic enclaves." The end of an era in Wisconsin, in accomplishing an acculturation measurable by demographers after the war,

---

3   Lawrence, "Forward," n.p.; Thompson, *History of Wisconsin*, 28, 31, 36; see also Michael E. Stevens and Ellen D. Goldlust, eds., *Voices of the Wisconsin Past: Women Remember the War, 1941-1945* (Madison: State Historical Society of Wisconsin, 1993). In 1940, Wisconsin had a German-language daily, two Polish-language dailies, a Finnish-language daily, and weeklies in eight languages among almost twenty ethnic newspapers, if with declining circulation numbers.

already would be evident in readers' letters to Griggs' column during the war years.[4]

Wartime work would bring women by the millions from rural ethnic communities to cities across the country, including Milwaukee, where newcomers would meet and "marry out" of ethnic groups that had defined their lives. Some would write of "love problems" that first had been the focus of Griggs' column, before readers redefined their forum to meet other challenges. Newcomers to urban life would include not only many migrant African Americans and Mexican Americans recruited for defense work but also prisoners of war, although German POWs hardly contributed to multiculturalism in Wisconsin. However, few Asian immigrants had settled in the state before Japanese POWs and Japanese American citizens from other states, who were unjustly incarcerated in the war years, including in a camp near Milwaukee that would make news owing to local residents' hostile reaction. For many reasons, writes Thompson, "customs and practices which were at the heart of each group's ethnic identity"— including gender identities—would decline. "The domestic turmoil brought on by the war frequently led men and women—but perhaps particularly women—to question that which they previously had taken for granted," he writes, and he cites media as a factor that would "threaten the persistence of unique traditions."[5]

Media also could perform a crucial role in retaining continuity for readers in communities across the city and state reached by Griggs' advice column, who reached out to other readers in return. Women in the war years increasingly would use Griggs' column as a form of community forum, while she increasingly would use the column as a community service, a "community clearinghouse" for referrals to social agencies. As her editor would recall, she researched "social service and religious organizations, the YWCA, the YMCA, public libraries" for recommended readings "and other educational services to guide people to authorized sources of help," such as professional counseling that Griggs could not provide. In return, many agencies would honor her for "valuable assistance in the community ... not only in counseling and writing on human relations but in directing young and old to their

---

4   Thompson, *History of Wisconsin*, 35, 55.

5   Ibid., 64-65, 82.

doors," as the second decade of the column would bring the first of many service awards for the *Milwaukee Journal* and its "Mrs. Griggs."[6]

Analysis of the sample of columns shows a significant increase in reliance on referrals to agencies, some recommended by readers, as well as an increase in their responses to each other, with three times as many such exchanges in the 1940s, compared to letters sampled in the 1930s. In addition to readers' replies, some referrals were "confidentials" from the columnist to readers whose letters never saw print. Another use of the column as a community forum, an indicator that the columnist had become embedded in the consciousness of readers of all ages, came in a 1941 letter on a runaway girl who had left a note for the writer, her worried mother, that "if she ever wanted to see her" daughter again, the mother was "to get in touch through 'Mrs. Griggs.'"[7]

Indicators of a culture already in transition came in final months of peacetime, in an early deluge of the letters of the sort soon to flood into the newsroom, although on a less weighty issue than impending war, as readers rallied to the defense of a popular pastime: bingo parties. In mid-1941, "Bette" wrote that her husband had ordered her to give up her bingo outing. The columnist counseled compromise, but did suggest that the wife curb her bingo habit, and her "mail swelled by several hundred letters," she wrote. Some respondents agreed with Griggs; one cited Biblical quotations on marital obedience, although interpreting the Bible as not requiring entirely abject subservience by wives. Others gave dire warnings that gambling addictions could begin with the seemingly innocuous bingo game. Responses reflected a local culture in which, as historian William F. Thompson writes, "gambling was more pervasive a pastime than many people were willing to acknowledge, though much of it was in the form of bingo games," often apparently sanctioned by being held in church halls. The next steps on the road to degradation, often only down the road from a church hall, were the slot machines then seen in many Wisconsin taverns.[8]

---

6   Lawrence, "Forward," n.p.

7   IQG, "'Tell Us Where You Are,' Is Unhappy Mother's Plea," *MJ*, May 26, 1941.

8   IQG, "Other Wives Comment Upon Angry Bingo Playing Wife," *MJ*, July 17, 1941; Thompson, *History of Wisconsin*, 25.

Again and again, Griggs would advise readers to avoid temptations of the tavern culture, a futile crusade in a Wisconsin with high rates of alcohol addiction. "A constant reader," the mother of a son overseas "with the Seabees," or Navy construction battalions, was "restless with worry," after her husband—who, "like many other men, liked to drink beer now and then"—had convinced her "to come along with him once in a while to pass a little of the time," taking along a young daughter. A neighbor had written to the son that his mother was "over at the tavern quite often with his little sister," which had upset him. "Awful people in this world will write gossip to our boys in the service, breaking down their morale instead of building it up," his mother wrote. Griggs also had no "respect" for the neighbor who had worried a son overseas and applauded his mother's "motive" to keep occupied. She counseled, however, that a tavern was not the place for a child and advised alternatives for worthier role models than the other women whom her reader had written of witnessing in the tavern, "drinking and smoking right at the bar with the men."[9]

Many men—and women—also were addicted to outings in the outdoors in Wisconsin, as a reader wrote of a culture in which hunting and fishing also were sacred rituals. Some readers rallied to defend wives' need for a social life of gaming or bar-hopping, and were shocked by the columnist's counsel to cut back on bingo and other local outlets. "Mirande," a faithful reader who looked forward to the column nightly, wrote that "you don't know much about husbands," although her letter revealed that her marital experience had been even briefer than that of the columnist. "If you think any spirited woman can stand for a man who tongue lashes her every time she wants to do anything besides wash dishes, you are a poor psychologist. It's time husbands understood what partnership means." Her bingo-playing—and her hats, her family, and her friends—had led to "terrible arguments" as "he said all I liked to do was sit and play bingo. I said all he liked to do was sit and fish.... It got so the only peace I had was when I was at a bingo game. So I decided to get back my freedom and play bingo if I chose and not have to listen to his fish stories." Divorced due to "incompatibility," she

---

9   IQG, "Son Gets an Unkind Letter About Mother," *MJ*, October 11, 1944.

had left him all that was left of the marriage: a cat, to which her former husband could, for all that she cared, "feed his fish."[10]

She was among several divorcees writing in the 1940s, a demographic difference from previous correspondents that emerged in the column's second decade. A constant that remained, among letter writers who self-identified by gender, was that more than 87 percent in the 1930s and more than 88 percent in the 1940s were women. However, a striking difference across the decades was age; of 40 writers identifiable by age in letters sampled in the 1930s and 68 in the 1940s, young adults and teenagers remained in the majority but declined significantly from 85 percent in the 1930s to 63 percent in the 1940s. Far more writers in the 1940s were in at least their late twenties, an age group that had comprised only 5 percent of writers identifiable by age in letters sampled in the 1930s but increased to almost 37 percent in the 1940s, including elderly readers at almost 9 percent of writers. As a result, more were married than in the prior decade, although in minimally significant numbers: Of 91 writers in the 1930s and 111 in the 1940s who self-identified their marital status, married writers increased from 27.5 percent of letters sampled in the 1930s to 31.5 percent in the 1940s. Widowed or separated writers remained few, although no divorcees had self-identified in letters sampled in 1930s, and that any divorcees self-identified among writers in letters sampled in the 1940s reflected increased divorce rates in every decade.[11]

Differences in ages of writers and in the contexts of women's lives were reflected in a significant decline in letters on "love problems," the initial intent of the column. Instead, the sampling in the 1940s measured a significant increase in letters on familial relationships. Of 117 writers in letters sampled in the 1930s and 168 in the 1940s, more than 57 percent in the first period had focused on romantic partners, while less than 40 percent did so in the 1940s—but familial issues almost doubled as a focus for writers, from little more than 16 percent of letters sampled in the 1930s to more than 30 percent in the 1940s. The increase came in worries about family members other than spouses; the latter remained at a similar level in letters on problems,

---

10   IQG, "Other Wives."

11   U.S. Census Bureau, *Census of Population: 1950, Volume II, Part 49– Wisconsin* (Washington, D.C.: Government Printing Office, 1952), 42.

from little more than 19 percent of such letters sampled in the 1930s to 17 percent in the 1940s.

Letters about living situations were at a low level in both decades, but the decline in Depression-era economic constraints and the increase in wartime transiency as well as in older letter writers would lead to fewer—if still a majority—living with parents. Thompson, a historian of the state, writes of the start of the tumultuous decade that, "for perhaps the last time in 1940, the people of Wisconsin had deep roots in time and place." Many of them lived with or near parents, whether in rural areas, small towns, or "city neighborhoods that had a coherence of known boundaries" in enclaves of residents "bound together by ethnic and religious kinship" and "secure and comfortable in surroundings that were known and familiar."[12] Of writers to Griggs' column who described their living situations in letters sampled, almost 86 percent in the 1930s had lived with parents, while 70 percent would identify as doing so in the 1940s. Even their letters would suggest that living at home would not guarantee stability for women in wartime.

Many women readers would remain in or return to parents' households in the 1940s, as husbands and fathers would go to war, and as housing shortages arose in Milwaukee, among cities with major defense plants even prior to U.S. entry into the war. In 1940, the draft began, as thousands of Wisconsin men registered for service in the regular military and "knew that it would only be a matter of time before they were called," Thompson writes. In mid-1941, a call-up came for the state's 32nd "Red Arrow" Division of the National Guard, immortalized in the Civil War as the "Iron Brigade," with more casualties than any other brigade in that war—a rate soon exceeded in World War II, when more than 90 percent of its troops would be among the dead and wounded. Also in 1941, buildups in production for Allies in the "Lend-Lease" program began, including in Milwaukee factories, well before the call to war came on a wintry Sunday in Wisconsin— "the day that shall forever live in infamy," as President Franklin Delano Roosevelt famously intoned after the Japanese attack on Pearl Harbor. Milwaukeeans heard him on WTMJ, the station owned by Griggs' newspaper—the call letters "TMJ" standing for "The *Milwaukee Journal*"—that had broadcast from the newsroom, near her desk,

---

12   Thompson, *History of Wisconsin*, 1.

in radio's experimental years. More recently, the *Journal* had experimented with closed-circuit television, but that medium's delivery to the consumer market was delayed as war halted manufacture of electronic devices for all but military needs. However, as the 1940s began, nine of ten Wisconsin households had radios to hear the station, the first west of the Alleghenies with clear-channel, FM capability, which helped to make the medium another crucial source of war news and communal support.[13]

Letters to Griggs referencing issues for women in wartime grew in great numbers. As historian Sara M. Evans writes, "women's most mundane activities"—recycling tin cans, buying war bonds, rationing food, writing to advice columnists—"were suffused with nationalistic fervor," but major decisions also had to be made. By mid-1942, the columnist often was asked "to advise whether girls should marry men who are going off to war," she wrote, and counseled that "cases are individual, that circumstances ... must be considered." The newlywed "Terry," already alone only a month after a wartime wedding, agreed with Griggs. The letter—typically laden with prose of governmental propaganda—recommended waiting to wed as a patriotic act.[14]

> A girl must have that something that helps her stand on her own feet, whatever happens, a courageous self-reliance and tremendous pride that carries her through every situation with flying colors.... The bride of a soldier, sailor or marine must keep these colors flying, or she will not be a credit to herself, her husband or her country. If she cannot keep them flying, she should stay single and not hamper the war.
>
> I was married in April, and a week later kissed my husband "good-by." I do not know what is ahead.[15]

If she could not know what was ahead, "Terry" was planning ahead, supporting herself and the war as a defense plant worker in Milwaukee and, with increased income, investing in war bonds.

---

13   Ibid., 26, 64-70; Patty Loew, "The Back of the Homefront: Black and American Indian Women in Wisconsin During World War II," *Wisconsin Magazine of History* 82:2 (Winter 1998-99), 84; Conrad, Wilson, and Wilson, *Milwaukee Journal*, 151.

14   IQG, "War Brides Need Courage, Self-Reliance and Optimism," *MJ*, May 28, 1942; Evans, *Born for Liberty*, 219.

15   IQG, "War Brides."

I have budgeted to the best of my ability, so that I am able to put a third of what I make into war bonds. If my darling comes back, and I feel that he will, we will have a nest egg, which he hopes to match. I work in a war production plant, and I am working hard, feeling that some of the work I do may help him and others ... on the path to victory.

I was working in an office ... but decided I could help more by getting into a factory.[16]

"Terry" also planned for a home of her own, taking cooking and sewing lessons weekly. "I don't have time on my hands," she wrote. "The days and nights pass swiftly." Griggs replied that her reader was the sort of "woman who need not be afraid to take a husband in abnormal times."[17]

The abnormality of wartime was as evident in Griggs' column as it was on the front page, as her readers wrote about the war in almost one in ten letters sampled for the entire decade. In months following the missive from "Terry," Griggs and regretful readers continued to counsel against rushed wartime weddings by "impetuous but immature" couples, as the columnist wrote. "A War Bride" replied to "Doomed" about her "defeatist attitude" toward unforeseen difficulties of wedded life, as "Doomed" had a husband at home, while "A War Bride" and others "would give anything to have the war ended and to be able to live a normal life," but wise military wives headed into marriage with knowledge of sacrifices ahead. Griggs and her readers often resorted to stereotypical sentiments, as when she wrote to "Strawberry Blond" to "stop this gallivanting around" and "concentrate upon your husband and marriage. Stop going to dances for the purpose of flattering your ego and pay more attention to your cookbook." An extreme example of a rush to wed in wartime came from "Troubled in Many Ways," engaged at only fourteen years old. Her fiancé, stationed in the Pacific, wanted her to vow to wed immediately upon his return. The columnist and her readers advised "Troubled" to first become reacquainted, after years apart.[18]

---

16   Ibid.

17   Ibid.

18   Ibid.; IQG, "College-Bred Couple Knows How to Meet Hard Times," *MJ*, February 25, 1942; IQG, "Promise Made at 14 Disturbs Engaged Girl," *MJ*, November 15, 1945.

"Polly" penned a letter about her wish, at twenty years old, to wed a "boy" whom she had met four months before. Their romance had consisted of roller-skating and movie-going, until he was called up for army camp and proposed marriage and a wedding within weeks. "Why shouldn't we take what happiness we can now? Others are marrying," wrote "Polly." The age-old argument had not persuaded their parents, as was evident in her next plaint—"Why can't our mothers see how earnest we are?"—nor did that persuade Griggs. "Polly" detailed a budget based on her pay of sixty dollars per month—far less than his—plus a newly enacted allotment for military wives. "Now that a bill has been passed allowing a serviceman's wife fifty dollars a month," Griggs replied, couples who had "met only last spring" also "believe as you do that they are sufficiently attracted and congenial to take a chance on marriage," but "congeniality plus the allowance of fifty dollars do not comprise a secure foundation for marriage. Even in normal times, I think a couple should see whether or not their romance will weather a winter," wise advice in Wisconsin. "In wartime, married life for newlyweds is not normal," Griggs wrote. "In six months' time, you may find it difficult to remember the color of eyes your husband has."[19]

War could change a man—or a woman, counseled Griggs, if facing motherhood alone for years, even for a lifetime. "If her husband doesn't come back," wrote Griggs, "a military wife had to be both 'mother and father' for the duration" or even decades ahead. Herself a widow, Griggs warned that military wives' allotment of "money will not recompense for loneliness" nor counter mistaken reasons for rushing to wed. A "confidential" reply, published without the letter that had prompted it, warned "Desperate and Heartbroken" to tell the truth to "the man whom you are thinking of marrying" rather than "make him think the child you are going to have is his." A similar letter turned into a sad saga, a "war tragedy" played out on her pages for readers, with a "confidential" reply, telephone calls, and other interventions by Griggs for a newlywed, nineteen-year-old military wife. "Ann" was suicidal. Pregnant by one soldier, she had married another soldier, due home on leave—and overdue to be informed of her pregnancy, at the least. Griggs immediately published a "confidential" to "Ann" to contact the

---

19   IQG, "Reckless Marriages Mustn't Follow U.S. Allotment Plan," *MJ*, August 28, 1942.

columnist with her name and address, received her reply, and arranged a referral to a counselor at an often-recommended agency. However, before "Ann" could take Griggs' advice, a "jealous relative" had related the truth to the husband, who had abandoned both the mother and her child by another man.[20]

The cautionary tales in the column, serving as social control in times of societal turmoil, warned "Polly" and other women of the worst that could result from wartime marriages. "When the war is over," as Griggs admonished "Polly," and if her fiancé "survives the world and comes home," he could "seem like a stranger." Problems with "strangers" arose, among signs of a changing world for Wisconsin women long secure in rural areas, small towns, or urban ethnic enclaves, until the war. On a first such letter on "strangers" to surface in sampling of letters from the start, Griggs worried that "Wondering" had met a man who was not "much of a gentleman" and had "an unpleasant way of showing it." A Michigan woman's more pleasant memory of an interlude in Milwaukee, where she had "associated with a stranger," gave Griggs an opportunity for humor, when she wrote that the writer also certainly had not met "much of a gentleman," as he had described himself as "a Journal man." However, apparently given the name given to the woman, Griggs avowed that he could not be a co-worker; indeed, in seriousness, she implied that no man who worked for her newspaper, with its high standards, would so deceive a woman.[21]

Her readers needed all-too-rare occasions for humor in the war years, when the news was worrisome. In the summer of 1942, when the impatient "Polly" already wrote of not wanting to wait for her fiancée at war to come home, the country had been at war for only eight months. However, casualties already had begun, and in the years to come, more than eight thousand Wisconsin men would come home in coffins, among more than four hundred thousand men serving from every state—and more than four hundred women in military auxiliaries, including many from Wisconsin—who would die in one of the deadliest wars in U.S. history. Griggs warned that "Polly" was

---

20   Ibid.; IQG, "Tell Us;" IQG, "Life and Death Cross in This War Tragedy," *MJ*, March 4, 1943.

21   IQG, "Reckless Marriages;" IQG, "Good Type of Husband Is Pictured by a Happy Wife," *MJ*, October 17, 1941; IQG, "Widow Longs to Pick Up Flirtation," *MJ*, October 28, 1946.

not ready for marriage and found "an authority" on military funerals as well as weddings. "The senior chaplain at Chicago's navy pier" had both buried and married many men, and to "young men who want to rush to the altar" and Griggs' readers, the minister counseled that it was not "wise to challenge fate at a time when the world is at stake."[22]

In 1942, women's fate and their stake in the war were altered by the federal government, with a massive propaganda campaign to persuade them to enter the workforce. For "Terry" and millions of already-working women nationwide, the war offered opportunity for better wages in factories at tasks that few women had been allowed to undertake before the war, owing to union contracts or unwritten constraints. Millions of women soon would work for wages for the first time, including in states such as Wisconsin, where women long had worked at a higher rate than in many states, although for lower pay. Their numbers and wages had declined during the decade of the Depression, with almost fourteen percent of state residents formerly in the workforce still without work by 1940—if, even then, more than a quarter of a million Wisconsin women comprised more than a fifth of the state workforce. Then had come "signs of a slowly returning prosperity," writes Thompson, such as the state's registration in 1940 of sales of more than three-quarters of a million automobiles—or "devil-wagons," as cars were called by Wisconsin parents who saw back seats as the devil's playground—before such temptation became more difficult to procure, as automobile plants' production turned to making military vehicles for the duration.[23]

An early Ford assembly-line factory in Milwaukee and other manufacturing sites swiftly retooled for defense production, and many went to triple-shift or overtime work—if they found enough workers. As historian Robert C. Nesbit writes, "the national emergency of World War II exploited what Wisconsin had at hand" in the then-thirteenth-largest state in the land: "industrial capacity" for "production of machines and other staples of warfare" and a "highly trained and productive labor force" both urban and rural, in an era when even

---

22   Ibid.; Congressional Research Service, *American War and Military Operations Casualties: Lists and Statistics* (Washington, D.C.: Congressional Research Service, 2010), 2. On Wisconsin women among wartime casualties, see McBride, *Women's Wisconsin*, 369-370.

23   Thompson, *History of Wisconsin*, 16, 22-23.

Milwaukee County retained more residents on farms than in twenty other counties in the state. The metropolitan area and southeastern Wisconsin—the main circulation area of the *Journal*—held almost half of all state residents, including almost a fourth of farm families in the state. They provided dairy products and other foodstuffs from the homefront to feed a force of more than sixteen million American men in the military, with more than a third of a million from Wisconsin. The unemployment rate in the state was negligible in 1942. By then, "the economy had absorbed available supplies of male workers" with many men away to war, writes historian Sara M. Evans, and "widespread recognition that only the employment of women" could meet the demand for defense work.[24]

With so many men at war, governmental propaganda campaigns called on women. They took on tasks "once viewed as inappropriate," historian Sara M. Evans writes, but the tasks that "suddenly became patriotic duties for which women were perfectly suited." Women also suited up in uniform, with more than eight thousand from Wisconsin in Army WACS, Navy WAVES, Coast Guard SPARS, and other auxiliaries, when women were not allowed in regular military; most enlisted as nurses. Family members filled in for many mothers away to war or to war work but could not meet all needs, as a letter from "Fifteen-Year-Old Girl" to Griggs attested. "Since my mother started to work last year" on the second shift, "I've done the cooking, scrubbing, ironing, dusting, and so on. I took over a woman's job," wrote the girl. Growing up fast for the war was a burden underscored by her words, as she "wouldn't mind doing it if my family appreciated it. But no." However, more than lack of appreciation had hurt her the most, as her mother had missed her graduation ceremony. Griggs was sympathetic but suggested that larger issues were at work in a working mother's schedule. "If she has a war job, her work is essential, and if she takes a day off, it might hamper the fighting overseas," she wrote; wartime workplaces constantly warned employees that absenteeism could cost a soldier his life for lack of supplies, weaponry, and munitions manufactured in Milwaukee factories. Griggs hoped that the girl

---

24   Ibid., 22-23, 93, 97-98; Nesbit, *Wisconsin*, 497-498, 527; Evans, *Born for Liberty*, 221.

would find comfort in considering "that the work your mother is doing may help win the war."[25]

Women workers became a financial windfall for another massive defense plant, Allis-Chalmers, a major beneficiary of federal contracts in the billions by the end of the war for many companies in Milwaukee County, which won 60 percent of all contracts in Wisconsin. The next-largest to win contracts was nearby Kenosha County, which had a history of more women in its manufacturing workforce; even so, the number of women working solely in its manufacturing sector by the war's end would exceed the number of all women in the county workforce in 1940. By comparison, in that year in Milwaukee, where unions were more resistant to women, Allis-Chalmers had employed only 144 women, 3 percent of its total workforce, well below the rate statewide for the manufacturing sector of almost one of five of working women even before the war, and in a state in which women comprised 22 percent of the workforce overall. By late 1941, Allis-Chalmers had to employ women, owing to a ramp-up of defense production even before an official declaration of war; women workers soon totaled 750 at Allis-Chalmers, although still less than 10 percent of its total workforce, which also had increased. By the war's end, women would comprise almost a fourth of the company's workforce—but that benchmark had been achieved by the end of 1943 in all industrial jobs in Milwaukee County, after a door-to-door drive to housewives. However, women in the county and across the country earned on average much less than men with less time on the job, even the women with prewar work experience.[26]

Perhaps owing in part to the prospect of paying less for more, employers long resistant to women in parts of their plants had become remarkably willing to change their ways and their workforce. In the first six months of 1942, they "raised their estimates of the proportion of new jobs for which women would be acceptable from 29 to 55 percent," Evans writes. Reactions of more conservative readers of the *Milwaukee Journal* were common across the country, according to *Fortune* magazine in 1943, when "practically no unmarried women

25   Evans, *Born for Liberty*, 219; McBride, *Women's Wisconsin*, 369; IQG, "'Home Keeper,' 15, Here's One for You," *MJ*, August 10, 1944.

26   Thompson, *History of Wisconsin*, 93, 97-98; Gurda, *Making of Milwaukee*, 311; Evans, *Born for Liberty*, 221.

left" for the workforce left only "the housewives." However, "sentimental people with strong, ingrained ideas about what women should or should not do" were among "many thoughtful citizens" who were "seriously disturbed over the wisdom of bringing married women into the factories," fretted *Fortune.* None of Griggs' readers in letters sampled wrote of difficulties in doing factory work, but readers did note redoubled burdens of also being housewives, when the U.S. census found that 99 percent of Wisconsin women did housework, while less than 1 percent of Wisconsin men did so.[27]

When women entered the workforce in force, co-workers—or their wives—could become "disturbed" by situations that arose or were feared on the factory floor. In the 1930s, when many women were forced out of the workforce, no letters about co-workers were found in columns sampled. In the sample in the 1940s, letters on issues with co-workers, if few, surfaced for the first time. Conflict could come from a co-worker's wife, wrote "A Puzzled War Plant Girl," who realized that her "predicament" was unlike others that had come up in the column.

> It isn't exactly a domestic problem. It isn't exactly a romance problem. I don't think it is an etiquette problem. Yet in a way, it is all three. I feel embarrassed, puzzled, and bewildered.... I was waiting for my boyfriend, who works in another department in the war plant.... It began to rain.... My friend was late, and I didn't want to get my hair wet, so I climbed in the nearest car.... I missed my handkerchief a little later.[28]

As her handkerchief "wasn't a good one," she "didn't think much about it"—until the next day.

> I heard that the wife of one of the men in my department had raised a big rumpus because she found a woman's handkerchief in her husband's car.... I heard that he is having a bad time at home, that his wife is accusing him constantly of unfaithfulness, simply because he stayed later than usual that night, and she found the hanky....
> I don't like to see a man being harassed and made miserable because of something I did.[29]

---

27   Evans, *Born for Liberty,* 221.

28   IQG, "Hanky in Husband's Car Created Situation," *MJ,* September 7, 1943.

29   Ibid.

Griggs advised "A Puzzled War Plant Girl" to be "courageous" and "clear this up" for her co-worker. However, his wife was a "stubborn, foolish woman," and to all of the wives of men in workplaces where women had been few, the former "girl reporter" gave a warning that, "with more husbands than ever in war plants where women are employed, wives should consider it patriotic" and "a matter of wifely loyalty and common sense to avoid senseless jealousy. The most foolish woman in the world is the wife who squanders a good marriage," Griggs wrote, "because of jealousy or suspicion over a bit of circumstantial evidence." The columnist's efforts to ease conflicts may have helped Milwaukee defense plants in countering national trends as war wore on; they retained and even gained in numbers, with almost two hundred thousand women in wartime factories in 1944. "Milwaukee is different," asserted a wartime employment official, owing to intensive recruitment of women—if also to lack of alternatives in "stable" industries.[30]

Many workers in the war effort were not in factories but on farms, where conflict with co-workers meant family conflicts. Wartime propaganda also called on farmers to feed both the homefront and military overseas, an effort in which Wisconsin was a major supplier, with almost half of residents still in rural areas. As Griggs wrote to a rural reader, facing loan debts on her land: "See that someone works the farm." Nearby, the International Harvester in Illinois held classes soon replicated across the country to train "tractorettes," women who could repair as well as drive equipment in fields, as many male family members and farmhands were drafted—until exemptions for agricultural workers—or enlisted. However, many younger women also left the land to enlist in military auxiliaries or for war work in cities. So also did rural minorities, whose numbers were minimal in Milwaukee until the war. Letter writers to Griggs rarely self-identified by race, but many may have had lives like that of Nellie Sweet Wilson. The motherless girl had grown up with grandparents on a Texas farm, where they had worked as slaves; then her father had moved to Milwaukee, where she had earned a high school degree during the Depression but found only work in domestic service for wages of less than fifteen dollars a month. She had wed and divorced and supported two daughters by the start of the war, when she sought work in a war plant for two years but was

---

30 "More Women in War Plants, National Trend Reversed," *MJ*, September 3, 1944.

told that there were no openings, "only to see white women behind her invited in for interviews," as historian Patty Loew writes. In 1943, in Wilson's third attempt at employment with A.O. Smith Corporation, demand for workers to fulfill a federal contract for manufacture of military aircraft propellers finally saw her hired at thirty-three dollars per week, three-fourths of the average for white women and little more than half of the average for white men in Milwaukee but far more than a maid was paid. As a result of similar disparities in rural and urban wage rates, a study found that most southeastern Wisconsin farms were worked by "partly disabled men" or women, "unseen and unsung soldiers of food production" for the war.[31]

Rural readers' letters described lives of farmwives and their families in wartime. "Farm Wife" wrote to support "A Worried Wife" regarding family conflict after a move to the city and to readers who had replied that urban life would be more costly, which was a "myth," she wrote.

> We buy many things at the same prices. Our taxes are just as high for ... schools, roads, and officials' jobs.... Our fire and police protection is far inferior. We have no municipal system of water and sewerage. If we want these comforts, we purchase our own little plants.... Electric and water maintenance bills [are] comparable to [those of] urban dwellers.... It just seems cheaper to live on the farm, because cash isn't all that is involved ... but some place along the line, it cost the farmer and his wife something.[32]

And the "farmer's wife has the same housework, maybe more," she wrote. Yet "urban dwellers" seemed to think that farmwives raised poultry and gardened "for a hobby," without paid wages. "Including produce and cash as income," she wrote, her husband averaged forty cents an hour.[33]

> What urban dweller would work for that? The farm hand and farmer both put in 16 hours a day, six days a week, and six to eight hours on Sunday. Any off-the-farm worker could live in grand style

---

31 Thompson, *History of Wisconsin*, 66-67, 85-87; Evans, *Born for Liberty*, 219; Loew, "Back of the Homefront," 85-86; Amy Rabideau Silvers, "Defense Work Led Wilson to Calling as Union Activist," *MJS*, January 31, 2008; IQG, "Reckless Marriages."

32 IQG, "Farm Youths Need to Live Their Own Lives," *MJ*, November 8, 1944.

33 Ibid.

if he worked an equal number of hours. People forget that the average farm is paid for by the work of the farmer, his wife, and children,
until the children are old enough to get city jobs.[34]

In sum, she wrote, "the young farmer's wife has to decide what will give
her and her husband the most happiness. If it's dollars and cents, run,
don't walk to the nearest off-the-farm job!" More than monetary reasons had motivated the move; an important factor for the young wife
had been benefits of urban life for children, long before they would not
have to go far for "city jobs."[35]

Another farmwife also supported the decision by "A Worried Wife,"
for her children's sake. "A Farmer Grandma" and her family had followed the column for years for affirmation that, compared to urban
readers, "our difficulties weren't so large that we couldn't settle them
among ourselves," but not "until lately did any of us believe that we
would have a subject for discussion" with "Dear Mrs. Griggs." The
writer knew of many "old-fashioned farms," like that of in-laws of "A
Worried Wife," who had resisted improvements or improved only
the barn, not the farmhouse. "Plenty of farmers get along with outside plumbing and primitive conditions in general," she wrote, yet "the
farmer and his family today are enjoying the largest change in the history of this country" and, with largess from war production and prices,
could afford to change their ways. Other "up to date" farmers accomplished modernization only because they "rob their children of every
penny they earn to buy more and more land" and "believed that their
children regardless of age were slaves" deprived of the fun of school
years when far from schools, as if "milking cows, looking after young
stock, and toiling in the fields should be all any boy or girl needs." In
such cases, wrote "Farmer Grandma," grown children were fully justified in leaving farm life, as "it isn't always the bright lights of the city
that draw these children away." But she knew that when they raised
these reasons within their farming families, "the fireworks start."[36]

Despite the work of farmwomen to increase crops to feed troops
overseas as well as other war workers on the homefront and Wisconsin
farmers' achievement of record production during war years, food

---

34   Ibid.

35   Ibid.

36   Ibid.

rationing and price controls also added to readers' worries reflected in letters on financial and familial woes. Shortages of commodities such as sugar and butter, both crucial to culinary culture in Milwaukee as a city that may have had as many bakeries as bars, "shaped the lives of every man, woman, and child in Wisconsin," writes historian William F. Thompson. Worse was meat rationing, in a culture reliant on a regular menu of German bratwurst or Polish *pierogies*—fried dumplings, often stuffed with ground beef—in requiring more creativity from housewives already coping with a time shortage, owing to war work or other shortages. Many had to take the trolley or bus for daily food shopping, after grocers had to suspend deliveries in gasoline shortages so severe that Milwaukee breweries brought back horse-drawn beer wagons.[37]

Families that finally had been able to afford cars coped not only with gasoline rationing but also with use of the lack of fuel as a creative excuse by teenagers. "Disgusted" opined that the columnist, like her parents, was behind the times in telling girls to take a trolley or bus and "not allowing them to go in cars" with teen-aged boys. "What with gas and tire rationing ... the bus and streetcar service to parts of the city is notably poor," she wrote, and rejection of a ride could "disillusion" a boy who had "saved his gas" for a girl, with impact upon her social "style" as well. "Mrs. Griggs, you and parents may not realize it, but nowadays, if everyone else can do things one girl can't, it cramps her style.... If the rest of the gang does it, it seems very stuffy of parents not to allow their daughters to do it." The argument that "everybody does it" did not sway Griggs in the 1940s any more than it had a decade before or would do in decades to come. "Think individually, not just as the 'gang' does," Griggs replied. As for admonishment that she "go back to your own youth" to recall "good times," as her ideas were as "as dated as those of some parents," the columnist drily wrote that "human nature hasn't changed since I was 13," a line likely repeated by readers who looked to her for help in discussions at local dinner tables.[38]

Families would recall dinners in shifts, owing to differing work hours and the housing shortage, a factor in an alleged rise in delinquency, as overcrowding drove teenagers out of the house to drive

---

37   Thompson, *History of Wisconsin*, 74-78, 83; Gurda, *Making of Milwaukee*, 313.

38   IQG, "'Parents Know Best' Is Challenged by Girl," *MJ*, June 4, 1943.

126   'DEAR MRS. GRIGGS'

around town in cars. "As told in the papers, the juvenile delinquency problem has been bad lately," wrote "Disgusted." More significant, with the worker shortage, was easing of child labor laws for hiring teenagers into the late hours, but Griggs and others in media missed that cause and focused on cars. A letter writer proved more perceptive, after being "stopped and questioned by police when out driving with her boyfriend," as Griggs wrote.[39] The boy blamed police persecution, but the girl blamed the social-control role of media, including the columnist.

> This "morals" drive throughout the city, the likes of which has never been seen before in this country, [is] making it tough on us decent girls who work the second shift.
>
> These nights, we can't even go for a ride with some age-old friends after dark without being stopped.... All of the police I have encountered have been insulting and insinuating.... We are "put down in the books" for relaxing after work.[40]

However, the writer was not riding and relaxing only with "some age-old friends," it seemed.

> Servicemen are being unjustly blamed for "pickups." If a girl leaves them alone, they won't look a second time. My girl friend and I are considered pretty ... yet when we walk down the avenue ... we are positively unnoticed and unmolested.
>
> If a young snip wants a date, wartime or no wartime, she'll get one by hook or crook, by flirting or wolfing. Why blame the war conditions?[41]

"The avenue" or "the av," as any Milwaukeean knew, was Wisconsin Avenue, the main street downtown and locale of a local USO. If she argued that "it isn't any different now than it was before"—before the war—the writer recognized "fast-moving times" of wartime as unusual: "In normal times, a girl asks for trouble by her conduct, and a fellow accepts," but "now, a girl asks and a serviceman accepts, merely because practically all fellows are servicemen." Griggs agreed, recalling her Chicago days as a reporter mistakenly stopped in police stations,

---

39   Thompson, *History of Wisconsin*, 79-80; IQG, "'You Started Morals Drive,' Girl Accuses," *MJ*, July 7, 1943.

40   IQG, "'You Started.'"

41   Ibid.

but also demurred that times decidedly were different for residents and police "trying hard to clear up a situation."[42]

The "situation" in the city's downtown, on "the avenue" and near the USO, where the likes of "Disgusted" and her friend liked to flirt, led to the largest flood ever of letters to Griggs—more than seven thousand letters in one week—and, more than ever, turned her column into a community forum for debate about wartime "morals." A colleague recalled that the record came in reaction to a "controversy" that "raged in her column over the morals of teenage girls … said to be behaving improperly with sailors," owing to the city's proximity to the Great Lakes Naval Training Station, only a train ride away in Illinois. A reader worried, "how can we even hope for victory and peace if girls become ruthless and corrupted?" City fathers proposed an early curfew for minors under the age of sixteen, which predictably brought protestations to Griggs by young readers. "Disgusted" wrote that a curfew would "cramp the style of teen-aged girls and unfairly punish the "innocent," who would "suffer with the guilty," while "An Angel" agonized that "this curfew business has got me down, as it has many others. It may cause a revolution." Another girl, "J.M.B.," rather hyperbolically asserted, "I thought we were fighting so we wouldn't have a dictatorship," but after reading the column regarding the curfew, the reader "wouldn't hardly care" if Germany won the war. "The kids of Milwaukee aren't going to take this lying down," warned "J.B."—to which Griggs replied, "cool down, honey." As ever more letters "deluged her desk," the columnist wrote, "we must face the fact that there is a girl problem in Milwaukee."[43]

The extent to which the columnist had created or at least contributed to exacerbating the perception of "a girl problem" is unclear from analysis of news pages as well as her page of the newspaper, but Griggs determined to provide the solution by assuming a social-mediator role of direct intervention that departed from her usual dispassionate

---

42   Ibid.

43   Ibid.; IQG, "Whitefish Bay Mother Views Wisconsin Av.," *MJ*, July 6, 1943; IQG, "Opposition to Curfew Forces Loud Protests," *MJ*, July 12, 1943; IQG, "Defiant Girls Won't Take Curfew Calmly," *MJ*, July 13, 1943; IQG, "Would Huge Canteen Cure 'Local Headache,'" *MJ*, July 14, 1943; IQG, "Boys Argue Against the Curfew for Teen Age," *MJ*, July 15, 1943; IQG, "What Can Girls Do If Curfew Ruins Plans?" *MJ*, July 16, 1943.

stance of journalistic objectivity. To mediate the conflict, she proposed and published a "pledge of good behavior" that her readers clipped, signed, and returned by the thousands, which the columnist personally delivered to City Hall to win one for the girls: The law set the curfew, at midnight, later than originally planned.[44]

The saga presaged a wider societal reaction regarding an allegedly increasing incidence of "juvenile delinquency" that went beyond city boundaries, as the issue later escalated to the state level. Hearings by a legislative Committee on Youth Problems signaled societal transitions to come in expectations of educators, with the recommendation that "the schools of Wisconsin wake up to their responsibility in educating future citizens by accepting the fact that their responsibility extends beyond ... imparting knowledge to an even greater obligation to train future citizens in how to live," including to "get along with other people in today's society" and "the most important responsibility of living— namely, that of parenthood and family."[45]

Among solutions suggested by the state curriculum committee attesting to the already-iconic status of "Dear Mrs. Griggs" was a compilation of her columns, distributed to schools as "better discussion material than any textbook." The committee opined that alleged "juvenile delinquency" was widespread, and that schools clearly were not serving a "large percentage of children who will not go on to college," although the columns came from letters penned by well-read young readers. The State-Wide Committee on Growing Into Maturity and Family Life of a Wisconsin Co-operative Educational Planning Program and a Wisconsin Co-operative School Health Program was assisted in selection of columns by a committee with representatives from the state Department of Public Instruction and state Board of

---

44   IQG, "Against Curfew? Why Not Pledge to Behave?" *MJ*, July 17, 1943; IQG, "If You Want Liberty Pledge Good Conduct," *MJ*, July 19, 1943; IQG, "Canteen Idea Offered Includes Teen Agers," *MJ*, July 20, 1943; IQG, "Indian Mother Pleads for Happier Juveniles," *MJ*, July 21, 1943; IQG, "Girls, Parents, What Goals Are You After?" *MJ*, July 22, 1943; IQG, "Do You Want Curfew? Pledge Good Conduct," *MJ*, July 23, 1943; IQG, "Curfew Here to Ring August 3/Council Sets Midnight Ban for All Under 16; Vote Is Unanimous," *MJ*, July 27, 1943.

45   "Schools: Recommendation No. 2," in "Report of Joint Interim Committee, 1945, Submitted to the 1947 Legislature on Youth Problems," quoted in IQG, *Growing Up*, n.p.

Health and the Milwaukee Health Department. The sixty-page book-
let included many young readers' letters and Griggs' replies, often reas-
surances that their concerns were "normal"—a catchword of the conformity that would characterize the decade to come, although Griggs
would employ the term otherwise in repeatedly pointing out that her
columns were evidence that "confusions and frustrations" of teenagers
were "normal" problems of adolescence and not the product of a current society." Thousands of copies of *Growing Up with Jim and Jean...:
Reprinted from the Columns of Ione Quinby Griggs* were distributed free
to students statewide in the 1940s and would resurface in discussion
of the topic of "juvenile delinquency" in her column as well as in news
stories, further legislative hearings, and the like for decades to come,
despite the columnist's plea for common sense.[46]

At least the sailors from Illinois who had been drawn to the de-
lights of Milwaukee, only to cause controversy—as mere mention
of the wicked state to the south could do in Wisconsin—had not
added to the housing shortage. Far more newcomers came owing to
defense factories' recruitment campaigns. "Housing was the commod-
ity most difficult to provide when it was in short supply," historian
William F. Thompson writes. "Practically nothing was built for fifteen years" of Depression and war, writes Milwaukee historian John
Gurda, with the result that "adequate housing was hard to find, and
the supply grew even tighter during the war." As early as 1942, the
federal government had identified severe housing deficiencies in sites
of significant war production in the state, especially Milwaukee, where
Griggs witnessed long lines of hopeful workers awaiting editions of
the *Journal*, hot off the presses for a head start on housing ads, that
caused traffic hazards for delivery trucks, until her employer set up
a separate site for distribution of early editions. *Journal* readers also
faced housing shortages in southeastern Wisconsin cities of Beloit,
Green Bay, Madison, Manitowoc, Oshkosh, and Sturgeon Bay, all
designated "critical defense housing areas" deserving priority in federal
funds for "prefab" housing and construction materiel. However, overcrowding continued, and landlords illegally raised rents and "refused
to rent to families with young children," especially for female heads of

---

46   Armstrong, "Issue on Teenage Morals;" IQG, "Advice to Teenagers of
      Yesteryear Holds True in These Times as Well," *MJ*, January 22, 1985;
      Wells, *Milwaukee Journal*, 265.

households. "Servicemen's wives with children were repeatedly turned away," Thompson writes, and workers recruited for defense industries "faced the choice of either giving up the job or leaving their families behind." In reply to readers' desperate letters, Griggs wrote that "doors are slammed many times when the wife of a serviceman or war worker ... asks for shelter with children" in a plea for landlords to "place patriotism and understanding of human needs above mere financial consideration."[47]

Griggs used her column to further understanding of families with housing issues, filling columns with letters from readers refused housing and telling their stories. In 1943, on the second anniversary of the attack on Pearl Harbor, came a letter from "Mrs. C.B.," mother of four and wife of a Milwaukee defense plant war worker doing overtime to meet production quotas.

> I am not the only mother who is worried with the need to find a decent place.... To rent a place, if one has children, is like looking for gold where there isn't gold....
>
> When I go from door to door to ask to rent a place that isn't too far for my husband to go to work, the doors are slammed in my face. I have had men tell me they preferred rats, dogs and cats to children.... We had to take a place thirty miles from Milwaukee.
>
> The house is worse than some barns. It was all we could find where we could take the children. We pay $25 a month rent and it has [no] water, lavatory, bath, or furnace for heat. The school is two and one-half miles from the house.[48]

Getting children to school with gasoline shortages—and only one car for a family in the 1940s—further complicated family life for a weary wife and even imperiled her husband's war work.

> We shop once a week. I get the children out of bed at 5 a.m. and get to Milwaukee with my husband at the time he goes to work. I sit with the children in the car until the stores open, then I shop and wait until my husband is through work, because there isn't gas enough for an extra trip. My husband is a war worker. He holds an important job.

---

47   Thompson, *History of Wisconsin,* 79-80; Gurda, *Making of Milwaukee,* 322; Wells, *Milwaukee Journal,* 338; IQG, "Place 'Child Welcome' on War Rental Signs," *MJ,* December 7, 1943.

48   IQG, "Place 'Child Welcome.'"

He drives thirty miles twice a day and works ten hours a day. This is getting him down.... If he can't get a place to live in Milwaukee, he may have to give up his job.[49]

The couple, both Milwaukee-born, had called the city home until the landlord sold his property, and a price-gouging new owner had raised the rent beyond their budget. "I don't expect you to find us a place," she wrote to Griggs, "but your column may reach the hearts of people who can help." In reply, Griggs "realized that many houses and apartments are already filled with other families or couples who can't be turned out" but hoped that readers could help "a hard-working father and mother ... turned away because of children," despite references. Calling their plight "a reversal of the things for which a democratic country stands," the columnist called upon her readers to patriotically "place 'children welcome' on rental signs" for the good of the country.[50]

Overcrowding occurred despite more sons away to war, with the return of daughters who were war wives—or widows. Many an adult woman in the 1940s lived under her parents' roof, often war workers helping to support parents, as did Alice DeNomie of Milwaukee. Although not apparently a letter writer to Griggs, her story illumines more lives of minority women in the era. She worked for the telephone company at fifteen dollars per week toward tuition at Milwaukee's prestigious Layton School of Art, until the war, when "school seemed pointless," as she would recall, for a daughter of a World War I veteran with other family members soon overseas in the Ojibwe tribal tradition of military service. The family also supported the USO, where she played cards, danced with troops, and was a popular volunteer: young, pretty, and "pretty innocent," she would recall. She found work at a war plant producing bomb sights, Perfex, at twice the pay of her prewar position. Part of her pay went to her parents to help to support a family of eight—and then ten, when her sister Mary Jane returned home as a war widow with a daughter, too.[51]

Families could be supportive but also contentious, a reason for an increase in letters on conflict in familial relationships. Problems with non-spousal family members—parents, in-laws, siblings, children

---

49   Ibid.
50   Ibid.
51   Loew, "Back of the Homefront," 84-89, 94.

—increased in letters sampled from little more than 22 percent in the 1930s to more than 27 percent in the 1940s, more than the number of letters about spouses or boyfriends. "Rise Above Feeling of Slights from Family" read a headline on a column on sibling rivalry that endured into adulthood. "Just because I'm the elder," wrote "One-Sided," she perceived parental "partiality" for a younger sister and her family. Her reader cited no recent reasons for continuing "childish resentments" that ought to be outgrown, as Griggs gently reminded "One-Sided." In contrast, however, a younger sister wrote with concern for a brother home from the war and living at home but enduring "discomfort" with his parents, as he no longer was a boy but was a grown man. The writer proposed a Milwaukee-style solution for him to have a place of his own—and for her to have him nearby: She would update a "rear house" behind her own in an older area of the city, where frugal immigrants often had built two houses on one lot. Griggs endorsed the plan but hoped that his need would not be long-term. "Maybe you can even introduce him to some girl," she wrote, and "one of these days, he may marry" and have "his own home."[52]

Moving out of parents' homes was not necessarily a solution for the fortunate who found vacancies in crowded boardinghouses, flats, or apartments. "Anonymous" complained about neighbors, although she had few companions and often was alone, owing to her husband's work. Griggs counseled the couple to consider whether he could find work closer to home or commute from "a more congenial vicinity," but with the housing shortage, advised her reader to "develop a less sensitive attitude toward others around you." Another reader had moved out on her own, only to have an aggravating neighbor. Griggs again advised "Barbara, Southside" to "develop diplomacy," reflecting the reality that finding another rental property often proved impossible in the era. "Learn to be diplomatic," Griggs also wrote to "J.M.," and "let your mother-in-law give advice," although she also advised that readers did not have to apply advice given by in-laws—or by the columnist. Simply "the giving of advice may satisfy her," Griggs wrote of the mother-in-law but perhaps about herself as well, as she had to be diplomatic when her forum became a resort for family feuds—and when relatives recognized themselves in readers' letters. A young father "had a fit" upon reading about his refusal to buy a baby buggy, as reported a relative who hoped that readers would write to "give this young man some 'medicine.'" Griggs suggested that the family stop writing and start focusing on how to help the young mother to get out of the house and get to a store to buy the baby buggy. But even a crib was beyond the means of the "Hopeful Mother" in a boardinghouse who could not find a better home for her "bureau drawer baby," as Griggs wrote. The letter brought an outpouring of community support, to the extent that the columnist had to arrange for a family services agency to help the "overwhelmed" mother sort through letters, cards, and calls with offers of housing from the column's community.[53]

Increasing concerns regarding familial relationships countered a decline in letters about romantic relationships, from more than 40 percent of 93 letters about relationships in the 1930s to less than 30 percent of 135 letters about relationships in the 1940s. A poignant letter that illumined the complications of war in a community that retained its ethnic ties came from a young reader whose fiancé was a POW—a German POW, captured in Africa and held by Americans. The couple had met in Milwaukee before the war, when he had visited relatives, but he had been required to return to Germany. However, as Griggs' reader hastened to write, "he is anti-Nazi and against the Nazi regime." She wondered whether they could wed after the war, without need for him to return to his homeland. The columnist replied that she had contacted the Red Cross, which recommended that he work with his camp chaplain and commanding officer. However, she expressed concerns that "he was a boy when you saw him last," years before, and had been "exposed to Nazism at its worst. Can you be sure he hasn't changed, that he is the same boy you thought you loved?... History will record that the strange hypnotic influence of the Nazi breed has converted many to its fold," wrote Griggs, and the columnist cautioned her reader to wait until she could "know him as he is today" or after the war, if that tomorrow ever came.[54]

---

53   IQG, "Brave Woman;" IQG, "Hanky in Husband's Car;" IQG, "Good Type;" IQG, "Agency to Help in Choosing Bureau Drawer Baby's Home," *MJ*, December 22, 1944.

54   IQG, "Girl Wants to Marry German War Captive," *MJ*, September 23, 1944.

Many readers joined war efforts to support the troops, including hundreds of state workers, most of them women—and Wisconsin Governor Walter Goodland and his wife Madge Risney Goodland—in assembly lines in a state office building in Madison in September 1944, in time to pack 21,600 Red Cross boxes for hospitalized troops overseas for holidays, months away. (Wisconsin Historical Society, WHS-13296)

Letters about dating declined from fully a fourth of topics in the 1930s to half that in the 1940s, and understandably so, with fewer men available during the war years for more than brief meetings, such as the sailors who had caused the city to consider enactment of a curfew. The dearth of men could lead to desperation as the long years of war seemed no nearer an end, a girl wrote to Griggs in a letter about a "fun-loving friend," who was "feeling very lonely," because "all her boyfriends are busy fighting for Uncle Sam." She was "an easy mark" for a man who "has lied to her and has been untrue. But she won't listen to me," and "he wants her to marry him immediately.... Don't you think that she should wait until the war is over, and her other friends return, so she can tell whether she is only lonely or in love with this man?" Griggs agreed that, again, the friend should "not consider marriage until after the war."[55]

The letter from "A Very Dear Pal" was published on August 15, 1945, the day after the unofficial "V-J Day"—the day of victory over Japan—which had signaled the end, at last, of the long years of war. When Griggs' copy had gone to press days before, because the "Green Sheet" and other feature sections were printed ahead of news sections, the columnist could not know that front-page headlines on August 14 would exclaim "War Ended! Truman Tells Nation." *Journal* readers had endured headline after headline on the front page that had changed their world in recent weeks, from the sudden death in April of President Franklin D. Roosevelt to "V-E Day" in May, marking the end of war on the European front, and in only the last week prior to "V-J Day," troops had dropped the first atomic bombs on Hiroshima and Nagasaki. "The bomb" forever had changed the lives of *Journal* readers, although they could not know then that the next war had begun, a war as yet unnamed: the Cold War. The continual threat of new conflicts afar also would have an impact on her readers. A woman would write of a "fiancé afraid of national problems," a man home from war but now wanting to "wait and see what the national situation will be" before they wed. Young readers, too, would write of "awaking to world realities."[56]

---

55 IQG, "It's Not Safe to Wed Man Minus Integrity," *MJ*, August 15, 1945.

56 IQG, "Her Fiancé Is Afraid of National Problems," *MJ*, July 7, 1947; IQG, "Youngsters, Awake to World Realities," *MJ*, September 26, 1946.

However, the worst years of fears of a new form of warfare were ahead. For now, World War II was over. By the time that the *Journal* hit the streets with huge headlines bannered across the front page, Milwaukeeans by the thousands had heard the news on the radio and had come to celebrate on "the avenue," the city's main street but a few blocks from the newspaper plant. For once, city fathers looked the other way, as servicemen snared victory kisses from any woman in sight. Among *Milwaukee Journal* reporters at the scene, a recent graduate in journalism "up the avenue" at Marquette University would recall that she had not kissed as many men in her four years of college, when few were on campus, as she did that day. Celebrations were smaller but as enthusiastic elsewhere in the state. On the same lakeshore in a city to the south, joining a jubilant crowd was Margaret "Marnie" Danhauser, the local favorite on the "Racine Belles" team later immortalized in *A League of Their Own*, a fictionalized film about the All-American Girls Professional Baseball League, based in the Midwest—where the Milwaukee Chicks were "world champions"—to maintain the sport, and its fan support, when male players had gone to war.[57]

As photos would attest, happy Wisconsinites statewide marked the day by holding up the historic front page of the end-of-the-war "extra" edition of the *Journal*, which printed a hundred thousand extra copies. Facing those readers displaying the front-page, banner headline was the back page of the "Green Sheet," with the last of Griggs' wartime columns, but far from the last on issues related to the aftermath of war and new issues for women. The marriage rate increased even more in the year after the war—to a number that would not be seen again in the state for almost three decades—and "war brides" wed overseas also would come to Wisconsin from many countries. A nationally syndicated cartoon in the "Green Sheet," next to Griggs' column on the last day of the war, depicted a bewildered bride being warned by her mother that "He's a nice boy, but remember, if you should have a little quarrel ... I wish he weren't so used to shooting Japs!" The issue of domestic violence also arose in the 1940s in letters to syndicated advice columnists "Beatrice Fairfax" and "Dorothy Dix," according to

---

57   "The AAGPBL Supports the Spirit of '45" at http://www.aagpbl.org/ index.cfm/news-item/62/the-aagpbl-supports-the-spirit-of-45, accessed December 11, 2011. The *Journal* reporter was Marian McBride, mother of a co-author.

historian David Gudelunas, as "certain taboos such as abuse" surfaced for the first time in such nationally syndicated columns in his analysis. The subject was not new to Griggs' readers, however, as they already had raised issues related to domestic violence in their column in the *Journal* for a decade, if often only implicitly, between the lines of readers' letters and Griggs' replies—but not always. Earlier in that year, the columnist had made her concern explicit in a "confidential" reply to "Mixed Up," whom Griggs had sternly advised not to "marry a man who ... struck [her] frequently."[58]

Other domestic issues would dominate life and letters throughout the postwar years of demobilization of millions of troops, as servicemen would continue to swarm downtown for years—and teenaged girls would continue to write to Griggs. As late as 1948, three "Disgusted Teen Agers" would claim to be civic-minded local boosters, attempting to bolster Milwaukee's reputation as a "friendly town," only to find their efforts twisted by "town boys," whose "talk can ruin a reputation" by referring to "girls who like to go out with servicemen" as "pickups." The patriotic trio wrote that military men deserved to "be treated with respect. They have won a war for us and are entitled to a joyous welcome in Milwaukee." Griggs agreed that the country owed heartfelt thanks to returning heroes but counseled that the girls, with an "exaggerated idea" of their role in extending gratitude, need not undertake the mission on behalf of Milwaukee.[59]

Many women readers faced an ungrateful country and never would recover gains made in the workplace, where they also faced a flood of veterans with preference in hiring under the new G.I. Bill. "As men were mustered out of the army, women were mustered out of the factories," writes historian Sara M. Evans. In Milwaukee, among almost thirty thousand laid off soon after Japan's surrender, "many of the furloughed workers were married women" and "were just as glad to go home," according to local historian John Gurda, although without evidence. However, a massive survey of women wartime industrial workers, including many in the Milwaukee area, found that 80 percent

---

58   IQG, "Three Big Influences of Marriage Explained," *MJ*, February 19, 1945; Gudelunas, *Confidential to America*, 56; Thompson, *History of Wisconsin*, 248; Galbraith, "Side Glances" [cartoon], *MJ*, August 15, 1945.

59   IQG, "'Pickup' Not Wise in Any Boy-Girl Meeting," *MJ*, August 12, 1948.

hoped to keep their wartime positions. A Milwaukee official of the federal war employment effort stated that, while some women workers "looked forward" to leaving for "the nursery front," many had "full confidence in their ability to have jobs" after the war. Their confidence in Milwaukee employers was misplaced. As Evans writes, "women knew that they, as well as men, had made victory possible," as had government propaganda to recruit women for war work, only to reverse to force them out of the workforce to return to stereotypical roles.[60]

Some women would succeed in staying in the workforce, as in the case of a "career girl" who held an executive position. However, in the late 1940s, she was "All Alone and Lonely," for reasons soon all too evident in male readers' replies. One wrote that "All Alone" undoubtedly was a "calculating" and "classy, costly, cold career girl" whose "heart wasn't on a par with her intellect" and who clearly could only make a man feel inferior. Another male reader doubted that a "career girl" would make a "swell companion" for a husband, not "willing to live on the money he earned." A third man was willing to compromise, if a "career girl" were "willing to work part time"—giving up her career. Griggs, a pioneering "career girl" of the press decades before, uncharacteristically ran the men's letters without replies, other than to term them "interesting."[61]

A few wives faced an unusual problem in their men's adjustment to civilian life in the period that Griggs termed "tough postwar years" for women, too. "Leta," a wartime bride, had met her husband only months before they had wed and he had shipped out. With his return to start married life, she wrote, "he makes me feel almost jealous of the army cook he had.... I'm really hurt. I wouldn't feel as badly if he had told me his mother was a better cook. But an army cook! How can a girl cook for a husband who criticizes her every time she lights the fire under the coffee pot?" He also criticized her shopping, if she erred in her calculations of their rationing coupon "points," and they had to do without meat for a few days. She had worked before and throughout the war, until his return, when he wanted her to quit work for housework. She felt such a sense of failure that she wondered whether she

---

60   Evans, *Born for Liberty*, 229, 237; Gurda, *Making of Milwaukee*, 323; "More Women in War Plants."

61   IQG, "Financial Figures Can Scare Good Man Away," *MJ*, November 1, 1947.

ought to return to work, leave their "cute apartment," and have him move to a boardinghouse for his meals. Several letters countered the popular lore about military rations, as "K.M.R." empathized on the woes of "cooking for a returned soldier husband" who did not "appreciate home-cooked meals as much as army meals." Their husbands missed military "he-man meals" of "well-cooked food and plenty of it, chiefly meat and potatoes," when they had to make a culinary adjustment to wartime meat rationing on the homefront. "K.M.R." had done double duty during the war; after long workdays, she also had "practiced a lot" to prepare for her husband's return with cooking lessons. However, another veteran's wife warned that many a man remained unrealistic, imagining that "the girl he thought could do everything so 'perfectly' isn't able to make hamburger taste like porterhouse."[62]

More often, women on their own as heads of households worried about how to put any food on their tables; whether or not they had worked before the war, many had to take lesser work at far lower wages afterward. For example, among the first let go from wartime factories in Milwaukee were minority women, such as Nellie Sweet Wilson, who was determined to stay off welfare, so she waitressed to support herself and her two daughters. Alice DeNomie also was let go but married a veteran so was able to move out of her parents' home into one of many "make-shift trailers" purchased by the city of Milwaukee and set up in a city park for veterans' families, facing the housing shortage. However, the trailer fell into disrepair that was dangerous for their newborn, and she and her husband again had to move home to parents—this time, her in-laws.[63]

Many readers desperately needed housing, and others took in boarders. To a reader who was "Miserable" living with family, Griggs had to reply that she could not use the column "to find homes for people." Also miserable was a teenaged girl whose bedroom, only an alcove, afforded little privacy or sleep, "with everyone in there all hours of the night," as her bedroom had been rented for years to her mother's cousin, "an old maid." Frustration also was evident in letters from "Fed Up"

---

62   IQG, "Returned Mate Talks About Wife's Cooking," *MJ*, March 24, 1944; IQG, "Major Interests Are Centered About Home," *MJ*, April 10, 1944.

63   Loew, "Back of the Homefront," 99-100; IQG, "Rally to Defense of Mother Bride Forgot," *MJ*, October 6, 1947.

and "Fed Up No. 2," to whom Griggs offered "housing suggestions" of experts that only revealed the extent of governmental inability to address the problem. Some readers reacted with sarcasm and ridicule. The column "read like it was written by the National Association of Real Estate board members, who believe that the housing shortage is a 'figment of the imagination,'" wrote "S.F." They advised "veterans and their wives to become modern Daniel Boones, to go build themselves shacks in the wilderness while the powers that be, who are responsible for their sad plight, live off the fat of the land." He called on "vets, millions of them if necessary" to form "a mass democratic movement" for a march on Washington to force federal action, as homeless and jobless veterans had done after wars before. He included among "powers that be" the *Journal* editorial board for "blaming the individual instead of the society that is responsible for this situation"—and expected that Griggs would not print his letter for his attacks on her integrity and her paper's "editorial slant." She did, commenting that the *Journal* could "afford to let it appear in this column." Another reader, "A Veteran Who Built His Own Shack," wrote that few could afford costs of land and lumber for a home, as he had done. "Some people think anyone can still chop down trees and build a cabin. This is 1948, Mrs. Griggs."[64]

Some families finally had found employment and housing. DeNomie's sister was able to move out of her parents' home; although war widows' allotment was insufficient in postwar years of high rents, she found a job with the *Milwaukee Journal*. Another *Journal* reporter, a veteran, returned to the newsroom, where he met the young Marquette journalism graduate who had made up for few dates in her college years with "victory kisses" in the city's celebration at the end of the war, and they became engaged. However, he was able to repeatedly defer setting a date by pointing to headlines about no housing to be had, until his exasperated but enterprising fiancée befriended *Journal*

64   IQG, "3 Attack Mrs. Griggs' Housing Suggestions," *MJ*, December 9, 1948; IQG, "Relative in the Home Annoys Teen Age Girl," *MJ*, May 14, 1948. "Coxey's Army," Civil War veterans, incurred arrests in the first march on Washington in the 1890s; "Bonus Marchers" from World War I in Washington in the 1930s incurred fatalities by federal troops, causing public outrage that led to the World War II G.I. Bill; see Lucy G. Barber, *Marching on Washington: The Forging of an American Political Tradition* (Berkeley: University of California Press, 2004).

pressmen to get "classifieds" hot off the presses, before housing ads
went out to long lines of readers waiting near the newspaper's plant for
copies. She found a flat, and the wedding went forward in 1946, the
year that the marriage rate peaked at a higher rate than had been seen
for decades—a rate not seen again in the century. That many newlywed couples faced high rents, the end of price controls, and runaway
inflation would force many families to struggle financially through at
least the first three years of the postwar period.[65]

Many letter writers wrote of financial problems in the 1940s, mainly in postwar years—well more than twice the tally in the 1930s, when
there had been less money to be had. Inflation, however, would double
postwar prices of many products and led to housewives' protests. As a
veteran's wife wrote in 1946, "life was pretty nice" in the war years, owing to the allotment for military families, although they "couldn't save
anything" for inevitable childhood illnesses and other bills. Balancing
a budget became "a toss whether coal or doctor bills can be paid," she
wrote. "Probably neither." Her husband also needed a new suit to seek
work. She needed a new winter coat. And, always, "the children needed shoes." Two years later, "with tears falling on this letter, as I write,"
another mother still faced the high price of shoes, when "children out-
grow clothes so quickly," and "food costs so much." Both were causes
of many arguments on finances that were "breaking up" a marriage
with "a man who argues with me about every penny I spend.... I don't
think it's my fault that prices are so high." In response, an older reader empathized with women working as "unpaid housekeepers, com-
pelled to beg for an extra penny.... Such a marriage partnership is no
partnership at all," she wrote, urging them to "end the farce." She had
been married for forty years, "short-changed all the way," and remained
"in the dark about [her] husband's earnings.... The man who insists
on handling the paycheck, not letting his wife know the full extent of
their income, has other things in his mind than being a fine husband"

---

65   IQG, "Scandal Ferret Adds Emotional Terrorism," *MJ,* January 2, 1947.
   Mary Jane DeNomie Aynes would become a pioneering television person-
   ality on WTMJ-TV, while the reluctant *Journal* reporter wed in 1946 was
   Raymond E. McBride, father of a co-author.

and "does as he pleases, while his wife is as good as in prison." She was filing for divorce.[66]

Griggs wrote to her readers that husbands were the ones who needed education on the impact of postwar inflation on household budgets. "There are more domestic squabbles over money these days than anything," she wrote. "Certainly, prices are out of line" for "rent, food, and clothing, three major necessities." Owing to war work, "the average wife had experience in money earning" as preparation for "household money management," but Griggs had researched several resources at the ready for readers, from Milwaukee Public Library reference librarians to Family Service Society staff to another woman legendary in the city. The founder and manager since 1920 of an innovative "woman's department" at the largest bank in the state, "Miss Kenny" "coached women in financial facts of life," both single women and "thousands of housewives" who "stopped daily arguments" by learning "how to discuss money matters more intelligently." A rare male letter writer attested that men also had to learn how to save. He penned for readers a "word picture of a young man's financial life in these tough postwar years," recalling that he had "hunted a job for four years during the late depression" and finally, for paltry pay, had "found a four-year apprenticeship"—cut short by the war that had cost him five years more in the armed forces. However, he had saved for night school and, upon return to civilian life, had earned high school and college degrees, as would other men on the G.I Bill, which would move them and their families into the middle class and into their own homes in the next decade—although some could not make the move until they also could afford cars, with lack of transit to new areas. Some could not even get cars yet, as retooling of auto factories from wartime use was slow, and demand was high; waiting lists were a full year in postwar years for even a "no-frills" sedan.[67]

---

66   Evans, *Born for Liberty*, 232; IQG, "Distressed Wife Asks Help to Pay Her Bills," *MJ*, December 27, 1946; IQG, "Domestic Fight over Money Not Necessary," *MJ*, February 12, 1948; IQG, "Wed 40 Years, Wife Doesn't Know Income," *MJ*, September 20, 1949.

67   IQG, "Financial Figures;" IQG, "Domestic Fight;" Gurda, *Making of Milwaukee*, 325. In 1949, the bank again made history in hiring a woman officer, lawyer Catherine B. Cleary, who credited "Miss Kenny" as her mentor. Cleary became the bank trust's first woman president and the

The return to prosperity did not promise an end to financial problems for families coping with a costly downside of local tavern culture:
excessive drinking, the largest category of family problems during both
wartime and postwar years. Letters on the issue increased in the 1940s,
as did alcohol consumption during and after every war. Women had
written of problems related to drinking in nonfamily relationships in
three letters sampled in the 1930s but wrote twice as many such letters in the sample in the 1940s. Far more evident was worry about excessive imbibing by family members. Women had written of problems
from alcoholism in family relationships in only two letters sampled in
the 1930s but did so in almost a dozen letters in the 1940s, for almost
a fourth of all letters about family problems. "Double Problems" worried for a friend whose family had driven him to drink, an "unhappy,
seemingly abnormal state of affairs" that had led him to "misbehave."
More typical was "A Faithful Wife and Mother," whose husband drank
"excessively" and exhibited subsequent "misconducts." She received
a typical referral from Griggs to contact a local "club" of Alcoholics
Anonymous (AA), founded a decade before. So did "Mrs. F.O.B.,"
whose spouse also drank to excess and "acted badly for a husband."[68]

Griggs was terse with a reader, "A.A.A.," who replied that "Mrs.
F.O.B." shared the blame, an increasingly prevalent perspective. The
"gendering of alcoholism," historian Lori Rotskoff writes, was typified
by the attack on "Mrs. F.O.B." as a "silly woman ... sitting home and
moaning about [her] husband's dubious pursuit of pleasure" and probably not keeping herself "attractive" and "interesting." However, advice
from "A.A.A." hardly accorded with the new, therapeutic approach to
alcoholism as an illness: "If he falls flat on his face in the doorway ...
let him get a cold." That alcoholism was not restricted to one gender
rarely was recognized by therapists but was admitted by letter writer
"F.I.C.," a "broadminded wife" whose husband "stayed out late every
night" but had not been as understanding when loneliness had led
her to weekly bowling and "stopping in a tavern afterward." She was

---

first woman director on major corporate boards; see McBride, *Women's
Wisconsin*, 124.

68   Thompson, *History of Wisconsin*, 25; Lori Rotskoff, *Love on the Rocks:
Men, Women, and Alcohol in Post-World War II America* (Chapel Hill:
University of North Carolina Press, 2002), 2-4; IQG, "Rise Above
Feeling;" IQG, "It's Not Safe."

"ashamed to say" that she now "enjoyed drinking, and when I drink, I forget lots of things," the cause of arguments and worry for their future. "It isn't helping marriage to frequent taverns," as Griggs agreed—but this time, she did not suggest AA, perhaps aware, as Rotskoff writes, that its "gendered fellowship" and "masculine culture" were predicated upon a belief that alcoholism was solely a male problem.[69]

Another addiction afflicted the family of a husband and father who was both sober and a "good provider" in the postwar economy, wrote a newly suburban reader, but he was not a "balanced family man," because of his gambling. The reader wrote that, instead of the promise of prosperity and the pursuit of happiness, problems now "happened all the time," and actually had become exacerbated by his escapist pursuits and her isolation, at home alone in the suburbs.[70]

> Until recently we lived far out, and if it hadn't been for neighbors, I would have been in a bad way. One time, I had sick children on my hands, had to sit up all night with them, and the next day carry water from a neighbor's because the pump wouldn't work....
>
> My husband couldn't help, because he was up until five at a poker game and he needed rest. I just got through hanging the clothes up when the pole broke, and the clothing went down in the mud. And was he mad when I called him out of bed.
>
> His life is one of poker games, golf, baseball, football—season tickets to all sports games.... He joined an exclusive country club, is in all the tournaments....
>
> The thing I need to know is ... we have a husband and father at home, not just someone who pays the bills. If he would only want to help me sometimes.[71]

Women in families first to move to postwar suburbs of Milwaukee, the era's fastest-growing area of the state, found that "suburban life had its discontents," as historian William F. Thompson writes, for mothers far from help from family or from "the help," domestic workers in the city.[72]

---

69   Rotskoff, *Love on the Rocks*, 3-13; IQG, "Major Interests Are Centered About Home," *MJ*, April 10, 1944; IQG, "Three Big Influences of Marriage Explained," *MJ*, February 19, 1945.

70   IQG, "This Isn't Picture of Balanced Family Man," *MJ*, July 11, 1948.

71   Ibid.

72   Thompson, *History of Wisconsin*, 228-230.

> It's difficult to get help in the home.... Financially speaking, we have a beautiful home, but I never have a dollar I can call my own. I have to beg for every penny, often under humiliating circumstances.... He's pleasant when everything goes his way, but let me suggest a ride or some small pleasure I'd like and he's unbearable....
>
> I can't go on any longer. Is there anything I can do to remedy this, besides divorce?[73]

Griggs gave a referral to marital counseling and recommended that "Mrs. J.M.R." set a deadline of only months for her husband to "revamp" and to "reevaluate, quickly, if he is to save his home and his future," or he would "one day ... be more bereft than the most dilatory bachelor."[74]

The letter about lonely life in postwar suburbs was a harbinger of the "housewife blues" that would become more prevalent in the next decade, when many women would be housebound mothers of the next generation, in numbers not seen in decades. The birth rate had begun to rise during the war; by the end of the decade, older siblings would wield power, like a letter writer who signed as "Will Baby Sitters Be Next to Strike?" The "baby boom" peaked in the postwar years, but high birth rates would continue throughout the next decade. A young mother and journalist, Betty Friedan, would write of the era that, after the decline in the birth rate during the Depression and then the deferral of dreams of domestic life owing to war, "a pent-up hunger for marriage, home, and children was felt simultaneously." As historian Sara M. Evans writes of the postwar period, "the consequence was the ferocious pursuit of private domesticity."[75]

The rising birth rate became a factor of life evident in many letters, including from unwed women writing of premarital sex and unplanned pregnancies. "Ann" hardly was alone in her "war tragedy," pregnant by one soldier but wed to another. Such cautionary tales in the column had not educated "Indignant Damsel," a lonely newcomer to town who lived with a relative and did not "frequent taverns" so was not "a cheap girl who goes out with a married man just for the sake of drinking." Nor was she a "gold digger" in accepting gifts from the man,

---

73   IQG, "This Isn't Picture."

74   Ibid.

75   Betty Friedan, *The Feminine Mystique* (New York: W.W. Norton, 1968), 174; Evans, *Born for Liberty*, 237; IQG, "Scandal Ferret."

a co-worker with whom she had lunch daily—and, at times, dinner. Her "suspicious" relative demanded that the daily meetings end. Did Griggs agree, or was she a modern woman, like "Indignant Damsel"? The columnist did not doubt her morals but warned that being a "subject of speculation among gossipy persons" could be unwise, as "the cocksuredness of many a girl has been her undoing." One reader already undone, "Wiser 21," unwisely included identifying information in her letter and received a "confidential" to write again with a name and address for information on how to "take this to court and prove that he is the father" and would have to pay child support.[76]

The column had come far from the era of consternation on the part of editors, as Griggs would recall, when her copy had included the word "pregnant"—and continued to go farther than the men may have imagined. Griggs continued to educate editors as well as readers with "frank talk," as she called it, often calling for anatomical terms rather than euphemisms still evident in news pages. David Gudelunas argues that, although media meant to target only women with such specialized features, "men, women, adults, teens ... all met" in advice columns in World War II, "arguably more so than in any other historical period" in his analysis, with an impact evident in the postwar period, a "dramatic topic shift in topical content" in advice columns, as "talk about sex became paramount."[77] That sex also sold papers may have aided in editors' acquiescence.

More letters referred to extramarital sex, as only three letters on the issue arose in the sample from the 1930s, with three times as many letters on affairs in the sample from the 1940s. "Lost Horizon," who had come face-to-face with her husband and the "other woman," who had told her that she was too "worked up," could only ask "how could any woman with five children not be worked up? I wanted to grab something off the counter and kill her. If I'd had a whip, I'd have whipped her. I wanted to claw her eyes out. I wanted to pull out her hair by the roots." Griggs accorded the letter a full column, giving a reply with a lengthy list of questions for "the aggrieved wife in a marital triangle."

---

76   IQG, "Luncheon Dates with Hubby of Another Woman Analyzed," *MJ*, June 23, 1942; IQG, "Son Gets an Unkind Letter," *MJ*, October 11, 1944.

77   Wells, *Milwaukee Journal*, 265; Gudelunas, *Confidential to America*, 3, 19, 53.

Another writer was "Still Young and Attractive," although nearing a silver wedding anniversary, and she did not want a celebration. Her husband was "keeping company" with another woman, and "it would be embarrassing to invite relatives and friends to congratulate us.... It would be a farce to pretend everything was going smoothly." Griggs agreed. She suggested a "nice dinner at home"—with their eight children—"that may shame him into self-analysis and a realization of what he is doing to his family." If he did not end the affair, however, the columnist listed agencies to assist in divorce planning to protect her and their children—and also recommended reading her next reply to a "Mrs. Happy."[78]

Although she continued to counsel readers to attempt reconciliation, Griggs increasingly recommended divorce, as did "Mrs. Happy" in a letter that directly addressed the once-taboo topic of sexually transmitted disease. Her ex-husband's "petty wolfing habits" had caused him to contract a venereal disease that had imperiled her health, and she had divorced the "philanderer." The level of detail in her letter may have imperiled his privacy, as letters did not always disguise identities and addresses, although the columnist removed most identifiers for publication. As her colleague and *Journal* historian Robert W. Wells wrote, "Griggs came to know more secrets than anyone else in the city. She sometimes felt that she knew about every cheating wife or husband in Wisconsin and a portion of Michigan" and points beyond. Although surrounded by sleuthing journalists, the columnist had stories that could "scoop" her colleagues, she told him: "I know of politicians who are carrying on, of women in love with their doctors, of men who are keeping two establishments, of women who read their husbands' mail and have detectives on the trail."[79]

Sex—premarital, extramarital, and even marital—increasingly arose in the letters in the 1940s, not only in Wisconsin but elsewhere as well, including in a new column in the wicked city south of the state border. The *Chicago Sun* had introduced "Today's Problems" in 1942, replaced in 1943 by a new column by Ruth Crowley, a nurse who also authored a child-care column. To avoid confusion, she adopted

---

78   IQG, "Wife Wanted to Whip Husband's Sweetheart," *MJ*, December 8, 1948; IQG, "Dad's 'Romance' Spoils Silver Wedding Plans," *MJ*, April 2, 1947.

79   IQG, "Dad's 'Romance;'" Wells, *Milwaukee Journal*, 265.

a pseudonym: "Ann Landers." In his analysis, David Gudelunas calls
Crowley's creation "the epitome of the modern advice column" and "a
clear departure" from still-dominant competitors and syndicated columnists "Beatrice Fairfax" and "Dorothy Dix." But their "lengthy dia-
tribes" of a "literary nature" and "sermonettes" no longer set the style
of advice columns, Gudelunas writes, with a coming "convergence oc-
curring within the genre" in a standardization of length of letters and
replies as well as in concerns of readers.[80]

The new "Ask Ann Landers" column in nearby Chicago looked remarkably like Griggs' creation. Crowley organized her column according to agendas of letter writers, including "lonely women left behind
during the war" and "looking for trouble as much as trying to escape
it," as Gudelunas writes. His analysis finds that Chicago readers—or
perhaps Crowley—were more preoccupied with sex than were readers
in Milwaukee, although the latter hardly had refrained from engaging
in "frank talk," too. Indeed, Griggs had been prescient in her harbinger
of the "modern advice column," a form that, writes Gudelunas, was
"maturing and settling into a pattern that would endure for the rest
of the century" as a community forum for readers and a clearinghouse
for referrals, mediated by a columnist with sometimes "sassy advice."[81]

In sum, Chicago's new column followed the format that Griggs had
debuted a decade before—a format that would become formulaic in
the advice industry in the next decade, under the next "Ann Landers"
and other competitors. Crowley's column endured only five years;
upon her newspaper's merger with the *Chicago Times*, she went on
hiatus. She would return in the next decade to revive her column, but
briefly, before being replaced by a newcomer who would claim as her
own creation the column's name and pseudonym that were established
by Crowley. The future "Ann Landers" was far from Chicago in the
1940s, when Esther "Eppie" Friedman Lederer lived in Eau Claire,
Wisconsin, where she and her husband moved during the war, soon
followed there by her twin sister and her husband. Pauline "Popo"
Friedman Phillips also would follow her into the "advice industry" as
"Abigail Van Buren," or "Abby." Whether they read the state's leading
newspaper is not known, nor whether both would be influenced by
the advice column in their state's leading newspaper, the *Milwaukee*

80   Gudelunas, *Confidential to America*, 81-91.

81   Ibid.

Journal. Lederer never would credit any of many of her predecessors among advice columnists for influencing her work but praised only her parents for instilling her "middle American values" and "morality." However, after his close analyses of the later columns, Gudelunas attributes their "straightforward style" as first "put in place" by Crowley in the mid-1940s.[82]

His analysis and others on advice columns across the country, but not in Milwaukee, miss the forerunner of the "modern column" already in place in Wisconsin for fifteen years by the end of the 1940s, after almost five thousand columns and countless letters—and by then, "Dear Mrs. Griggs" was known well beyond Wisconsin's borders. When her column had marked its tenth anniversary, she even had merited national media attention in the most popular magazine of the period. In part, the *Saturday Evening Post* profile of Griggs served as the magazine's apologia to the columnist, according to a colleague. Griggs had sent a "scorching retort" to the magazine for a "merciless piece" that had disparaged her professional sisterhood, women journalists, as "Paper Dolls," who "invaded hitherto inviolate masculine precincts" of many allegedly new "beats" for women—"finance, politics, sports, and the police beat"—in World War II. All, of course, had been covered by Griggs and other women at major metropolitan newspapers, decades before.[83]

A recent assessment by a *Saturday Evening Post* archivist admits to "condescension" and "unapologetic contempt" toward women journalists by the authors. Both men, they had affirmed that "ancient prejudice still holds firm" among editors "suffering the dames under protest," due to "sisters in the lodge exercising their right to ask scatterbrained questions and to go native with unprofessional behavior that is embarrassing to colleagues on the same assignment." The authors concluded that "candor compels most editors to admit they will take a dumb man of erratic social habits over a smart gal every time," as many an editor did after the war, when no longer under duress to employ women "for

---

82   Ibid., 88, 93-95; Fox, "Ann Landers, Advice Giver;" "Eppie Lederer, 1918-2002."

83   "What to Do;" Armstrong, "Mrs. Griggs Really Cares;" "It Happens Here," *MJ*, September 3, 1944; Stanley Frank and Paul Sann, "Paper Dolls," *Saturday Evening Post*, May 20, 1944, 20-23; IQG, "They Dance All Over Pop's Heaven," *Saturday Evening Post*, December 9, 1944, 24.

the duration." At the time, in response to Griggs'"retort," the magazine
offered her an opportunity to submit an article and published her feature on her"girl readers" in wartime,"jive-happy" at a "jazz heaven" at a
Milwaukee dance hall. The *Saturday Evening Post* also sent a reporter
to interview Griggs and to pen the accompanying profile.[84]

More important to Griggs may have been recognition of her efforts
on their behalf by women journalists in Wisconsin, who honored her
in 1946 as "Woman Journalist of the Year." However, her work also
had endeared her to male readers, especially veterans' groups that
would honor Griggs in years ahead—not only in the post-World War
II period but also again and again, after more wars that would bring
her more readers from the front. As the *Saturday Evening Post* had
reported, Griggs had gained a greater and even worldwide following
from "the boys in most camps and close to all battlefields" on many
continents as well as women and girls whose letters had deluged"Dear
Mrs. Griggs" by the thousands weekly during the war.[85]

Readers' letters to the column already had chronicled their lives
during a decade and a half of societal upheaval, from the Depression
through World War II and the onset of the Cold War. As postwar
years of recovery came to a close in 1948 with a return to economic
stability and new prosperity, readers of the column would continue
to record for posterity their concerns amid more war, changes, and
challenges in the decade to come—when, despite new competitors in
the"advice industry," her faithful readership only would grow for"Dear
Mrs. Griggs."

---

84   Jeff Nilsson,"War, Work, and Women," *Saturday Evening Post*, accessed
      at www.saturdayeveningpost.com/2010/07/16/archives/then-and-now/
      war-work-women.html; Frank and Sann,"Paper Dolls," 20-23.

85   "Mrs. Griggs Wins Journalism Honor," *MJ*, May 13, 1946; "Helped
      Veterans, Trio Wins Honor," *MJ*, April 13, 1949; Armstrong,"Mrs. Griggs
      Really Cares."

4

Postwar Prosperity and the 'Problem That Has No Name,' 1949-1960

As the nation, the Midwest, and Milwaukee neared the mid-century mark, prosperity and stability returned for many readers of "Dear Mrs. Griggs." Images of women happily home from wartime work in factories to raise families pervaded not only the print culture but also the new television shows that broadcast into homes across the country. The shows would be connected by national networks in 1950, spurring sales that would make "television consoles" central in most American homes by the end of the decade and would change more than décor: Television would change the dynamic of family life. Griggs also would appear to be ubiquitous as televisions, even capable of appearing in two places at once to early adapters of the new technology in 1949, when she made her television debut on her employer's station. That same night, she sent a surrogate to accept an award from a statewide veterans' organization, given in gratitude to Griggs for her crusade in her column for their postwar care. "The audience assumed that the substitute was Mrs. Griggs," reported the *Milwaukee Journal*, "and it became slightly confusing when Mrs. Griggs on television and the 'Mrs. Griggs' who received the award didn't exactly resemble each other."[1]

A semblance of happy family life soon to be projected into millions of readers' homes and become pervasive in the culture during

---

1   Unidentified newspaper clipping, *MJ*, n.d., Griggs File, Journal Sentinel Library, Milwaukee, Wis.; see also "Helped Veterans, Trio Wins Honor," *MJ*, April 13, 1949.

the decade to come would confuse many viewers, who would write
to Griggs of their far different realities. Despite media images of stability in the 1950s, the decade would be marked by dramatic changes in marital status and family structure, size, and lifestyle with the
impact of the "baby boom" and of the urban sprawl to booming new
suburbs. "The typical depiction of the decade" did not "deal with major
social change," as Wisconsin historian William F. Thompson writes.
The "comfortable" life, compared to that of their parents in decades
of the Depression and war, meant that "most people were anxious to
avoid demands and tensions of such times." Instead, they "sought satisfaction and security in jobs, marriage, and family, a new home in the
suburbs, and two cars in an attached garage." Of course, "most people"
who would find fulfillment and security in the workforce were a minority of Wisconsinites: men, for whom, "more than ever before, jobs
and income were secure." Even men who again went to war in Korea
would return to reap economic benefits of the new G.I. Bill. As for
the majority of Wisconsinites, "women went along with ... marriage
and raising a family [as] the best and most desirable ways of fulfilling
themselves," writes Thompson. In other words, for many of Griggs'
readers, the 1950s would mean a regression to dependence upon men
for security as well as "domesticity and large families," the ideals that
"were an integral part of the dream"—a dream reliant on a new reality
for women to marry younger for greater fertility.[2]

Many readers in maternity wards would turn or return to "Dear Mrs.
Griggs," in a decade dominated by the "baby boom." One was "Help!"
The young mother of three, herself hardly past her teens, wrote "I have
a new baby, loads of work, and very little sleep. I could burst into tears
at the drop of a diaper pin. How much longer can I keep a rein on my
temper? I'm so tense I feel something will snap soon…. Sometimes,
I think I'm losing my mind. I'm caged in day after day after day." Her
younger son, a "handful," only heard her "criticizing and scolding" daily.
"Am I abnormal?" asked "Help!" The problem was her lack of help,
replied Griggs, who wondered about the whereabouts of her husband
at night and "what he does to help." Similar pleas came throughout the
era from other readers, such as "Planning the Future," who wrote that
she "slaved," while her spouse went to sleep. "The man I married isn't
a husband" but "really, just a man in search of material comfort…. We

---

2   Thompson, *History of Wisconsin*, 253, 615.

no longer need him, his family or his abuse." Griggs worried that her reader was "overweary" from expectations to host large family events, described in her letter, and advised that she stop planning future events, without household help that typically had been available to past generations of young mothers with many children.[3]

The demographics of the "baby boom" decade forever altered life in Wisconsin. Among "important changes taking place within the state" owing to its soaring birth rate, writes historian Robert C. Nesbit, especially evident was the construction of schools to cope with the "explosive growth of the suburbs." Many mothers of school-aged children would return to the workforce later in the 1950s to afford their families' newly suburban lifestyle, although for far less economic reward than in their wartime work in factories. Even in the 1950s, seeds of the "Rustbelt" era ahead would be seen in a relative decline in manufacturing statewide and in a "rapid rise of clerical, sales, service, and public-employment sectors" with "the entrance of more and more women into the workforce," Nesbit writes—especially in teaching, as the boomer babies became school-aged children. Amid major economic expansion for the city and state, the two-income family—and its stresses—would become more common, but not until later decades for the letter writers with young children in the 1950s. The societal phenomenon of many working mothers of pre-school-aged children remained decades away, but childrearing and housework led housebound "Mrs. B." to write an ardent letter to let "Dear Mrs. Griggs" know that the "Green Sheet" long had become a guilty habit—through two marriages and many children—to "ease the mind at the end of a nervous day," when she "waited eagerly each night for years to read your column."[4]

In the era of the "baby boom," both housebound mothers of young children and working mothers, whether home from maternity wards or workplaces, would find the newspaper's late-afternoon home delivery not workable with schedules of fast-growing families. As an indicator of the impact of the "baby boom" in Wisconsin in the 1950s,

---

3   IQG, "Mother Hates One Son, Loves Other Children," *MJ*, January 2, 1954; IQG, "Domineering Women Get Strong Criticism," *MJ*, January 4, 1960.

4   Nesbit, *Wisconsin*, 532; IQG, "Cash Request Irks Relatives Invited to Silver Wedding," *MJ*, December 2, 1960.

when the total population increased by 15 percent, the number of children of school age increased by 42 percent across the state. The rate was far higher in the Milwaukee metropolitan area, where "the 1950s were the years when tens of thousands of Wisconsin families, with steady employment, no significant inflation in the cost of living, and growing numbers of children, rushed to suburbs in hitherto unprecedented numbers," Thompson writes. The population of the multi-county Milwaukee metropolis would surpass one million, and Milwaukee County's population would increase by almost 20 percent during the decade, with well more than a hundred thousand new residents in the city alone. As a result, although the metropolitan area added almost a thousand homes per month, the housing shortage continued—veterans' families awaited "temporary" housing until almost mid-decade—and led many out of Milwaukee to surrounding towns, such as one with a growth rate of more than 70 percent in the era. "Dad put Mom and the kids in the station wagon and moved to the suburbs," as Thompson writes, which "seemed to most people to be the place where one could best enjoy the good life."[5] Some of Griggs' readers, however, would discover a downside.

In suburbs ever more distant from the city for commuting spouses, housebound mothers faced isolation for more hours in the day. "Above all, get out somewhere," counseled a mother of eight in her letter to other readers. "My husband says a woman's place is in the home, and I agree, but I add, 'a little recreation helps her to appreciate her home.'" Her recommendation for "recreation" was to attend PTA meetings. As Thompson writes, "signs of discontent" with "the mundaneness of suburban life" would be seen in "working-class wives … raised in the cities" but "disoriented in the suburbs," far from family and "old networks of friends and confidants." Historian Sara M. Evans sees the suburbs as "female ghettos," with men away all day, until new subdivisions had sufficient settlement for women to emerge as "community builders," similar to the role of their foremothers in "frontier towns." Until then, they could continue to find a sense of community in their readers' forum that they had built in the newspaper, albeit that weary mothers would await peaceful hours after children were abed. The mother of eight counseled another letter writer with a "hectic life" to find "time

---

5   Nesbit, *Wisconsin*, 503; Thompson, *History of Wisconsin*, 228-232, 253, 618, 716; Gurda, *Making of Milwaukee*, 326, 343.

for yourself" to read—although she often found time only by "putting the 5 year old on the bed with me"—for comfort in "comparing problems" with other mothers' worries and woes, as "some, I feel, have worse ones."[6]

Content of readers' letters again reflected the context of the time, as marital and family concerns greatly increased during the dozen years from 1949 through 1960—peak years of the "baby boom"—and issues of "love" and dating drastically declined. In the column's first years, from its inception in 1934 as "advice to the lovelorn" through 1940, more than half of sampled letters had focused on "love" and dating. From 1941 through 1948, during and after World War II, readers had continued to reframe the column as a community forum on many issues, as dating had decreased to become the focus of less than 40 percent of letters sampled. Now, from 1949 through 1960, dating issues would decrease drastically to 14.5 percent, less than a sixth of letters sampled. Not that issues such as allegedly dated dating etiquette disappeared, as was made clear in the early 1950s in a memorable letter from seven soldiers on the front in the Korean conflict.

> We, the undersigned, wish to go on record disapproving your answer to "Right or Wrong." As we are all young men, serving our country in Korea, we think that a fellow should go to the door for his date, instead of honking in front of the house.
>
> If we had a daughter and her b.f. sat out there and blew his horn, we would ask him, "What else did you get for Christmas?"[7]

However, the content analysis shows that women readers continued to be the majority of letter writers, although far more women than girls, among letter writers from 1949 through the 1950s.

Marital status made a significant difference in the decade among women letter writers, like Wisconsin women in general. Less than a decade prior to the period, in 1940, more than half of Wisconsin women in their young twenties had been single. By the end of the 1950s, less than a third of Wisconsin women in the age group would

---

6 Thompson, *History of Wisconsin*, 228-232, 253, 618; Evans, *Born for Liberty*, 247, 250; IQG, "Laughter Tonic Aids All Married Couples," *MJ*, July 23, 1957; IQG, "Cash Request."

7 "Angel of the Green Sheet, That's the Journal's Ione Quinby Griggs," *Little Journal* [company newsletter], September 1953, n.p., in the Journal Sentinel Library, Milwaukee, Wis.

be unmarried. Among Griggs' readers, marital concerns had been the
focus for only a fifth of sampled letters in previous decades—20.7 percent in the 1930s and 19.4 percent in the 1940s—but became the
focus of almost a third, 32.1 percent, of letters from 1949 through
1960. Family issues had markedly increased in the 1940s from the first
decade of the column and continued to do so, accounting for less than
a sixth of letters sampled in the 1930s, at 14.7 percent, but almost
doubling to 27.0 percent in the 1950s.

While women continued to comprise almost nine in ten writers of
letters sampled—and most writers to Griggs during the decade of
the 1950s did self-identify by gender—the priorities of the primarily
women readers of the column would reflect shifts in marital status and
maturity that again would be representative of the larger community.
Teenagers or younger adults had accounted for more than eight in every ten letters in the 1930s and for almost two in every three letters
in the 1940s, at least of approximately a third of letters sampled in
which writers had revealed their age groups. Now, in letters sampled
from 1949 through 1960, more than two-thirds of writers would disclose their age or general age group—a proportion more similar to
the three-fourths of letter writers who revealed age groups in David
Gudelunas' analysis of "Ask Ann Landers" under columnist Ruth
Crowley in Chicago until the mid-1950s. However, her column had
continued to attract a younger readership. Not until the next writer
under the *nom de plume* of "Ann Landers" would that column witness a shift to older women readers and their issues.[8] That shift began
sooner in the counterpart column in Wisconsin, where teenagers and
young adults would account for fewer than three in ten of letters to
Griggs throughout the 1950s.

The continued younger readership of Crowley's "Ann Landers" column in the city to the south affords other opportunities for compar-
isons with Griggs' column, especially in the trend to more married
women among her readership. The analysis of Crowley's column in
Chicago finds a shift to more married women among letter writers
only in the latter half of the 1950s, after the coming shift in authorship
of that column. In contrast, Griggs' column already had attracted an
older, adult readership. From fewer than one in ten letter writers to

---

8   Thompson, *History of Wisconsin*, 248-249; Gudelunas, *Confidential to
     America*, 88.

Ione Quinby Griggs in the late 1940s or 1950s. (Courtesy of Western Springs Historical Society)

"Dear Mrs. Griggs" columns sampled in the 1930s and few more than a third sampled in the 1940s, older readers' numbers soared to seven in ten—69.7 percent—writers of letters sampled from 1949 through 1960. As a result, married readers also increased. Of letters sampled in previous decades, fully two-thirds to three-fourths of writers to Griggs had self-identified their marital or single status; now, four-fifths of writers did so, disclosing a striking difference across the decades: From fewer than a third of letter writers sampled in previous periods who had self-identified as married, the number now more than doubled to almost three-fourths—71.1 percent—from 1949 through 1960.[9]

Perhaps most important, "Dear Mrs. Griggs" would remain a source of constancy to her regular readers of her sole-authored column, while readers elsewhere, amid other changes in their lives, would have to cope with a coming shift in columnists under the "Ann Landers" pseudonym. In the initial decade and a half of Griggs' column, "love" had been the focus of more than half of sampled letters, while marital and family concerns had accounted for little more than a third of sampled letters. Other categories, such as work, had accounted for less than an eighth of letters. Now, in the 1950s, "love" issues would be a focus of less than a sixth of the letters in "Dear Mrs. Griggs." In contrast, according to Gudelunas, Crowley's column in Chicago continued to focus on "love and relationships," a leading category with approximately 40 percent of letters to "Ann Landers" and equal to its number of letters on marital and family issues.[10]

Rare among Griggs' readers was "Old Maid," who was happily unmarried. "You can talk all you want about happiness in marriage, but those who say there isn't much, tell the truth. I remember too well my folks' fighting," she wrote. Now, when she would "notice how married folks nag each other and sneer, calling attention to each other's failings in public," she wondered "how much they must berate one

---

9   Ibid.

10 Ibid., 89. Gudelunas' analysis of the "Ask Ann Landers" column under Crowley from the mid-1940s to mid-1950s uses different categories than does this study. He codes topics of letters to Crowley as "courtship questions" at 26 percent and "premarital concerns" at 15 percent, for 41 percent of letters; "marital relations" at 28 percent and "parent-child relationships" at 13 percent, also for 41 percent of letters; and "all other topics" at less than 5 percent of letters.

another in private." Also rare in the 1950s among letters to the column were writers who self-identified as working women, such as one signed as "Underpaid Secretary."[11] Instead, marital and family issues increased in letters from less than a third of 150 letters sampled from 1934 through 1940 to little more than half of 155 letters from 1941 through 1948 but motivated writers of almost two-thirds of 159 letters sampled from 1949 through 1960.

The marked rise in letter writers' marital concerns came as women in the late 1940s and 1950s married more and married younger than had their mothers, their grandmothers, even their great-grandmothers. Nationwide and in Wisconsin, of women and girls fourteen years of age and older, less than 60 percent were wed in 1940 but almost 66 percent were wed in 1950, owing to more marrying at younger ages. The median age at first marriage for women had been almost 22 years in 1900, had dropped to little more than 21 years by 1920, then had begun to rise to 21.5 years of age in 1940. But the trend had reversed by 1950, when the median age at first marriage for women would fall to its lowest point in the twentieth century, 20.3 years of age—women barely out of their teens, a statistic that would remain unchanged throughout the decade. More men also married than did those in previous generations—although a lower percentage of men in Wisconsin than nationwide—and at younger ages than had men before them. The median age of men upon first marriage of almost 26 years old at the start of the century had dropped to less than 22 years old in 1950, a statistic that also would remain unchanged even on the eve of the 1960s.[12]

The unchanging statistics on marital status throughout the 1950s would mask frustrations for many young housewives and mothers that would not be recognized nationally until the next decade, upon publication of the bestselling book, *The Feminine Mystique*. The term, as historian Sara M. Evans writes, "defined women's place in the postwar, family-centered, prosperous, middle-class lifestyle." However, the stories that author Betty Friedan would relate already were evident

---

11 IQG, "Old Maid's Mental Closet Holds Fears," *MJ*, September 28, 1951; IQG, "One Girl Got Husband, Other—'Sugar Daddy,'" *MJ*, April 10, 1951.

12 Evans, *Born for Liberty*, 249, 253; U.S. Census Bureau, *Census of Population: 1950, Volume II, Part 49–Wisconsin*, 42.

in those already told by readers who essentially authored most of
the "Dear Mrs. Griggs" column. A reason that Friedan's book would
resonate nationwide also was evident in that, although she surveyed
Eastern, college-educated women, they would voice discontent similar
to that of many women in the working-class city and suburbs served
by Griggs' column—including discontent with social-control messages in media, from newspapers to magazines to radio to new television shows that aimed at women in the era. Friedan, also a journalist,
would introduce her study with a telling phrase soon to be famed:
"the problem that has no name," for the frustrations felt in the 1950s
by women, who were silenced by media social-control messages that
they ought to find fulfillment only in the dual ideals of domesticity,
childrearing and housekeeping.[13]

The "problem that has no name" was evident in the names on letters
in Griggs' column, in women's pseudonymous signatures—"Afraid
and Lonesome," "Bewildered," "Weary," or "Wondering"—and also was
evident in a coding of sampled letters utilizing Maslow's theory of a
"hierarchy of needs": The category of concern for "self-actualization"
that had surfaced in less than 3 percent of letters sampled in past decades would be the focus of 15.6 percent of letters from 1949 through
1960. "Hope Has Ceased to Spring" felt a pervasive sense of failure.
"I've always kept hoping and trying," she wrote to Griggs. "I work
harder than my sisters, yet their housework gets done, while mine is
still a mess." That morning, her husband had left on her breakfast plate
a newspaper clipping about a woman who was a "resolution breaker,"
a "constant failure" who "resolves in vain ... to stay on her budget" or
to "read a certain book." Her "habit of failure" could be contagious and
ruin a man's career as well, according to the clipping that had started
her day, courtesy of her helpful husband. Griggs, although a journalist, dismissed the media message and the implicit suggestion that a
marriage ought to be based upon an imbalance of power. "He isn't a
teacher, and you are not his pupil," Griggs replied. His judgment was
poor, as they were to be "partners in marriage," she wrote. She offered
a referral to an agency that could help with budgeting—and a recommendation that "Hope" bring along her husband to ensure that he, too,
took on household responsibilities. Griggs closed the column with a

---

13   Friedan, *Feminine Mystique*, 1; Evans, *Born for Liberty*, 246.

separate paragraph addressed to the husband, suggesting that he had to change his "attitude."[14]

The lower average age upon marriage in the 1950s led to rising fertility rates, as mothers started childbearing years at younger ages and had larger families. Griggs and her readers agreed repeatedly that fathers had to help more, despite counter-messages that new media now broadcast directly into new "family rooms" of the 1950s. In the Milwaukee area alone, her newspaper's annual consumer survey charted the sales of television sets in the new decade to an extraordinary number of "early adopters" of the new technology as soon as supplies hit stores. At the start of the period in 1949, for Griggs' on-air debut, less than half of one percent of local households had television sets. However, only two years later—after the first national networks in 1950—more than half of households had televisions, and almost all area homes had televisions by the mid-1950s. Millions of televisions, writes historian Suzanna Danuta Walters, projected an image of "a period of happy and fulfilled homemakers waxing freshly washed floors and beaming brightly at their broods through their suburban picture windows," an image all too evident in the early "sit-coms," such as the "hugely popular" show that had debuted in 1954: *Father Knows Best*.[15]

Griggs' column also grew in popularity in the era, despite competition from television, as her readers simply did their best, coping in part by turning off the television and turning to the newspaper, or at least the back page—because many print media, even in "women's pages," also revealed a bias for an all-knowing *pater familias*. Even print media whose purpose purportedly was to provide balanced advice picked an array of "experts" with misogynist messages. For example, *Parents' Magazine* quoted University of Chicago psychologist Bruno Bettelheim, a Freudian who blamed unfeeling "refrigerator mothers" for autism and pontificated that "the completion of womanhood is largely through motherhood, but the fulfillment of manhood is not achieved largely through fatherhood." By then, in the mid-1950s, mothers had been vilified for a dozen years in a series of popular books

---

14   IQG, "Wife Finds Piece on Failures at Her Plate," *MJ*, July 1, 1953.

15   Gurda, *Making of Milwaukee*, 327; Suzanna Danuta Walters, *Lives Together/Worlds Apart: Mothers and Daughters in Popular Culture* (Berkeley: University of California Press, 1992), 74.

by "experts" with telling titles such as *Generation of Vipers*, *Maternal Overprotection*, and the especially vicious *Modern Woman: The Lost Sex*.[16]

The columnist and her readers clearly attempted to counter media messages of the era, which undermined mothers' confidence. Not surprisingly, letters to the column came from many writers worried about themselves, their abilities, and indeed, their identities. Such concerns from mothers had been minimal in past decades, surfacing in less than 2 percent of letters then, when many women had gained confidence in enduring the Depression and in the workforce in World War II. However, despite the alleged stability of the 1950s, maternal lack of confidence now surfaced in 8.8 percent of letters. Similarly, despite the prosperity of the period, media messages that promoted home ownership also strapped young couples at cost to their home life, with an increased emphasis upon keeping up appearances. After decades of Depression-era privations and wartime shortages, home ownership had become possible for more Americans, with federal programs in the postwar period that promulgated "the American Dream" through subsidies for mortgages, automobiles, and freeways that would fuel the fast growth of suburbs in the 1950s.

Even at the start of the decade, in a revealing exchange with Griggs and other readers, a young "Mother" admitted mistakes made with new neighbors and unfenced yards, but she had mended fences and pleaded for understanding. She was "fatigued," not only from overwork but also from boredom or "lack of change. What I need is a few evenings away from my own four walls and child, a release from staying in so much," she wrote. "I haven't been anywhere without my child for seven months"—but "babysitting and movies are too much of a luxury.... The trouble is it's financially impossible," even with a helpful husband, a good provider. "We've put everything into our home" and were "trying to finish our home and yard," she wrote, while their child was "growing like a weed and needs shoes every three months" and "the cost of living is skyrocketing.... We are simply caught in the squeeze of inflationary prices." Indeed, prices did soar again in 1950, a second wave for consumers so soon after a postwar wave of inflation.[17]

---

16   Walters, *Lives Together/Worlds Apart*, 81.

17   IQG, "Wild Mutt to Blame; Neighbors Make Up," *MJ*, October 11, 1951.

Complaints also came for new homeowners with families who became freeloaders. "I'm at my wit's end," wrote "One Who Wants to Do Right," a mother of three "who needed lots of attention," as did a new home with three bedrooms and a sun porch, she noted with pride. She had "visualized a first summer" in their home "as one of wonderful enjoyment and peacefulness ... for the first time in my married life. Last summer, we were in a small apartment." However, that cramped housing had kept away her sizeable family—she had half a dozen siblings—and his. Now, relatives planned to visit the city, so she faced a summer of "cooking and entertaining a big number of kinfolks (hubby's and mine)," who planned to "drop in" without warning. "I'm all nerves," she wrote. In reply, Griggs took a turn at letter writing, penning a recommended response for her reader to post in the mail to her family, including information on nearby hotels. However, the next letter writer had few such alternatives in an area far from Milwaukee, in the land known to Wisconsinites as "up north." She and her "hubby" had saved for years for a summer cottage to get away from it all in the sparsely populated rural north woods of the state, only to have far-flung families follow them almost as far as the border with Canada. One relative even pouted when fishing was poor, wrote "Muskie," who yearned for "peace and privacy." Griggs again counseled her reader to get the gumption to refuse or at least to restrict visits.[18]

Readers also assisted newcomers to a new country, such as several British "war brides," or to a new region for a transplanted "Southerner" now in the Midwest and also housebound with a new baby. The latter wrote of loneliness during long days, with older children in school. "If it were not for my work about the house, the radio, and the newspaper, my spirits would have dropped lower than the Wisconsin temperature at times.... I have talked to salesladies, the postman, people on corners, just anyone who would give me a feeling of friendliness." Griggs referred her and other readers to a newcomers' club, where they would be welcome. However, to a mother-in-law who had not made welcome her son's English war bride, Griggs gave sterner advice. "You didn't approve of his choice," she wrote, so her reader "should go the farthest to achieve harmony" with the daughter-in-law now stranded "in a strange land." Another English war bride found some local customs decidedly strange and had advice for her countrywomen on hospitality in the

---

18   IQG, "Remember, Kinfolks, a Home Is a Castle!" *MJ*, May 10, 1955.

Heartland: "Don't offer tea to Milwaukee people," she wrote. "Have coffee."[19]

More war brides would arrive during the decade, now from Korea, as readers' letters again reflected fears, not only for troops overseas but also on the homefront in the Cold War. As local historian John Gurda writes, "as the physical horrors of World War II gave way to the gnawing anxieties of the Cold War," local media reported "that major cities, particularly industrial centers like Milwaukee, were prime military targets." The new form of war, however, also had a very physical presence for residents in suburbs, where "Milwaukee was ringed with Nike anti-aircraft missile installations," along with a site on the lakefront in the city's downtown. Civil defense drills also "lent a sinister undertone to a period usually remembered for innocence and optimism," Gurda writes. The city alone soon had hundreds of fallout shelters, filled with one thousand tons of supplies.[20] New homes near a massive Nike missile site in Waukesha were advertised with private, underground shelters to avoid neighborliness in the event of nuclear war.

Governmental propaganda amid a second "Red Scare" echoed even in debate about another war of the era, a war at home that raged among readers who foresaw the certain end of civilization in the faddish fashions of the younger generation, early in the Fifties. That Griggs gave readers a role in setting the column's agenda was evident in the ongoing debate on cultural values, as when all of the era's conflicts merged in the worldview of "An Admirer" in 1950:

> I have five children at home.... I also have a boy in the service. He is in Korea fighting the Communists and all that communism stands for. We at home aren't asked to go to the battlefront to sacrifice our lives, but it's the duty as well as the privilege to help all that we can on the home front....
>
> I don't think boys and girls have realized these outfits and haircuts might give comfort to those who want to plant wrong ideas in youthful minds.[21]

---

19   IQG, "Boy, 19, Earns $60, Is Allowed Only $15," *MJ*, January 10, 1955; IQG, "English War Brides Offer Bit of Advice," *MJ*, January 19, 1952.

20   Gurda, *Making of Milwaukee*, 324-325.

21   IQG, "Clothes Issue Agreed on at Family Meeting," *MJ*, December 1, 1950.

To the possibility that "ducktail" haircuts, pegged pants, or pedal-pushers gave aid and comfort to the enemy, Griggs could only respond with good wishes for the soldier son of her admirer.[22]

The Cold War "politics of fear" arose again in another debate about whether girls ought to wear slacks, when another letter writer chastened children to beware of dressing "as if you were in Russia." Griggs replied with gratitude to a more sensible parent, who sighed for the loss of "the sweet little school girls" but suggested that children needed to wear snow pants in wintry weather in Wisconsin. The columnist was less kind to two teenaged girls, "Ernie" and "Pauline," whose letter attacked parents who "blame a large part of the country's mess on us, but it's all their making" in "this godless civilization." Griggs suggested that the girls study their history books "more carefully and extensively" before deploring all progress. "News travels faster due to modern inventions," she wrote from the newsroom, "but human nature isn't worse."[23]

Griggs also replied tersely to a reader who had rudely ogled a teenaged girl in "saddle shoes, angora socks," and a "*babushka*"—a localism in Milwaukee for a head scarf—with an "unsightly" long skirt. The "New Look" from fashion designer Christian Dior featured longer hem lengths, after the end of wartime shortages of fabric needed for uniforms. "Femininity was back," according to historian Sara M. Evans. "Skirts dropped to within inches of the floor," with cinched and belted waists, and "well-defined bosoms," she writes, owing to the restrictive and rigid "foundation garments"—girdles—that symbolized American women's "exit from the male industrial labor market" and more "polarized images of femininity and masculinity" in media. Some rebellious, long-skirted daughters in the era would be among parents shocked in the next decade by high hems of "miniskirts" and a return to wide-legged, "bell-bottomed" trousers that had been popular in the 1940s, before form-fitting "capris" and "pedal pushers" of the 1950s. Debates about dress codes and other aspects of childrearing would occupy many readers in their homes and their column, captured in the headline, "Clothes Issue Agreed on at Family Meeting." The concept of a "family meeting" also characterized the era, writes Evans, as the "strict

---

22   Ibid.

23   IQG, "Girl Reveals Facts of Poor Marriage Start," *MJ*, June 3, 1954; Evans, *Born for Liberty*, 238.

regimen of 'scientific' childrearing" was replaced by advice popularized by a pediatrician, Dr. Benjamin Spock. His bestselling book in the postwar period preached for more "permissive" practices in parenting, with the result that "mothers operated with fewer rules and greater responsibilities."[24]

While the Korean conflict as well as the Cold War arose in many columns on unrelated topics—Griggs scolded a father who was rarely home that "these are serious times," when "our country is preparing to defend our homes again"—as soldiers and "sweethearts" also appealed to Griggs to assuage their fears, again. The conflict took local troops to Korea from 1950 well into 1953, when a rare male letter writer worried about a lack of letters from his "sweetheart back home." He wrote that "the truce was signed," and "maybe that's what the trouble is, maybe folks back home think that it's all over here." He wrote, "but they're wrong, very wrong." The troops still were stationed in Korea, living on "mess kits" and in tents and "old prisoner-of-war shacks," where "it still gets mighty cold in winter, and threats of renewal of this mess constantly hang over our heads." The privations had been bearable when, during the war, his fiancée had written "every day, but now I'm lucky if I get a letter from her three times a week.... I have told her what mail means to us fellows over here. It's our No. 1 diversion, as there isn't anything to do here except talk or read when we aren't on duty.... No matter how busy a civilian can get, one doesn't get so busy one can't write often. I know! I used to be one!" He also "used to be" a college student, still the status of his fiancée, "fairly busy" because she carried a heavy courseload. The columnist cautioned him to "avoid harassment that may affect her studies"—and then addressed a paragraph to "University Sweetheart" to consider "shorter letters if it means more of them" for the sake of "your boyfriend's morale. I am sure he won't mind."[25]

The end of the Korean conflict did not end the Cold War, and troops continued to be stationed overseas, while their wives continued to write letters about their worries well into the mid-1950s. One letter writer, "GI Jo Jo," worried that she was "disloyal" for wanting her husband home and drew letters of disapproval from other military wives.

---

24   Ibid.; Evans, *Born for Liberty*, 243.

25   IQG, "Wife Cites Incidents That Griped in 1950," *MJ*, January 9, 1950; IQG, "GI in Korea Pleads for Fiancée's Letters," *MJ*, July 29, 1953.

"That little lady thinks she is 'unfortunate' for having a young husband in service," wrote a mother of a toddler with a baby on the way—and a husband heading overseas for a two-year military stint. "If she should write letters that worry him, then she may have something to worry about." However, "First Aid" encouraged the worried reader to have "faith in herself and her husband" amid "world tension that creates such situations.... Whatever you have seen on TV and in the newspapers or have heard over the radio has nothing whatever to do with your life and his, so count it out." She reinforced the need to write letters to soldier-husbands, relating "the case of a cousin," a German officer in World War II, who had been "taken by the Russians very early in the war." His wife had written daily, despite never receiving letters in return, nor could she "be sure if he was alive or not" until 1955, when he was one of the first POWs released by Soviets, at last.[26] The letter served as a reminder of how recent in public memory and dominant in the era was World War II.

Now, as the midpoint neared in the more prosperous decade of the 1950s, a generation of readers had grown up with "Dear Mrs. Griggs" for two decades since its inception in a markedly different time, in the depths of the Depression in 1934—but as significant as changes in women's lives was continuity in their concerns. Alcoholism was a constant, often tied to abandonment or abuse, as in the case of the "Discouraged Wife," who had abandoned a relationship, but all too briefly. Her husband drove off for drinking sprees that went on for hours. However, if she went out, she had to "get home on the dot." He insulted her, and he hit her, repeatedly. "After he hit me the last time, I got up my nerve and left him," taking the children with her, she wrote. Then came a familiar cycle of abuse: "When he located me, he was terribly worried ... and looked after the children and me real nice and was pretty good for a time," she wrote. "But now he is back in the inconsiderate rut," repeatedly reminding her that he had been "roped into marriage" by a premarital pregnancy. Griggs replied that "he 'roped' himself into marriage" but, unusual for her, recommended only that the wife "be patient ... and he will grow out of it"—without

---

26 IQG, "He Couldn't Answer But She Wrote Daily," *MJ*, January 17, 1956. On release of surviving German POWs, see Robert Moeller, *War Stories: The Search for a Usable Past in the Federal Republic of Germany* (Berkeley: University of California Press, 2003), 40-42.

a word of advice regarding domestic violence and the likelihood of its return in the relationship.[27]

Another letter writer appealed to readers as well as to Griggs for "Advice Needed." In her young twenties with two children, she and her husband had wed in their teens and had been happy for a few years, until "one day we did have a quarrel that lasted longer. It seemed to be the beginning of the trouble that happened later," she wrote. Her husband "became restless," refused to discuss his issues, quit work, and "soon the bills began to pile up," forcing them to move from "a lovely apartment in a nice neighborhood" to "a place that was a shambles," she wrote, while he only worsened and "tried to drown his problems in drink." Repeated cycles of apologies and promises finally "became too much for the children and me," she wrote. She had left him, and he had left town. Now, years later, he had written to her that he had "been through a lot and was a changed person" who would behave better, if she would take him back. "Mrs. Griggs, I've also been through a lot," wrote her wary reader. The columnist recommended readings and referrals to agencies as well as asking an acquaintance to act as an "ambassador" to first meet with the prodigal spouse and give goals to be met—joining Alcoholics Anonymous, getting a job—to prove "not only repentance but evidence" of newfound "emotional maturity." Her readers also replied, often with similar advice from sad experience. Only one offered the opposite advice, as her husband had "proved that he had changed." They had reconciled, remained wed a decade later, and she "really hoped the lady who wrote you will give her husband another chance."[28]

However, physically abusive spouses rarely deserved "another chance" in the minds of the columnist or her readers. To "Too Much," a mother whose children also were endangered by domestic violence, Griggs gave her reader's lengthy letter and her reply an entire column for discussion of the husband's escalating behaviors, from excessive drinking that delayed meals to repeated verbal abuse about meals, when he finally arrived home only to "make cracks" about food that had to be reheated for him. He also had begun to abuse their children, the letter writer wrote. "Once he put the child in the bathroom

27   IQG, "Marriage Is Rough After Wrong Start," *MJ*, October 9, 1959.

28   IQG, "Should This Woman Take Husband Back?" *MJ*, April 16, 1956; IQG, "Education Is Possible for Any Boy or Girl," *MJ*, July 19, 1956.

and locked him in … and he forgot about him, going back to sleep. The cries woke him up, and he spanked the youngster," she wrote. "My husband shows no sense when it comes to punishing them, so I have forbid[den] him punishing them at all." Then came the day that had caused "Too Much" to write to the columnist, when "to get at the baby he slapped the other child so that he flew across the kitchen floor. Now, Mrs. Griggs," she wrote, "no matter how busy I am, I don't slap the children." She had slapped her husband, however, as "he deserved it. He never apologizes." Griggs replied with a paragraph to each parent that neither a child nor a spouse ought be "slapped" or "endangered." Surprisingly, Griggs gave only her rather routine counsel to respect and discuss each other and their issues.[29]

More often, and especially for younger readers endangered by domestic violence, Griggs gave recommendations from her roster of referrals to reputable community agencies, as in the case of "Confused, Frightened, and Desperate." The young victim of domestic violence, both physical and verbal abuse by her father, became yet another case in which the columnist and her readers concurred that fathers did not always know best. Nor could "Confused" count on her mother, who was abusive by her absence; both parents went to a neighborhood bar almost nightly and left the fourteen-year-old to babysit both a toddler and an infant. Classmates had come to visit the girl, for which the father had beat her. He then had relented and allowed the girl to invite friends again, but had reneged and beat her again. Then, her parents had forced her to accompany them to the tavern, where her father publicly humiliated her in front of laughing bar buddies. "I've begged them to send me to a 'home' if I'm 'no good and dumb,' but they refuse," the girl wrote to Griggs. The columnist counseled that "a father's ridicule of his teenage daughter before a bar line-up" was "deeply disturbing," as were other parental behaviors, and provided information to make an immediate contact at a local agency, the Children's Service Society.[30]

Alcoholism, abuse, and domestic violence arose in several letters, often also interrelated to topics of marital infidelity and premarital sex, the subject of several letters sampled, which was not a significant increase from previous decades. The detailed nature of such discussions for decades did underscore a difference from other columns analyzed

---

29   IQG, "Wife Cites Incidents."
30   IQG, "Father Belittles Girl in Line-up at Bar," *MJ*, September 2, 1958.

by scholar David Gudelunas. Not until the mid-1950s, for example, did he discover similarly "explicit sexual discussion" in the "Ask Ann Landers" column in Chicago, well after forthright debates by women readers of the advice column-*cum*-community forum in Milwaukee had discomfited some of Griggs' male colleagues in the newsroom. In the interim, media and American culture forever had been altered by publication in 1953 of the "Kinsey Report" on the extent of sexual experiences in American society—for example, a finding that a fourth of women college students engaged in premarital sex—and front pages had caught up with seemingly innocuous back pages of newspapers, where few topics were taboo, and women readers' discourse went into detail, without euphemisms and allusions that characterized news columns, compared to readers' letters and columnists' replies.[31]

Although the number of letters on extramarital sex was not significant nor significantly increased, in comparison to past decades, women readers writing to Griggs were somewhat more likely than in past to act assertively, as aggrieved wives or girlfriends or as the "other women." Not that another woman—or man—necessarily was the cause, as the columnist wrote to an unforgiving "Martha," informed by her husband of his affair after ten years of marriage. Griggs warned that an "estrangement between a husband and wife is usually far along before the 'other man' or 'other woman' makes an appearance. A lot has happened to affect marital harmony." She devoted the rest of the long column to quoting a marital self-help book, a popular genre in the period. When "One Who Wants to Do Right," one of the "other women" in a five-year affair, wrote to ask how long she ought to wait for a married man, she received a curt rejoinder from the columnist—and worse from readers. "Who do you want to 'do right' by? Obviously, yourself," replied Griggs, advising her to "get right out of this man's life.... I doubt if he ever has meant to leave his wife." Readers agreed, some apparently doing so in colorful language. Griggs noted that, despite the column's sometimes explicit discussions, boundaries remained and

---

31   Gudelunas, *Confidential to America*, 89; Evans, *Born for Liberty*, 249. The second "Kinsey Report" in 1953 on female sexuality from interviews with six thousand women garnered greater public reaction, in part as Indiana University in "the Heartland" seemed an unlikely site for sexuality research; see Alfred C. Kinsey, Wardell B. Pomeroy, Clyde E. Martin, and Paul H. Gebhard, *Sexual Behavior in the Human Female* (Philadelphia, Penn.: W. B. Saunders, 1953).

had required that some letters be edited to be suitable for publication in a "family newspaper" in Milwaukee.[32]

That the wife had learned of the affair also resonated with readers, who often wrote of the difficulties of re-establishing trust in relationships. "I have been considerably interested in some of the recent letters printed in your column regarding cheating," wrote "Worried." He had "been engaged to a Milwaukee girl while employed in a distant state," and he had "kept hearing very disconcerting things about her sneaky activities, dating other fellows." Despite their "stormy engagement," they had wed—but she refused to give up her photo albums of "all that other stuff in the past." He said that she had been "secretive" about the albums but also had "flaunted" the photographs, which didn't "jibe," wrote Griggs. From his description of marital discussions, she gathered that he had wed "a spirited woman who may rebel at accepting a verdict that possession of silly old pictures proves she isn't trustworthy at this time.... Get on with the marriage!" Yet she and her readers understood that there were times to give up on a marriage—as in the case of "Snooky," a woman divorced for decades. But "my conscience still bothers me," she wrote, because she had left her husband after he "became impotent"—a term not at all common in the columns of a "family newspaper," next to comics and crossword puzzles in the entertainment-oriented "Green Sheet," in which the word "pregnant" had discomfited some male editors in the column's earlier days in the 1930s. By the early 1950s, media had progressed little. Television network marketers would not allow Lucille Ball in "I Love Lucy!" to be "pregnant," although she could be "expectant."[33] But Griggs again proved imperturbable, perhaps implacable, as she put the term "impotent" into print. She and her women readers eventually would have

32   IQG, "Infidelity Is Result, Not Start of Trouble," *MJ*, July 17, 1952; IQG, "Sister Gives Another Side of Story," *MJ*, January 8, 1959.

33   IQG, "Should Old Pictures Cause This Ruckus?" *MJ*, October 11, 1955; IQG, "Troubled Ex-Wife Is Seeking Advice," *MJ*, October 13, 1958; Wells, *Milwaukee Journal*, 265; Rick Mitz, *The Great TV Sitcom Book* (New York: Richard Marek Publishers, 1980), 46; Jude Davies and Carol R. Smith, "Race, Gender, and the American Mother: Political Speech and the Maternity Episodes of *I Love Lucy* and *Murphy Brown*," *American Studies* 39:2 (Summer 1988), 33-63.

impact, as once-*verboten* topics in Milwaukee's press would move from
her back page to the "news" pages.

That advice columns acted to counter societal constraints rarely is
recognized by media scholars—and constraints in the era of Cold War
ultra-conservatism and "politics of fear" were severe in a state where
readers elected and re-elected Senator Joseph McCarthy. Reasons
debated by historians include several factors in the electorate, identified by Wisconsin historian William F. Thompson, which also inform understanding of Griggs' readership. McCarthy's "unusually
attentive audience" at home included a "high proportion of first- and
second-generation foreign-born," writes Thompson, who were "determined to clear themselves of any taint of alienism and to establish
credentials as '100 percent loyal Americans.'" Also a factor was "a particularly strong streak of moralism" in the state, whose population
included a high proportion of regular churchgoers, especially in conservative Lutheran synods and the Catholic church, which could be as
strident as was McCarthy in opposition to Communism. The power
of Catholic voters in the state would wane in the period and prove un-
predictable in the 1960 presidential campaign, when John F. Kennedy
would win Wisconsin's crucial primary, then the first in the country.
In the end, however, his Catholicism would become a major issue and
cost him the state, according to political scientists. However, early in
the era, state Catholics' strong support of McCarthy helped him to
win office. A graduate of Milwaukee's Marquette University, whose
journalism school trained many in the state's media, he became sav-
vy in how to put pressure on the press. When the *Milwaukee Journal*
joined in opposition to McCarthy, "a position of some peril," writes
Wells in his history of the newspaper, "the senator struck back" by
calling for a boycott of the state's leading media voice. Subscription
cancellations flooded in from areas such as the Fox River Valley, a
stronghold of Catholicism, from whence McCarthy came. News desks
needed to be cautious. However, Gudelunas writes, the same controversial topics that raised conservatives' ire could "appear far less sensational in the context of advice columns" and could continue to "fill a
significant cultural silence by serving as a site for national discussions
about sexuality."[34]

---

34   Wells, *Milwaukee Journal*, 367-376; Thompson, *History of Wisconsin*,
     531, 686-687; Gudelunas, *Confidential to America*, 3. On McCarthy and

In other words, the "advice industry" continued to transform the newspaper industry. As an advice columnist said from "the female perspective" in addressing an annual convention of the American Society of Newspaper Editors, "this problem of what women read in the papers is what turns editors old and gray before their time, because the favor of the fair sex is the real circulation-builder.... It is the 'little woman' who decides what paper shall come into the home." Editors accustomed to deciding the agenda of topics suitable for public discourse, who often considered such conversation best reserved for readers' bedrooms, now saw sexual topics increasingly and brazenly discussed in their newspapers, in advice columns, "alongside questions about husbands who hog blankets in bed," Gudelunas writes. The effect of embedding sexuality into the typical mix of such mundanities of life in columns often placed on pages with comics and crossword puzzles helped to make headway in efforts to "normalize controversial subjects" and "maintain an audience not particularly attracted to topics concerning human sexuality."[35]

In the working-class city of Milwaukee, topics related to sexuality apparently were not at all *verboten* and both attracted and maintained a readership that made Griggs' column the most popular page in her increasingly popular newspaper. With every revelation from her readers, her readership only grew more, as did circulation. By the end of the decade, the daily *Milwaukee Journal*—the "Green Sheet" did not grace the pages of the Sunday editions—would reach more than a third of a million homes in metropolitan Milwaukee, with more readership statewide. Her column also increased readership of other resources that she recommended, as librarians learned to anticipate an increase in calls from patrons for books promoted in the column. In appreciation of her patronage, the Milwaukee Public Library created an exhibit displaying her other honors as well as examples of the "books and pamphlets that Mrs. Griggs has recommended," reported

---

the *Journal*, see also an analysis by its political reporter, later a professor of journalism: Edwin R. Bayley, *Joe McCarthy and the Press* (Madison: University of Wisconsin Press, 1981). On the 1960 campaign and Catholicism in Wisconsin, see Andrew R. Baggaley, "Religious Influence on Wisconsin Voting, 1928-1960," *American Political Science Review* 56:1 (March 1962), 66-70.

35 Gudelunas, *Confidential to America*, 3, 19, 53, 70.

the *Journal*. The newspaper's own switchboard operators also had learned to anticipate readers' calls by monitoring the back page of the paper as much as the front page, after Griggs recommended a book to a parent who requested help in explaining the "facts of life." Almost five hundred calls came into the switchboard, requests for more recommendations of readings on sex education.[36]

In the 1950s, little progress had been made in sex education, as attested by many letter writers like "Married at 15," writing as late as 1960 in a debate on the dangers of not providing information on "facts of life" and on strict parenting that had precluded her from having friends.

> My mother didn't encourage me to confide in her.... She never told me any of the real facts of life, only hinted at things.... In my ignorance, all I could gather was that if a boy touched me anywhere at all, like putting his arm around me or kissing, I'd have a baby. It scared me, but loneliness bothered me more.... So I sneaked out....
>
> At 13, I had a chance to meet some boys ... years older and soon was dating one behind my parents' back. I decided my mother didn't know what she was talking about, because holding his hand didn't make me pregnant.... I became adept at lying....
>
> Today I regret very much having done this, but I feel that if my parents had shown faith in me, and above all had talked with me plainly about sex and life, instead of making everything seem so shameful, alarming and vague, I would have confided in them.[37]

A dozen years later, at the end of the decade, she wrote that "one thing is certain": Her twelve-year-old daughter would "have a different deal than I had." The mother, not yet thirty years old, wrote that they had "long talks," and "she has faith in me. If parents do right, I don't think 15-year-olds will want to wed," as "a girl needs to learn so many things

---

36   Ibid., 10-11; Conrad, Wilson, and Wilson, *Milwaukee Journal*, 186; Wells, *Milwaukee Journal*, 386-398; "Library Exhibit Honors Mrs. Ione Q. Griggs," *MJ*, September 17, 1953; Russell E. Smith, "Hinterland Columnists," *Editor & Publisher*, November 27, 1947. The newspaper's Sunday circulation surpassed half a million in the 1950s.

37   IQG, "Girl Got False Facts of Life From Mother's Half Truths," *MJ*, September 6. 1960.

before tackling the serious job of marriage." Her daughter already "knew the truth about things"—that is, about sex.[38]

Advice columns offered sex education not often available elsewhere in the era. Too many readers had to rely on "typically useless" and dated dating manuals, according to Gudelunas. "Women (if not men) were oftentimes able to find detailed information in a somewhat unlikely place," the information included with "female hygiene products." Otherwise, readers could turn only to advice columns "issuing their own brand of sexual education" that "proliferated in the mass media," including women's magazines, but newspaper columns could be "a unique bridge between the formal and informal curricula pertaining to human sexuality" in "talking about ... topics not discussed in the classroom." Columnists could offer an "authoritative, instructional voice" in experts interviewed and readings recommended, he writes. And newspaper columns could "reach out to the general readerships" of "men, women, adults, teens, those who normally avoid sexual content and those who thrive on it." All could "meet in the few column inches of the newspaper advice column" for information on sex—which, as ever, sold more papers.[39]

The *Milwaukee Journal* led media worldwide in 1950 in advertising volume, which would only increase during the decade with a growing readership—including Griggs' audience. National media increasingly focused on the newspaper's successful formula, although reporters from magazines such as the *Saturday Evening Post* puzzled about the peculiarities of the "Green Sheet" and the popularity of "Mrs. Griggs." As she continued to reap awards, her newspaper continued to reap the rewards. After its third Pulitzer Prize in 1953, the *Journal* ranked in the top ten of newspapers nationwide in a poll of editors; they accorded the newspaper third place for journalistic quality, after only the *New York Times* and *Christian Science Monitor*. The *Journal* would double in revenues during the decade and grow to sixteen hundred employees.[40] Best-known among them would not be the publisher nor Pulitzer Prize winners but the beloved "Mrs. Griggs," grandmotherly moderator of the community forum found in the back pages, where

---

38 Ibid.

39 Gudelunas, *Confidential to America*, 19.

40 Wells, *Milwaukee Journal*, 386-398.

her women readers wrote the newspaper—and, decade by decade, re-framed the definition of "news."

As in past decades, readers turned to their forum to write of pre-marital sex and unwanted pregnancies, but many letters offer partic-ular poignancy as a record of the plight of women and girls in the last decade prior to the introduction of "the Pill." The first oral contracep-tive would become available in 1960, but only to married women in many states, including Wisconsin; not until the next decade would the Supreme Court outlaw state laws prohibiting "the Pill" for single women. In the 1950s, Griggs' readers who practiced birth control still relied upon methods that had proved unreliable for centuries, such as the "rhythm" method allowed by the Catholic church, which remained the predominant faith by far in churchgoing Wisconsin. The inevita-ble result was evident in lives of letter writers like "Discouraged Wife," who had wed too young.

> I married at 17 and won't beat around the bush—it was a case of "have to." Now I am tied down with babies and a husband with no respect for the work I do....
>
> Everything I do has his ridicule or indifference.... I'm penned in with the children and would like a little time out, but he seldom offers to look after the children.... I wash the car, clean the garage, cut and trim the lawn, besides caring for house and babies!
>
> Believe me, if he had to follow my footsteps, he would be a pretty tired guy.[41]

Another wrote to Griggs to reach her younger readers, in continuing a discussion in the column from its beginning, but with wisdom from which the writer, "Wiser Now," had not benefitted.

> Mrs. Griggs: Maybe my true life experiences will be a warning to some girl who now is on a reckless path. I was a member of a teen "gang." I don't imagine I was any different than any other girl in the "gang," but I didn't put on any brakes.
>
> I thought it was smart to cut high school classes. I thought it was smart to drink, smoke and "pick up" fellows. I thought I was having a thrilling time. I didn't even think I was heading in the wrong di-rection. I met a fellow.... I believed him.

---

41   IQG, "Marriage Is Rough."

> I was too dumb and blind to see that he really wasn't in love with me. He had no respect for me, and I should have known it from the start. I found I was pregnant.[42]

She wrote to Griggs that, had she "read the column before it happened, I might have seen how wrong I was" to marry too young, and not "the kind of marriage" for which she had hoped.[43]

"Wiser Now" led a loveless life, because her husband blamed her for their failure to prevent pregnancy. The letter was classic, so concisely capturing the era for women that it could have been among rare hoaxes that readers—and colleagues—attempted to test Griggs. However, "Wiser Now" had provided her name to the columnist, who requested that she continue to write with "more about your married life. Perhaps I can help to make life bearable." Both her husband and "Wiser Now" also were "older now," and "even if he was a reckless boy, and you were a too-gullible girl, a lot might be salvaged if you would stop feeling sorry for yourselves" and for the couple to put the past behind them, because they were parents whose children needed a better future. However, Griggs closed her reply with a sense of resignation: "It's worth a try."[44]

"Prodigal Daughter" had a different story to tell in a letter replete with terminology often only whispered in the era, such as "out of wedlock." At twenty years old, she already had been married and divorced, because her ex-husband had not wanted children. "In the months that followed" the divorce, she wrote, "I went 'wrong.' That's all I can call it." Her mother and sisters had known for months that she was pregnant, but now her father and brothers knew, and "naturally, it has caused a great disturbance in the family," as did her wish to keep her child.[45]

> One brother stated that no man would want a woman like me if I had an "illegitimate child" with me. I admit I'm in no position to give the child the good home it should have ... but I am willing to try. I have a good job ... but would still be unable to hire anyone to care for my child after I returned to work....

---

42 IQG, "Girl Reveals Facts."

43 Ibid.

44 Ibid. On her colleagues' hoax letters, see Wells, *Milwaukee Journal*, 265.

45 IQG, "Family Against Girl's Wish to Keep Baby," *MJ*, April 22, 1957.

> Mrs. Griggs, I don't want to give up my own flesh and blood! I can't![46]

Owing to her parents' health, they could not raise the child, she wrote, and a sister and brother-in-law had agreed to adopt "but now want no part of it."[47]

Another reader with no help from her family in the offing, "Prodigal Daughter," had sought other sources of support, with contradictory results. Her minister arranged a visit to an orphanage, and co-workers advised her "to keep the child, that if I don't, I'll regret it later on, but it's easy for them to talk," she wrote. "They won't have the responsibility. I will!" The father was in another state, "in jail for an affair with another girl who is also pregnant," she wrote—but actually for bigamy, as he had married there, while "the divorce wasn't 'final' here," she wrote. She had decided to not inform him of the pregnancy. Griggs could only agree and, in reply to her reader's request for a referral to "board the baby for a year," she recommended counselors who could help her to "weigh the pros and cons carefully." Griggs also gave her own counsel that, no matter her decision, she ought to "avoid tagging the coming child [as] 'illegitimate,' as "a child is never 'illegitimate.'" By then, she had served as godmother for many progeny of readers, wed or otherwise. Her newsroom regularly updated a record of the number of newborns named for the columnist; a colleague reported that they included "a set of Seattle twins, Ione and Griggs."[48]

Another constant from previous decades' columns was a number of letters from happily married readers, not seeking advice but seeing a need to counter the messages of marital misery—although almost all also noted how much they looked forward daily to reading of the woes of others. "Oldsters" had their "spats," they wrote, but never about a spouse who "liked to get 'soused,'" and a "Mrs. B." was happily wed, a second time, to a husband who helped "wash, iron, and do everything else that relieves me or makes me happy when he comes home." Most heartwarming for Griggs was hearing again from a writer from Nebraska named "Marie," who had not wed two decades before,

---

46   Ibid.

47   Ibid.

48   "Ione Quinby Griggs Is Subject of Article in Pageant Magazine," *MJ*, February 13, 1950.

when her parents had opposed her marriage to a Milwaukeean. "In the Thirties, they disapproved, because he didn't have any money," as Griggs recalled for readers in introducing the letter from "Marie." In the interim, the man had wed and became a widower before he and "Marie" had met again—but "her parents still disapproved," because he had not become "a man of 'property.'" They "had threatened to disinherit" their daughter, in her forties and still at home. They relented, "Marie" finally married her Milwaukeean, and now wrote to report that the newlyweds had "driven by the Journal building" on their wedding day in gratitude to Griggs for her advice to the bride. However, a colleague recalled Griggs' reaction as actually "a little indignant at such wanton display of spinelessness," because her advice had been to tell the parents to "bequeath their property to a home for cats," for all that "Marie" cared.[49]

Griggs continued to refuse to directly do matchmaking or fundraising, although she also welcomed opportunities to connect readers to do so and to promote worthy causes—and even personally intervened in some cases, especially for readers with disabilities. As the decade opened, the Disabled American Veterans association honored her for "continued interest" in their cause, and a national magazine, *Pageant*, headlined Griggs as "Wisconsin's Conscience" for her good works. A case noted in that article, and in many accounts by colleagues since, was of "a cross-eyed country girl" who signed her letter—perhaps with irony—as "Iris." She was mocked by boys even in church, writing that "When I get up to sing in the choir ... the boys snicker and cross their fingers." The columnist offered comfort, of course, but accounts of ensuing events again vary. Griggs would recall that she mentioned the girl's plight to a colleague's neighbor, a nurse at Marquette University's medical school, who suggested its *pro bono* surgery option. The columnist contacted the parents, who "put little stock in doctors, and thought Iris was just 'putting on airs' ... but consented to an operation," as a colleague wrote, who also recalled that the two-dollar nightly bed bill was paid by the girl from her "egg money." Griggs later recalled, though, that "the parents were objecting to the idea of having to send money" at all, "so I wrote to them and told them it wouldn't

---

49 IQG, "Laughter Tonic Aids All Married Couples;" IQG, "They're Happily Wed after Column Advice," *MJ*, December 6, 1954; Mosby, "Heart of Milwaukee," 54.

cost anything. The fact is, I paid for the bed." In the end, no matter the details, a colleague wrote that "the result was a stunning blond girl with perfect blue eyes. Now the girl is married and has two babies," both "with perfect eyes"—as the newsroom knew, because Christmas cards with gratitude to Griggs, and with photos, came for years. In another case, a mother of a child with mental retardation and a neighbor in their duplex who had a child with cerebral palsy "helped each other out" and sought other parents in need of support. Griggs gave more than routine readings and referrals; she promoted a Milwaukee "march"—in modern terms, a "walkathon"—for services for people with disabilities, with a goal of eight thousand marchers. Thanks to readers of "Dear Mrs. Griggs," the goal was more than met.[50]

The case of "Iris" added to local lore about Griggs, often repeated in reportage on the column, as was her personal intervention to prevent a suicide. The "Hinterland Columnists" feature in a professional journal for journalists nationwide, *Editor & Publisher*—"the Bible for the trade," as the *Journal* termed it—reported on the rescue that saved a reader, and sold an ad.[51]

> Occasionally she has to get out and personally get into a mess to try to help somebody.... One night, late, a cab driver phoned her and told her he had a would-be suicide in his cab, whose wife had run away with their children. The man couldn't make up his mind whether to shoot himself or walk into the lake, unless he could get his wife back.[52]

Griggs' no-nonsense response became legendary, often repeated in later versions of the event.

> Ione put on her hat, marched downstairs, and told the man to stop talking foolish.
> "My wife's left me," he told her. "Unless she comes back, I'll kill myself."
> "Nonsense. Get in touch with her. Tell her you love her."
> "I don't know where she is."
> "Run a want ad in the Journal asking her to come home."

---

50   Mosby, "Heart of Milwaukee," 52; IQG, "Dear Mrs. Griggs," 36; IQG, "Father Belittles Girl."

51   Mosby, "Heart of Milwaukee."

52   Ibid.

But the ad in the "Personals" column brought no response. Mrs. Griggs finally tracked down the wife's attorney and arranged a meeting. Before the reunion, Ione ordered the husband to buy a corsage and two orchestra seats to a show and to make a reservation at the most expensive restaurant in town. Overwhelmed by such attention, the wife went home.[53]

Versions varied as to the lasting success of Griggs' intervention. One claimed that she later got another call, this time a daytime call to the newsroom from the Journal lobby, where the husband wanted to see Griggs. She was alleged to have said that she thought, "Oh, here we go again." However, "he had come to introduce me to his children," who "seemed to positively adore their daddy." Another account stated only that "the couple must have lived happily ever after," as "otherwise, Ione would have heard from them," because she eventually heard from everyone.[54]

Few readers went unheard in her column, or so it seemed, no matter how small were their worries—or the readers themselves—as Griggs brought together one of her youngest followers with one of her oldest for a story that ran in the news section, reminiscent of her "stunt stories" at the start of her career. A seven-year-old girl's parents had contacted the columnist about their "heartbroken" daughter, because her puppy, "Inky," had been stolen. Ninety-one-year-old Mary McCloskey read the column and called her son, whose dog of the same breed recently had pups, all gone to good homes but for the last of the litter—the one that he had kept for himself. He was willing to give up the pup and contacted the columnist; he also was an amateur magician and concocted a plan. Griggs made arrangements with the girl's parents and a staff photographer, who doubled as her chauffeur, as she did not drive. The girl was promised a magic show but was unaware of the surprise planned by the puppy's owner: He pulled "Inky No. 2" out of his silk top hat for a photograph that ran across half of a page and enthralled Milwaukeeans. Griggs relied on readers for other magical moments, regularly reuniting them with lost wedding rings—so honest were her readers that even large diamonds were returned—or family heirlooms and photographs, often forgotten in clothing and furniture

---

53   Wells, *Milwaukee Journal*, 264.
54   Ibid.; Armstrong, "Mrs. Griggs Really Cares."

given to charitable groups or sold in garage sales.[55] The latter were limited to warm weather in Wisconsin, where the "lost-and-found" letters to Griggs became a sign of spring as reliable as late blizzards, and readers' pleas on pale-green newsprint of the "Green Sheet" resembled the shade of green shoots emerging in gardens from the snows.

Accolades continued for the column in popular national and even international media in the 1950s. In addition to the headlines hailing her as "Wisconsin's Conscience" in the paean in *Pageant*, she was "The Heart of Milwaukee" in *American Mercury*, and "The Angel of the Green Sheet" in *Coronet*—or "*De Engel van de Groene Pagina*" in Dutch, when a translation of the article ran in a women's magazine in the Netherlands, *Libelle*. Letters asking for advice arrived from overseas; as a Hollander explained to a *Journal* colleague, his country lacked such advice columns, "because of a generally accepted belief that no one would be sufficiently interested in the problems of others to reply to the letters." Each magazine article retold now-familiar tales of readers' woes from crossed eyes to premarital pregnancies to lost items, and almost all articles were freelanced by the columnist's male colleagues. Writing about Griggs had become a source of side income—indeed, almost a local industry in herself, if again for the benefit of others.[56]

Accolades extended even to academe in 1957, with inclusion of her work from her earlier career—her book, *Murder for Love*—in a scholarly journal. The book published in the 1930s on the notorious "murderesses" whom she had met was cited in an article in the *Journal of Criminal Law, Criminology, and Police Science*. Scholarly attention would have gratified Griggs, who had betrayed a self-consciousness about her lack of higher education. The piece, by a professor from the University of Bonn enamored of deeper meanings discovered in his topic of the "American Desperado," discoursed on a woman murderer executed in the 1920s and relied on reportage by Griggs. The excerpt of her work was ensconced among reports of treacherous murderers as told by Nero in ancient Rome and a Marquess of Brinvillier

---

55   "Angel of the Green Sheet;" Mosby, "Heart of Milwaukee," 54; "Magician Pulls Puppy from Hat, Makes a Young Lady Very Happy," *MJ*, December 30, 1959.

56   Mosby, "Heart of Milwaukee;" 51-55; "A Dutch Treat for I.Q.G.," *MJ*, October 28, 1954.

in medieval France, with Shakespearean quotes from the mouth of the fictional Lady Macbeth in merry, murderous olde England.[57] All made for heady company for the columnist, conscious of never having earned a college degree.

The topic of education topped front pages nationwide late in 1957 as well as some letter writers' priorities. Soviets' success in the "space race" in November 1957 with Sputnik, the first satellite, initially was met by panic on the part of some Americans who warned of attacks from the skies. However, longer-term benefits would lead to more funding for schools to prepare more students for college and more funding for college students. The impact in a working-class city was evident in letters with contrasting viewpoints on a college degree, or even a high school degree, in earlier and latter years of the decade. For example, a year before Sputnik soared in the skies, "Emotionally Immature But Average" wrote of having "a fairly good job," an apartment, "a car and some other things an average teenager craves," despite lack of a high school degree. He admitted that, at times, he wished that he had the degree and could go to college, although he saw no economic reason to do so—but also blamed his parents for not pushing him to do so. In an era when the G.I. Bill for veterans of World War II and then the Korean conflict had raised the average age of college students considerably, Griggs responded to "Emotionally Immature" that many a grown man had gone back to school to get one or more degrees and gave referrals. Not that a degree was a guarantee of wisdom, as Griggs could only agree with a reader whose "educated husband" was "as self-centered, self-indulgent, and demanding as a preschooler," she wrote. "He may be high in I.Q. but low in E.Q. (emotional quotient)," Griggs replied. "I wonder how he won you!" In contrast, in post-Sputnik years, more typical was a letter from a mature and "prospective college boy" seeking academic advising from the advice columnist. "College Boy" received referrals to local campuses' career-advising centers but also assigned readings: a list of free booklets on many career fields, although the columnist recommended a journalism major.[58]

The repeated use by readers and the columnist of gendered terminology, such as "college boy," reflected the stereotypes but also the

---

57   Hentig, "Pre-Murderous Kindness," 371.

58   IQG, "Education Is Possible;" IQG, "Choice of a Career Puzzles Schoolboy," *MJ*, July 8, 1959.

Griggs' readers still debated the worth of college degrees for women in 1956, when students at the then-women-only Alverno College in Milwaukee held a "white-glove" event for newcomers to campus, as fashions regressed for women after the war to a return to gloves, hats, and ladylike crossing of the legs at the ankles. If the fashions were typical of the era, the students were not; fewer women went to college in the 1950s than in the 1920s—although enrollments soared across the country after the war, but because millions of men became the first in their working-class families to attend college, owing to one of many G.I. Bill benefits: taxpayer-paid tuition. (Copyright 2014 Journal Sentinel, Inc., reproduced by permission)

realities of an era when few women earned degrees—fewer in the 1950s than in their grandmothers' generation, decades before. In the 1920s, women had comprised more than a third of college students nationwide, although only 8 percent of all eighteen- to twenty-four-year olds in Wisconsin had enrolled in college by the end of that era. Then, women's numbers had declined even further on campuses in the Depression, when men's numbers had not. By 1940, few more than 2 percent of Wisconsinites held college degrees, most of them men—a gendered trend that had increased after the war, owing to the G.I. Bill. By the 1950s, few letters sampled from Griggs' column came from women with college degrees or girls with aspirations to higher education. The state's postwar birth rate, soon to peak at almost one hundred thousand births per year, meant that more "baby boomers" graduated from high school in Wisconsin than in earlier eras, and at a higher rate than in most states. More girls earned high school diplomas than did boys, despite a state law that allowed school districts to force pregnant girls to drop out. More high school graduates in Wisconsin went on to college than in other states, with fully a third of high school graduates in the state on campuses by the end of the 1950s, which was four times as many as in their parents' generation and twice the national average in their own era. However, more men than women went to college in Wisconsin, again because of the G.I. Bill for veterans of the Korean War as well as World War II. For the men, the number of University of Wisconsin campuses multiplied, as ten state teachers colleges became state universities in the mid-1950s—but the teachers colleges that formerly had mainly served women students now became dominated by men. For years to come, women would comprise little more than a third of students at the Madison campus and a minority on most campuses.[59] For most women in Wisconsin, the opportunity to earn higher education and better employment to achieve their aspirations would have to await the modern women's movement, decades away.

Older women yearned for the opportunity for more education, as two in the University of Wisconsin Extension administration found when they canvassed women students to take results to regents for more funding for yet more returning women students. In 1958 in

---

59 Thompson, *History of Wisconsin*, 568-569, 767; Nesbit, *Wisconsin*, 529-530, 547.

186   'DEAR MRS. GRIGGS'

Madison, former professor Dr. Katherine Clarenbach and former legislator Ruth Bachhuber Doyle's statewide canvass of women students in non-degree coursework offered by the UW Extension found that most were in Milwaukee, most worked outside their homes, and most wanted more courses for career advancement as well as educational enrichment, because only a third had completed high school. Few women nationwide had been encouraged to seek college degrees in the decade, writes historian Sara M. Evans, and those with degrees "remained limited primarily to female-dominated fields such as nursing and teaching." And teachers had come under attack in the 1950s as "frustrated females" who were prey for Communists, according to the Congressional House Un-American Activities Committee. They and other working women had witnessed a decline in their pay during the decade, compared to the pay of men in education and most employment categories, as many women with college degrees had become discouraged from careers and succumbed to the dominant "domestic ideology." However, as college enrollments rose in Wisconsin to almost a third of all eighteen- to twenty-four-year olds by the end of the decade, mainly men delaying entry into the job market, so did debate in media nationwide and in the most-read newspaper page in the state about the need for women to return to the workforce.[60]

As the end of the 1950s neared, a divisive debate among readers of "Dear Mrs. Griggs" foreshadowed those that would arise nationwide among women—and men—in the next decade, after publication of *The Feminine Mystique*, about balancing work and family. The issue had festered for years between the lines in letters, but a full debate began in 1957 with two letters that Griggs ran in one column, which

---

60 University of Wisconsin System Women's Studies Consortium, *Transforming Women's Education: The History of Women's Studies in the University of Wisconsin System* (Madison, Wis.: Office of University Publications, 1999), 15, 37, 41-45, citing Gerda Lerner and Joyce Follet, "Documenting Midwestern Origins of the Twentieth-Century Women's Movement, Oral History Project," Wisconsin Historical Society Archives; Marian McBride, "Political Pioneer," *MS*, February 24, 1965; "Remembrances Celebrate a Pioneering Feminist," *MJ*, March 13, 1994; Evans, *Born for Liberty*, 244, 265; Claudia Goldin, Lawrence F. Katz, and Ilyana Kuziemko, "Homecoming of American College Women: The Reversal of the College Gender Gap," *Journal of Economic Perspectives* 20:4 (Fall 2006), 133-156.

she introduced with the "practical idea" that a woman "have some job experience to call on in the event she must support herself or her family later." First came a letter from "Listening," who had received her diploma only months before. "I'm glad I went to college but happier still that I am going to be married in the not-too-distant future," she wrote. "Don't you think I am wise to get married soon instead of having a 'career'?... My parents seem disappointed that I am not putting my 'college training' to work by getting a job." Griggs cautioned that work experience was crucial "insurance" for "every woman," no matter her educational level or marital status, as husbands "became ill or died," while divorce had "catapulted" many women into the workforce. Her reader's degree and skills were "fresh," so she ought to "get a job and work for a while, longer if necessary," after the wedding as well. Griggs also advised "Listening" to listen to advice forwarded by the writer of the next letter.[61]

"A Happy Professional Working Mother" expressed her unhappiness with media and other letter writers who reinforced social-control messages and criticism of working mothers. However, her ire led her to impute their intent as envy in an *ad hominem* attack that enraged other readers and deflected from the central issue of the debate. "I have come to the conclusion that some are written by women who are jealous of a woman working outside the home," she wrote. "The jealousy is probably due to the fact that they aren't qualified to hold a job in the business or professional world or are inefficient housekeepers unable to do their housework in half the time it takes others.... Some of us can accomplish quite a bit more during those hours." Evidence supporting the latter part of her statement, at least, surfaced in studies of expectations for housewives in the era, when the new "electric servants" advertised as "labor-saving" did not necessarily increase efficiency. A national study in the mid-1950s found that, in comparison to fulltime "homemakers," employed women with families and homes of similar sizes spent half the time on housework. A study of Wisconsin fulltime "homemakers" found that they averaged more than fifty hours per week on housework, seven days a week—far more than the forty-hour, five-day workweek of their husbands. Although a male historian refers to household appliances as "indulgences" of the 1950s, calling them luxuries that compensated for women's "sacrifices

---

61   IQG, "Diploma Not Enough for Late Years Job," *MJ*, July 31, 1957.

of the war years," many appliances did reduce labor in terms of back-breaking housework tasks.[62]

Appliances did not reduce hours on housework, however, as time taken by housekeeping tasks remained essentially the same—and almost entirely done by women—as in decades before, when a survey had found that women in Wisconsin did 99 percent of housework, while men did 1 percent. As demand for electrical power increased, tripling in Wisconsin in only two decades after the war, so did demands on women's time. For example, sales of electric washing machines also tripled in the 1940s, compared to a decade before, but could complicate tasks; a forty-eight page "home laundering guide" accompanied one manufacturer's machine and hardly reduced laundry time, writes historian Susan Strasser, because it added to reading time. Indeed, as home washing machines had replaced many laundries that went out of business, once-weekly laundry became a daily chore, because families had more clothing. Home freezer sales also increased after the new frozen dinners of the 1940s were redesigned and reframed as "TV dinners" in the 1950s, the era when, local historian John Gurda writes, "the most popular electrical 'appliance' of the postwar period was undoubtedly television." However, popularity of frozen foods would contribute to the disappearance of home delivery of dairy, bakery, and produce trucks that long had enlivened the streets of Milwaukee and many suburbs—as well as the days of homebound *hausfrauen* in discussions with the milkman, baker, and "vegetable man" about dinner menus.[63]

A letter from "A Happy Professional Working Mother" provided evidence of a different debate, referring Griggs and other readers to a rare exception to most media messages of the era in a prescient report in 1957 on working women. Griggs gave the rest of the column to another article by widely read economist and financial reporter Sylvia Porter, a counter-message calling for educated women of the country to return to a workforce with a shortage of skilled workers. The article summarized results of a survey by the U.S. Department of Labor of more than 80,000 women college graduates in 1955, when 46 percent wanted to work after marriage and only 12 percent planned to "work only as necessary." Most had only "minimal interest in applying the

62   Ibid., Strasser, *Never Done*, 267-276.

63   Gurda, *Making of Milwaukee*, 327; Strasser, *Never Done*, 267-276.

knowledge and skills they had obtained," Porter wrote of "an attitude toward employment that gives scant encouragement to a nation suffering from a severe shortage of skilled workers." She did not address the shortage of career choices for women in the era, although sixty percent of women graduates surveyed had training to teach in school districts coping with the "baby boom" but made clear that "most won't remain teachers if they can get a husband or find some other way out," Porter wrote, warning that "the women will bitterly regret [that] as they reach their thirties and forties." By contrast, many women of that age in the mid-1950s, who had worked in World War II, had raised their families, or had older children, were returning to the workforce.[64]

A statistic "startling" to Porter, from the federal study, showed that working-class women had regained their wartime numbers in the workforce. In Wisconsin, as William F. Thompson writes, "a large number of women always had worked for wages and salaries," fully a fourth of the state workforce even at the start of the 1950s. More went back to work, reflected in the growing number of two-income families needed to afford middle-class lifestyles. However, in a decade when increases in individual incomes were almost double the increases in the cost of living, others worked not for financial reasons but "to fill a void in their lives," as Porter wrote of the problem that finally would be given a name in the next decade, in *The Feminine Mystique*.[65]

Readers of "Dear Mrs. Griggs" found, in Porter's words, a foreshadowing of messages on signs to be seen in feminists' marches in the modern women's movement, more than a decade away.

> The re-entrance of the older married woman into the labor force is one of the most startling aspects of this phase in the development of "womanpower." Out of the 21,000,000 women working today, almost half are in the 35-64 year age bracket.
>
> They are returning to work not only to earn more money but also to gain new interests, to fill a void in their lives. But how is the current woman college graduate going to [do] when all she has to offer when she applies for a job is a yellowed college diploma?[66]

The study did not address underemployment—part-time, underpaid—for millions of married women whose return to work was a

---

64   IQG, "Diploma Not Enough."

65   Ibid.; Thompson, *History of Wisconsin*, 255-256, 263-267.

66   IQG, "Diploma Not Enough."

significant factor in "massive growth" of the workforce in the 1950s, as historian Sara M. Evans writes. Despite the growth of more than 40 percent in professional women in the workforce in the period nationwide, their numbers were unchanged in Wisconsin. And despite the growing number of women in college in Wisconsin, where their numbers would double in the decade from the mid-1950s forward, most new jobs for married women were in sales or clerical work, the occupational categories for fully half of employed women in Wisconsin in the 1950s—and previously populated primarily by unmarried women. Historian William F. Thompson writes that married women "provided the state labor market with elasticity," if "often to their collective disadvantage" in lack of job security. Or, as Evans notes, the shift in the workforce resulted from the "sharply reduced supply of single working girls."[67]

Another study predicted that daughters of the women of the 1950s not only would be more likely to remain single but also would not let their skills "become rusty during fifteen or more years of domesticity," as Porter put it. They would emulate their grandmothers in the early 1940s who had found fulfillment in working—if in factories or offices —while raising families.[68]

> Each new generation of women in our land is growing up with more respect for the woman who has held a job, and yes, for the one who continues the dual roles of job holder and homemaker. This changing attitude of women themselves toward work is one of the most significant findings....
> The "I never worked college graduate" may find her own daughter considers her oddly old-fashioned.[69]

Griggs agreed, to an extent, writing that those so fortunate as to go to college needed "to follow up ... with sufficient experience" to "qualify for self-supporting or family-supporting jobs."[70]

---

67   Evans, *Born for Liberty*, 253, 261; Thompson, *History of Wisconsin*, 249, 267, 271.

68   IQG, "Diploma Not Enough."

69   Ibid.

70   IQG, "College Graduate's Career—Motherhood," *MJ*, August 12, 1957.

Debate continued, when "A Happy Professional At-Home Mother," a former teacher for a year—wrote to defend her departure from the workforce a dozen years before, after the war.

> Mention is made of teachers not staying in the field if they can "get a husband or find some other way out." There ought to be nothing alarming in almost 75 percent of our women college graduates wanting not a "career" but marriage and motherhood.
>
> Nor should those who thus choose ... be made to feel that they are betraying their education and their country. May I suggest it is not women "escaping" into marriage and motherhood who are responsible for the shortage of skilled workers, nor is it the role of college-educated women necessarily to fill this shortage.[71]

Low pay had not led her to leave the field, wrote the former teacher, as "the causes of our 'labor shortage' in certain fields," were not "materialistic." Instead, she quoted a college president—a male—who had addressed college women to warn that "masculine tactics of aggression" were dominant in workplaces and counter to "values" that had sent the letter writer happily home.[72]

The rest of the happily-at-home reader's letter primarily echoed media mantras of the era that, as the initial letter had stated, put a primacy on motherhood rather than recognizing a need to reform workplaces to allow women to manage both families and careers. "The choice is not motherhood or a career," wrote the onetime teacher, although without addressing that remained the only choice, even by law or by local custom and "unwritten law," in some career fields and school districts. As Evans writes, the education sector was in transition, with need to "expand so rapidly in response to the baby boom that retaining prejudices against married women teachers" eventually would prove "impractical." However, lack of adequate child care also would leave many women with no choice but to be at home like the letter writer counseling—or consoling herself and others—that "motherhood is a career, the glorious one for which woman was made female," as "woman's nature is made to complement man's, not compete with his to their mutual disadvantage." She closed with a tired "strawman" tactic of claiming that "a great many thinking people"—unnamed—"fear for the ultimate consequences of a society which urges women to assume

---

71   Ibid.
72   Ibid.

the dual roles of jobholder and homemaker.... These fears are real. We are seeing their realization today." The letter filled the column with more "fears" and would have filled more of the page; Griggs had to apologize, however, for having to edit the letter "for lack of space."[73]

Although glad that the letter continued an important discussion, Griggs wrote, she had to point out that the happily at-home mother had misstated the columnist's point: That Griggs had grounded her reply in regrets related in letters by other readers who had to work, whether in struggling, two-income families or as the sole support of their families. Recognition of a growing number of female-headed households was rare in media, writes historian Sara M. Evans, which more often "evoked moral condemnation rather than social concern,"[74] but not from Griggs.

> Letters from widows, deserted wives, wives of invalids, and others who have been out of college for years show that many "educated" women find it difficult to fill business or professional jobs as necessary, due to lack of experience earlier in life.
>
> I don't say they should work after marriage but do believe it is wise to gain experience ... as a measure of insurance, as you did in teaching for a year.[75]

The debate would continue for the rest of the decade but went unresolved by her readers.

One irate reader was an "elderly teacher" whose letter, as late as 1960, could have come a century before, because she blamed societal woes on "domineering" women, returning to the workplace. They also were faulted for becoming increasingly involved in politics, although fewer than five percent of elective offices nationwide were held by women, and in Wisconsin, the legislature again was all-male as the decade ended. Yet women, wrote the older reader, had made "weaklings" of men, who merited "healthy fear from their wives and children. For Pete's sake, Mrs. Griggs," she wrote, "advise men to ... quit being pushed around like three-year-olds by their wives!" Griggs tersely replied, "I see no trend toward domineering wives and weak, ineffectual husbands"—except on television. The myth that women were to be feared was fed nightly on televisions into almost every home by then,

---

73   Ibid.

74   Evans, *Born for Liberty*, 251-252.

75   IQG, "College Graduate's Career."

when only a few strong "sit-com" characters such as Donna Reed—
occasionally depicted as a working woman, a nurse—and Harriet
Nelson in *The Adventures of Ozzie and Harriet* reversed the dominant
"father knows best" theme. "Of course," Griggs reminded her readers,
"TV characters aren't representative."[76]

The lack of resolution to the ongoing debate foreshadowed discussions to come in the modern women's movement, by then less than
a decade away. But first, before women's rights again would gain the
media agenda and public awareness, African Americans' civil rights
movement would fill front pages and television screens in the new
media synergy in the 1960s, if often for activist tactics that had been
undertaken throughout the 1940s and 1950s but had garnered few
headlines. In part, the press reflected the mindset of many Americans,
especially Midwesterners, who held to the pretense that racial discrimination was restricted to the South. That deflected headlines then—
and historical attention since—from the fact that, ever since the
Great Migration from the South, many major events in the civil rights
movement had occurred in the Midwest that foretold events to come.
For example, almost two decades before a tactic in the South would
capture the media's and country's attention in 1960, the Congress of
Racial Equality, founded at the University of Chicago, had staged
lunch-counter sit-ins in 1942 in that city and had pioneered other
tactics of nonviolent action for enforcement of laws on public places
and housing in the Midwest, well before CORE had headed south to
hold workshops to train a new generation in its methods. So had the
NAACP, the oldest of civil rights organizations since its founding in
1909—in response to lynchings in the Midwest—as the NAACP's
Ella Baker had won integration of schools in the East, and Constance
Baker-Motley authored the *Brown v. Board of Education* brief that had
won the landmark Supreme Court ruling in 1954 to integrate schools
nationwide, also based on a case in the Midwest. However, historian Thomas J. Sugrue writes, "hard-fought struggles in the North" had
begun to "slip into historical obscurity" and be "eclipsed" by battles in
the South, soon to be "discovered" by new television networks and
other media. They downplayed that "Northern civil rights protestors
had developed and perfected strategies" to integrate schooling and

---

76   IQG, "Domineering Women;" Evans, *Born for Liberty*, 247; McBride,
Women's Wisconsin, 430.

housing—and that the Midwestern civil rights movement's tactics of sit-ins and "grassroots boycotts, led largely by groups of mothers" had "inspired activists around the country to demand equal education" and other objectives.[77]

Yet advice columns rarely had confronted issues of race, again reflecting mainly white readership of mainstream media. If columns often had been ahead of front pages in addressing issues of sex, gender, ethnicity, and even class, they had been behind their times regarding racial issues raised in Midwestern cities with sizeable communities of color, such as Chicago. In 1950, Milwaukee had been home to few more than twenty thousand African Americans, accounting for little more than three percent of the city's population. By the end of the decade, the "late Great Migration" to Milwaukee, a generation later than to most cities in the North, almost tripled their numbers to more than sixty thousand. However, as the city experienced great growth in every group, African Americans would comprise little more than eight percent of its population by 1960. That was their lowest proportion in the fifteen largest cities in the country, yet Milwaukee was the most racially diverse part of Wisconsin as home to almost all African Americans in the state. Indeed, almost all resided in one aging neighborhood near the *Journal* newspaper plant. Not for decades would courts conclude that, since 1950, the city "had administered the school system with the intent to segregate." As a result of segregationist housing laws as well, African Americans living within sight of the *Journal* remained almost invisible in daily lives of readers—and editors and reporters. All also remained blind to the "restlessness of the state's minorities," writes Wisconsin historian Robert C. Nesbit. As William F. Thompson writes, "the city's elected and civic leadership," including the *Journal* publisher, also "remained largely indifferent" to reports of "intolerable" conditions in the "inner core" neighborhoods near the newspaper plant.[78]

---

77 August Meier and Elliott Rudwick, *CORE, A Study in the Civil Rights Movement, 1942-1968* (Urbana: University of Illinois Press, 1975), 13-14; Thomas J. Sugrue, *Sweet Land of Liberty: The Forgotten Struggle for Civil Rights in the North* (New York: Random House, 2009), 142-144, 168-181, 208-212.

78 Governor's Commission on Human Rights, "Negro Families in Rural Wisconsin: A Study of Their Community Life" (Madison, Wis.:

Soon to awaken in the 1960s to many societal problems that had gone unnamed by media on the front pages, readers who rarely raised issues of race on the back page of the newspaper in their community forum, Griggs' column, did report a rising discontent among women that also would emerge in wider public discourse with publication of *The Feminine Mystique*. Few women would march in the streets for their rights for a decade, although many minority women and others with them would march in the streets of the city in the 1960s—including the street where the columnist lived, and where she and her colleagues worked, a street that would be the site of urban riots. The era ahead, writes historian Sara M. Evans, "would shatter illusions of stability in the '50s and challenge American society in the '60s to live up to its values." Even readers who held no illusions regarding race, gender, and once-unimaginable issues would continue to turn to their community forum for a sense of continuity, amid conflicts to come in the 1960s.[79]

Governor's Commission on Human Rights, 1959), Wisconsin Historical Society Archives, Madison, Wis.; Nesbit, *Wisconsin*, 533; Thompson, *History of Wisconsin*, 532-534; Gurda, *Making of Milwaukee*, 360-361.

79   Evans, *Born for Liberty*, 262.

5

The Sixties Engender Debate on Sex and Gender, 1961-1970

The 1960s would prove pivotal for women, for Wisconsin, and for the world in ways not fully foreseeable then, although a medical breakthrough on the market in 1960 for women would remake Wisconsin and their world: "the Pill." As historian Elaine Tyler May writes, most of the male developers and advocates of the first oral contraceptive did not fully foresee "its potential to liberate women," while women perceived that "the pill" was "precisely that," because birth control meant "control over their lives." In Wisconsin and across the country, the impact of a more reliable form of birth control than any before became evident as the "baby boom" came to an abrupt end. In the very Catholic state of Wisconsin—the focus of the country in 1960 as the state with the first presidential primary, won by Catholic candidate John F. Kennedy—the birth rate peaked in 1960 and began to decline in 1961, for the first time in decades and throughout the decade, because even many Catholic women defied their church's decree against "the Pill."[1]

As lawmakers in the majority of states also had decreed that prescriptions for "the Pill" would be available only to married women, legions of single women and their doctors became lawbreakers in Wisconsin, with the collusion of their beloved columnist, the grandmotherly Ione Quinby Griggs by then in her seventies, who added

---

1   Elaine Tyler May, *America and the Pill: A History of Promise, Peril, and Liberation* (New York: Basic Books, 2010), vii-ix, 10; Thompson, *History of Wisconsin*, 252, 262.

Planned Parenthood to her regular roster of community agencies to recommend to her readers. Another sign of the times would be letters from readers suggesting that she was behind the times, in tumultuous times ahead in the 1960s, although Griggs would remain well ahead of most Wisconsin lawmakers. As the 1960s began, all of the legislators in Wisconsin again were men, who would maintain the state's ban on "the Pill" for unwed women for another decade. By the mid-1960s, a few women would win election to the state legislature, including one against a male opponent with the campaign slogan, "it's a man's job." However, single women who wanted better jobs or just job stability would not wait for legislators to allow legal access to "the Pill" that would make possible more professional careers for women. By the mid-1960s, owing to "the Pill," birth rates would drop nationwide to the lowest level in three decades, since the depths of the Great Depression, when the "Dear Mrs. Griggs" column had begun—and when women finally had won an end to the nineteenth-century laws that had banned even the dispensing of information on earlier methods of birth control.[2]

The year 1960 also marked the end of an era for the city of Milwaukee and the beginning of its population decline for the rest of the century. The twelfth-largest city in the country in the 1930s, when Griggs had arrived, Milwaukee had dropped but rebounded to ranking as eleventh-largest in 1960, with a peak population of almost three-fourths of a million residents—but would begin a decline to drop to twelfth-largest city in the U.S. by the end of the decade. Suburban sprawl, however, would maintain population growth in Milwaukee County and beyond, in the multi-county metropolitan area that was home to many of her readers, whether longtimers or newcomers driving through the city to ever-more-outlying towns. As populations of most major Midwestern cities in the "Frostbelt" also would decline during the decade, at an even faster rate, Milwaukee

---

2   Thompson, *History of Wisconsin*, 262; Rita Rubin, "The Pill: 50 Years of Birth Control Changed Women's Lives," *USA Today*, May 8, 2010; McBride, *Women's Wisconsin*, 435; J. R. Ross, "From First Female Lawmakers to Farrow, Times Have Changed," *MJS*, April 27, 2001.

would remain the tenth-largest metropolitan area in the country in the mid-1960s.[3]

As for "Mrs. Griggs" and her following of women readers across the city and region, none could foresee that her career as an advice columnist had reached only its halfway point, with another quarter of a century ahead for their collaboration in the column. Already in her seventieth year as the decade opened, Griggs had outlasted many an editor and publisher. Few remained from the era when she had joined the *Journal*, prior to Social Security, so not even a newsroom full of reporters could attest to her age. She courteously but resolutely continued to refuse to provide her birth year on personnel forms. Not that her editors, nor the publisher, nor even the new chairman of the board—one of a few co-workers predating her at the newspaper— would dare to question their now-iconic columnist with answers always at the ready for readers.

The tiny columnist, who loomed large for her following—which included ever-younger colleagues—had continued to faithfully appear at her desk daily, ever in her trademark hat, without fail. Then, in 1961, a headline in the Journal Company's employee newsletter exclaimed that "Ione Misses Work for First Time in 27 Years!" The first hospitalization in her life unsettled the columnist, not only owing to need for minor surgery but also owing to her fame. She asked the nursing staff not to introduce her as "Mrs. Griggs from the *Journal*," lest she have to listen to others' woes, while recovering from her own. However, as she shared with co-workers, her "roommate told me her troubles, anyway." Returning to the newsroom, Griggs again appeared as ageless as her advice, almost always helpful—although testy, at times. Her counsel on a page headlined "A Polite Way to Say 'None of Your Business'" seemed counter-productive, and even rather astonishing for an advice columnist, when Griggs stated that "it is poor manners to ask questions" on personal matters. The woman well-practiced in artful evasion about her age for almost half a century archly asserted that, if nosy

---

3   Marc V. Levine and Sandra J. Callaghan, *The Economic State of Milwaukee: The City and the Region* (Milwaukee: UWM Center for Economic Development, 1998), 11-22.

sorts "persist, pierce their seemingly insensitive hides by asking how they would like a barrage of questions about their private doings."[4]

Her ability to adapt throughout a journalistic career of forty years by the 1960s would be put to the test amid societal changes. Some readers would challenge her advice in the decade that would become known for youthful rebellion and a "generation gap," while a younger generation again would turn to "Mrs. Griggs." A rebellious mood actually was more widespread by gender and age, as older workers witnessed the beginning of the decline of industrialization in a region that would come to be dubbed the "Rustbelt." The impact upon workers included those in her plant in 1961, in "the only major strike in the *Journal's* history," writes its historian and reporter Robert W. Wells of newspaper unions' futile resistance to computerized production. For a few days, the management even dropped advertising for news in abbreviated editions, although the *Journal* would remain among the nation's top five newspapers in advertising linage. When the strike led a management without historical memory of wartime newsprint shortages to again drop the "Green Sheet," history repeated itself, as "reader protests quickly forced its return," Wells writes. Milwaukeeans would have their comics, their crosswords, and their "Mrs. Griggs."[5]

The advice columnist remained a constant in readers' daily lives, despite other changes at the newspaper with import for the city and state. The Hearst era ended in Milwaukee in 1962, and the city nearly became a one-daily-newspaper town, until the *Journal* bought the *Sentinel*. Some *Journal* staffers switched. The "Green Sheet" staff stayed on, as did the section's formula, despite changes to come in other sections and in new columnists. Sadly, one featured column of the era was not new but needed to be revived in the 1960s, a weekly compendium of local news from the *Journal* called "Dear Joe: Your Letter from Home," begun during World War II but now sent to Milwaukeeans in the military in Vietnam. Wartime for millions of men again meant opportunity for women at the *Journal*, where the managing editor stated that women journalists "had two advantages in getting hired:

---

4   Wells, *Milwaukee Journal*, 254, 336, 399, 412, 423; IQG, "Ione Misses Work for First Time in 27 Years!" *Little Journal*, July 1961, n.p.; IQG, "Reader Wants a Polite Way to Say 'None of Your Business,'" *MJ*, September 4, 1964.

5   Wells, *Milwaukee Journal*, 327, 400-419.

Fashion rebellions of "the '60s" remained ahead early in 1963, and readers' issues often resembled those of the 1950s, as did finery donned by a mother and white-gloved daughters at a "tea party" in suburban Brookfield in Waukesha County, soon to become the fastest-growing county in the country, as population declined in the city of Milwaukee. (Copyright 2014 Journal Sentinel, Inc., reproduced with permission)

DEAR MRS. GRIGGS'

They weren't being drafted and they smelled nicer." The comment about aromatic advantages "would have been scorned as sexist a few years later," writes Wells, when the modern women's movement would have impact on the news and on the newsroom. Wisconsin women, national leaders in the movement, would take the editors to task, and more stories by and about women's issues would appear that were new to the "news side"—but not new to readers of the back page of the newspaper, where they and their columnist had discussed premarital pregnancy, marital affairs, divorce, and more for decades.[6]

Larger societal upheaval soon to have impact on readers' daily lives remained ahead, as the decade opened with little sign in readers' letters of discontinuities or discontents with their lives. Instead, most sampled letters differed little from those of a decade before. Readers rallied to the column's calls for help, such as a memorable plea on behalf of a reader unable to provide a "steady supply of mother's milk" necessary for survival of a sickly infant. "Griggs found enough *Journal* subscribers who were not only willing but able to fill this unusual request," writes Wells, "so the child survived." One reader would "wet nurse" the child for a full year, until he could be weaned to cows' milk—no doubt also supplied by readers on dairy farms still within the *Journal* circulation area. Griggs would relay regular updates for her readers as the boy grew, and the newspaper would continue to reference the story, and its columnist's role, into the next century.[7]

Readers also continued to write of disputes with neighbors, tenants, landlords, or in-laws, although as often owing to in-laws visiting too often as to in-laws who never visited at all. Yet letters also came signed from "Happy Reader," and even "A Happy Teen Ager." Others offered innocuous requests, such as prayers to ease relatives in pain or pangs for lost pets. One reader even requested housekeeping hints, a commonplace among other advice columnists, but not from Griggs. This time, she again did not opine "on the question of draining dishes after washing them, in preference to drying with a towel" but cited "good, conscientious housewives" as opting for sanitary benefits of "the draining method," which the letter writer had described as "my

---

6   Ibid., 33-34, 403-419.

7   Ibid., 265; Jim Stingl, "Woman Literally Gave of Herself to Save Sick Infant," *MJS*, November 17, 2009.

'lazy woman's' method." Griggs replied that her reader hardly was lazy, as she was a working wife.[8]

In sum, life seemed humdrum in Milwaukee, the Midwest, and the nation in early years of the decade, until the day in November 1963 that massive presses of the *Milwaukee Journal* stopped upon news of the assassination of the president. Word arrived in the noon hour in the newsrooms of the Midwest, "barely in time to make the final edition," recalls *Journal* historian and reporter Robert W. Wells. Presses then rumbled for hours in floors below the newsroom for a hundred thousand "extra editions," and the *Journal* lobby was "jammed with people waiting to buy papers," he writes of a day that ended an era in American politics—and its print journalism. Television networks preempted regular programming for days and nights that would turn many regular readers into viewers, especially for "breaking news" on which broadcast media could score "scoops" on the press. Some readers, however, would perform the ritual of framing the historic front page that day. Few would do so for the back page, the most popular page of the newspaper, which also had stories to tell of everyday lives of readers of Griggs' column in the "Green Sheet," which was printed days ahead. On that historic day, readers found a timeless discussion on downfalls of gossip and "griping" by "the girls" at neighborhood *kaffeeklatsches* of a reader, "Ex-Mrs. Discontent," who was happy to have abandoned the unhappy gatherings.[9] More attacks on Milwaukee's once-beloved *kaffeeklatsches* would arise in a lively debate, later in a transitional decade, as Teutonic traditions and terms became less visible and more nostalgic.

Wider discontent in tumultuous times for women in Wisconsin and elsewhere arose amid issues of civil rights and civic dissent as well as a youth rebellion that would take a toll on family life, but the column would be a source of constancy in lives of Griggs' readers. The gender of most correspondents also remained constant, as 85 percent of the letters sampled in the 1960s came from women and girls. The number of older adults authoring letters sampled in the decade now declined to little more than half of their level of participation in the

---

8   IQG, "Widower Interested in Widow, But What Is She Interested In?" *MJ*, July 26, 1963.

9   Wells, *Milwaukee Journal*, 412-413; IQG, "Wife Soured on Fault Finding and Griping at Kaffeeklatsches," *MJ*, November 22, 1963.

previous decade, when such readers had penned almost seven in ten or 69.7 percent of letters sampled. Instead, in the 1960s, few more than a third or only 37.6 percent of letters sampled came from older readers. Rare in the column for his gender and age was "Worried," a widower wondering whether he was sufficiently "classy" to court a widow critical of his clothing and companions. Griggs worried, too, as "it is tragic at any time to make an unfortunate marriage, especially so after a man is past 40"—an age that must have seemed ancient to many of her new correspondents in the 1960s.[10]

In the decade when readers would witness the rise of the modern women's movement, their columnist witnessed more of a girls' movement, with a return to a far younger following. After reaching more mature and married readers in the 1950s, and despite her own longevity and that of her column, her constituency in the 1960s returned to an age group as young as had been readers in the column's initial decades in the 1930s and 1940s, when Griggs had marched on city hall with thousands of petitions from girls at war with the "city fathers" for a proposed curfew to curb flirtatious behaviors with sailors and soldiers on downtown streets. In the 1960s, writers self-identified by general age in 117 of 164 letters sampled, almost seven in ten of all letters—similar to the percentage in the previous decade and far more than in an earlier era—and almost six in ten writers were teenagers or young adults, perhaps reflecting her readers' generational angst.

A common topic of young readers' complaints was parental and societal criticism of their clothing, companions, fashions, and "fads and music." So wrote reader "No Hidden Meanings," soon after "Beatlemania" came to Milwaukee with the British band's first tour. The phenomenon of their young, female, and frenzied cohort of fans had seemed frivolous, until police forces in the city and elsewhere had faced streets filled with sizeable mobs of girls, screaming for the mop-topped musical group. Media delved into deeper motivations of "Beatlemania" in the era, as does historian Susan J. Douglas since. She argues for the significance in women's history as well as music history of the 1964 tour of the "Fab Four" at "a critical point in evolution of girl culture" that created a "sense of cultural and social collectivity" through media for a generation raised with television and transistor radios. In the adolescent response, she sees "seeds of female yearning

---

10   IQG, "Widower Interested."

and female revolt" soon to evolve into a movement, when a media-savvy generation in the streets would return as women marching for their rights. Their "yearning" also came in the context of troubled times, argues Douglas, as the boyish band served to lessen a sense of loss for girls in the era, who had seen a young president assassinated on their television screens and were witnessing increased deployments and deaths of their brothers and others in the Vietnam War.[11]

Similar media reports at the time wearied Griggs' young reader, "No Hidden Meanings." The girl opened with a polite promise that she regularly read Griggs' column for advice that had proved "excellent most of the time," so her reader hoped for help in understanding why media and others subjected teenagers to mass analysis. "Why must there be hidden meanings behind everything teenagers do?" she wrote. "Psychologists tell people that our music and fads are 'related to some type of rebellion.'" She ridiculed the search for "some kind of theory to explain our way of life. Why can't we wear our clothes, tease our hair and listen to our music without having someone explain the whys and wherefores to our parents? Why can't we do these things because we like them?" Grandiloquently, she wrote that she represented "teens of various races, religions and social standings" in eliciting the grandmotherly Griggs' opinion on "fads and music in connection with so-called 'hidden meanings.'" The columnist replied that "an interest in music of any kind is beneficial," and many fads were "healthy outlets." The onetime follower of "flapper" fashion and "bobbed" hair warned, however, that "teasing" hair was "a stupid practice, whatever psychologists think it suggests." Readers continued to wage the debate for years, as in a letter from "One Half of Two Generations" about a parent who belittled teenagers for feeling "picked on" for fads. "This sounds like we are a bunch of babies," but "all we're asking is that our ideas be understood," wrote the young reader. "Call it the generation gap if you want to," but teenagers were not so superficial, she wrote. Instead, it actually was "a gap between ideas."[12]

---

11   Susan J. Douglas, *Where the Girls Are: Growing Up Female with the Mass Media* (New York: Times Books, 1994), 98, 113-120; Jonathan Kasparek, "A Day in the Life: The Beatles Descend on Milwaukee," *Wisconsin Magazine of History* 84:2 (Winter 2000-01), 14-29.

12   IQG, "Teen Ager Perplexed at Effort to Analyze Activities of Teens," *MJ*, January 12, 1965; IQG, "Use of Brute Force by Dad Won't Work, Girl,

The gender and youth of the majority of her readers also engendered debate on alleged sexual permissiveness in the 1960s, although at the same time—on the same day—that letters begging for basic information suggested a naiveté on the part of parents, reluctant to provide the "straight talk" of advice columns. Clothing, or lack of it, figured in two letters in one column. "Nineteen" had to reply to a boyfriend's request that she pose for photos for "a certain magazine that publishes pictures of girls. They're called 'playmates,'" she wrote. The columnist was well aware of *Playboy* and advised that her reader not "discard your sense of what is right" nor her clothing. "Too Far?" requested readings on "facts of life," as the sixteen-year-old did not know "much more than a ten year old." She also appealed to parents to "take time and explain sex to your children. Then maybe they'll get to sleep at night instead of staying up to write letters to Mrs. Griggs. God bless you, Mrs. Griggs." The blessed columnist agreed that "it is a crime in this enlightened age for teenagers to be kept in ignorance." She gave the girl a reading list—and a caution that "your information that no harm can come to a girl who is fully clothed is false."[13]

Many letters echoed those of earlier eras, as former teenagers who had bedeviled their parents now were parents deploring similar behaviors, such as "petting" and "necking." Hardly new practices, both merited more debate in the column than did major events in the eventful era. The first letter, published on a Valentine's Day, came from a fifteen-year-old who feared that her parents would "ruin everything" if they knew that she was going "steady" and wearing a boy's class ring—a "necking ring." She signed her letter as "Am I Too Young?" and received replies from readers of all ages agreeing with Griggs, who essentially answered "yes." The columnist wrote that, although "few boys or girls" had not "sampled some necking," even "smart, decent people a lot older have run into trouble through necking." Apparently, some people a lot older—parents—used the column for discussion with daughters. Another fifteen-year-old, "In Need of More Advice," wrote that a talking-to had led her to agree to give back a boy's ring, but she

---

14, Says," *MJ*, April 14, 1969.

13   IQG, "Man Startles Girl Friend, 19; Asks for Near Nude Photos," *MJ*, August 20, 1964.

faced a dilemma of how to do so and remain friends. Griggs gave the girl a helpful script.[14]

A few outraged teenagers' replies employed rhetoric that foreshadowed a rebelliousness soon to be seen beyond the column in the 1960s. "We belong to an era of our own," wrote one, but "our parents cannot see," as her generation "can't express themselves with words so they use gestures"—as some would do in photographs that the newspaper would not print. Another found the words to express herself with frankness not evident in earlier disagreements with Griggs.[15]

> My gosh, lady, if a girl waits until 15 or 16 to "get to know the opposite sex," she'll probably get married at the ripe old age of 45.
>
> Just because you're old doesn't mean you should force your dumb ideas on us…. In the olden days when Mr. Griggs (poor old chap!) married you, he probably drove his horse and buggy with a chaperone in the back seat! I could write better answers than you.[16]

The rejoinder from Griggs attempted humor but suggested a rare defensiveness, as she "was glad to give space to the views" of teenagers "defending or arguing the issues of necking and going steady"—and that the letter gave her "a good laugh … on a day when the mail [was] unusually heavy" during the controversy. The letter also brought memories of "how Mr. Griggs loved his big Buick!… But if he had had a horse and buggy, I am sure he would have driven it with a flair and would have charmed the chaperone out of the back seat, if there had been one."[17]

Although many elders empathized with the columnist, one older reader subtly implied that Griggs' advancing years hampered her ability to give advice. His hilarious letter revived her droll wit. She wrote that many men had written to her—"young, middle aged, single, married, serious, skeptical, hopeful, remorseful, happy, befuddled, sad, sober"—but she had to doubt the sobriety of this writer, who claimed that fortifying effects of a favored local brew were required for readers

---

14   IQG, "Girl Wears a 'Necking Ring,' Says She Knows When to Stop," *MJ*, February 14, 1966; IQG, "Neckers in Teen Age World Not Sold on I.Q.G.'s Advice," *MJ*, February 28, 1966.

15   IQG, "Neckers in Teen Age World."

16   Ibid.

17   Ibid.

to face "frighteners" in letters to the column, adding to "one upsetting thing after another." Nor could he find comfort in "Green Sheet" comics—"Judge Parker," "Mary Worth," and more—that reminded him of current events or topics that resembled those in her column.[18]

> I usually check first to see if Judge Parker has the number of those peace people. Then I tolerantly turn to see if Mary Worth is still horning in on other folks' business....
>
> I am becoming a bit concerned about Cherry's love life in Mark Trail, or rather the lack of it. How long does a chick with a figure like that have to wait.... Maybe she should write you! Unlike my wife, I pace no floors over those characters.
>
> Frankly, I prefer Major Hoople. I can identify with him.[19]

"Major Hoople," a fusty figure from the past, provided solace to the writer—as did "opening up the sixth beer" in the requisite preparation to "pitch into reading your column," he wrote.[20]

> Learning to live with the "bomb" is a breeze when you consider some of the heart stoppers you have to cope with daily or nightly.... Take the problem, "to neck or not to neck." You and I are definitely on the opposite side[s]....
>
> I lean toward that first part, "to neck," provided that it isn't with a member of my wife's bridge set, a pretty gabby group if you ask me, one that's given to bragging.... I admire you for letting us know how you stand on 'necking,' even if you backed the wrong side.[21]

He complimented her for not allowing "winds of public opinion" to "blow you off your course" but wondered whether she could relate to "kids" in the era of television, as "back in your day and my day, wireless radio" was the new technology. He had found her wisdom timeless on "free-loading relatives" and so-called friends: "You have gotten to me! I don't complain when some cheapskate friends serve a 'no-brand beer.'" He also had progressed in coping with current events, realizing that the real news was not on the front page: "When I dash over to pick up the Journal on my neighbor's front porch every night, I now whip

---

18   IQG, "Reader's Got the Bomb Figured, But Sneaky Cat Spells Trouble," *MJ*, June 17, 1967.

19   Ibid.

20   Ibid.

21   Ibid.

to the back of the Green Sheet first, because that's where the exciting stuff is. Then, even if the old crank of a neighbor comes and grabs the paper out of my hands, I'm cued in on what's going on," because he read "Mrs. Griggs." The recipient replied that she was happy to have his letter, "even if it is after the sixth beer. It is usually the wife who writes me when her husband has reached the sixth or more."[22]

More often, young readers welcomed her advice on societal mores in flux, often evident at school dances. Letters from students in Catholic schools offer context for understanding the array of emotions in the era, from bewilderment to anger, when rules shifted without warning—as did suddenly modernized church practices for their parents as well. In the mid-1960s, the papal convocation colloquially called "Vatican II" caused changes for clerics and lay faithful alike. Local laity may have felt the most discomfort from lapsing of the longtime ban on meat on Fridays, although that religious practice had become a cultural ritual, and the weekly "fish fry" remained a mainstay in Milwaukee restaurants, bars, and church basements. Catholics had to relearn rites of worship, however, after abandonment not only of the Latin mass but also of the requirement that women cover hair with hats, *babushkas*, or "chapel veils." Soon, nuns no longer wore veils, if they remained in the sisterhood at all. Many renounced vows and left the religious orders, as did many priests. One who continued to wear the collar made headlines in Milwaukee for his activism: Father James Groppi. Assigned in 1963 to an inner-city parish and soon advisor to the NAACP Youth Council, he organized a group called the NAACP Commandos that joined in civil rights protests underway and starting to escalate in that pivotal, transitional year of 1963. At other parishes, even the once-innocuous Catholic Youth Organization's dances became cause for controversy in the column. "I'm Catholic," wrote a young reader, who asserted that "even at CYO dances that are watched over by priests and sometimes nuns, the kids will neck."[23]

Confusion and conflict about cultural norms went well beyond parochial schools, as their public school's shifting strictures also brought a group of "Baffled Freshmen" to the column by 1966. Their letter led Griggs to question whether "school leaders [were] being unreasonable" regarding arbitrary "edicts" imposed without warning. Her young

---

22   Ibid.

23   Ibid.

readers were reasonable, about dress codes so detailed as to require that "girls dress decently with an average of skirts about three inches above the center of the knee," and that boys "not wear their hair exceptionally long" in "Beatle cuts," they wrote, nor were they "hoods," a localism for those who "smoke and drink a little and try to act big." However, that code was clearly stated and disseminated in advance. Not so for school events, where "close dancing" caused a contretemps with a school administrator, although parents had "watched us dance" and did not object. Above all, the writers objected that "a reason hasn't been given us," a common plaint in the 1960s. The columnist also questioned whether school officials were acting reasonably but advised her young readers, "fast growing out of childhood," that they had to accept the inevitable "penalties we all pay for growing up."[24]

Younger readers had to accept an inevitable power imbalance in their schooling but soon would be on campuses, where college students' mantra by the mid-1960s became to "question authority." In all, surprisingly few younger readers questioned the elderly authority figure most popular with their age group in the era, or they may have seen her in the mediative role of many grandparents. She proved resistant to shock when "Confused Madison Co-ed" wrote of moving in with a boyfriend, without benefit of marriage but with benefits that Griggs did not discuss. She provided a balanced discussion of potential pitfalls to her reader, who could not have known that the columnist had comported with cultural rebels of an earlier era in Chicago's "bohemian" crowd in the "roaring Twenties." Griggs also empathized with a proud grandmother of a male student at the state campus in Madison who refused to participate in graduation rites. "This is one more rebellious thought that may strike a boy or girl of this age," she wrote, although also pointing out that, in comparison to the sense of community at high school events, "big college commencement ceremonies" could seem "superfluous." Whether either she or her reader had attended recent events at Madison was questionable, because Griggs referred to the ceremonies as promising to be "dignified," when protesters planned disruptions. However, media coverage across the state often had not fully conveyed that antiwar protests continued to escalate in the state capital, in reaction to the escalating conflict and call-ups of many grandsons gone to

---

24   IQG, "Teens Can't Understand Edict to Stop Dancing 'Too Close,'" *MJ*, February 23, 1966.

Racial issues arose in readers' discussions in "Dear Mrs. Griggs" as civil rights protests began in the city as early as 1964, when a mother and daughter donned cold-weather wear to march on a picket line with CORE, the Congress for Racial Equality, prior to court-ordered integration of Milwaukee Public Schools to counter the effects of highly segregated housing patterns. (Wisconsin Historical Society, WHS-4993)

war, like the brother whose little sister had shared his letter of advice with Griggs' readers. A sad constancy of the column would be wartime letters again, and increasingly, during the decade.[25]

By mid-decade, young people in particular—those most likely to have to go to war, like the proud grandmother's male graduate—were questioning authorities from schools to campuses to city streets as well as at home. Antiwar protests began by mid-decade in Wisconsin, where the state campus in Madison became a major center of antiwar activism in the country, and similar protests arose at the state campus in Milwaukee. The city also was the site of civil rights rallies and hundreds of nights of marches against racist residential laws in the city soon to be known nationwide as "the Selma of the North" for its resistance to ending its segregation. Such societal concerns increased in sampled letters in the category of "other" issues. Few were counted from early decades of the column, for less than 5 percent of sampled letters, but those with "other" issues had doubled to 10 percent in the 1950s and now doubled again to 20 percent in the 1960s, reflecting raised awareness of concerns that rarely had arisen for readers in previous periods.

Few writers self-identified by race in any era, although most apparently were white, as were more than ninety percent of residents in the city—and ninety-nine percent in the suburbs—and as were readers who raised the issue of racial prejudice in the 1960s. Their discussion went for weeks in 1966, a year prior to escalating racial conflict that would culminate in urban riots. Mothers focused on effects of racial discrimination on families raised in a city and society that countered efforts at childrearing "without hate in their hearts," as "Worried Parent" wrote of "a relative with ugly prejudices" who "might influence children" with his words.[26]

> This relative ... has been very prejudiced about a certain minority
> group and speaks out more and more about it.... This relative cuts

---

25   IQG, "Bossy, Know It All Hubby Even Takes Over Kitchen," *MJ*, June 22, 1967; IQG, "Little Sister Gets Advice from Brother in Service," *MJ*, July 22, 1967; IQG, "GI on Leave Spent More Time With Girl Than With Parents," *MJ*, August 31, 1964.

26   IQG, "Relative With Ugly Prejudices May Influence Young Children," *MJ*, February 15, 1966; IQG, "Workshop to Fight Prejudice Bore Fruit for Many Parents," *MJ*, February 24, 1966.

these people down in front of my children. Children ... don't sprout
prejudices themselves. They get them from adults.

I sincerely want my children to grow up without any hate in their
hearts.... I don't believe this relative realizes that the children are
old enough to know what is being said. He probably thinks it goes
over their heads or in one ear and out the other.

The fact is children are smart enough to grasp a lot of things.
They are old enough to repeat what they hear, not maliciously but
innocently. The remarks could take root in their minds.[27]

The issue had come into homes across the country by 1966, when children watched television broadcasts of the violent reaction to the civil rights movement in the South. The issue also had come into the letter writer's home and marriage, discovering differences about raising children in a segregated society—but she would go forward on her own, if she could determine what to do.

Since this relative is not on my side of the family, I am hesitant
to make an issue of it. I don't want to cause bad feelings.... My
[spouse] seems to think I am taking this whole thing too seriously.
What can I do? One [child] has just started school, and I don't want
the child ... repeating prejudiced remarks or thinking prejudiced
thoughts.[28]

She closed with gratitude for help from Griggs and her readers, whose discussion would reassure her and others that they were not alone in confronting the issue. Griggs first counseled her reader that her spouse ought to be the one to confront his relative but also advised the mother and others in a reply with a message far more directive than was commonplace for Milwaukee's columnist.

This is what you should do at home. Teach your children that
prejudice is unkind, unfair, dishonest, inhumane, and ignorant. Get
through to the children in terms they will understand, but see that
the meaning is clear. Impress on their minds and hearts that it is
only fair to judge another person's worth by his conduct, not by
his looks, his nationality, his race, or anything for which he is not
personally responsible.

---

27   IQG, "Relative With Ugly Prejudices."
28   Ibid.

If there is love and respect in your home, you can develop the
right attitudes in your children toward people with different
backgrounds.[29]

The column elicited responses from other readers, indicative of wider
concern in the community.

The mother's plea regarding racial prejudice "impelled" another reader to share resources from a recent event, and Griggs gave an entire full
column to the issue. "Local Mother" agreed that relatives influenced
children, "in subtle ways, if parents are not alert," and that "the problem of teaching goodwill and combating prejudice is a very real and
important one for every thinking parent." A group of other "concerned
mothers with a variety of backgrounds from the Greater Milwaukee
area" had met "to learn and discuss the type of problems that concern
'A Worried Parent,'" as "our children will be the leaders of tomorrow,
and we must see that they grow up to be leaders of good will." The
Milwaukee Public Library had provided a booklist for children, and
attendees had compiled suggestions "on just what things, big and small,
each family could do to create good will in the hearts of their children
and in the community," she wrote. Mothers had deemed the event a
success and planned more. For her readers, the columnist researched
and reported on sponsors—a roster of organizations, from the League
of Women Voters to Catholic, Jewish, and Protestant groups—and
Griggs proffered publicity for the workshops in the works.[30]

Griggs gave the Milwaukee mothers an opportunity as guest columnists of a sort by also researching and publishing their suggestions,
well-intentioned but unintentionally revealing the extent of segregation in the city. For example, the mothers suggested that others occasionally "shop in another neighborhood" and "attend church in the inner core," the area segregated for African Americans in the city. The list
was revealing of the women's naiveté in their suggestion to residents
of "the core" to "take your family to a suburban church," indicative of
an inability to anticipate racism that African Americans encountered
outside their designated area in the city.[31]

---

29   Ibid.

30   IQG, "Workshop to Fight Prejudice."

31   Ibid.

Discuss the issues of prejudice with your mate.... Read books in the field of intergroup relations.... Encourage your children to read books dealing with other religions, races, and nations. Think through the ways in which you as a family can deal with day-to-day questions of prejudice.... Avoid talking in the family circle about "they" and "them." Teach that stereotypes of any kind are wrong.[32]

Other suggestions also revealed readers' lack of recognition of African American experience as differing from that of earlier ethnic groups and also indicated how deeply embedded in local institutions was a similar lack of understanding. For example, readers suggested that to "attend the holiday folk fair" would be educative, a reference to a longstanding event celebrating the city's ethnic heritages—but primarily those from Europe, with little inclusion of other continents of origin. Readers recommended visiting the Milwaukee Public Museum to "learn about other cultures," although its recently opened exhibit on the "Streets of Old Milwaukee" that allegedly celebrated the city's multicultural history mainly marked the Germanic ancestry of many of the museum donors.[33] Decades later, another building belatedly would be added to the exhibit to also acknowledge a pioneering African American family, which was significant in the city's past.

Amid media attention to the antiwar movement and to the African American civil rights movement, another groundswell for the rights of women also was rising, with Wisconsin roots. In the 1960s, the modern women's movement would merit little notice in media nationwide, including in the news section of Griggs' newspaper. However, women found ways other than news pages to "network" from 1963 forward, a year that proved to be pivotal. First came the publication of journalist Betty Friedan's book, *The Feminine Mystique*, on "the problem that had no name," the frustrations of women caught in the 1950s culture of domesticity that continued for many readers, like a letter writer to the column who had come to adulthood on the cusp of the transitional time. In 1963, she had graduated from high school, had wed two weeks later, and had two children in the next two years. At twenty-one years old, she already was "Old at Too Young an Age," as she signed her letter about "something lacking in life" as "an old married lady" and

---

32   Ibid.

33   Ibid.

wondering whether she had more to offer, other than being a wife and mother.[34]

In 1963, the modern women's movement had begun to organize, arising from a first-ever Presidential Commission on the Status of Women, appointed by President Kennedy and chaired by former First Lady Eleanor Roosevelt. She had delivered its report regarding pay disparities and discrimination, detailed in exhaustive data, with recommendations that Kennedy signed into law in the Equal Pay Act of 1963, only months prior to his assassination. The next year, gender bias in hiring also became illegal with a last-minute amendment that added "sex" to the list of outlawed causes for discrimination that were encoded in the Civil Rights Act of 1964. However, as historian Sara M. Evans writes, "the inclusion of sex" was considered "a bit of a joke," and federal enforcement of the law would be lacking for decades, without support of the subsequent presidents. The presidential commission on women's status continued to meet annually, and some states established similar commissions that accomplished more. Among the first was in Wisconsin, under Dr. Kathryn "Kay" Clarenbach of Madison, who was adept at making news.[35]

Just as the "news side" of the *Journal* newsroom had missed signs of a rising women's movement in issues discussed on the back page of the newspaper in Griggs' column, a major story in 1966 relegated to its "women's pages" made the front page of the *Milwaukee Sentinel.* Historian Marcia Cohen credits the latter newspaper as first in the country with the story of the founding of the National Organization for Women at the annual meeting of state commissions on the status of women, a story with a "local angle" for Wisconsin with the selection of "Kay" Clarenbach as first chair of NOW's board. Cohen writes that the "tall, dignified" academic was selected despite Easterners' suspicions of her and other Midwesterners as "unlikely insurgents in stockings, high heels, and proper suits." NOW's first headquarters were in Clarenbach's home in Madison, and other founders included Milwaukeeans—a labor activist, an African American leader, women religious at local colleges—who, with others from Wisconsin, comprised almost a third of its founders. Although their work rarely would

---

34   IQG, "She Knocks Sister-in-Law for Favoring Booze Over Kids," *MJ,* July 12, 1969.

35   Evans, *Born for Liberty,* 274-277.

make news, their goals were not new to Griggs' readers, whose issues resonated in NOW's statement of purpose for "full participation" in society "in truly equal partnership with men" and NOW's emphasis on education to improve women's incomes, as almost half of women worked for pay—usually low pay—in the 1960s.[36]

That Griggs gave girls and women a forum for discussion as well as encouragement to gain education, careers, and self-sufficiency—as she had, decades before—somehow made her a standard-bearer for feminism in the mind of a male reader, "Big Mouth," an apt moniker among pseudonymns obviously provided by the columnist. "Browbeaten" by women, so "Big Mouth" claimed, he equated equality with "superiority" and, as so often in the era, he also confused the common courtesy of opening doors with common sense in opening employment in workplaces.

> Many women seem determined to have complete independence and recognition … sacrificing their femininity and the love and respect they seek from a man. Women apparently have the feeling that is primarily for the benefit of their sex and are going farther, calling for followers in a movement not just for equality but for superiority.
>
> They want to compete with men in business and professions … but expect the same man whom they have browbeaten all day to open doors for them in the evening.
>
> How can the protective instinct of the male be stimulated by the superior-acting female … marrying for the sole purpose of having a legal whip to scream nonsupport.[37]

He lacked support for his claim that feminists wed and bore children for the sake of non-support. However, also based on nameless sources, he reassured readers that such women were few, as a vague, "vast" number wanted only to "fulfill their place in life," like his wife—who was a "nut."

> The vast majority of women still get married to have a home, raise a family, assist their husbands, and rightly fulfill their place in

---

36   "Madison Woman Heads US Group," *MS*, August 1, 1966; "Women Form Action Group," *MJ*, August 1, 1966; Marcia Cohen, *The Sisterhood: The Inside Story of the Women's Movement and the Leaders Who Made It Happen* (New York: Fawcett, 1988), 134-138.

37   IQG, "A Runaway Wife Is Missed; Family Wants Her to Return," *MJ*, November 26, 1963.

life.... But by certain modern standards ... in several national magazine articles, this vast majority of married women [is] considered
"some kind of nuts."
        I thank my lucky stars that I found one of the uncomplicated
"nuts."[38]

Griggs mildly rebuked "Big Mouth," based upon "years of receiving
thousands of letters" from women who acted "responsibly and compe-
tently" for "husbands, children—and themselves." If hers was far from
a feminist statement, it reflected her long-published beliefs. She would
not countenance subservience, however, and adroitly combined in the
same column a letter from a "Truck Farmer's Wife." Her chronically
unemployed husband had not wanted their child and had "unpleasant
traits," from tantrums to "cussing a lot." In sum, he was "ornery." Griggs
warned the husband that "a truck farmer should know that what he
sows, he is going to reap."[39]

        Despite the rural reader's letter on marital discord, the contrasts
between the 1950s and 1960s for Griggs' following were reflected
in a marked decline in discussion of marital issues, which in turn reflected the fast-growing numbers of single women nationwide and in
Wisconsin during the decade. Marital issues had been the focus of
more than half of letters sampled in the 1950s—an increase from less
than a third of letters in previous decades—but were the focus of less
than a fifth of letters sampled in the 1960s. The number of marriages in Wisconsin now began to rise, but only because of the number
of "baby boomers" reaching maturity, Wisconsin historian William
F. Thompson writes. More couples awaited more maturity, with a
rise in the average age upon first marriage for women as well as men.
However, in proportion to the larger population, historian Robert C.
Nesbit writes, the "single state" in the state had declined from more
than half of Wisconsin women aged twenty to twenty-four years old
in 1940 to less than a third by 1960, "when attitudes favoring marriage, family, and domesticity were at their height."[40]

        The stigma applied to single life for women continued into the
1960s and engendered one of the decade's major debates in "Dear Mrs.
Griggs." First came a letter from a wife "Disgusted With Widows,"

---

38   Ibid.

39   Ibid.

40   Thompson, *History of Wisconsin*, 248; Nesbit, *Wisconsin*, 503.

because her husband wanted to devote time to his widowed sister's young child. "I think that having to 'father' her child is a lot of hog-wash," she wrote with a callousness that continued for paragraphs and, in turn, disgusted the widowed Griggs and readers like "Another Widow But Not Helpless," who complimented the columnist for her reply. "Usually, you are too easy on some of these complainers, but you certainly put this woman in her place," she wrote. Others, however, felt "lost emotionally because we are made to feel that society has no place for us" as "fifth wheels," as one wrote. Another also had been "in-tolerant of widows" until she became "the extra woman likely to be a liability to the hostess," while an "extra man at a party is seen as an asset." However, a letter from a "Happy, Adjusted and Independent" widow offered hope for others—although the onslaught of letters led to another from a "Much More Maligned Spinster" who "had to blow off steam after reading about the 'sad lot' of widows," envious of their "half loaf of widowhood," as at least they had memories of marriage.[41]

Griggs' attempt to assuage her reader led another to excoriate the columnist for extending neither pity to "poor spinsters" nor her usual "psychological excuse" for the "single problem."[42]

> Like other people, you just can't see any psychological excuse for her problem or any need for sympathy. Nor do you tell her where to get help as you do the frigid wives, divorcees, alcoholics, and so on....
>
> Why didn't you say she was "to be pitied," so humanity would at least be led to grant us spinsters a little sympathy and understand-ing? You told this spinster that not having the blessings of married life wasn't a sound excuse for a barren, miserable life....
>
> It is you "thought leaders" who cause the misguided attitudes to-ward spinsters whose lives are hard and lonely.... Teach the truth

---

41   IQG, "Brother Helps Widowed Sister, His Wife Doesn't Like Situation," *MJ*, July 22, 1964; IQG, "Extra Man's an Asset at a Party But Not So With Spare Woman," *MJ*, August 17, 1964; IQG, "Widower With Four Children Tells of Plight of the Lonely," *MJ*, August 21, 1964; IQG, "Only a Woman Offered to Help When Elderly Man Fell on Bus," *MJ*, August 25, 1964; IQG, "Workshop Is Slated at YMCA on Preparation for Marriage," *MJ*, August 26, 1964; IQG, "Lonely Spinster Tells Widows to Be Thankful for 'Half Loaf,'" *MJ*, August 27, 1964; IQG, "Spouse Lied About Her Past, Husband Found Out, Left Her," *MJ*, August 28, 1964.

42   IQG, "Reader Wants a Polite Way."

about spinsters who have been made into psychological cripples....
Many mothers make their daughters into spinsters, emotionally or psychologically crippling them, so they will have household
drudges....

And the rest of the relatives expect the spinster to be a free
drudge for them, too!

....A column like yours that influences the thinking and relationships of so many people should be careful not to promote intoler-
ance and lack of understanding for any unfortunate people, and this
includes spinsters.[43]

Griggs readily agreed that her reader might need "psychiatric help, or
at least education in living," and offered her usual referrals to community resources.[44]

Griggs also reiterated her optimistic outlook on the single life. "The
woman who has reached a certain age and never married would, in
my opinion, resent being pitied," as "some of the finest, best balanced,
happiest women" whom she knew happened to be single and would be
"shocked and horrified to be tagged 'psychological cripples,'" she wrote,
nor had their mothers "brainwashed" women who "prefer single life
independence to marriage." To the reader's query as to how the columnist would feel if also "deprived" of a husband and family, Griggs
replied revealingly, as a longtime widow, that she had missed having
children but could "see no point in missing a good life or being sorry
for one's self. The way to live life is to grapple with it each day and
make the best one can of it." More often, she was sympathetic to other older women alone, such as a widow who feared moving from her
home now beyond her means. "Even in the seventies," wrote Griggs,
"new friends can be made, if one is outgoing and receptive."[45]

The trend to marital bliss now reversed. By the end of the 1960s,
single women were 45 percent of all Wisconsin women, a higher proportion than in most states, as "the state of single-ness" lost its "stigma."
The number of single women soared to levels not seen since 1940,
writes historian Robert C. Nesbit, not "as a consequence of another
depression, or of women deciding not to marry, but more a factor of

---

43   Ibid.

44   Ibid.

45   Ibid.; IQG, "Should Widow in Her Seventies Move from Familiar
      Contacts?" *MJ*, February 11, 1965.

women postponing marriage" for college or for work, "in a marketplace that now had more job opportunities for them." By the end of the decade, in most of the state's cities and even small towns, "the state of singleness no longer had a stigma attached to it, and fewer high school graduates continued to live at home" but lived alone or with "other singles," Nesbit writes. Historian William F. Thompson also notes that also contributing to more "never-marrieds" in the 1960s were "older and widowed persons" and a divorce rate starting to rise "steeply upwards" in the late 1960s in Wisconsin and nationwide, a rate that would double in less than a decade. Still, in the 1960s, the number of marriages also increased with the rate of population growth, and of all women ever married, fewer than one in ten had been divorced.[46]

Letters on divorce came from writers of all ages. A twelve-year-old suburban girl wrote to Griggs that her grades had dropped as her parents were getting divorced, and her mother was dating and displaying "a new personality that I don't like and a fast temper" in "fighting" with the writer and her siblings. As the writer's grade-school graduation neared, she feared a "big fight" and wondered how to prevent it. "Where in all this is your father?" wrote the columnist, with consoling words and counsel to stay calm amid the chaos of her home, and with stronger words to the mother to attend to her children's unhappiness. Another writer, eighteen years old, wished that her parents had divorced rather than have "an atmosphere thick with unhappiness" in her home; however, they had stayed together to save for college. "Divorce, I'm sure, they consider out of the question because it is going to take so much money to finish educating us," she wrote. "It ties them to an existence they must find miserable and, believe me, I would rather quit school and be uneducated, going to work to support myself," she wrote. The reply counseled that resort to divorce court also could cause misery and hardly was a "cure-all." Griggs suggested that the writer speak to each parent to seek marriage counseling, telling them "that you and your sister care enough to want them to live together happily, not just stay together as a sacrifice for you."[47]

---

46 Nesbit, *Wisconsin*, 503-504; Thompson, *History of Wisconsin*, 248.

47 IQG, "Girl, 12, Is Confused and Hurt by Divorce Plans of Parents," *MJ*, June 14, 1961; IQG, "Should a Child Tell Parents They Should Get a Divorce?" *MJ*, January 16, 1962.

As the decade brought more letters from lonely single parents as well as their children, Griggs gave increasing recognition to the reality of increasing divorce rates, and especially gave regular publicity to organizations that arose for single parents and their families. First references in the column came for "Parents Without Partners," but she would add new organizations to her roster of recommendations such as "Double Duty, Inc.," a group for which Griggs could vouch, as she had "watched it grow from the first meeting" and had received good reports, she wrote. A letter writer detailed its activities at length, such as guest speakers for parents and summertime activities for children on their own, as the letter writer noted that "the one parent in a family more often than not works." Another difference from the 1950s was a sensible directive for one family activity, a visit to a submarine at the lakefront: "Mothers are asked to wear slacks."[48]

Reassuring to younger readers dealing with divorce may have been an entire column of letters from others in "blended families" who praised stepfathers. They wrote in reply to a letter from a young divorcee and abandoned mother about her fiancé, a prospective stepfather who worried as to whether he could succeed in the role, and they also wondered about whether to proceed with adoption. In reply, the columnist invited "a reader or two" to "add reassurance" from their experience, and the response was far greater than Griggs expected. One remarried mother wrote that she had stayed up past midnight and could not go to sleep without penning her letter to put in the morning mail about her husband, who also had worried before they wed but had been "a wonderful father" to her son from her first marriage as well as to more children from their own marriage. "And believe me," she wrote, "when the boy is in trouble, my husband is the first to stand by him." They had foregone adoption, because her first husband continued to be in contact with his son, although two more remarried mothers wrote with similar admiration for their children's stepfathers who had adopted children from former marriages and were "real dads" with "happy, adjusted families." A stepdaughter, "Girl Graduate," also wrote of her "very nice stepfather who has been wonderful" to her mother and "much more like a father than my real father," but she faced a dilemma for "blended families," because schools and other societal institutions had not adapted to new realities; her high school restricted

---

48   IQG, "Organization Is Great Help to Family With One Parent," *MJ*, June 3, 1968.

tickets to graduation to two parents, and her "real father" wanted to attend. The columnist encouraged her to talk to a teacher about the possibility of another ticket; if not, she counseled the girl to "let your stepfather know how grateful you are to him for his care and devotion." The lead letter in the column devoted to the topic came from a rare male letter writer, a stepfather who happily signed as "Dad"—despite the second marriage also ending in divorce. However, his now-adult stepson, with children of his own, still so addressed him, wrote the writer "honored to be called 'dad' and 'grandpa' by these wonderful people, whom I consider my own." That no letters sampled similarly discussed stepmothers may have reflected another reality: Divorced women, especially with children, were less likely—or less willing—to remarry than were men.[49]

More often, letters came to the columnist from divorced women coping with too-typical emotional and financial costs of single motherhood in poverty and lack of adult companionship. As historian Sara M. Evans writes, many women of the era who had headed from high school into marriage lacked understanding of their "competence" when unpaid, with little preparation for self-sufficiency after divorce, as "few recognized the social and economic vulnerability of their position as housewives."[50] For example, "Lonely Woman," in only her mid-twenties, had five children, had no child support or familial support, and had to move to a new neighborhood.

> It has always been hard for me to make new acquaintances. I am so lonely....
>
> My kindergarten daughter's schoolwork is suffering because I am not happy. I have no money for baby sitters, no friends I can impose upon to babysit.... I haven't a car and it is quite impossible to take five children under 6 on a bus. Cabs are out because of the price. My relatives all live in the east. My in-laws refuse to associate with us.... Have you any suggestions for entertainment, not only for myself but for my children?[51]

---

49 IQG, "Yule Gift Giving Has Become a Real Hardship for Couple," *MJ*, December 4, 1963; IQG, "Readers Say That Stepfathers Often Prove to Be Real Dads," *MJ*, December 17, 1963; IQG, "He Has Two Jobs to Support the Family He Seldom Sees," *MJ*, July 8, 1961; Evans, *Born for Liberty*, 302-303.

50 Evans, *Born for Liberty*, 267.

51 IQG, "Divorcee with Five Children Under 6 Finds Life Lonely," *MJ*, April 11, 1961.

Griggs advised her to not give up on mass transit, suggesting that she avoid rush hours and rely on "many a kindly bus driver" to get her brood to parks or the zoo, where she might meet other mothers. Griggs also advised her to "put male association in the background for the time being," because of her admitted "lack of mature attitudes" that had led to her numerous children; that, in turn, had kept her housebound and lonely, without time and mobility to meet other adults.[52]

The divorcee's story suggested that debate on perceived sexual permissiveness was not restricted to actions only of the young. However, despite a decline in discussion of marital issues and rise in unmarried and younger readers, letters did not return to previous levels on "love" and dating issues at the column's inception as "advice to the lovelorn." Discussion of dating was the focus of less than a fourth of letters sampled in the 1960s. Instead, discussion increased of issues in all other categories, especially family conflict separate from marital concerns. Family conflict had more than doubled as a focus of letters sampled— from 22 percent in the 1930s to an average of 45 percent in the 1940s and 1950s—and increased to more than half, 52 percent, in the 1960s.

Issues with in-laws continued. "How do you cope with an older member of the family who reacts gloomily to every good thing?" asked Griggs in prefacing a letter from a reader who had "reached the end of her patience" with a mother-in-law who disapproved of her son's gift to his wife, the "good thing" being a mink coat. The columnist counseled medical checkups in the case of personality changes but agreed that, based on the writer's long list of incidents for years, her in-law's personality had not altered. Griggs gave similar advice to a young mother who had tolerated a mother-in-law's criticism of the writer's tasty foods and her taste in furnishings but sought help in how to handle medical advice for her children that contradicted their pediatrician. For "Help, Please," the columnist delineated the difference between advice and interference, "as long as there isn't any mistreatment or neglect…. When this isn't the case, outsiders, including relatives … should keep hands off and tongues still." Griggs again gave the same advice to "A Concerned Grandmother" of a widowed daughter-in-law, left alone to raise five children, who occasionally left them with the writer. However, she claimed that the daughter-in-law spent "five nights a week drinking and dancing" and came home "in wee hours of

---

52   Ibid.

the morning," an account greeted with skepticism by Griggs, as the in-law was called upon only occasionally—and could see even less of her grandchildren, if she continued to criticize unverified concerns.[53]

The return to a younger following also was reflected in concerns regarding their entry into the workplace. That girls and young women turned to Griggs on the issue is intriguing, but perhaps she was the sole "career woman" that some knew, since far fewer of their mothers in the 1950s had held aspirations for careers. Work issues tripled to 12 percent of letters sampled in the 1960s, compared to 4 percent or less in previous decades; that is, for the first time, work issues reached the level of at least one in ten letters sampled. Younger writers focused on problems in finding work in a decade when gender bias in workplaces would be outlawed under a new Civil Rights Act but not enforced by a new Equal Employment Opportunity Commission that refused to end sex-segregated "help wanted" advertising that separated job openings for men from those for women. Media on the news side led by the *New York Times* also belittled the law for gender equality. Closer to home, in the city that was the center of employment in the state, the *Journal* rebuffed the respected leader of the state commission on the status of women and NOW founder Kay Clarenbach, when she requested that the newspaper follow a federal recommendation to end sex-segregated listings. She turned to the *Sentinel* to state that "one big newspaper in this city has said that over its dead body would it change the format on classified advertising," although both papers followed corporate policy. To Clarenbach and others, the Journal Company replied—with a revealing pronoun usage—that it was "up to the advertiser if he wants to discriminate." Not for another decade, and only after many others in the press did so, would the Milwaukee newspapers abide by federal recommendations to finally end sex-segregated job listings. The *Milwaukee Journal* had felt little pressure in its market, where most women still held "low-paid, low-status jobs," writes Evans, so they could not "identify with clear-cut dilemmas" of college-educated women seeking careers in a "gender-segregated economy.... Even

---

53   IQG, "Husband Gave Her Mink Coat; Mother-in-Law Gives Scowls," *MJ*, January 12, 1961; IQG, "Young Mother Says In-Laws Give Advice on 'Do It!' Basis," *MJ*, November 29, 1963.

younger women preparing for professional vocations found themselves caught" in the aftermath of the 1950s culture.[54]

Girls aspiring to traditional, feminized professions also faced obstacles. Twins together penned a letter as "The Look-Alikes," who volunteered as hospital "candy-stripers" in hope of careers as nurses' aides, whom the girls had admired, after enduring bedridden years owing to health problems that imperiled their high school diplomas. In an empathic reply, Griggs hoped that they would avoid overwork and "try to keep well." Their letter and one from a motherless girl recovering from rheumatic fever, enduring an extended hospital stay "in the same old room for weeks," elicited encouragement and advice from many readers, who wrote of overcoming health conditions and homebound years. For readers with disabilities, the discussion provided a visibility that rarely was evident in media of the era. For a reader with dwarfism seeking friends, Griggs had research at the ready on organizations offering social activities and assistance for employment, especially extolling "Little People of America" and its local founder. A Milwaukee schoolteacher of lesser height but large ability, she also was past president of a local Business and Professional Women's Club chapter, had a children's radio show, and was "proof that size doesn't limit a person's ambition, success, or accomplishments," Griggs wrote.[55]

Not to slight her readers of greater height, when a tall teenaged girl wrote of few dancing partners, Griggs gladly publicized a "Toppers" group. For readers such as "Popular But Tubby," she promoted "TOPS (Take Off Pounds Sensibly)." All were indicative of increasing, unhealthy concern with self-image, especially among girls. Griggs and her readers addressed the problem in other columns, well before medical practitioners and other media warned of bulimia, anorexia, and

---

54   Marian McBride, "Mothers Limited by Law," *MS*, November 9, 1967; Evans, *Born for Liberty*, 274-277. Marian McBride was the mother of a co-author of this study.

55   IQG, "Twins Want to Finish School, Find Obstacles in Their Way," *MJ*, November 23, 1963; IQG, "Faced With Long Stay in Bed, Girl Thinks She'll Go Crazy," *MJ*, November 25, 1963; IQG, "'Going Crazy in Bed' Gets Tips From Readers Long Bedridden," *MJ*, December 9, 1963; IQG, "Husband Admits His Faults, Wants to Avoid a Divorce," *MJ*, August 14, 1967; IQG, "14-Year-Old Fears Being Called 'Ice Cube' If She Obeys Mother," *MJ*, October 28, 1963; IQG, "Short Folks, This Is for You: 'Little People of America, Inc.,'" *MJ*, November 27, 1963.

similar syndromes. Others with invisible disabilities also faced discrimination. A mother wrote of her "strong and husky" son with epilepsy, seizure-free for years yet still facing hurdles in hiring in the "big, warm city" of Milwaukee. Griggs gave a referral to an organization for people with epilepsy and welcomed responses from readers willing to give him work.[56]

The motherless twin girls, however, faced a greater obstacle to their education: their father. Owing to hospitalizations, the seventeen-year-olds still were high school sophomores. They wanted to stay in school, but their father refused to support them past their next birthday, because he did not "believe it's necessary for girls to finish high school so isn't inclined to help us any more than he has to," they wrote. "We are ambitious, but there seem to be so many things in the way.... We do want to finish high school very badly," they wrote, so had sought part-time work but found no openings. In addition to her usual encouragement about overcoming "obstacles that seemed insurmountable," Griggs gave a rare glimpse into her childhood, when an immigrant classmate had "braved a class of six-year-olds" to learn English and eventually had earned a college degree. Her reminiscence from the 1890s actually was apt in the 1960s, with Wisconsin's influx of immigrants and migrants into a bustling *barrio* in her city and surrounding agricultural areas. With the example of her classmate's "courage," "determination," and route to success, she recommended agencies and resources for tutoring "to get ahead faster" in school.[57]

Not a word was addressed to the father who was against girls graduating even only from high school, but Griggs' disapproval was evident, and her emphasis on gaining an education was familiar to her readers—including dozens who self-identified as students in letters in the 1960s, a sign of changing opportunities for women. A significant

---

56   IQG, "Girl's Behavior Cheapens Her, She's Concerned About Future," *MJ*, December 2, 1963; IQG, "Graduate's Parents Rewarded for Their Love and Sacrifice," *MJ*, June 6, 1966; IQG, "Fat Wife Blames Her Figure, Garbage Pile-up on Husband," *MJ*, June 9, 1966; John S. Clogston, "Disability Coverage in American Newspapers," pp. 45-58 in Jack A. Nelson, ed., *The Disabled, the Media and the Information Age* (Westport, Conn.: Greenwood Press, 1994).

57   IQG, "Twins Want to Finish;" Thompson, *History of Wisconsin*, 246-247; Rodriguez, et al., *Nuestro Milwaukee*, 6-7.

increase in women college students still was a decade away nationwide, and yet another decade away in Wisconsin. However, in the columns sampled in the 1960s, of more than fifty letter writers who self-identified as working, nonworking, or as students, almost half—47.1 percent—now were students, compared to less than a fifth of letter writers who had self-identified similar statuses in the previous decade. That more young women planned not just on jobs until marriage but on careers, so were staying in school and college, affected their living arrangements—and those of their parents—in the decade when the phrase "generation gap" became commonplace in public discourse. That the 1950s had been anomalous in lower levels of women's education and of those living with parents also was evident in the column. Almost two-thirds of letter writers then who had identified residential status had not been living with their parents, not only because they had been an older cohort of writers to the column but also because women had married at a younger age than in the 1960s.

In comparison, in the 1960s, at least six in ten young writers of the letters sampled were living with their parents, an increase again to almost as many as the seven in ten who had done so in the 1940s. However, some still were leaving home too soon, like runaways described in letters about family conflicts in the 1960s. One came from a "Distracted Mother" followed by a letter from another mother with a missing daughter. The second was divorced, but the first also had raised her children alone, for reasons unstated, and the daughter "had grown up fast" in helping with a sibling. In retribution, she repeatedly ran away from home, determined to "hurt" her mother worried past "distraction" that her daughter was only hurting herself. Griggs agreed and addressed the girl directly to "get in touch.... You evidently have some faith in me. Tell me about your troubles so I can help you. Added suggestion: Getting out on your own and working isn't as easy as it sounds. It can be pretty tough if a girl hasn't finished high school."[58]

As more girls did earn high school degrees in Wisconsin, their earnings allowed them to leave home. "Among the young women who did not continue beyond high school," writes Wisconsin historian William

---

58   IQG, "Distracted Mother Wants Her Girl, 16, to Come Home," *MJ*, December 10, 1963; IQG, "Errant Spouse Cured as Wife Opened Mouth, Put Foot Down," *MJ*, January 2, 1964; Thompson, *History of Wisconsin*, 249.

F. Thompson, "many delayed marriage in order to take advantage of the greater number of employment opportunities open to women," at last, as of the late 1960s, although their earnings rose only slowly. "Popular stereotypes notwithstanding," he writes, most households of singles in the state "were not composed largely of students, divorced persons, or unmarried couples living together"—"living in sin," as some parents put it. Instead, most were older widows like Griggs, as women were living longer and "less likely than men to remarry after divorce or the death of their spouses." Again like Griggs, a majority of "both the young and old singles lived alone," he writes. However, more than before were young workers, especially the single women by the late 1960s who "felt more free and able than they had in the 1940s and 1950s to live apart from their families, either alone or with other single men and women." Few conflicts with roommates arose in letters to the column, compared to conflicts within families.[59]

As reflected in readers' letters, Wisconsin's college campuses witnessed more women students in the 1960s, although the greatest growth in their numbers remained ahead. The state rate actually lagged behind the nation, despite a doubling in the number of undergraduate women within a decade by 1963. Their numbers would double again in the next dozen years, leading to almost tripling of the proportion of women in graduate and professional schools in the state, writes Thompson. Examples in the column included "J.," a college student elsewhere in the Midwest in the mid-1960s, who wrote home to Griggs about a goal of going on to graduate school to be a veterinarian. Few women students found role models on campuses in the professoriate, however, even in the late 1960s, when some women faculty in Wisconsin would face denial of tenure for volunteering to take on teaching overloads to offer the first courses in women's studies in the state. To fill the faculty gap, students also offered noncredit courses, although one would recall that her campus women's organizations found more interest in finding models for bridal shows.[60]

Women college students' letters also were likely to focus on campus social life, although often revealing of larger issues in transitional

---

59   Thompson, *History of Wisconsin*, 250.

60   Ibid., 251; IQG, "Girl Blasts Former Friend, Calls Her Show-Off and Flirt," *MJ*, April 13, 1965; McBride, *Women's Wisconsin*, 441; UW, *Transforming Women's Education*, 69-79.

times. "A Concerned Coed" asked, "do all college boys have liberal ideas on sex?" As "A Concerned Ed" replied: "Yes, they do." He defended his gender, however, as seeking more than sexual relationships and advised her to "get your message across tactfully from the start," although admitting that a man "may get so mad that he couldn't care less about certain girls' ideas. He may be so upset, he will not believe you," which was the predicament of "A Concerned Coed" and the point of her letter. "A Male Student" from the state university at Madison doubted her in a "slight defense" of his gender that slighted "A Concerned Coed," blaming her for "doing something to encourage" her dilemma, despite her statement to the contrary. A similar message came in an arrogant missive from "A Right Guy," who had read "with amusement" the letter from "A Concerned Coed." He gave his credentials for giving her advice as a claimed respect for "cute little coeds who are really fun to be with" and asked "A Concerned Coed" if she was "asking for the treatment" that she received. "That is, do you appear with too short, too tight clothes, ratted hair, extreme makeup, and puffing away at a cigaret?" Or, worse, was she "pushy"? One male correspondent admitted concern for the "coed" but could offer no advice, so he closed with hope that "perhaps Mrs. Griggs can help with this." As for the columnist, she hoped that other male respondents were not "a representative poll." Griggs stated as a "certainty" that "girls don't want boys to date them for what they can get out of them" and advised finding "ways on a campus for finding out the personality and character of a boy or girl." The advice column was not the way, as Griggs advised "A Right Guy" for closing his letter with the offer of a date with "A Concerned Coed." The column's "rigid policy" was to not serve as a dating service, Griggs reiterated in her standard statement, and stated more sternly in his case.[61]

Yet throughout the 1960s, as younger readers wrote of aspirations for college and careers, the column may have served as a reminder of realities in a transitional time for women, among them older wage-earners who waged again an ongoing debate with "stay-at-home moms." A "Working Mother" wrote of her suburban family's need for a second income for a second car. She unleashed many letters from the likes of "Mother Paid With Love, Not Money"—not that they did not want to

---

61   IQG, "A Concerned Coed's Letter Really Riles Male Students," *MJ*, June 2, 1966.

work, as most wrote that they stayed home for lack of good child care. The mother unpaid for her work at home, a Phi Beta Kappa college graduate, had left behind a career not when she became a mother but, she wrote, when she became weary of unsuitable sitters. "Nonworking Mom" echoed the concern, as did "A Mother Who Is Mad," who had resisted her husband's requests—he "needled constantly" on financial needs—that she return to work. She had refused and now called on other readers as "mothers of the world" to "take heed! Quit your jobs" to "solve the delinquency problem." She blithely wrote of re-entering the job market when her children were grown, despite repeated cautions from the columnist and readers regarding difficulties faced by increasing numbers of displaced homemakers with outdated skills.[62]

"Stay-at-home" letter writers who lamented the lack of reliable child care in the era and area lacked ability or will to link their individual experiences to larger societal needs to improve work opportunities for women. "Gail" wrote of a rare employer providing child care, a school bus company offering the benefit to attract mothers seeking work—if part-time—but unable to do so "because of baby sitter problems." As "Educated to Help Others, But Not Myself" wrote, "What can I do? I have children." She needed another paycheck, as her husband was "a big shot to all the barflies" and would "buy groceries for every woman he meets but his wife.... A man must have rocks in his head to behave like this after many years of married life," she wrote, but she lacked child care to find work. Griggs recommended her roster of employment agencies, but telling of the times was that none offered assistance in obtaining reliable, affordable child care.[63]

Another writer, "Same As 'Educated to Help Others,'" was atypical in having held a high-level position with a higher income than had her husband—indeed, her four husbands. The last of the lot, however, "was not satisfied until I quit and stayed home to look after him," she wrote. Now, she had "no income, no job," and sought work as well as child care. "I learned too late, after four marriages, that it's hell on earth if you don't pamper a husband's precious ego" and out-earn him,

---

62   IQG, "Motherhood's Satisfactions Outweigh Career for Her," *MJ*, April 12, 1968.

63   IQG, "Three Sisters Have Problems: Their Mates Drink Too Much," *MJ*, November 30, 1963; IQG, "Sassy Son Troubles Mom, Is a Slap the Right Answer?" *MJ*, August 29, 1967.

she wrote. Griggs could recommend an agency to assist in finding child care but could not resist observing that her reader had "evidently picked the same type four times.... If you do cast an eye around for a fifth mate, look long and carefully," she wrote, reassuring her that "all men are not like this." Too many men in the era, however, held to a medieval view of husbands' control of wives and their wages. Feminists' campaign to revise marital property rights laws remained decades away from their first success, which they would win in Wisconsin.[64]

More typical was the letter from "What Am I?" about a two-income family's finances, in which her income was less than that of her husband. As historian William F. Thompson writes, gendered pay disparity was among reasons that, "for more and more mothers"—although still a minority in the 1960s—"suburban life had its discontents," because married women often lacked geographic mobility, and suburbs offered fewer work opportunities and lower pay. "As their children grew older and required less of their time and energy, some women began looking for activities more personally satisfying" in the 1960s, he writes. "More married women ... became interested in finding jobs to help pay for vacations or college education for their children, or to resume jobs and careers that had been interrupted when they married and began their families." However, he writes, "most women looking for jobs found fewer opportunities in the suburbs than in the central cities"—in part owing to loss of mass transit in metropolitan Milwaukee, with the demise of "interurban" electric train lines in and out of the city in the 1950s—with the result of a surfeit of suburban women seeking work and finding lesser wages, if they could find work.[65]

"What Am I?" was a mother of four earning four hundred dollars a month, while her husband earned half again that amount. Yet he squandered her income as well as his own, which had led to unpaid bills and to her "nerves," including fear of further pregnancies. He "used the weapons of sex and money," Griggs wrote in a reply that was unusually straightforward, owing to the columnist's outrage at the husband's further demand that his wife pay him for "babysitting ... for an hour or so with the children," refusing to recognize parental responsibility as well as partnership in marriage. Neither the writer nor the

---

64   IQG, "Parents Work, Dad Wants Pay to Sit With Their 4 Children," *MJ*, July 12, 1965.

65   Thompson, *History of Wisconsin*, 231-232.

columnist argued against the commonplace usage then of "babysitting" for fathers' care of children, a term never used for mothers' care. Griggs focused first not on marital finances but on her reader's immediate need to ease "nerves" by taking control of marital sex. "Fear of another baby," wrote Griggs, "must be terrifying to visualize" with "a man who puts himself before payment of bills" and recommended her usual roster of family financial planning agencies—and family planning, with the address of a Planned Parenthood clinic downtown on Milwaukee's main street, decades prior to protests that would close clinics across Wisconsin. Indeed, in her era, Griggs freely publicized Planned Parenthood appeals for volunteers to assist in lowering costs for "this much-needed service to women."[66]

Another husband felt that he owned his wife's wages to spend as he wished, even on vacations on his own. After "Mrs. H." had lost her job, "Mr. H." and the law saw her checks for unemployment—from her earnings, banked in a state fund—as, like her paychecks, his property.

> I have worked for 12 years outside my home. I've done all the housework besides, with no help from my husband. He has insisted that I turn over the greater portion of my money for upkeep of the home, allowing me no voice in spending it. He has never once been appreciative.... He has badgered and harassed me, telling me what a terrible cook, housekeeper, and budgeter I was.... I'm beginning to think I can live without him.
>
> He goes to Florida twice a year, and if I can't go, "it's just too bad," he says. He is close-fisted at home, but with everyone else, the sky is the limit. He makes enough to support the family without me working but spends so much in taverns [that] I should give him my unemployment checks? Not while I have my right mind. He plans to go to Florida....
>
> Let him go! I'll hang onto my checks. If he tries to grab them away from me, I'll see that he gets his walking papers with a divorce

---

66   Ibid.; IQG, "Yule Gift Giving Has Become a Real Hardship for Couple," *MJ*, December 4, 1963. Wisconsin's landmark marital property law, passed in 1984, took effect in 1986; see McBride, *Women's Wisconsin*, 449, and Catherine B. Cleary, "Married Property Rights in Wisconsin, 1846-1972," *Wisconsin Magazine of History* 78:2 (Winter 1994-95), 110-137.

action. I'm tired of being a servant who must finance my 'boss's' vacations and take his abuse. I am past 50, and I am tired.[67]

Griggs replied that a wife was not "required to give unemployment checks to her husband so that he can enjoy Florida vacations! Keep your checks"—in part to prepare for life on her own. The columnist recommended agencies to help to "get all the figures together," "give you some facts to counter your husband's claims," and protect her own funds from him and his wastrel ways.[68]

Complaints of time in taverns, a constant in the column and in Wisconsin, also came from sisters headed for divorce and signing their letter "We've Had It!" Published in the same year as *The Feminine Mystique*, their letter indicated increasing frustration of wives of alcoholics with "double burdens" of housework and the workplace but also their increasing assertiveness.

> This column has been much discussed in our family of three sisters. For each of us, marriage is at a breaking point. Why? ... The older [our husbands] get, the worse they act. All are drinkers who are out at least four nights out of seven. They cannot afford these toots. The young children ... go without necessities, and this includes proper food, because 'dear father' drinks up many dollars that should go for groceries.

One sister, especially, wrote of her situation after decades of marriage to an alcoholic husband.

> I have worked nearly all of my 21 years of marriage, paying the bills ... because of [his] drinking. I am 40 now, tired and nervous.... I work, come home, walk in the door and work some more, until I fall into bed. I cook meals, bake, clean and mend. I ... finagle to buy groceries and pay all medical and dental bills.
>
> Every payday, "father" gives me just so much out of his check. It's never enough.... He plunks in a chair as soon as he gets home ... then goes out and gets drunk. I would like to know what there is in it for a woman who is exhausted and disgusted.... Nothing works. I left my husband once and started divorce, but that didn't scare him.
>
> I don't like divorce but feel I may have to go through with it or I will end up in a mental institution.[69]

---

67   IQG, "Man Demands Spouse's Checks for His Vacation in Southland," *MJ*, December 6, 1963.

68   Ibid.

69   IQG, "Three Sisters."

The letter reverted to a collective voice in the conclusion that "our men drink too much but deny they are alcoholics. They say we are the ones at fault but won't consult marriage counselors. So what to do?" Griggs replied in straightforward terms about a husband and father who "drinks up the groceries": "Buy food for yourself and the children, but don't buy any for him" and save any earnings, in anticipation of divorce. "If he wants to eat well, he will have to provide the money. Ditto for your sisters' husbands! It might get through to them that their wives mean business."[70]

Another writer had lost her business owing to her alcoholic husband's debts that left them "penniless," but that was not the worst that had led her to leave. She had become pregnant, but "there was so much mental cruelty that I lost the baby," she wrote. She also had lost a daughter sent to a relative for her safety, after the husband had "trouble with the law," landed in jail, but had not "given up his jaunts in saloons," where he acted like a "teen age Romeo"—although he was "a gray-haired, balding coot." She had left at last, but he begged for her return. Griggs told her to only "try life with him again" after he had, "for a length of time ... lived a sober life."[71]

As ever, Griggs gave a referral to Alcoholics Anonymous as well as Al-Anon for families of alcoholics, as she did for "A Drunk for a Father," another girl in danger of domestic violence.

> I must talk to someone about our family problem. My father is a drunk. Every weekend he goes out and gets terribly drunk. He doesn't become happy ... like some drunks, but mean.
>
> His meanness even sent my mother to the hospital. He doesn't work much, so my mother has to support the four of us children. This really means she supports six....
>
> Maybe he'll bring home $10 a week on the average. My mother can't take it much longer. Will you please tell me where she can get help so we will be rid of him? She tried to divorce him once.... If he could even be sent to jail, it would help.
>
> He doesn't treat us kids right, isn't even half a father.... Isn't there some law?[72]

---

70 Ibid.

71 IQG, "Wife Says Her 'Balding Coot' Acts Like a 'Teen Age Romeo,'" *MJ*, November 28, 1963.

72 IQG, "Tenants Lack Responsibility, Discouraged Landlord Insists," *MJ*, December 5, 1964.

Griggs reiterated her advice to "tell mother to talk to the district attorney's office" but, tellingly of the times, her reply was not heartening. She did not suggest that abuse so severe as to cause her mothers' hospitalization would merit the full force of the law, prior to the modern women's movement's later work for enforcement of domestic violence laws. A "habitual drunk"—a legal term that Griggs used repeatedly, deliberately, and carefully—could be convicted "under the Huber law, staying in jail nights and working days to earn money to be given to the family." She had to hedge even on that hope, however, as enforcement "would depend on circumstances."[73]

Letters also suggest an increase in women alcoholics, less likely than were men to find effective treatment. Some attempted to hide alcoholism in an affront to a caffeinated ritual to Wisconsinites that caused a series of letters on suburban life. A reader reported that women in her suburb gathered in "spiked kaffeeklatsches," as soon "as their husbands leave for work." Other readers wrote in outraged denial of such despicable behavior in the suburbs, attempting to deflect discussion to a defense of the allegedly "awful suburban hausfraus." One penned a paean to the pastoral life in the suburbs, where women "kept too busy" to drink—if only owing to their need to drive their children to activities, when not babysitting others' children. The writer finally admitted that "there may be a few drinking mamas" in their up-to-date kitchens or even drinking and driving out of the ubiquitous cul de sacs of suburban road designs. Another truthteller wrote about a neighbor who "can't get out of bed to face the day without her tranquilizer" in the "little paradise" of "ideal living," because "wrongdoing housewives in our wonderful suburbs" soon succumbed to "a lot of pressure" for conformity and "worry more about trying to fit in the same groove as the neighbors"—but most were "more interested in milk bottles than beer bottles."[74]

Others hoped that readers of the column would recognize themselves in horrific accounts of alcoholism. "A Heartsick Relative" wrote of a reader's worsening behavior, writing to Griggs that the woman "reads your column as soon as the paper arrives. Maybe if she sees this

---

73   Ibid.

74   IQG, "Wives in Suburbia Spike Talk About Spiked Kaffeeklatsches," *MJ*, July 21, 1964.

in print, it will hit home, making her think" of her impact upon her children and others in the family.[75]

> She has been tagged by all who knew her as a habitual drunk. Her fine husband and children never know what to expect when they return home each day. Her drinking changes her into a raving, insulting maniac.... At holiday time, it is more of a problem.... You may suggest not offering her a drink, Mrs. Griggs....
>
> She has entered our home at noon, already drunk.... We also cannot eliminate her, because of her three children. They look forward to being with their cousins, aunts, and uncles.... But when one walks in half-stewed, what can we do?[76]

Relatives had met about seeking medical treatment, but her husband had resisted "and told us to mind our own business." The writer appealed to Griggs as "the last resort" to reach her reader.

> Maybe you can say something to make her pull herself together. Something has to be said so that she will start realizing why the family has canceled some birthday and anniversary celebrations in the last few years, why neighbors have stopped coming in for coffee, why her young ones seldom ask to bring friends home. You are the last resort.[77]

Griggs agreed that the relatives could not allow an alcoholic to ruin the traditional "get-together" that could be "blessed" for family life "but it can be a nightmare if one drinks too much" and was "inflicted on the gatherings." She suggested separate events for the children and their cousins. She also directly addressed the husband with referrals, but Griggs gave the greater part of her reply with a referral for the wife, her reader, to contact a counselor at Alcoholics Anonymous.[78]

A relative of another alcoholic mother worried about abuse of her youngsters, wondering "what can be done to help the children before it is too late?" in an appeal to Griggs and readers.

---

75   IQG, "Three Sisters;" IQG, "Dad's in Jail, Mother Drinks; Girl, 15, Considers Suicide," *MJ*, August 18, 1964; IQG, "Family Gatherings Imperiled by Woman, a 'Habitual Drunk,'" *MJ*, December 19, 1963.

76   IQG, "Family Gatherings Imperiled."

77   Ibid.

78   Ibid.

She has a serious problem. Maybe if she reads this, she will collect her senses.... She is a heavy drinker, likes her freedom. She doesn't look after her children.... [The baby] hasn't developed because her mother pins the sheets about [her] to keep her in bed....

We dropped in for an unexpected visit and found the oldest child home alone. The front door was unlocked. The television was on.... She never did come home while we were there. We checked with neighbors, and no one knew of her whereabouts.

This has happened other times.... I know this is not a healthy at-mosphere.... She and her husband fight a lot, and I think she takes out her anger on the children.[79]

In a strongly worded reply, Griggs stressed that it was "important to get immediate help for these two innocents." If the father would not act, her "humane, conscientious" reader had a duty as a "concerned adult relative" to contact the county protective services unit. "The chil-dren can be helped," she wrote, as could the couple in marital counsel-ing—and the mother with treatment.[80]

In the 1960s, research and treatment in alcoholism rarely served women well, owing to continued assumptions that all addicts were male, despite evidence in popular culture such as the increasing in-cidence in advice columns of letters on women's "drinking problems." Historian Lori Rotskoff writes that feminists eventually would ad-dress alcoholism but, like foremothers in the earlier women's move-ment, would tie drinking to domestic violence with women as victims rather than as alcoholics and abusers. As for substance abuse, histori-an Michelle Lee McClellan writes that refusal to recognize "lady lush-es" included the American Medical Association, which "denied that drinking during pregnancy posed any danger." Even if correctly diag-nosed, women "faced tensions and contradictions as they sought treat-ment" tailored to "a predominantly 'male' disease," she writes. More of-ten, they were misdiagnosed, especially the "'respectable' middle-class housewife who drank at home" and was treated with medications that only added another addiction. As for wives of alcoholic men, they were advised to "exhibit patience" with partners and sublimate their lives to support alcoholic spouses, emotionally and financially, according to Rotskoff. Regarding Al-Anon, an organization primarily for families

79   IQG, "She Knocks."

80   Ibid.

of alcoholics, she writes that "throughout the 1960s ... the primary focus remained the same: to help women cope with the challenge of living with an alcoholic spouse" in "marriages based on traditional gender roles." Al-Anon aimed "to minimize the legitimacy of women's anger" with their lives, but in the 1960s, they "began to apply aspects of the emerging feminist critique" to their lives and to the alcoholism that made their families dysfunctional. As a result, Al-Anon would "encourage members to assert more autonomy in their marriages"— but not until well into the next decade.[81]

For most women, the potential for impact of feminism on many aspects of life remained only a promise that would not come soon enough in the 1960s. Many of Griggs' readers may have been unaware of the modern women's movement during that decade, despite involvement of local leaders in national organizations, owing to little media coverage of their cause compared to other movements. In 1966, in the same year as the founding of NOW, African Americans escalated civil rights activities in Milwaukee. In 1967, after nightly marches for months, the city's "inner core" erupted in riots that began with an incident near the Journal—and Griggs' residence—in an area soon under a curfew with call-up of National Guard troops for armed patrols. However, her column was on hiatus, and Griggs was on vacation, in worrisome weeks for Milwaukeeans. Even when the column was not on hiatus, direct reference rarely was made to news events, not the purpose of the back page of the paper, in the view of Griggs and her readers, as their letters set the agenda of the column. They focused more on societal issues and not as much on the "news," which is defined as event-oriented and was the focus of the front page.[82]

Not until the end of the decade did women's news move to the front page, if only for a day, as women created events to win attention to their issues. As a result, "the new movement suddenly gained visibility," as historian Sara M. Evans writes. NOW called on women in 1970 to

---

81   Rotskoff, Love on the Rocks, 240; Michelle Lee McClellan, "'Lady Lushes': Women Alcoholics in American Society, 1880-1960" (Ph.D. diss., Stanford University, 2000), 164, 228.

82   Gurda, Making of Milwaukee, 371; "National Guardsmen Patrol Area Where Riot Erupted," MJ, July 31, 1967. The column was on hiatus from July 24 to August 15, as marches resumed, and in early September; see "On Vacation," MJ, July 24, 1967, and September 4, 1967.

mark the fiftieth anniversary of the Nineteenth Amendment for woman suffrage—and demand action on the Equal Rights Amendment that had languished in Congress for almost fifty years—by marching out of their homes and other workplaces for massive marches in streets nationwide. Response was overwhelming even to the organizers, and the movement at last won coverage on every television network, in major news magazines, and even on the front page of the *New York Times*. "Thousands of women marched and demonstrated in cities across the country," writes Evans, "some of them taking a stand for the first times in their lives," even some in small towns across Wisconsin and the Midwest as well as Milwaukee and every major city in the country.[83]

In the *Milwaukee Journal*, the women's movement finally made the top of the front page, if reporting "mixed support" from both women and men mocking the event in 1970. The news story in the *Journal* found that "few women actually walked off the job either at home or in the thousands of offices where they answer the telephone, type the letters and keep the files in order," with no mention of less stereotypical work and workplaces. The woman reporter may have been responsible for a subtle reference to the unpaid work of housewives at home as work, if the extent to which her work survived her editors' copy pencils cannot be known. Other than mention of a few "demonstrations," including one downtown by a handful of women costumed as housewives, pregnant brides, and "Playboy 'bunnies,'" the story also omitted reporting that a contingent of women activists also had marched that day on the *Milwaukee Journal* itself.[84]

Inside the main news section, the *Journal* did print "demands of the Milwaukee Women's Strike Day Committee," including many issues that had arisen in readers' discussions in Griggs' column: equality in education and employment, accessible and affordable child care, prevention of domestic violence, and more. The women especially called on the Journal Company "media complex" to refuse "ads that degrade women's bodies to sell products," to end its sex-segregated "separate want ads," and to "stop stories that trivialize women" as well as

---

83   Evans, *Born for Liberty*, 288; "Bringing Feminism to Business," *MJ*, May 8, 1985.

84   Jo Sandin, "Women's Strike Day Gets Mixed Support," *MJ*, August 26, 1970. The account of the march at the *Journal* is based on observation—and participation—of a co-author.

"cheesecake photos." That day's *Journal*, however, included not only the front-page story trivializing the nationwide event but also an opportunistic, full-page ad promoting beauty products by calling on women to "Liberate the Way You Look," as "Beauty Is Every Woman's Right," pages of sex-segregated "want ads"—and a staple of the "Green Sheet": a "cheesecake photo" of bathing beauties.[85]

The demands concluded with a declaration of support for the ERA but warned that its passage into law would not again let women be "lulled into complacency." On the back page of the newspaper that day, Griggs' readers hardly were complacent, but their concerns underscored the feminist concern for over-emphasis on women's appearance. A wife worried that she had not kept up her looks to keep her husband, while another reader looked askance—and apparently could not help but keep looking—at the appearance and activities of "sick suburbanites" with "free sex ideas" allegedly exhibited in "love-in gatherings" in the city's working-class suburbs on the South Side. Griggs, while agreeing in general on the "bad taste" and "stupid behavior," doubted that her reader was "a regular witness of 'love-ins' and wrongdoing" and requested information as to whether her reader had easily viewed events from her windows, after "waiting for the show to begin … in someone else's backyard," or perhaps had required a telescope.[86]

Winning visibility for women's issues would continue to prove difficult in the decades ahead. Other movements would make more progress, and more movements would arise. Some were signaled in Milwaukee women's "demands," which were not observed in sampled letters sent to Griggs, such as gay rights. Some issues soon to emerge on the societal agenda, however, had not been noted in the "demands" but had been discussed in the column, such as the rights of people with disabilities. Foremost at the end of the decade was the antiwar movement. The longest war in the country's history continued to escalate in Vietnam, as did the "war at home," where killings of students by troops caused massive protests that closed hundreds of campuses in 1970. As a fourteen-year-old had written to Griggs only months before in a prescient letter, that her parents hit her in arguments was not winning her agreement any more than did "violence on campuses,"

---

85   "Demands Detailed by Women Strikers," *MJ*, August 26, 1970.

86   IQG, "Wife Eats Her Heart Out Over Mate's Lunch Dates," *MJ*, August 26, 1970.

because "our minds aren't going to be changed by hitting us. To stop us, we'd have to be beat to a pulp," as were campus protesters. But they would prevail, because "fighting isn't the answer," she wrote. "Maybe discussion is better." Griggs, who had given that counsel in some-times-volatile discussion in her column for decades, could only agree.[87]

She also often had counseled that, if words failed, a resort to ac-tion could be required for resolution for women's progress. Feminists' fight for equal rights competed for coverage in the Journal with the aftermath of tragic events in the antiwar movement in Wisconsin, where typical rhetoric of the time—"strikes," "demands," and "demon-strations"—may not have resonated well with many readers after a wearying, worrying decade of news not only of war but also of the assassinations of a president and other political leaders, fatal racial ri-ots in Milwaukee and other cities, antiwar unrest on campuses, and headlines that had shocked the state only days before: The story on feminists' "strike" shared the front page of the Milwaukee Journal with a story on a student killed in a bombing of Sterling Hall at the state campus in Madison by antiwar activists. His son and daughters were fatherless, as were thousands of children after years of war.[88]

A shared sense of loss increasingly was evident in letters as the long decade ended at last. "Lonely," who also was fatherless, and whose mother had to work fulltime, wrote of missing his brother serving in Vietnam, as was the fiancé of "L.P." Also lonely, she kept busy with work and night classes but turned to Griggs and her readers for advice on "how to remain cheerful" with worsening war news at the end of the decade, which was "devastating," she wrote—as it was for families of more than fifty thousand Wisconsin men and women who would serve in the longest war. Their words of longing also would be evi-dence that the losses of war were among the continuities across the decades in women's lives and in their letters to "Dear Mrs. Griggs."[89]

---

87   IQG, "Use of Brute Force."

88   "Police and FBI Question Youths in Bombing at UW," MJ, August 26, 1970.

89   IQG, "Sharp Words End Romance But Pride Is the Big Pain," MJ, October 13, 1969; IQG, "Teenage Girl Wants Out, Can't Ever Please Mother," MJ, January 3, 1970; Kenneth B. Black, "Foreword," xiii, in Sarah A. Larsen and Jennifer M. Miller, Wisconsin Vietnam War Stories: Our Veterans Remember (Madison: Wisconsin Historical Society, 2010).

6

The Modern Women's Movement and Writing on Their Rights, 1971-1980

As the decade of the 1970s opened, and the *Milwaukee Journal* filled front pages almost daily with news of politicians' increasingly opposing views of the Vietnam War as well as news of the "war at home" by antiwar protesters, women readers wrote on the back page of the newspaper about their varying experiences of the war, with stories of its impact on their lives. The repetitive reportage in the news section on battle after battle echoed in the last section, the "Green Sheet," not only in the revived *Milwaukee Journal* column called "Dear Joe: Your Letter from Home" but also in the column that had endured for decades, "Dear Mrs. Griggs." Both had brought comfort to families of military from Milwaukee and across Wisconsin in World War II. The content of both columns often would recall the past for older readers in the 1970s, another decade of societal change and political chaos, when little else in their lives would seem the same.

Readers' letters about the war in Vietnam would be reminiscent of those in past, and often almost identical in wording, as in a debate in "Dear Mrs. Griggs" about "Dear John" letters from home to troops overseas. "Just a Concerned Mother" earned a scolding from Griggs and scorn from readers for "carrying ugly tales," as one wrote regarding rumors that a military wife in Milwaukee had been unfaithful. "Mrs. Griggs: May I be one of the first to applaud you for your reply," wrote "Here's Hoping," because "when the mother wrote her son about rumors she had heard, she undoubtedly lowered his morale. And in the war zone is where a young man's morale needs to be kept high. The man in Vietnam is in a fighting area. Writing him stupid letters … could be the last straw." Others concurred and also consoled the young

wife, as the letter suggested that jealousy of her may have motivated
her mother-in-law. More fortunate in her new family was "Anna H.," a
Vietnamese war bride in her "wonderful adopted country." She missed
her homeland, however, as did other "newcomers" from her country
who had married into Milwaukee families, she wrote. She hoped to
establish a "war brides club," which Griggs gladly agreed to promote in
her column to help to make the women welcome in Milwaukee.[1]

More than ever before, Griggs and her readers would turn their
column to promotion of a plethora of clubs: "Y-Pals" for "friendless
teens" to "Half Notes" for the more musically inclined to entertain elderly neighbors; "Mobile Wheels" and other organizations providing
services for the aged; the perennial "People Without Partners" that
would, by the end of the decade, reach out to readers among increasing
numbers of the divorced in the 1970s. These and many more groups
mentioned apparently grew greatly in the era, as evidenced in columns
sampled in this analysis. The growth in "associational memberships" in
the era also would be gauged by political scientist Robert D. Putnam
in a groundbreaking book published decades later, *Bowling Alone*. The
sport long had crossed race, gender, and class lines in the city, where
local union organizers had forced the American Bowling Congress to
end "white males only" rules decades before, only increasing its popularity and making metropolitan Milwaukee among top markets for
the "reality television" of the day, "Bowling for Dollars," in its 1970s
heyday. By then, fans or "pin pals" in the Milwaukee market even supported two competing bowling shows; one would remain on the air
after the show ended elsewhere, as bowling lanes spread to suburbs to
maintain market size despite a decline in the city's population during
the decade to come, the first decline for the city in more than a century. Deindustrialization swept the Midwest, spreading the seeds of an
economic decline as well, soon seen in Milwaukee and similar cities in
a region dubbed the "Rustbelt" during the decade. But the city would
retain its ethnic and working-class character, symbolized by beer, by
baseball, and—as also seen in the 1970s on the nostalgic television

---

1   IQG, "War Bride from Vietnam Suggests Forming a Club," *MJ*, March 1,
      1971; IQG, "Reader Is Sick of Attending Showers for Shotgun Weddings,"
      MJ, March 23, 1971.

Bowling, like bingo, became almost addictive for many Milwaukeeans, according to contributors to the "Dear Mrs. Griggs" column, in the city that was home to the American Bowling Congress. Some took their outings to the lanes less seriously, such as the Wonder Bread women's team, costumed to resemble the popular product's familiar, colorful, polka-dot packaging. (Wisconsin Historical Society, WHS-8339)

"sit-com" *Happy Days*, allegedly based in an otherwise often-mythical Milwaukee—by bowling.[2]

The city and the *Milwaukee Journal* circulation area then boasted many bowling leagues, a sign—similar to Griggs' advice column—of "social connectedness." Putnam employs the term in his study of a decline of "social connectedness" in subsequent decades, which he traces to the Vietnam War, Watergate, and other events in the 1970s. Using the sport as a measure of societal malaise in the aftermath of

2   Robert D. Putnam, *Bowling Alone: The Collapse and Revival of American Community* (New York: Simon and Schuster, 2000), 38-42, 48-64; Doug Schmidt, *They Came to Bowl: How Milwaukee Became the Tenpin Capital* (Madison: Wisconsin Historical Society Press, 2007), 8, 48, 65-67, 215-217; Eric Fure-Slocum, *Contesting the Postwar City: Working-Class and Growth Politics in 1940s Milwaukee* (Cambridge, Mass.: Cambridge Press, 2013), 195-202; see also Dick Golembiewski, *Milwaukee Television History: The Analog Years* (Milwaukee, Wis.: Marquette University Press, 2008).

the tumultuous times, he notes that the number of Americans bowl-ing would increase, but more would bowl alone, without "pin pals" in leagues of their own. Putnam distinguishes "traditional civic organiza-tions" from "support groups," as the latter are "inner-directed" on pri-vate life more than public life and carry no "social obligation," so they function more like Griggs' column-*cum*-community forum, with no requirements for participation, if some of her faithful readers wrote that they had been unfailing participants for decades.[3]

That the column in which Griggs promoted clubs and "support groups" as a public good contributed to "social connectedness" in the city and even beyond is evidenced by many appeals to Griggs and her readers, often from afar. In a memorable example as the decade opened, a letter from a Michigan reporter and onetime Milwaukeean came to the column—and to other newspapers across the country—on behalf of a boy in her town, dying of kidney disease. The reporter begged readers to collect Betty Crocker coupons toward purchase of a dialysis machine. Griggs rallied her readers to the cause for months; in the end, they contributed more coupons than from any other lo-cale in the country. They "put Michigan to shame," wrote the former Milwaukeean. "I should have … knocked on Wisconsin's door first!" As much as a decade later, readers would continue to reference their communal response in the coupon campaign and ask for reports on the boy. Griggs and her correspondent in Michigan would oblige, gladly.[4]

That Milwaukee and the *Journal* had the longest-running advice col-umn in the country, a column not nationally syndicated but based in its city and circulation area, had contributed to the growth of clubs, civic organizations, and causes that regularly relied on Griggs for pub-licity. Her regular readers knew to look to her column for appeals for causes, which usually came at the end of the column. Some readers commonly received top-of-the-column treatment, such as people with disabilities, who sought Griggs' support in greater numbers. She also earned the gratitude of veterans and their families for giving encour-agement to readers such as "Anna H." Her letter ran at the top of the column and as the topic of the headline, to bring attention to another

3   Putnam, *Bowling Alone*, 38-42, 48-64.

4   IQG, "Partly Blind Farm Wife Sees Only Hardships Ahead," *MJ*, January 12, 1971; IQG, "High School Honor Student Changed Quickly in College," *MJ*, January 27, 1971.

generation of "war brides" brought to Wisconsin. "In every overseas conflict where Americans served," Griggs wrote, "a number have wed girls of that area and brought them to their hometowns to live. The Vietnamese conflict isn't an exception."[5] Her words typified the columnist's message to millions of readers for many decades, conveying continuity amid conflicts overseas as well as the "war at home," which even would contribute to toppling a president, Richard M. Nixon—one of three presidents in three years in the mid-1970s. Constant political upheaval of the era also would contribute to a much-discussed "credibility gap" in public trust of institutions, while "Mrs. Griggs" would remain a trusted institution by readers in Milwaukee and beyond in the Midwest.

Griggs also would maintain her mediative and generally non-judgmental role, but for a few failings, as she also faced a range of societal issues raised by readers in the 1970s that would be exceptional even for her column and as she neared her ninetieth year by the end of the decade. As she wrote to a reader, she could only agree that "people of all ages can do amazing things." In her eightieth year, at the start of the 1970s, Griggs' accomplishments garnered an award from her peers in the Milwaukee Press Club, which was even older than Griggs as the oldest press club in the country. At the same time, however, the oldest press club in the country would not admit her or other women to membership and remained adamantly all-male. As the decade opened, and as many counterpart press clubs across the country yielded to accepting women as members, male journalists in Milwaukee only increased their resistance and their condescending coverage of five years of petitions, picketing, and protests by women journalists in the city, a saga that provides context for understanding Griggs' media milieu. The next year, when another woman journalist won a prestigious club award but refused the honor, men amended the press club's

---

5   IQG, "War Bride;" IQG, "Dad's a Do-It-Yourselfer, Family's Exhausted, Unhappy," *MJ*, October 11, 1971; IQG, "Partly Blind Farm Wife;" IQG, "Wife Admitted an Affair, Should He Forgive Her?" *MJ*, January 3, 1972; IQG, "Smiles Greet Girl's Wish to Be California Actress," *MJ*, April 21, 1972; IQG, "Girl Feels Friendless; Parents Won't Listen," *MJ*, April 25, 1973; IQG, "Married for Security, Now Woman Worries," *MJ*, July 27, 1973; IQG, "Runaway 'Heard a Voice,' Now Happy Back Home," *MJ*, January 24, 1977.

constitution to considerably complicate procedures that would be needed to amend it again to admit women.[6]

As male fears mounted of a "flood" of women in the elite "working press" category of members, the club's board felt no shame in reassuring members that relatively few women had been hired by men—some members also were the very men in management of virtually all-male Milwaukee newsrooms. Then, in 1971, the leading male bastion of the profession, the National Press Club in the nation's capital, fell to pressure from women in the field as well as women in politics and business; most members of press clubs were not in the media but joined for access to influence journalists, so many other women's progress also was slowed without such informal and useful contacts. Finally, facing a lawsuit that threatened its endowment, the men of the Milwaukee Press Club relented in late 1971. The next day, the club president and its membership chair, Bennett F. Waxse of the *Journal*, escorted several women from newsrooms to the club for lunch, led by Ione Quinby Griggs. She posed for a photo—wearing a hat, of course—at the formerly men-only bar, famously adorned by a massive painting featuring a nude female figure, "Emma," appreciated as even more well-endowed than the country's oldest press club.[7]

The oldest advice columnist in the country remained imperturbable then and throughout the decade, despite the issues raised by readers in her daily mail. At the start of the decade, for example, in a single column—the same column in which the letter from the Vietnam "war bride" led the array of the day—Griggs' readers debated premarital sex and extramarital sex, sexually transmitted diseases, abortion, and other signs of the times. In one reply to a previous letter from a student who had defended premarital affairs, "Fellow American" resorted to Biblical terminology in reminding younger readers of end times ahead, as if "'anything goes,' a nation or city can finally go, too." Deploring "this new morality," the flag-waving letter writer suggested that the

---

6   IQG, "Woman Stayed Too Long with Cheating Husband," *MJ*, March 11, 1978; Kimberly Wilmot Voss and Lance Speere, "Way Past Deadline: The Women's Fight to Integrate the Milwaukee Press Club," *Wisconsin Magazine of History* 92:1 (Autumn 2008), 28-43. Earlier press clubs preceded the Milwaukee Press Club, founded in 1885, but elsewhere had not endured.

7   Voss and Speere, "Way Past Deadline," 28-43.

Ione Quinby Griggs (second from left) in the country's oldest press club, in Milwaukee—and in 1971, the last press club in the country to admit women as members—on the first day when women finally were welcome as members, and she was the first woman escorted past its doors by club membership chairman Bennett F. Waxse (standing), also of the *Milwaukee Journal*. Other colleagues at the *Journal* included (at Griggs' left, left to right) Patricia Roberts, Mildred Freese, Barbara Abel, and Barbara Strain; also, at Griggs' right, was Genevieve G. McBride, one of the co-authors, then an editor at the *Milwaukee Courier* and the *Milwaukee Star* and formerly among the first "copygirls" hired at the city's other major daily newspaper, the *Milwaukee Sentinel*, for a job for aspiring journalists that long had been restricted to "copyboys." (Courtesy of Milwaukee Press Club Collection, Archives, University of Wisconsin-Milwaukee Libraries)

student could benefit from her coursework, writing that "if you knew your history, college girl, you would realize" that what had "happened to Rome and to Sodom and Gomorrah" could occur again in her city. The comparison to Rome, at least, was flattering to Milwaukee, more often called the "American Munich" for its resemblance to the solid, stolid European city of similar heritage and mores. Sly selection of the next letter in the same column may have amused Griggs' most astute readers, as it attested that "Fellow American" had overstated an old-fashioned morality of a mythical past. The letter replied to another reader, pregnant after an extramarital affair, who had sought advice as to whether to tell her husband. "One Who Knows" counseled that she not do so, not only from her own experience but also based on advice of her "confessor." Only her minister knew, wrote "One Who

Knows"—and as her spouse still did not know, decades later—that their "oldest boy who had been a real joy" to her husband was not his.[8]

In another frank discussion of unintended pregnancies, readers replied with "their two cents' worth," as one adoptive mother wrote, about options for an "Anguished" grandmother-to-be. The topic of unwed, unplanned parenthood had been a constant in the column from its inception, although the incidence of letters on the topic slightly increased in the 1970s. More significant was that "Anguished" wrote not about a daughter but about a son; as he was unwilling to marry his girlfriend, she was going to give up their child for adoption. Also significant was that readers' responses not only explored options but also exhibited more societal acceptance of unwed mothers—and an end to the common practice of sending girls far from home, as Griggs had helped to do from the first years of her column. Now, wrote "Been There," as "pregnancy of unwed girls is becoming more frequent ... whether or not to 'keep the baby' is a decision that must be made by the individual mother and must depend on circumstances." Her circumstances had led her to opt for adoption, "a sad chapter" in her life that had led to "a happy ending." As for "Anguished," readers agreed that adoptions often were unhappy endings for grandparents, who rarely again saw grandchildren given away, unless they later sought their origins. The topic brought letters in the late 1970s from adoptees, such as "Searching Adult." She was encouraged in her search by a reply from "Bitter Forfeit," who finally had been found by a grown daughter.[9]

Other alternatives were available by the 1970s, as Griggs and her readers advised, with more opportunity for women to be self-sufficient. "Little seems to be heard about those who make it on their own," wrote Griggs in introducing a letter from "Deserted and Penniless" of "one woman's report of taking care of her family, working her way from the ground up" with "stamina and determination," to "encourage others to do the same." In reply to attacks on "welfare mothers," Griggs countered in the column that day with a letter from "One Who Won't

---

8   IQG, "War Bride."

9   IQG, "Parents Contemplate Adopting Son's Unwanted Child," *MJ*, February 1, 1971; IQG, "Alcoholic Father Reformed, His Family Is Proud of Him," *MJ*, January 24, 1973; IQG, "Wife Puts Her Foot Down on Husband's Snowblowing," *MJ*, December 18, 1978.

Give Up." Five years before, at the age of fifteen, she had resisted pressure to give up her son for adoption and endured "an embarrassing experience in court" when the father "tried to deny his paternity." Despite proof of his paternity, he paid minimal child support, so she went back to business school, while working as she could to support her son and to minimize their welfare dependency. She soon would graduate with her diploma, and with Griggs' congratulations.[10]

Readers also referenced options including not only adoption but also abortion, if subtly. It was not an option for most women in Wisconsin in the early years of the decade, prior to the legalization of abortion by the Supreme Court in *Roe v. Wade* in 1973. Until then, the status of abortion still was contested in the state, a situation that exemplified need for federal action by the Supreme Court. In Wisconsin, despite a district court decision in the early 1970s that abortion was legal under the state constitution, physicians continued to be arrested and prosecuted, so that women who went to the sole abortion clinic in the state found it open one day but closed the next. The district court ruling remained under appeal, pending before the state high court, which eventually would overturn the ruling—only to itself be overruled by the U.S. Supreme Court. In the interim, only weeks before the discussion in Griggs' column by "Been There," "No Rights," "Anguished," and others, another clinic offering abortion services had opened in Madison. In Milwaukee, with the only other such clinic in the state, the *Journal* would report that a handful of hospitals also allowed physicians to determine their patients' medical need to end pregnancies. As a Planned Parenthood counselor said, "a woman could always get an abortion in the city if she knew which doctors to see." However, writes historian Laura Kaplan, Wisconsin's attorney general openly defied the federal district court in "announcing that the state would not comply with the ruling," and that he would continue with a crackdown. As a result, few physicians were willing to risk their practices and their patients as prey for prosecutions. For those few, as one woman found when sent across the state to Milwaukee to the sole willing physician in the city, their

---

10   IQG, "Deserted and Penniless, She Made It on Her Own," *MJ*, January 4, 1978.

practices were "swamped with local patients." She could not wait, and she went home.[11]

Alternatives took Wisconsin women across the state border, even out of the country, according to one of fifteen Milwaukee ministers who formed a "Clergy Consultation Service on Problem Pregnancies," which joined the roster of Griggs' referrals. Clergy counseled Wisconsin women to fly to Mexico or the few states that had—and enforced—legalized abortion, especially New York. Other women went to Chicago for illegal services from a famed women's collective called "Jane." The minister counseled many married couples coping with "honest birth control failures," she said. However, other than abstinence for the unwed—as the practice hardly was conducive to wedded bliss—the minister counseled that the most effective form of birth control was the oral contraceptive. But "the Pill" continued to be an illegal, "indecent article" under state statutes for unwed women at the start of the decade. In Milwaukee, most unmarried clients had not practiced birth control, according to another minister quoted in a *Journal* series in the early 1970s, published not as news but in "women's pages"—by then, aptly but unfortunately renamed by male editors as the "Spectrum" section, which brought to mind a gynecological instrument. The series came well after debates on the issue in the advice column on the back page of the newspaper—and by then, the Madison clinic had been raided by police and then closed, until the state Supreme Court would be superseded in 1973 by the U.S. Supreme Court.[12]

Similarly, no matter the official stance regarding state law repeated on the front page of the newspaper, readers of the back page knew the reality regarding availability of contraceptives for single women in Wisconsin. Although few physicians risked prosecution for abortions

11 Jean Otto, "Unwanted Pregnancy Forces Agonizing Decision," *MJ*, April 4, 1971; Jean Otto, "Controversy Surrounds Birth Control, Abortion," *MJ*, April 6, 1971; Laura Kaplan, *The Story of Jane: The Legendary Underground Abortion Service* (Chicago: University of Chicago Press, 1995), 79-80; Evans, *Born for Liberty*, 291-293. On the Madison clinic, see also Annie Nicol Gaylor, *Abortion Is a Blessing* (Madison, Wis.: Psychological Dimensions, 1976).

12 Otto, "Controversy Surrounds Birth Control;" IQG, "Husband Is 'Mama's Boy,' and His Wife Resents It," *MJ*, January 21, 1971; IQG, "Girl Feels Friendless; Parents Won't Listen," *MJ*, April 25, 1973; Wells, *Milwaukee Journal*, 432.

until the courts settled the issue, at least during that decade, far more were willing to disregard state law still banning the prescribing of contraceptives for single women and for others under the age of twenty-one years, unless they had parental permission. "A Happy Person" blithely reported that "many doctors will give the pill to girls. My parents don't even know that I am taking it, and I wasn't 21 when I started" as a college student. "Confused Mother," however, wrote to readers for reassurance on her handling of a high school-aged daughter's request for "the Pill."[13]

The debate went for weeks, finally eliciting an epistle from "Edgar Establishment," a rare male writer to enter the fray. His attempt at curmudgeonly humor failed to amuse the columnist. She disliked his dismissive tone toward serious discussion and parental concerns, when he wrote:

> I am still laughing over that letter sent in by the mother of the girl who dashed home to get permission to take "the pill." Egad! Can't the younger generation make any decision for themselves anymore? My own mother was busy enough trying to decide what my dad wanted for dinner ... to take time out to decide if daughter could have a "pill" or sonny boy should drink bourbon or brandy. I never bothered her.[14]

He applauded "a ray of hope" for the younger generation in a recent letter from a girl to Griggs.

> She made up her mind about premarital sex. She probably decided wrong, but at least she did not have to call a family caucus. Along with coping with rising taxes and air pollution, parents just don't have time to squeeze in things like that.
>
> Now, if these young folks expect us of the establishment to get things worked out, they are going to have to quit pestering us with their small problems.[15]

"'Sonny boy,'" retorted Griggs, "I don't think you have grown up." Scolding him for "scoffing" at "serious family problems," she suspected

---

13   IQG, "Mom Burns Child's Fingers, Calls This Discipline," *MJ*, January 13, 1971; IQG, "Son Pleads With Father for Love and Understanding," *MJ*, February 7, 1971.

14   IQG, "Son Pleads With Father."

15   Ibid.

that he was "a bachelor who doesn't know that a parent has other duties than paying taxes." Griggs again pointed out that "the girl you laugh about is a minor and would have had to get her mother to sign for 'the pill' unless she got it illegally from other sources."[16] Although Griggs could not counsel breaking the law, her selection of letters about alternatives acted to inform readers—as did stories in news sections.

For some readers, however, alternatives would be few. Bans on "the Pill" continued by some faiths even after 1972, when the U.S. Supreme Court ended legal bans for single women. But even afterward in Wisconsin, "A Happy Person" had not informed her parents that she was on "the Pill," as "they would be very hurt, if they knew, because their beliefs are different." The columnist advised honesty, true to her personal convictions. However, honesty in marriage also was a guiding principle for Griggs, who faced a difficult task in counseling a Catholic reader who had "never felt happily married" for thirty years, owing to her refusal—or, it seemed, her husband's—to practice forms of birth control that continued to be proscribed by the Vatican.[17]

> Mrs. Griggs, I am writing to you as a last resort after a recent flareup with my husband. I don't know of anyone else to talk to. I can't talk to any of my friends about my marital life.
>
> Friends and neighbors think we have a perfect marriage. Little do they know!
>
> The problem ... ever since I married is the attitude my husband has about sex.... When we married I didn't want to become pregnant right away.
>
> We are both Catholic so any kind of birth control except the "rhythm" method was a no-no for us. My husband, especially, has a strong conviction about this....
>
> When I refused to have sex with my husband, he called it a "mortal sin." After our last child was born my guilt feelings and phobias became more intense.[18]

She had become "nervous," a "worrier ... insecure and emotional," or so she was told by more men, when she sought help. Her physician "said it was emotional," so she "sought the help of a psychiatrist. All I learned

---

16   Ibid.

17   IQG, "Mom Burns;" IQG, "Disagreement Over Sex Threatens a Marriage," *MJ*, August 1, 1977.

18   Ibid.

was that I must learn to accept myself as I am," she wrote. She did not mention having turned to her parish priest, a revealing omission. As for her husband, he was not accepting—and the problem became hers, if she asserted herself regarding sex and became the "aggressor," which also was a "no-no" in a belief system based on women's submission.[19]

> Not a day in my 30 years of marriage [has] gone by that either my husband or I have brought up something about our sex life…. He seems to be waiting for some miracle that will turn me into a sex pot….
>
> I have begged and pleaded with my husband to let me decide when to have sex, which I guess would make me the aggressor, instead of forcing me….
>
> When I don't try to please him … he manages to make me feel guilty.[20]

She was the one, her husband said, who had to "straighten out" her "sex life"—also revealing, if he also saw his "sex life" as separate, with no concept of sex as a mutual act. He also did not approach sex as an act of "tenderness." As a result, the reader was left with "religion and guilt."

> I don't know how we have stayed together this long. I have probably stayed due to insecurity (no means of support if I left him) [and] thoughts of religion and guilt.
>
> I don't know why we are torturing each other by staying together when neither of us is happy…. All I have wanted was a kind word or tenderness.
>
> My husband thinks that if I could straighten out my sex life, all would be well.[21]

She signed herself as "Waiting With Hope" for a kind word, after three decades of marriage.

"Sex is important," asserted Griggs, a statement that may have startled new readers not familiar with her straightforward style, which had not altered, despite her age. In attempting to provide hope that her reader had not received from medical professionals, the columnist had to avoid the wrath of Catholic faithful and their church, which remained a strong force in the city, despite increasing numbers of "fallen away" in the decade. She first affirmed the teaching of the church that

---

19   Ibid.

20   Ibid.

21   Ibid.

sex was important for procreation, the sole purpose in the eyes of the Catholic church at the time. Then, she anticipated the logic of a later papal proclamation that sex also ought to be "unitive" in marriage—or, as Griggs' put it, sex ought to "give personal pleasure" in a "mutually happy sex relationship." Happiness hardly was possible, however, if not taking into account "the number of children that parents can decently support, and the mother can take care of" and the "tenderness" that her reader sought. As for the husband, "I think that he is the one who needs instruction and counseling on sex," wrote Griggs, giving a referral to Catholic Social Services—and adding a missive directly addressing the husband, as she admonished him to "go with her to this agency!" and reiterating that the issue in their relationship and "sex disharmony" was his.[22]

While the legality of abortion and contraception seemed settled in Wisconsin, at least for the duration of that decade, the issue of unintended pregnancies continued to come up in readers' letters as a regular topic in the column. A year after the high court's ruling on oral contraceptives for unwed women, "A Girl," nineteen years old, wrote that she had informed her boyfriend that she was pregnant, and "he just said to 'get rid of it'.... I'm really scared.... Now I don't know what to do." As she had done for decades, Griggs recommended referrals for unwed mothers from her roster and family planning classes for the future. Griggs also noted that, despite the writer's suggestion to use her initials in publishing the letter, the columnist had created another signature, as even initials could be identifiers—an indication that, although increasing, societal acceptance of unwed mothers was not as widespread in the region as some older readers feared.[23]

For younger readers, that the women's movement and others also had won the goal of making family planning available for all women, no matter their marital status, would be among reasons that more went to college and on to careers, nationwide as well as in Wisconsin. "The new feminism had made a lasting impact on higher education," historian Sara M. Evans writes. Women's college enrollments had begun to increase in the 1960s, but many graduates by the 1970s still

22   Ibid.

23   IQG, "Girl Feels Friendless." On the ban on oral contraceptives for unwed women in states including Wisconsin until *Eisenstadt v. Baird* in 1972, see May, *America and the Pill*, 118.

were stopped from going on to graduate school. Class-action lawsuits were filed for the purpose of exerting political pressure. As a result, Congress acted in 1972 by enacting Title IX, banning gender discrimination at educational institutions receiving federal funds. By the end of the 1970s, women would comprise a majority of new students at campuses nationwide—but not in Wisconsin, which began to lag behind other states in women's status and would remain below national norms in their educational attainment and incomes into the next millennium.[24]

Even in Wisconsin, more women graduates than before would go on to graduate studies for careers in fields where they had been but a token few. In professional schools nationwide, women's enrollments soared from 5.4 percent of law students in 1970 to 28.5 percent of law students at the end of the decade and, in the same period, from 8.4 percent to 23 percent of students in medical schools. In Wisconsin, more than a century after the first woman in the state university's law school, a study found that a "trickle" became a "flood," as first-year women law students doubled in the first year alone of the decade, when the school's prestigious *Wisconsin Law Review* had its first woman "executive." A former Miss Wisconsin, she would graduate first in her class and be on the bench as a judge by the end of the 1970s, when almost a hundred women would comprise 40 percent of first-year students at the law school. The state university's medical school, however, had a more colorful history. As late as the mid-1930s— when Griggs' column began—a dean had established the unwritten practice of rejecting women applicants for the sole reason that they might marry and have families, although men also married, propagated, and left medical careers at the same rate as did women. As late as the 1970s, interviews on marital and childbearing plans were required only for women applicants, not for men—but for the husband of an applicant. He was interviewed regarding his wife's plans for a medical career. The school would alter admission procedures at last, in the late 1970s, when women would swell the entering class. They soon would comprise more than a fourth of the graduating class, a rate not seen since the 1920s, which had been all too briefly promising for women

---

24   Evans, *Born for Liberty*, 300; Amy B. Caizza, *The Status of Women in Wisconsin* (Washington, D.C.: Institute for Women's Policy Research, 2002), 5-6, 33-62.

aspiring to higher education, the era when Griggs had begun her career after her own brief foray onto campus.[25]

Despite her age, the columnist's readership remained relatively constant by demographic measures in the 1970s, including many younger
readers, which may have meant that the column served as a community forum not reliant solely on the columnist. As new generations of
women turned to the advice columnist, she continued in turn to adapt
her advice, especially to young women dating in the era of "the Pill"—
at least, when it became legal for unmarried women in Wisconsin—
and she held to ageless principles that rarely dated her. Griggs schooled
herself on shifts in sexual mores in Milwaukee and even more rapid
changes in laws in Wisconsin as well as nationwide in the early 1970s
regarding preventative practices, such as contraception, for the sake of
her readers in an era of misinformation about "all this free love and sex
before marriage," wrote a reader. She was weary of bridal showers for
"shotgun weddings," which Griggs agreed were in poor taste, although
the goal was worthy. More often, she adapted to the times, and even
to public celebrations of pregnant brides, as she reminded readers that
any occasion of marriage was preferable to the alternative of more letters about unwed mothers and abandoned children.[26]

Male letter writers remained an anomaly in the 1970s, as they had
throughout the decades of "Dear Mrs. Griggs." In answer to an accusation from "Misogamist" that Griggs gave gendered advice, she coolly
stated the obvious reason: She knew her audience, her readers who
often wrote regarding gendered issues, because "more women over the
years have written me." She also reported recently receiving more letters from male readers than in earlier decades. The analysis of letters
sampled, however, found no significant change: Of letter writers who

---

25   Jean C. Love, "Twenty Questions on the Status of Women Students in
     Your Law School," *Wisconsin Women's Law Journal* (Summer 1997), 405-
     415; "Miss Wisconsin Goes On to Be Chief Judge," *MJ*, October 3, 1985;
     "Women Lawyers on the Increase," *Gargoyle* 2:1 (Autumn 1970), 6; Ruth
     B. Doyle, "Women and the Law School: From a Trickle to a Flood," in
     Marian J. Swoboda and Audrey J. Roberts, *Wisconsin Women, Graduate
     School, and the Professions* (Madison: University of Wisconsin Board of
     Regents, 1980), 65-73; Rima D. Apple and Judith Walzer, "Medical School
     Remembered: Women's Experiences at the University of Wisconsin,"
     Wisconsin Academy Review 31:1 (December 1984), 14-17.

26   IQG, "Reader Is Sick."

self-identified by gender—fewer than in some prior decades at about a third, or 36.3 percent, in letters sampled in the 1970s—women remained nearly nine of every ten contributors to the column. Teenagers and young adults continued to comprise more than half, or 52 percent, of writers of letters sampled in the 1970s, of the many readers who self-identified by age. Interestingly, more young readers in columns sampled in the 1960s had criticized the columnist as hopelessly out of date than in columns sampled in the 1970s. More typical of the time was a gushing and "Thankful Girl" who wrote to Griggs, "I always read your column. I have to compliment you on all your advice," which the teenager termed "fantastic." That the fifteen-year-old fan also had written to give public expressions of gratitude to her parents, however, may have led her readers with teenaged daughters to wonder whether the letter was a hoax.[27]

A significant decline in a related category of analysis of the column, and a departure from national demographic trends, suggests that Griggs had a growing readership in the 1970s of young, working-class women not yet part of the trend to enrollment in college by others of their age and gender. Although the columnist's younger readership had remained relatively constant, of the approximately one in five letter writers sampled who self-identified as to their working, nonworking, or student status, those who self-identified as students declined from almost half in the 1960s, 47.1 percent, to less than a third in the 1970s, 31.3 percent. They may simply have been less likely to so self-identify, when their student status was more likely with soaring college enrollments. Or they may have been less likely to so self-identify in the column, after antiwar protests at the state university in Madison had led to a bombing and death of a student in 1970.

Readers' debates repeatedly showed that shockwaves from the Madison antiwar protests still reverberated across the state, with a backlash against campus life anywhere—at the time that enrollments of women students started to steadily increase in the 1970s, at last. Their numbers remained well behind enrollments of men, because G.I. Bill benefits paid for college for veterans now home from a new war, as the bill had done for decades by then for millions of veterans from wars before. However, other concerns of a "Worried-Sick Father"

---

27   IQG, "Introspective Session Helped Him Quit Smoking," *MJ*, January 15, 1976.

of a "coed" at an unnamed campus had caused him to write to the column. His progeny had been a prodigy, "a daughter any parent could be proud of" in high school years, as "a cheerleader, a member of prom court and National Honor Society"—apparently in order of importance—and "a normal, well groomed, studious moral young adult who knew right thinking," until she had come home from college.[28]

> She had altered her choice of attire, being casually clad in faded bell bottom jeans, hiking boots, a very odd belt with a strange beaded little sack attached to it, and an old Air Force flight jacket. When she removed this last item, my wife and I were horrified to observe that she had apparently misplaced her brassiere.... A number of people we hadn't met dropped in. To be frank, they all appeared to be hippies.
>
> She didn't ... attend church with us the next day.... Her language was quite crude.... She is not the girl she once was. She has changed so much in one semester.[29]

Griggs reassured her reader that, regarding "the young people you called hippies," their apparel "needn't mean they are identical to those who call themselves hippies. Right or wrong, a fun type or otherwise, this type of dress has spread." Griggs recalled the "flapper" fashions of her younger years, when media had conflated clothing fads to mean far more in terms of lifestyle and ideology than for all but a few women in her era. She also downplayed the daughter's "crude words" as "bravado," albeit hardly an "excuse".... But it is hard sometimes to differentiate between those who dress and talk the part and those who take on the serious vices," as she advised the father.[30]

As for fears of the "vices" and of a daughter "on drugs," Griggs considered behavior such as "vague" replies and a reluctance to disclose "whereabouts" to have another explanation: The girl was a teenager. However, a reader found that advice as naïve as were the worried parents. "I fear your advice wasn't enough," wrote "E.C." The description of the daughter left "little doubt but that she is on drugs and has sold herself cheaply," owing to the evils of higher education.[31]

---

28   IQG, "High School Honor Student."

29   Ibid.

30   Ibid.

31   IQG, "Colleges Can Be Corrupters, Father of Freshman Warned," *MJ*, February 6, 1971.

"Worried Sick" should apologize to his daughter for not knowing enough about the facts of life where drugs and influences on campuses are concerned to have warned her....

She should have been told what many colleges are like today. She should have been shown that a greater effort would be made to corrupt her than to educate her. She should have known that girls are taught on campuses that they should demand sexual license.... She should have been warned that marijuana is now so prevalent on campuses that the beer depots know when a shipment arrives, because the beer sales drop so dramatically.

"E.C." warned of one area of study that parents ought to fear most, however, for its promulgation of undefined "new values" that undermined old-fashioned family values: the sociology major.

They are encouraged by some teachers, especially in the sociology department, to gear their behavior to what is accepted rather than to what is moral....

One of the first things many students are told when they get to college is to forget the lessons that their parents have taught, that "new values" apply. If she is a sociology student ... one of the first papers she would ... write would be a family criticism....

There is one hint that I can give a parent ... and that is to keep [their children] out of the sociology department if possible. If a course in sociology is demanded for graduation, and there is no escape from taking it, warn your young people that they will be taught to forget their previous convictions regarding morality, that they will be seduced into accepting the myth that individuality is gone, and that society must be served.[32]

Not that any major was a safe haven to shelter students from the horrors of inculcation into serving society. The English major also was suspect for promoting literacy. Lest "your lovely young daughter" fall prey to "the college corrupters," warned "E.C.," the writer exposed the most insidious and stealthy of academic strategies to steal children's minds by persuading students to read books. "Many colleges," as "E.C." wrote, "require readings of the foulest and most corrupting books published, calling them 'literature.'" Others called them the classics.[33]

That revelation resonated with "R.M.J.," a prescient "helicopter parent" prior to coining of the term. In her mid-thirties, she had "become

32   Ibid.
33   Ibid.

a college coed" not to expand her education but to surveil campus life for "insight into problems" ahead for her children. "The advice of 'E.C.' is absolutely correct," she wrote. "Anyone who doubts what is going on at campuses should take a daytime course in freshman English or sociology and find out for themselves"—as she had done, enrolling in an introductory English course taught not by faculty but by a teaching assistant, a graduate student. She apparently had expected a tweedy sort, but her teacher was a "hippie."[34]

> On the day of my first class my instructor sat cross-legged on the table before us. His stringy hair hung down to his shoulders.... The shirt he wore was once white but now was soiled, and the sleeves were tattered to shreds at the elbows. The pants he wore were faded denims with holes.... He wore several strings of "love beads" around his neck.[35]

In addition to her review of sartorial standards of graduate students, the reader had concerns regarding the first day's course content on sex—or "homosexualism"—drugs, and rock 'n' roll.

> What I learned in that course no parent would be able to determine beforehand.... This first class was ... a lecture supporting anti-American activities, plus advocacy of free love and drug use. The classes that followed were spent in much the same way....
> I learned more about drugs than I did about English. I learned the going price of hashish and the advantages of homosexualism....
> I heard a detailed account of each rock festival which took place and the immorality that went on.[36]

The reader "became so repelled by the propaganda" that she had filed a complaint, although her account was contradictory on whether her complaint was with the department or college at the campus, unnamed but apparently the state university in Milwaukee. Her letter also implied that its faculty had gone on strike, although the campus had been among hundreds across the nation that had closed owing to student strikes after killings of students by military forces at Kent State and Jackson State campuses in other states—and only at the semester's

---

34 IQG, "Mom Became Coed, Found College an 'Immoral Mess,'" *MJ*, February 16, 1971.

35 Ibid.

36 Ibid.

end. That her faculty had ensured that students earned credit now earned the faculty no credit from an unhappy reader.

> All this I heard and more, in vulgar terms, with profanity and filthy words used frequently.... When a teachers' strike occurred, I made four long distance calls, attempting to learn what had happened to my class.... Weeks later, I learned that my class would not be resumed and I would be graded on work done prior to the strike.[37]

Griggs gave the letter a terse, one-sentence reply. Throughout the debate, she had published as many or more letters from the likes of more temperate contributors to the column, such as "A Happy Parent" of college students, who reassured readers that the daughters of "Worried Sick" parents were atypical, as only "a few students do lose their heads and can't take advanced schooling in stride." In her typically mediative stance, Griggs acknowledged "a good thing to realize the need for awareness on the part of both children and parents" as to pitfalls of campus life but cautioned that "we don't want to discourage [getting] college or university education."[38]

The debate's undercurrents did raise a range of relatively new issues for many readers, arising early in the decade and recurring for years to come in the column, such as drugs and homosexuality—issues that were new not solely for older readers, and not solely on campuses. Some parents' letters on drug use had surfaced in the 1960s, most often when their progeny had admitted to use on an experimental basis, and letters also claiming only infrequent drug use had come from college students. In the 1970s, letters to Griggs about drug use greatly increased, and often from or about younger users in high schools and even middle schools—and so also did letters from and about runaways, which had come to the column for decades but now more often were linked to drug use. Early in the decade, an extended exposé in the "women's pages" of the newspaper entitled "Girls in Trouble" with the revelation of an "underground runaway railway" fed fears of parents, and references to the series would continue in Griggs' column for years. For example, a letter from "The Mother" detailed the agonies of the search for a daughter made worse when "stories of an 'underground for runaways' have come to me, making me feel sick and angry." Griggs

---

37   Ibid.
38   Ibid.

also referred to her *Journal* colleague's series but only to reassure her reader that nothing in her letter suggested that the daughter was either on drugs or "underground" and gave a referral to a Pathfinders agency, which had arisen to assist runaways and, if they wished, in reuniting families. The agency would become one of her most-oft cited referrals in the era.[39]

Some young readers defended their generation from sweeping generalizations, as did "A Member of the Other 98%." In reply to an attack on "those no-good teens," the aggrieved reader replied that "the majority of teens don't drink, smoke, or experiment with pot." Some who did do so, however, wrote to defend their drug use, primarily of "pot," and assert that it had no impact on their grades or other aspects of life. Others, however, wrote that they had succumbed to peer pressure and sought advice to escape it. "Right on the Edge," a suicidal girl who had progressed to "LSD," wrote to Griggs: "You are the last person I still have any faith in. Hurry or it may be too late." The columnist replied that she could understand "the desire to relate to those of your generation;" her reader, however, needed to "not follow the herd" and "not imperil her health, her peace of mind, or her future." To the girl's reasoning that her drug use was in part retaliatory to demonstrate "freedom" from parents, Griggs replied that "real freedom is in not being impaled on artificial precepts." Glad that the girl was a regular reader and had written, if in "desperation," Griggs penned a particularly personal reply. "You know where I stand," she wrote, "not because I am of a different generation or don't believe in youthful pleasures, but because I know certain things add up to disillusionment and sometimes disaster." Griggs gave referrals to agencies for the girl and her parents, with an appeal to her reader to write again.[40]

---

39   IQG, "The Case of a Runaway from a Mother's View," *MJ*, March 31, 1973; Jean Otto, "Girls in Trouble," *MJ*, September 26, 1971; Jean Otto, "Girls in Trouble: Teens See No Way Out, So They Run Away," *MJ*, September 27, 1971; Jean Otto, "Girls in Trouble: Parents of Runaways Ask Themselves, 'Why?'" *MJ*, September 28, 1971; Jean Otto, "Girls in Trouble: Runaways Tell Their Story," *MJ*, September 29, 1971; Jean Otto, "Girls in Trouble: Runaway Found, Authorities Seek Answers," *MJ*, September 30, 1971.

40   IQG, "What Should Mother Tell Daughter Who Smoked Pot?" *MJ*, February 8, 1968; IQG, "Husband Fears for Safety of Baby, Depressed Mother," *MJ*, April 23, 1968; IQG, "His Friends Smoke Pot, Want Boy

Columns on the issue increased in the later 1970s among sampled letters, now including several by or about adults doing drugs. "A South Side Mother" fretted for a neighbor's children who came to her door for money for bus fare to their grandmother's home for food, as their parents' grocery money had gone to drugs. An adult wrote that he had started "smoking pot" in college and continued to do so with no effect on his work record, although admitting that others "got so stoned" that they could not "function at the job the following day" or "take some speed the morning after 'turning on,' in order to function properly." Letters on the issue—primarily on "pot," with some mention of "sniffing glue" or other substances—rarely abated for long. In the late 1970s, readers waged a weeks-long debate, begun by a younger user, "Pot Smoker," about the "harmlessness of marijuana," to which the columnist replied with studies claiming otherwise. "Another Pot Smoker" followed, writing that Griggs was "fair most of the time, looking at views from both sides, but that this time you were one-sided.... Well, just what do you recommend to relieve tensions or ease anxieties? What do we do when we feel depressed?" Some "weak kids" succumbed to peer pressure. He had been "one of those weaklings.... But after a month of being stoned, I became my own person." Griggs devoted the rest of the column to her research, especially addressing most depression as "normal" and pointing out that the impact of masking emotions with "pot" could counter requisite learning to cope with realities of life. In reply, a self-styled expert signing himself "Master of Arts, Master of Sciences" sided with young readers. His letter was a lengthy treatise demeaning any of the above who dared to doubt beneficent effects of drugs and attacked Griggs for allegedly abdicating impartiality, his "understanding" of the role of a newspaper reporter, revealing that he did not understand the role of a columnist.[41]

---

to Join Them," *MJ*, August 8, 1970; IQG, "Troubles Mount for Girl Who Considered Suicide," *MJ*, April 26, 1974; IQG, "Boy Friend Was on Drugs, Ended Up in Institution," *MJ*, March 20, 1975; IQG, "He's a Ranting Drudge, She's Had It, Up to Here," *MJ*, April 14, 1975.

41   IQG, "Worker Says He Handles Pot Better Than Drinking Men," *MJ*, August 24, 1971; IQG, "Can Upset Neighbor Do More Than Complain?" *MJ*, September 17, 1974; IQG, "From One Young Adult, a Song of Gratitude," *MJ*, February 28, 1975; IQG, "Was Mrs. Griggs Wrong to Point Out 'Pot' Danger?" *MJ*, June 28, 1978; IQG, "Mrs. Griggs Taken to Task for Her Information on Pot," *MJ*, July 2, 1978.

Letters came from parents, from a "Junior High School Teacher" of "hopheads," and from college faculty conducting research on drug use—although almost all on any side in the debate throughout the decade agreed with "Rational" on the irrationality of the illegality of "pot" and the legality of alcohol with its impact on lives, a telling point in Wisconsin. As a younger "pot" user put it, "why should middle-aged or old people feel obliged to take a drink ... which can rot the gut or kill brain cells?" A young adult, "Rational," had continued "pot" use since college and claimed his work was unaffected, compared to alcohol's impact on co-workers.

> The group goes out to relax twice a week in a more socially accepted way. They hit two or three local bars and come to work the next day with splitting headaches. It takes two or three cups of coffee to start them functioning. If their ... legal method of unwinding is better than mine, I fail to see it. Alcohol has not been proven to be better than pot....
>
> Yet alcohol is legal and marijuana is not.[42]

The middle-school teacher offered the rare reply to take exception with the argument, which she had heard not only from students but also from parents excusing the behaviors of her students.

> I am furious at the continual comparison between alcohol users and pot users.... It is deplorable when people become alcoholics, but saying that pot is no worse than alcohol is only begging the question. We have far too many people misusing alcohol.
>
> We do not need additional multitudes muddling their minds with marijuana.... We could have "1984" before that year. Drugs could be used to control people. Perhaps that book about "1984" was more prophetic than anyone realized.[43]

When the year 1984 would come to the column, the debate on drug use would not abate—but it never would bring as many letters as did the topic of alcoholism and its impact in Wisconsin.

More letters continued to come to the column on alcoholism, including more on women alcoholics, a topic that had increasingly stymied readers in previous decades. A male reader, "Disgusted With It All," wrote to Griggs after almost two decades of marriage that "life

---

42   IQG, "Was Mrs. Griggs Wrong;" IQG, "Worker Says He Handles Pot."

43   IQG, "Teacher Describes Effects of 'Pot' in Her Classroom," *MJ*, June 30, 1978.

is a living hell" with a wife who hated him and drank "a bottle a day," blaming resentment about their financial situation with rising mortgage payments and a growing family of "growing kids." Griggs gave her usual referrals of Planned Parenthood for family planning as well as financial planning and a local agency for alcoholism counseling; she apparently no longer recommended Al-Anon, with its shortcomings in counseling women. The columnist heard from many younger readers on the issue, such as a girl who had grown up too soon with a "mom drinking ever since I can remember" and had to raise her siblings. She finally sought help when her mother's boyfriend "started beating on them," and her mother also got "belt happy." The girl had gone to police and to "different people, telling the story over and over. All that was done was to take me away," she wrote. Now her mother prevented her from seeing a "littlest sister," which was "tearing apart" the older girl removed from the home. Griggs recommended a local agency for child abuse to find a resolution and hoped that the girl would write again.[44]

For men, she continued to recommend Alcoholics Anonymous, as in a reply to "The Husband," who had been helped by the organization—as "The Wife" had not been helped by Al-Anon in the couple's saga that played out on the back page of the newspaper for readers, and for weeks. He had initiated the series, first writing to Griggs to extol the wonders of single life after also initiating a divorce, because he had met a new love at that ubiquitous setting for sin and iniquity in the city, the bowling alley, where beer was thrown down gullets faster than balls down gutters. Griggs wrote that "he admitted drinking" could have contributed to ending his marriage of more than twenty years, and she advised him to "go to A.A." In a second letter, he said he had "joined A.A., wasn't drinking a drop and wanted his wife back" in his life, but Griggs gathered that there might be more to the story and invited "The Wife" to give "her side."[45]

---

44   IQG, "Husband and Wife Battle Over High Cost of Living," *MJ*, October 23, 1973; IQG, "Drinking Mom Makes Life Tough for Children," *MJ*, October 22, 1977; IQG, "Job Offer;" IQG, "Mom Who Disciplined Is Left Out While 'Children' Coddle Their Dad," *MJ*, October 11, 1979.

45   IQG, "Wife of Alcoholic Gives 'Her Side' of Home Conflict," *MJ*, April 22, 1977.

> I have been reading your column for years and have the highest regard for your answers but would have to write a book to tell all that has happened in our marriage....
> My husband is a "problem drinker".... I'm not saying I'm perfect.... But I wasn't a chaser as my husband was, nor a drinker. While he was running after other women, spending money and drinking, I was home taking care of our children.[46]

Their stories differed, too, as to who had initiated divorce—and not for the first time.

> Years ago when he spent the weekend with my "best girl friend," I filed for divorce.... My husband followed me and said he would change his ways if I would go back to him.
> He also intimated he would take the children away from me if I didn't stop considering a divorce. Yes, we went back together, but I never heard the end of my "mistake."
> I really did try to make our marriage work, but it wasn't three weeks before he was with another woman.... I went to Al-Anon, the group for wives of alcoholics, and my daughters went to the Ala-Teen group.[47]

She had received more help, though, from meeting with a psychiatrist than from Al-Anon. She gained understanding that her husband "felt so guilty he was probably using me as an excuse for his drinking"—although he had begun drinking at the age of fourteen, before they had met.[48]

> These past two years his drinking got worse.... The children begged him to get help.
> But he wouldn't.... I was very lonely, Mrs. Griggs, for years. It's not much fun to sit home and have a husband get drunk every night. My children told me to get out of the house, so I wouldn't have to put up with that kind of life....
> I filed for divorce about a month ago. It was to save my sanity and the children's. They were so emotionally upset, afraid to bring their friends home, because of their father....

---

46   Ibid.
47   Ibid.
48   Ibid.

The children do love him, but they have lost respect for him. There have been incidents.... My husband said he would seek help and quit drinking, but he has said this before.[49]

Her report "conformed to the pattern of many an alcoholic," wrote Griggs, as she had suspected. In hope that their decades of marriage would not "go down the drain," she wondered whether "The Wife" could consider postponing divorce pending proof that "The Husband" was hewing to the A.A. program. Either way, she deserved "encouragement," wrote Griggs, who again wrote nothing in her reply regarding Al-Anon and gave a recommendation to a different organization.[50]

The never-ending letters on alcoholism and other addictions had come to the column for decades, but the daily mail to the newsroom in the 1970s still could bring issues new even to the columnist said to have seen it all. "This is the first complaint of the kind that has been made to me," she replied to a reader, although Griggs was "not greatly surprised." Her reader, however, was surprised by her boyfriend's "hobby" and felt "really weirdo" asking for advice on an unusual situation; she had included her name and address—not published—to assure Griggs that the letter was not a hoax. The columnist posed her questions to her readers: "Do girls have more puzzling dating problems today than the girls of other years? Has the tendency toward long hair styles changed the boys so that they are adopting other styles of adornment and pastimes usually claimed by girls?" The boyfriend's "pastime" was knitting. "It struck me as very strange, but when I got used to the idea I let it ride," her reader wrote, until an "adornment" had made her "wonder" as well. "Did you ever hear of a guy whose ears are pierced … because he thought it was 'cool'?" The columnist advised that, if his "conduct is commendable in other areas," she saw no need for concern—except about her reader's conduct, as she ought not get "serious" about a boy if his hobby "bothered" her. As for his accessory, Griggs rather liked the new style for men—not that it was new, she noted, writing that "some old time pirates wore earrings, although in one ear only. Maybe your boyfriend thinks of himself as a swashbuckler." A male reader who also had adopted the accessory, "Studded Lobes," wrote that more than "gay" men pierced their ears, as attested by his wife, with historical references from ancient times

---

49   Ibid.

50   Ibid.

to the practice among manly, "early Romans and Egyptians." Griggs advised only: "Don't start wearing your wife's earrings." For "Studded Lobes" and like-minded readers, Griggs again also conducted research in retail and could recommend shops for Milwaukee's most fashionable men, if they wished.[51]

A cross-dressing husband in "drag" also was a first for the column, and perhaps for the newspaper. In introducing the letter from "Suburban Reader," the unflappable Griggs asked whether a wife determined to be adventurous and seek new experiences, such as "lap dances" from talent at a Milwaukee "male go-go" bar, should complain if encountering the unexpected?[52]

> My girlfriends and I wanted to go to one of those new places in Milwaukee that have male go-go dancers.... I never complain when my husband goes out to play cards or bowl with his friends, so I wasn't surprised that he didn't object to me going out with the girls, although I didn't say just where we were going....
> One of the dancers, a good-looking fellow, came down and sat on my lap when he had finished dancing.
> All of a sudden a "woman" rushed up yelling, and when "she" got close, I realized it was my husband dressed as a woman. He was wearing one of my wigs and a pantsuit from his sister... He told me to "hush up" and pretend he was my mother and leave with him.[53]

She was shocked and humiliated, but her issue was her husband's behavior back home, where he stated that the spouse whose actions were suspect was not him but "Suburban Reader."

> I was so embarrassed I could have fallen through a crack in the floor. He later justified his actions by saying he had to keep an eye on me, and the dance on my lap proved his suspicions that I needed watching. I thought this was pretty lowdown and sneaky, maybe even perverted of him to do this to me, and I would like to know what you think.[54]

---

51   IQG, "Confused Coed Discovers Her Boyfriend Knits," *MJ*, February 11, 1971; IQG, "Does Son Suddenly Change When He Reaches Age of 13?" *MJ*, March 11, 1971.

52   IQG, "Hubby in Drag Bustles Her from Male Go-Go Joint," *MJ*, February 11, 1976.

53   Ibid.

54   Ibid.

Griggs hoped that "Suburban Reader," otherwise happily married, could somehow "see the humor of the situation" and be glad that her husband did not go to "female go-go places" to be similarly entertained by a dancer who might "leap onto his lap." The columnist, however, failed her reader in not focusing on the issue of her husband's attempt at psychological projection to foist blame on his wife. Griggs did hope that "domestic harmony" might return for her reader and suggested that it was best achieved "if both husbands and wives are aboveboard" about "evenings out they don't do together"—no matter whose closet provided the clothes to do so.[55]

With more working women than for decades before, the issue of sexual harassment also might have been expected to surface more than before as well. A rare instance in letters sampled in the 1970s, however, was another mention of homosexuality. The letter came from a male reader, who wrote that harassment had come not on the job but in the job-seeking process, as a result of meeting an alleged personnel manager in a bar. The writer also claimed that the job offer had been retracted, not only because of his refusal to engage in sex but also because the potential employer had retreated and stated that the opening would go only to "a black man." Griggs criticized the veiled racism in the letter, which was rare in her column, if not in the community, and pointed out the illogic of the alleged excuse related by her reader. However, Griggs gave referrals for filing complaints against companies for "false pretenses." As for an undercurrent of concern about homosexuality in the missive from the reader, he had signed his letter as "Engaged to Marry," with an expression of worry as to effects on his wedding plans if events became known. She assured him that there was no shame for anyone with a reputation for honesty, and advised that he ought to inform his fiancée. The columnist closed with advice for jobseekers of any gender that "bars are poor places to find legitimate prospective jobs."[56]

As for women in the workplace, Griggs' readers in the 1970s reframed their ongoing debate to reflect the growing numbers of working

---

55   Ibid.

56   IQG, "Job Offer in Bar Turns Out to Be a Different Proposition," *MJ*, June 1, 1978. On the issue of race in letters sampled in the 1970s, one writer self-identified as African American; see IQG, "Black Woman Tells of Help She Received in Greendale," *MJ*, January 11, 1972.

mothers. The proportion of working women among writers of letters sampled significantly increased in the 1970s to almost four in ten, 38.5 percent, of all who self-identified their working or nonworking status. The proportion of women letter writers in the paid workforce would almost double in a decade to a level not seen in letters since the 1940s. Their letters reflected trends across Wisconsin and the country by the end of the 1970s, when more than half of all women would be out of the house and on the job, with impact also on men in their families and in the workforce. "The growing number of working women" in Wisconsin, writes historian Robert C. Nesbit, redefined "domestic and family arrangements," as "whether women held a paid job" had impact on many factors for themselves and their families, such as their housing, their neighborhoods and schools, and "the amount of disposable income available for education, leisure, and recreation," and especially "the age at which they married and started families" and "the size of their families" that they now could plan and afford.[57]

The debate for decades in the column about working mothers now focused far less on whether mothers of younger children would work—"periodically, people giving 'pros' and 'cons,'" as a reader put it—and focused more on advice shared among readers on how mothers somehow would do so, working both in their homes and in their paid workplaces. Readers and Griggs repeatedly tied the issue of working mothers to need for their income in the inflationary economy of the 1970s, especially early in the decade. But more was at work in moving more mothers of younger children into the paid workforce, which continued even after inflation eased. By the end of the decade, mothers of older children were more likely to work than were women without families; fully three-fifths of women with children from six to eighteen years old would be in the paid workforce. In a greater societal change—and challenge—almost half of mothers with children under six years of age would be in the paid workforce by the end of the decade.[58]

"A Weekend Warrior" penned a primer for other mothers on how to make working work. She was a registered nurse, with four children born in five years, so her family had needed more income. She had gone

57   Nesbit, *Wisconsin*, 503.

58   IQG, "Mom Works on Weekends to Help Fight Inflation," *MJ*, July 9, 1979; Evans, *Born for Liberty*, 301.

back to work every other weekend to be home on weekdays—when she "seemed to be the only mother home these days" in her Milwaukee neighborhood, she wrote.[59]

> Since I returned to work every other weekend, I've been able to buy all the "extras" we want. One of my neighbors seems jealous…. She doesn't realize that a nurse works hard…. When I described how hard I worked, she said, "blood makes me sick." It can make me feel sick, too, but a nurse learns to hold her breath or wear a mask at times. There are always things in a good job a person has to put up with.[60]

Nursing was not that different from parenting in many ways, she wrote—and men could master it—although she always had planned on having children. She had not planned on a nursing career when in high school in the 1960s, and when an R.N. did not need a college degree.[61]

> If a person can change a baby's diaper, she can learn to be a nurse's aide. I told this "gal" so and got her a job as an aide for good pay, but she only lasted two weeks.
>
> Nothing worthwhile is easy in this life…. I never planned to go into nursing. It was my third choice. The first choices didn't have enough security for a woman….
>
> My husband is helpful, but he never changed a diaper until I went back to work.
>
> Now he's an "old pro" at not only diaper changing…. Incidentally, he's a much better father, also husband. He appreciates me, knows what it's like to look after children.[62]

As much or more than the working status of a father, in a new era for many men as well as women in the 1970s, a mother's working status affected the affordability of her family's size, spacing, and housing space and place, as "A Weekend Warrior" would state in her letter. She personified state historian Robert C. Nesbit's later assessment of working mothers' impact.

---

59   IQG, "Mom Works."

60   Ibid.

61   Ibid.

62   Ibid.

I had my children first. Having a house came second. When my
children were tiny I was almost ashamed to open the door, because
the carpeting was threadbare and the furniture falling apart. But I
knew I could always work to get new things later, while I wasn't sure
I would be young enough or healthy enough to have babies if I kept
putting it off. I was older than many when I married....

To all the young wives out there: Don't despair.... Mothers, try a
weekend job. It might solve your problems.[63]

For all of her careful career and life planning in past, however, and
perhaps owing to her high-demand field, the reader did not foresee
the problems in future for women who followed her well-intentioned
advice to take what would be identified and termed, a decade later,
as the "mommy track." The landmark study of setbacks in advancement in their careers and thus in their incomes—and family income—
would be another landmine that would explode myths and would revive again, for a new generation of readers, the debate about working
motherhood.[64]

Letters still abounded about marital bliss or its lack, often in new
terms that reflected the times. "Man-Made Robot" was "beginning to
feel like a robot wife, from keeping house and the budget to making
love in the bedroom" and to feel not only shut out but also "shut off"
like a machine. Griggs also replied in a reference to the times that
"this may be a computer age," but she reaffirmed her age-old advice
in directly addressing the "insensitive" husband. "I am blunt," she concluded unapologetically, after writing to her readers that she recently
had "heard a man tell a woman,'marriage is on the way out!' That was
stupid," asserted Griggs, who could attest from her daily mail count
that marriage remained a mainstay for materiel for an advice column.[65]

However, intriguing in analysis of the column's contributors may be
an indicator that marital or single status as a means of defining themselves simply became moot for many women by the 1970s. Three-
fourths had self-identified their marital or single status at the start
of the column in the 1930s. Then, numbers doing so had declined

63   Ibid.

64   Felice N. Schwartz, "Management Women and the New Facts of Life,"
     Harvard Business Review (January-February 1980), 65-76.

65   IQG, "Wife May Counterattack as Mate Shuts Her Off," *MJ*, April 13,
     1971.

to two-thirds of letter writers self-identifying their marital or single status in the 1940s, prior to a reversal again, when those self-identifying by marital or single status had soared to four-fifths of writers of the letters sampled in the self-conscious 1950s for women. The rate of women's self-identification by marital or single status had seesawed again in the next decade, with a decline to two-thirds of writers of letters sampled in the 1960s. Then, the trend continued steadily downward, as little more than half, or 52 percent, of writers of letters sampled self-identified their marital or single status in the 1970s, the lowest level of letter writers doing so in decades to date of the "Dear Mrs. Griggs" column. Of the writers of letters sampled, and of writers who self-identified marital or single status in the 1970s, a slight decline from the previous decade in numbers of those who never had married, approximately one in four, was countered by a slight increase in the number of married letter writers, reflecting national demographic trends toward a peak marriage rate during the decade.

Indeed, the rate of first marriages increased to a peak in the mid-1970s unmatched since the post-World War II period, as "baby boomers" who had delayed marriage did wed at last, at a later median age than in many decades. At the century's start, median ages at first marriage had declined for women from 22 years old in 1890 to 21.9 in 1900 and for men from 26.1 years old in 1890 to 25.9 in 1900. Both continued to decline to 21.2 and 24.6, respectively, in the 1920s, before a slight rise by the 1930s, when Griggs had begun her column. By the end of that decade, median ages at first marriage in 1940 were 21.5 years old for women and 24.3 years old for men, but the trend again had reversed in the post-World War II period and beyond. By 1950, median ages at first marriage had hit an all-time low of only 20.3 years old for women and 22.8 years old for men, both unchanged by 1960. Then came the impact of "the Pill" in the 1960s. By the start of the 1970s, median ages at first marriage had risen to 20.8 years old for women and 23.2 years old for men, and both would rise more during the decade than in any decade before. By the end of the 1970s, the median age for men at first marriage would be near records at 24.7 years old, almost matching their median in 1920—while women would wait to first wed until a median age of 22 years old in 1980, a high that had been unmatched for almost a century, since 1890. However, the divorce rate also rose steadily in the 1970s and would not peak until the next decade.[66]

In contrast to "never marrieds," multiple divorces and multiple marriages became more the norm in society and in the column. "Third Time Around" wrote of a "shaky" marriage; she was suspicious of her husband, also remarried, when he often would "go to a gas station and be gone longer than he should," she wrote. The reader admitted to remarrying solely for "material security," which Griggs called clearly reason that her reader had "missed the boat this third time around," because marriage required a better foundation. The columnist provided her usual roster of referrals for marital counseling but also asked her reader to examine whether she was being reasonable or over-reacting to unfounded suspicions, based on insufficient information in her letter. Griggs' response differed to readers with evidence of life with "chronic philanderers," so many that it seemed that adultery was a chronic societal condition in the early 1970s—or that wives' acceptance was on the wane. "Non-Believer," "Miserable in Marriage," and other readers wrote more missives about reaching the end of their patience than had writers of letters sampled in previous decades. All were wives ready to end marriages of many decades. "I'm getting too old to fight this sort of thing," wrote a reader in recounting life with "a ladies' man."[67]

Another reader, a great-grandmother, still felt forced into her unhappy marriage, long after having been engaged at the age of fourteen and pregnant at sixteen years old, when she had gone unwillingly to her wedding. "I can't see myself suffering any more. So if I had it to do over again, I'd give him one more chance, no more. I don't think it's worthwhile to go through all I have, all these years," she wrote to Griggs. Her reader's only reward had been her children, then dozens of grandchildren and now great-grandchildren. She could not leave her husband but sought solace from the columnist, who advised finding

---

66 Evans, *Born for Liberty*, 177, 237, 253, 265, 302, 316; Thompson, *History of Wisconsin*, 248; U.S. Bureau of the Census, "Estimated Median Age at First Marriage, by Sex, 1890 to the Present" (Washington, D.C., 2006).

67 IQG, "Married for Security;" IQG, "Mate Roams, Wife Snoops, It's Been Going On for Years," *MJ*, January 15, 1972; IQG, "He's a Ranting Drudge."

comfort as an "influence for good" with grandchildren to "help them avoid … hurts and injustices suffered" by her reader. "Speak plainly to them" about marriage, wrote Griggs to the matriarch. "Give it to them straight."[68]

Owing to improved birth control, marriage no longer automatically meant decades of childrearing for women with more options in the era: married or single, whether never-married or divorced and single again; married, with or without children; single, with or without a family to raise. "Baby boomers" not only had delayed marriage for a higher age at first marriage than in decades but also had delayed starting their own childrearing years. Media reported the trend in headlines about a "baby bust," until maternity wards in hospitals again would overflow in the late 1970s, with some mothers-to-be enduring labor in hospital hallways in Wisconsin. As state historian Robert C. Nesbit writes, "young couples marrying later also delayed beginning their families, and on average they preferred to have fewer children than had their parents," who had birthed the "baby boom" with sizeable families in the 1950s and 1960s. By the end of the 1970s, the average family size in Wisconsin would decline to 3.3, "only slightly more than one child per set of parents," as Nesbit writes—that is, in those households that had two parents.[69]

More significant regarding marital status may have been the number of households now headed by single women with families. Of little more than half of writers of letters sampled who self-identified their status, one in six—15.8 percent—in the 1970s was divorced, widowed, or separated, more than double the percentage in all previous decades of the column of writers of letters sampled who had identified their status. More in the 1970s were single mothers than in the decades before. "Will Someone Please Remember the Children?" was a divorced reader at the start of the decade, whose letter pleaded with others to also oppose "a radical anti-marriage movement," actually a "men's movement," whose founder had sent a missive to newspapers nationwide that had run in the column. He argued, against all data, that divorce financially benefitted women. Instead, historian Sara M. Evans writes, "divorce had devastating economic consequences for

---

68   IQG, "Sad Life With 'Chaser' Detailed by Grandma," *MJ*, February 4, 1975.

69   Nesbit, *Wisconsin*, 504.

many women" in the 1970s, when "in the first year following a divorce, the standard of living for men increased 42 percent and for women it decreased 73 percent." As another of Griggs' readers wrote in reply to the missive from the anti-marriage advocate, he acted from "bitterness and self-pity" and actually sought "male liberation from marriage"—no matter that he termed it "divorce reform" of laws according any rights to women—and he was "overly preoccupied" with "the need for revenge" on his ex-wife. "He is concerned only with his pocketbook, not the life of the child he has participated in producing," she wrote.[70]

"Will Someone Please Remember the Children?" described her experience, as a working-class woman coping with the economic impact of divorce on herself and her young children.

> I can only describe divorce as an agonizing experience....
> Life for myself and my two small children became an almost impossible fight for survival. It is very difficult for a woman to earn enough to provide for a family and pay a babysitter while she works, and be a good mother.
> In spite of the fact that this struggle and the hard facts of reality resulted in the frustrations that poverty can produce, including malnutrition, we made it.[71]

While mothers of younger children would become more than half of working women by the end of the decade, well more than half of mothers who became heads of households in the 1970s already were in the paid workforce in Wisconsin.[72]

> We made it in spite of ... my children's father [who] does not believe he has any moral obligation to help provide for the children he rejected. He has been quite successful in evading his responsibility, and successful in pursuing a selfish mode of living....
> This type of individual is the loser, no matter how much he gains materially at the expense of others.[73]

The "others," the children too often forgotten in criticism of working mothers, were the reason for "divorce reform," she wrote, but not as the

---

70   IQG, "Is Parental Advice Best in Children's Marriage?" *MJ*, February 2, 1971; Evans, *Born for Liberty*, 302.

71   IQG, "Is Parental Advice Best?"

72   Nesbit, *Wisconsin*, 503.

73   IQG, "Is Parental Advice Best?"

"men's movement" meant. The soaring divorce rate had so overloaded the system that judges rarely came into a case until the end of a process replete with delays, too late to rectify decisions on custody and child support already made by lesser court commissioners, less concerned with "real justice" than with division of property.

> The courts are too busy, and sad to say, far too impersonal. If reform is needed, it is in this area. Court schedules are jammed, often inefficient, and family court commissioners are case-hardened and too overburdened ... to administer real justice.
>
> Incidentally, alimony rarely is awarded in Wisconsin, if the woman is able-bodied and has no dependent children. If alimony is awarded, it is usually a supplement to child support and is most often [time-limited or] suspended when a mother goes to work, which she invariably must do, unless she goes on welfare, which I didn't do.[74]

Regarding custody, she wrote, "you cannot, no matter the problems with the ex-mate, put a price tag on human beings ... the children, or use them as pawns in a silly battle to win. Win what?" Her question was prophetic regarding the "men's movement" founder whose missive had begun the series of letters. Then, he was only beginning his crusade, which he would wage for decades and finally lose in his state's high court, ending his appeals and freeing his ex-wife from further legal fees to retain her property under the divorce decree. The case fueled a feminist campaign for new laws for women's property rights, which would win its first success in Wisconsin, but not for another decade more—after many more letters to Griggs on the issue of divorce reform.[75]

If women would win equal rights under the Constitution, men would benefit, wrote a local "men's movement" leader in another letter to the column, a clever ploy. His fellow "anti-marriage movement" advocate's letter had "much truth in it," wrote the Wisconsinite of "a rising feeling in this country that marriage is not the answer for a fulfilled life." He positioned himself as seeking "divorce reform" for women's sake, owing to "emotional trauma" that they endured at the end of marriage as well.

---

74   Ibid.

75   Ibid. The nationally known "radical anti-marriage advocate" was George F. Doppler, author of *America Needs Total Divorce Reform—Now!* (New York: Vantage Press, 1973).

He did not, however, address data on economic trauma to women and children in divorce but opined—without similar evidence but claiming to state "known fact"—that "courts do impoverish the male" with the "imposition" of child support, so that "the male is penalized in a divorce action." He admitted, however, that women suffered as well, because "the male" increasingly tended to react to the court order by eluding it—and paying no "penalty" at all. "The male takes off, and she either has to go on welfare or she has to go out and support the family," he wrote, in an argument that needed work as much as did women without support. In the end, the "men's movement" advocate argued for his "divorce reform" to be accomplished by "equality under the law" for women—the aim of a proposed federal Equal Rights Amendment or ERA that woman suffragists first had penned for Congress, where the bill had been submitted by a member of the House, who was a nephew of Susan B. Anthony, almost fifty years before.[76]

In the next year, the debate would move from the back of the newspaper to the front section, if still far from the front page, when the ERA finally passed in Washington in 1972 and went to the states for ratification. Wisconsin's leader of the "men's movement" welcomed "this position on women's lib," as "equality of the sexes is a good thing," he said. "The emancipation of women ... has deprived men of their rights," he said, in a news story that otherwise quoted feminists in Wisconsin, who immediately undertook work toward winning ratification of the ERA. Wisconsin legislators acted swiftly to approve the bill. That brought Illinois activist Phyllis Schlafly to the state almost as swiftly to stage her first attack on the ERA, a crusade that would become her life's work. First, Schlafly so muddled the issue in Wisconsin with her claim that a federal ERA would mandate "unisex bathrooms" that, in a referendum, voters rejected a minor rewording of the state's historic ERA that had been on the books for more than half a century —where it would remain, as originally written, rather than with the wording to reflect laws enacted in the workplace in decades since. As

---

76   IQG, "Wife Plans Spending Spree to Punish Fool of a Husband," *MJ*, February 3, 1971. On the local "men's movement" leader, Lee Haydock of Milwaukee, he variously described himself as founder, board chair, or director of a Wisconsin Institute for Divorce but "refused to describe the number of members" other than that most were men; see "Group Works to Help Ease Pain of Divorce," [Madison, Wis.] *Capital Times*, April 12, 1975.

for "divorce reform," Wisconsin would be among the first states with "no-fault divorce" by the end of the decade. No matter how well-intentioned were women who worked for the law, however, it would realize the aim of the "men's movement" in further reducing the incidence of alimony—and, as a result, the average income of Wisconsin women, who would fall farther behind national norms for women with every decade ahead.[77]

As debate over the ERA also would extend into the decade ahead, the proposed law did not surface in readers' debates by name but continued as an undercurrent in letters sampled. At the end of the 1970s, proponents neared the number of states needed but also neared the first-ever deadline imposed by Congress for ratification of a Constitutional amendment. They won an extension for a few more years to win the few more states needed, including the state to the south of Wisconsin, Schlafly's home state of Illinois. In the interim, many readers of the column and even the columnist indicated apparent acceptance of changing mores about marriage and more.[78]

A series of readers' letters in the late 1970s came on premarital relationships, which also became news, when the Milwaukee police chief's continued unwillingness to cope with women in the department culminated in the surveillance and firing of two officers for "cohabitation," although they were engaged. Unlike the chief, most readers accepted or at least acceded to the change. "His Mom" shared the "shock" that had been expressed by others upon learning, one wrote, that their children were "shacking up." Her grown son and his girlfriend were "living together without benefit of a wedding ceremony," she wrote. "We don't condone this lifestyle." They had, however, "given love and good wishes" to him and the "lovely person" with whom he lived, along with her daughter from a former marriage. "They seem to get along better than most married couples we know," wrote the reader, if with resignation. The columnist commended her "compassion" and may have shocked faithful readers, who well knew her faithful promulgation of marriage,

---

77   Dorothy Austin, "State Women Leaders Laud Bill Approval," *MS*, March 23, 1971. The article and many others incorrectly state that the Wisconsin referendum in the 1970s in Wisconsin was for the state's first ERA, rather than for an amendment to that historic first state ERA in the country, still the law; see McBride, "'Forward' Women," 79-136.

78   Evans, *Born for Liberty*, 304-307.

when Griggs agreed that "adults choosing to live together rather than marry because of the marital failures they see around them" and the "fear" of divorce was understandable.[79]

Issues of divorce and child custody hardly were resolved among readers, however, nor would other age-old debates be settled in remaining years of the column, as it neared its half-century mark—and as Griggs neared her ninetieth year. As ever, even as the "computer age" came to the newsroom, the seemingly ageless Griggs proved her adaptability again. Replacing a few typewriters at a time at mid-decade, the first "video display terminals" unnerved even many younger newsmen. As one recalled, "it didn't help that these alien machines were called VDTs," which "sounded a bit too much to some of us like a sexually transmitted disease." Management sought volunteers—or victims—to pioneer in the often-frustrating new ways of putting out the newspaper. Reporters recalled that "stories vanished and refused to return" on the system that was "crashing all the time" and "only too happy to eat or lose your story when it was half done." Many were unwilling to master complicated new keyboards and codes, and at least one opted for retirement, rather than adapt to another new technology. Griggs, however, gave it a go. "She might have let out an 'oh dear' once in a while," a news clerk near Griggs' desk would recall, yet she "learned enough about the computer to keep putting out her column. She must have been close to eighty then," guessed the awed colleague. Actually, of course, Griggs already was an octogenarian, but her age remained the columnist's closest secret. She maintained her record of having missed hardly a day in the office, as she neared half a century at the *Milwaukee Journal*.[80]

Even in its final years ahead, her column on the back page of the newspaper also would continue to maintain relevancy owing to readers whose letters at times in the 1970s had reflected front-page headlines,

---

79   IQG, "Lifestyle of Grown Son Accepted by His Mother," *MJ*, December 19, 1978; Katherine Skiba, "2 Engaged Officers Spied Upon, Fired," *MJ*, September 14, 1978. On coverage of the firing of the officers, other "cohabitation" incidents in the state, and readers' reaction, including the cited letter to Griggs, see also Elizabeth H. Pleck, *Not Just Roommates: Cohabitation After the Sexual Revolution* (Chicago: University of Chicago Press, 2012).

80   Wells, *Milwaukee Journal*, 442-444; Jim Stingl, "35 Years Ago, We Traded Typewriters for Terminals," *MJS*, May 31, 2011.

from drugs to divorce to environmentalism in the state that had pioneered "Earth Day" at the start of the decade. Other issues in letters sampled again had been harbingers of headlines still ahead, as "news" that rarely would be seen in newspapers for a decade or more. For example, the issue of "smoking pot" had caused considerable debate among readers, while a lone letter among those sampled on the more ubiquitous smoking of a legal substance, tobacco, led to little discussion. Its banning would become a major crusade meriting extensive coverage in years to come. Similarly, readers had written for decades of workplace situations that suggested sexual harassment, a term coined only in the mid-1970s. The first few court cases came only in the late 1970s—more than a decade before the term would become more commonplace parlance in a society that still would wrestle with the concept, when it would become the focus of the country and televised Congressional hearings on an appointment to the highest court in the land.[81]

Readers' many letters on other issues that had occasioned infrequent coverage as "news" in Wisconsin, such as birth control bans, provided better reading than did the straight reporting of legislative bills, votes, and vetoes. As for abortion, which at least had moved forward to the "women's pages" during the decade, the issue finally would become front-page "news" in many newspapers nationwide in the next decade—but even then, reporting rarely would resonate with the impact of readers' letters in the column in the *Milwaukee Journal* on realities of their lives. Perspectives of women readers on many issues would continue to differ from the "news" in their conversations with each other and with their "Dear Mrs. Griggs," as they entered the final years of their unusual collaboration on the column, which again would bear witness to a return of an era of conservatism in the country—or, for feminists, a "backlash against American women."[82]

---

81   IQG, "Introspective Session"; IQG, "Mother Abused, Beaten, Laughed at by Big Sons," *MJ*, February 5, 1971; IQG, "Dad's a Do-It-Yourselfer, Family's Exhausted, Unhappy," *MJ*, October 11, 1971. On sexual harassment, see Susan Brownmiller, *In Our Time: A Memoir of a Revolution* (New York: Dell, 1999), 279-294.

82   On the term "backlash" to describe a 1980s "counter-assault on women's rights," see Susan Faludi, *Backlash: The Undeclared War Against American Women* (New York: Three Rivers Press, 1991; rev. ed., 2006), 18-19.

7

The End of the ERA and the End of an Era in Milwaukee, 1981-1985

In the final decade of "Dear Mrs. Griggs," when the column would set a record in the "advice industry" in surpassing fifty years in print, the aging columnist who seemed to have seen every aspect of human nature would witness age-old issues for women that now would be front-page news. At the time, neither Ione Quinby Griggs nor her readers had the terminology not yet coined for discussions of issues such as "acquaintance rape" and "stalking," but that did not deter their debates on the back of the newspaper about those and other issues in women's lives. The column again proved topical and even prescient in coverage of issues that would emerge on the news agenda and even on the front page in the coming decade. At the same time, at the start of the decade, headlines heralded a "conservative revolution," claiming a return to "family values" that would not necessarily serve many families of the women in working-class Milwaukee who comprised most of the column's readers. They could vouch, as a slogan of the modern women's movement in the previous decade had declared, that "the personal was political." However, by mid-decade, Griggs' readers would lose the venue that had provided opportunity to participate in public discourse, the column that had served as a community forum for more than half a century.

Few discussions proved so personal to women, and so politicized in the era, as those on the issue of rape. It had come to the fore in the 1970s, when feminists first had won reframing of rape laws in Wisconsin and elsewhere. The issue especially won wider public consciousness with women's "Take Back the Night" movement, which then had come to Wisconsin in marches and "speak-outs" of rape survivors and their supporters in Milwaukee and elsewhere at the end of the decade. A landmark study soon to be undertaken on sexual assault would be published only as the column came to an end, in mid-decade, when both scholarly and popular publication, the latter in *Ms.* magazine and then in other media, would explode the myth of solely "stranger rape" and expose continued refusal of authorities to recognize a need for further reform of laws, practices, and prosecution of perpetrators and of medical and media treatment of rape survivors.[1]

Years prior to the start of the landmark study on sexual assault, "A Rape Victim" had spoken out in the column about her experience, which reflected societal reluctance—and officials' refusal—to address the issue. The banner headline on the column that day, with the words "brutal," "raped," and "sex nut," was especially jolting in juxtaposition with "the funnies," the comics on the same page of the "Green Sheet" feature section.

> I was 23 years old, a very independent young woman. I had heard of rape for years but thought, "Hell, I would be able to get away from anyone who tried to rape me!"
>
> ....I gave a ride to an old high school acquaintance. He had at one time been friendly with my brother, also had met my father.... I

---

1   IQG, "She Thought Passenger Was Friend But Was Raped by a Brutal 'Sex Nut,'" *MJ*, January 22, 1981; Daryl J. Olszewski, "Statutory Rape in Wisconsin: History, Rationale, and the Need for Reform," *Marquette Law Review* 89 (2006), 695-697. On the initial study of rape that began in 1982, and the first scholarly publications, see M.P. Koss, K.E. Leonard, D.A. Beezley, and C.J. Oros, "Non-stranger Sexual Aggression: A Discriminant Analysis of the Psychological Characteristics of Undetected Offenders," *Sex Roles* 12 (1985), 981-992; see also M.P. Koss, C.A Gidycz, and N. Wisniewski, "The Scope of Rape: Incidence and Prevalence of Sexual Victimization in a National Sample of Higher Education Students," *Journal of Consulting and Clinical Psychology* 55:2 (1987), 167-170. For the first popular publication, see Ellen Sweet, "Date Rape: The Story of an Epidemic and Those Who Deny It," *Ms.* 14:4 (October 1985), 56-58. For a book-length treatment of the study, by a journalist, see Robin Warshaw, *I Never Called It Rape* (New York: Harper and Row, 1988). On another report of rape to Griggs' column and her handling of a possible hoax letter, as the writer alleged that the rapist claimed to have written to Griggs and received her "go ahead" to rape, "because of the loose lifestyles today," see IQG, "Story That Rapist Told His Victim Is Preposterous and Ridiculous," *MJ*, October 14, 1982.

thought I was safe with him.... It didn't occur to me that a few years could make a difference in a young man.

I am 5 feet 2 inches tall and at the time weighed 105 pounds. This fellow was 5 feet 11 inches in height and weighed 175 pounds. He had ... turned into a "sex nut," and being in a car with him, I didn't have a chance.[2]

She contacted police but they discouraged her from pursuing prosecution of the rapist.

With my clothes ripped, I went home. My mother ... panicked, so I had to call police, but I decided not to press charges. I feared that under the circumstances, having once known the guy and offering him a ride, I couldn't make the charge of rape stick.

Even the police thought it would be fruitless. So three years later this "nut" who ... raped me is running around free. As for myself, I am pretty locked up inside me, fearful to be left alone, afraid if I go outside by myself, someone will be watching for me to harm me.[3]

I let first step to recovery, years later, was writing to Griggs—and to other readers, for their sake.

I feel like a prisoner. I have a daily battle with myself. Some days it's better for me, some days worse. I decided to write this letter to warn others, hoping to prevent them from going through the same horror, also as a step to help myself. I hope it will keep other girls or women from being as ignorant and gullible as I was.[4]

Griggs reassured her reader that her "report" would help others, perhaps to take "precautions"—but more important for her reader was recovery and return "to a normal life, physically, mentally and emotionally," she wrote. "I pray that no woman who reads today's column will ever be raped, but if she is and survives the experience, does she know what she should do to cope with her emotional well-being?" For "A Rape Victim" and other readers, Griggs gave an extensive list of referrals to recently established "crisis lines" and services in several counties and informed her readers that the counselors would accompany rape victims to hospitals and to police.[5]

---

2   IQG, "She Thought Passenger Was Friend."

3   Ibid.

4   Ibid.

5   Ibid.

The issue of rape repeatedly arose in the column in the 1980s. A reader who had "never told anyone before writing a first letter" to Griggs about "acquaintance rape" wrote a second time that her "secret was out." On a date, she had encountered the rapist, reacted from "painful memories of feeling brutalized," revealed the reason to her boyfriend—and had not heard from him since. Worry for him had motivated her to write again, but Griggs advised her to focus more on herself, again giving a referral for counseling to recover from the trauma that still affected her relationships. Another reader wrote of marital rape—also not by that term, another concept yet to be widely and legally recognized—in a letter labeled by Griggs as "one of the worst battered-family stories that has come to my attention" in half a century. "Can you bear hearing one more battered wife's story? One more about battered children?" began the letter about a "husband who goes into a rage and beats me if I don't feel like sex when I'm overtired— as I'm likely to be with seven children." All were under twelve years old, two "still in diapers," wrote "Battered," who had wed at the age of sixteen. Her husband, jailed three times for battering, had returned each time to inflict worse. The result, despite her "precautions," was repeated pregnancies. "Battered" worried more for her children, however, and wondered whether a women's shelter in Milwaukee provided counseling for them. "Yes, children can be helped," replied Griggs, urging her to "get away from the batterer as soon as possible. You will be guided as to steps to take in planning a life of safety, security, and peace of mind." Griggs gave the rest of the column to her research on Sojourner Truth House, a referral to be repeated often in the remaining years of the column.[6]

The first shelter in the modern era in Milwaukee for battered women and children, the Sojourner Truth House had been founded only a few years before, but the first facility had fast become overcrowded. A larger site had opened by the 1980s, a year before "Battered" wrote to the column. In the coming year, reported Griggs, the women's organizations that had founded the shelter predicted need to house a

6   IQG, "Battered Wife Is Told About Help Offered by Sojourner Truth House," *MJ*, March 10, 1982; IQG, "What Can Woman Do If Boyfriend Leaves After Learning of Rape?" *MJ*, January 28, 1983; IQG, "Many Books Can Help Parents Alert Children About Sexual Abuse," *MJ*, June 29, 1984.

thousand women and children. One may have been "Help!" who worried whether she would be welcome, because her batterer was a live-in boyfriend.[7]

> I can't take the pain of abuse any longer. I don't know where to turn. I am getting to be a nervous wreck. I have been living with a man … for the last three years. I have a child by him. The last year has been a nightmare, a year of physical and verbal beatings, lying and cheating. He is drinking and using drugs, I have told him to leave, but he won't.[8]

Her experience explained why women continued to work for new domestic violence laws—or at least enforcement of existing laws, rather than lectures from the authorities on the benefits of marriage. No law required that victims be married to receive protection from police, no matter their personal and moral beliefs, but her reader informed Griggs that doing so could be difficult.

> There must be some action I can take, legal or otherwise.… I contacted the police in my district twice. The first time the officer said nothing could be done because I'm not married to the man. The second time I was told I had made my bed so now must lie in it.
> Something has got to be done. All I want is for him to leave the house where I pay rent so I won't be available for his abuse.… Not being married to him, paying the rent and owning all the furnishings should make it easy to get him out, but it isn't.[9]

Griggs again gave a referral to the shelter for battered women, after researching her reply and receiving assurance that readers could call Sojourner Truth House as a shelter for all women, "wed or unwed," as well as children. "You don't have to stay in this mess," she wrote. "You and your daughter would be helped in every way," she wrote in urging her reader to "get the shelter's help as soon as possible" and seek child support to "scare him into leaving of his own accord," wrote Griggs

---

7   IQG, "Battered Wife;" IQG, "Abused by the Man She Lives With, Woman Hopes Somebody Can Help," *MJ*, October 22, 1983. The shelter, now part of Sojourner Family Peace Center, continues to operate in the city.

8   IQG, "Abused by the Man."

9   Ibid.

After the decade of antiwar protest, and after the 1970s opened with a campaign for the Twenty-Sixth Amendment to the Constitution to lower the voting age to eighteen years old—and with celebrations of the anniversary of the Nineteenth Amendment for full federal suffrage, five decades before, in 1920, just as Ione Quinby Griggs had begun her journalistic career—the number of women students at Pulaski High School in Milwaukee equaled the number of male classmates sworn in as new voters in 1980 by teachers Anne Canarie and Donald Soucie. Some of the new voters may have been among the young readers who remained faithful followers of "Dear Mrs. Griggs" into the 1980s, with debates about women's rights and another federal amendment campaign in the first state with a state Equal Rights Amendment, won in the Wisconsin constitution in 1921. However, her readers would see the revived campaign for a federal ERA end only a few states from victory with the requisite number of ratifications, as some states rescinded as a result of an anti-ERA campaign. (Copyright 2014 Journal Sentinel, Inc., reproduced with permission)

of the abuser.[10] Paradoxically, the columnist was encouraging a threat of child support to encourage paternal abandonment. Apparently no reader called her out for doing so, including judges and others in local officialdom, who often wrote that they were regular readers but rarely wrote regarding the egregiously gendered inactions increasingly reported by readers.

10   Ibid.

Griggs had begun the decade by defending her favorite agencies, but letters sampled suggest that she gave up doing so for some, perhaps owing to several factors in the politicized era of failure of both the ERA and efforts to reform other women's rights laws. When "Help!" wrote to the column in 1983, women's rights had become more controversial than in previous decades, after reaction in the 1970s to the *Roe v. Wade* ruling had aided a rising "conservative revolution" by 1980 that would end many women's hopes for an Equal Rights Amendment. The deadline imposed by Congress came in 1982, almost sixty years after women first had proposed the Constitutional amendment. However, the ERA remained three states short of the requisite thirty-five states' ratifications to become law—and although more than that number of states had ratified. Anti-feminists since, however, had swayed a few states to rescind their ratifications.[11]

Wisconsin, one of the first to ratify a decade before, had stood firm for a federal ERA. Its historic first state ERA also still stood, although the law had been so little used that journalists then—and historians since—incorrectly stated that the state lacked its own law. As a result, some *Journal* readers seemed resigned to apparent failure of the modern women's movement. Others determined to redouble efforts to win progress in other ways. "I saw that my personal agenda for me as a woman probably would never be met in my lifetime," said one, but for her daughters, she worked for "a better tomorrow." Her story and another on the ERA, a "brief," ran on inside pages; more coverage of a massive Constitutional amendment campaign could be found only in "women's pages." The *Journal* front page that day did include a story on women's rights, on a mother illegally denied custody, although elsewhere in the country. Only the column on the back page of the newspaper consistently covered local child custody cases, as reported by readers.[12]

Child custody laws, policies, and practices remained in a state of confusion in Wisconsin in the 1980s, when "Help!" wrote of the unpredictability of courts in contested custody cases, increasingly a concern in the column—another gendered issue, in addition to rape,

---

11   Evans, *Born for Liberty*, 306.

12   Joy Krause, "ERA Has Been on the US Agenda Since 1923," *MJ*, June 30, 1982; Lois Blinkhorn, "A New Day Dawns as Chapter Closes on Women's Rights," *MJ*, June 30, 1982; McBride, "'Forward' Women," 79-136.

about which readers provided perspectives too often lacking elsewhere in the newspaper. Worry for her child was the reason that "Help!" had felt helpless, as the abuse "got so bad" that she had considered suicide but wrote, "I wouldn't kill myself and leave the child I had by him. I wouldn't want him to get custody of her. Think of the life she would live." Anger at courts motivated another reader, "A Column Fan," to write of a case of removal of a child from relatives in the adoption process and return of the child to an abusive parent. Griggs replied, "there probably is no greater tragedy than the wrongful shuffling about of a child in the tender, impressionable years" and called for revision of custody laws, if indirectly, in writing that others ought to "consider" doing so.[13]

Griggs heeded her role as an advice columnist, not an editorial writer. She only could reply with resources for her reader to "possibly help the child," returned to a possibly abusive home. As for "whatever happened in court," she increasingly retreated from defending judges, court commissioners, and other officials in divorce and custody cases, writing that it was not for her to "judge" causes of the judicial "postponements" and "paperwork errors" that cost parents custody. After reading many letters alleging repeated failures of her favorite agencies and the courts, Griggs was glad to publicize efforts for reforms. A letter from a professor at the local state university gave Griggs praise—gratifying to the columnist who had not completed college—for help in finding participants for and publicizing "exciting" results of a "wife-beating" study that found need to reframe women subjected to spousal abuse, not passive victims but proactive survivors devising "various strategies and techniques" and resources for "violence-free lives."[14]

Griggs' retreat from referrals to longtime sources did not signal a retreat from moderating divisive discussions in the increasingly

---

13   IQG, "Who Is the Loser When Toddler Is Given to a 'Neglectful' Mom?" *MJ*, September 14, 1982; IQG, "'Beating Wife-Beating' Project Brought Some Enlightening Results," *MJ*, September 5, 1981.

14   IQG, "Who Is the Loser." For an example of another request within the same week for Griggs' assistance, a request for participants for a study of breastfeeding, see IQG, "Her Co-Workers Want to Muzzle Wagging Tongue of Hypochondriac," *MJ*, September 10, 1981. For an example of a letter to the column from an official, see IQG, "Judge Takes Issue with Woman Who Claimed Mom Was Not Guilty," *MJ*, July 16, 1982.

conservative final decade of the column, when women comprised more of her contributors than in any previous period. Of writers who self-identified by gender, women comprised more than 90 percent in letters sampled. In recommendations to attempt to resolve conflicts, however, she continued to refrain from a reflexive preference for her most faithful readers. For example, in the case described by "Column Fan," a court had returned the child to a mother described as neglectful, a placement with which Griggs had disagreed.

Her fairness again was tested in a readers' debate about custody, among the last columns in which she first gave a fervent defense of her favorite social agencies, until adamant women readers wrote repeatedly of troubling experiences with social workers as well as other officials involved in contested cases. The women's letters unleashed a campaign by "men's movement" proponents, who returned in greater numbers to contribute to the column, compared to their few letters found in previous decades. Then, they had worked with women legislators for "no-fault divorce" reform, first proposed twenty years before, who finally won the law in the late 1970s. A legal scholar argues, however, that lawmakers in Wisconsin, with a "penchant" for impetuous legislation, did not act wisely to anticipate sometimes-disastrous impacts of "no-fault divorce."[15]

Contributors to the column did focus on the effects of the new "no-fault divorce" law in Wisconsin on child custody laws, not brought in line with divorce reform until a decade later. A woman reader blamed "the women's liberation movement, striving for equality," for having "helped to bring about this situation" of mothers no longer receiving alimony, owing to divorce reform—and then, "in the best interests of the child," also denied custody by courts for lack of ability to support their children as well as could fathers. That caseworkers calculated the higher likelihood of fathers following court orders for child support, only if they had custody, also had worked against mothers seeking custody, as readers wrote. By the mid-1980s, many reports of such cases

---

15   Joseph A. Ranney, "Anglicans, Merchants, and Feminists: A Comparative Study of the Evolution of Married Women's Rights in Virginia, New York, and Wisconsin," *William & Mary Journal of Women and the Law* 6:3 (2000), 544-548, 556. On post-1920 laws in Wisconsin relevant to women and gender, see also Joseph A. Ranney, *Trusting Nothing to Providence: A History of Wisconsin's Legal System* (Madison: University of Wisconsin Law School, 1999).

beyond Griggs' column would cause a wider crusade for changes again in state laws, with the support of the women's movement for equitable standing in courts for both genders.[16]

In the interim, readers such as "Been There" castigated the columnist for "naiveté" in her advice on non-support. "Mrs. Griggs, you are unaware of the immensity of this problem," she wrote, citing national and local statistics on divorce, custody, and court-ordered child support.[17]

> By the end of the first year after the divorce, 40% of the women don't get support money for their children. After the second year, the percentage is 60%, and [it] increases as time goes by.
>
> Thousands of women are in this predicament, carrying the whole responsibility of support for the children.... Is it any wonder these women feel like outcasts from a society that screams about women on welfare but takes no trouble to correct a situation?[18]

The columnist's "'should-have' attitude" to women was not helpful, her reader wrote, when the courts in Milwaukee and elsewhere in Wisconsin admitted their lack of effort in forcing fathers who had abandoned families and flouted laws to comply with court-ordered child support.[19]

> Most of the fathers have "disappeared." Their whereabouts are known to the courts, but the red tape involved and the multitude of cases make it impossible to achieve any results.... I have been more fortunate than most.... I have never been on welfare.
>
> But I tried repeatedly to get court-ordered support from my children's father and failed. I consider our court systems extremely lax in providing assistance....
>
> They continue to pass the buck by saying that their hands are tied, that our laws here don't cover ... even though they have correct addresses for the fathers.
>
> The position of these mothers is sad.... The unfairness of the present attitude and legislation is deplorable.... The present laws regarding support are a joke. If people would just keep in mind

---

16   Ibid.; IQG, "There Is No Substitute for Mother Love, Woman Says," *MJ*, November 30, 1981.

17   IQG, "Divorced Mother with Family Backs Idea of a Support Group," *MJ*, September 5, 1984.

18   Ibid.

19   Ibid.

that the support is for the children, not for the mothers, the attitude of society would change and the laws would show improve-
ment.[20]

Griggs carefully parsed her comment that had prompted the response
from "Been There" and agreed that "more is needed than additional
legislation," but she was not sanguine. Enforcement by courts was
lacking "not only because of lack of staff but of money," and in a conservative era, the expected outcome "could be an outcry from taxpay-
ers." If her reader was willing to "give time and effort, besides writing a
letter," toward organizing for change, however, Griggs would give her
support to a support group, gladly forwarding letters of interest from
other readers.[21]

Despite the women's movement's support of gender equity in divorce, custody, and child support, some male contributors to the
column promoted a preference for fathers' custody of children in divorce—even fathers refusing to marry the mothers of their children
or obey child-support orders. Their immoderate letters may have influenced Griggs in her shift in referrals after debates on child-custody
laws earlier in the decade by readers, as legislative resolution remained
in flux until the end of the decade. Many letters came from mothers,
such as "Fifteen Years of Hell," who had lost custody of her children
five years before. She blamed Milwaukee County social workers—often recommended by Griggs—empowered by a clause in the state's
"no-fault divorce law," a compromise with Catholic lobbyists that required couples to receive counseling from social workers, whose custody recommendations carried crucial weight in family courts.

> The decision was unfair. My ex-husband wouldn't admit how
> cruel and abusive he had been to me. He beat and otherwise abused
> me.... Milwaukee County Social Services Department either was
> deceived by my husband before the divorce action or deliberate-
> ly blinded themselves as to why I fled this man and my children,
> fearing to let anyone know where I was. I was like a beaten ani-
> mal whose life had been threatened over and over. I was so afraid I
> shook at the mention of my husband's name....

---

20   Ibid.
21   Ibid.

The children had seen him beat me, even take a butcher knife to my throat.[22]

She had been forced to remain in the dangerous situation, because women fleeing abuse could be seen by social workers and courts as abandoning their children. When they had awarded custody to the father, she no longer was in physical danger. The order had enabled him to employ a new form of emotional abuse, however; he had "kept moving" to keep the children from her for years.

Last year ... I got a phone call from one of the children. He had run away from his Dad.

He told me his father had threatened his life. It was his third run-away attempt.... He is with me now and has improved remarkably in school.... Although my income is low, I am totally supporting him. His father is aware of this but won't give me custody.

Due to harassing phone calls forbidding the boy to speak to his brothers ... the boy doesn't want to talk to his father.... I have opened up ways for my ex-husband to communicate with this son, even though I am not given that privilege with the children still with their father. I am gravely concerned ... about the other children.... I can't afford a good lawyer to represent me so I can see the other children.

I wait each day to hear from them and am fearful that one of these days, I will hear of their deaths.... I see no help in sight.[23]

Griggs attempted to defend social workers by blaming her reader's lawyer, presuming poor legal representation in her case. The columnist referred her reader to the Legal Aid Society; its huge caseload, however, hardly recommended it for "Fifteen Years of Hell," as her ex-husband was well-off, with a family that funded his costly law firm and continual flights from justice.[24]

As letters came from mothers who had lost custody of their children, Griggs also could count on letters from custodial fathers in the 1980s. "K.R.P.," from a "fathers movement" that apparently had encouraged the letter campaign to the column, issued vituperative demands— twice—that another reader engage in public debate. His target, "Seen

---

22   IQG, "Mother Who Lost Custody Now Says the Court's Decision Wasn't Fair," *MJ*, September 13, 1982.

23   Ibid.

24   Ibid.

It All," replied that he refused to engage with "a man whose pen spits venom, attacking women in general." Also "active in the 'fathers movement'" was "Custodial Father," who criticized the columnist for alleged gender bias in her carefully balanced reply to "Responsible Mother." Griggs retorted that he ought to "refresh his memory" and reread the column, as "there was no bias there, and none was intended." She had not said, as he claimed, that fathers were not "capable" as "custodians, or that all mothers were responsible." Indeed, she wrote, her statement "that 'some fathers' would know more about what went on in the lives of their children if they had the responsibility of custody" was exactly his argument, although he also had admitted in his emotional, illogical letter that fathers "skip out on child-support payments" and "visitation rights." He blamed their bitterness on costly lawyers, although the costs of court battles were borne by both sides.[25]

"Custodial Father" made a hobby of going to the courthouse to check on the divorce and custody records of casual acquaintances and others unknown to him. He claimed evidence that "even if the mother murdered the child during the custody trial right in front of the judge," fathers could not win in the courts. That he had custody of his daughters contradicted his claim, but they had "the best 'mother' possible in their paternal parent," he asserted, citing as "fact" that mothers committed "two-thirds of child abuse" and that "mother love" was "folklore." He closed his communiqués with contact information for a "fathers movement" organization, for which he had not been the best spokesman. Griggs printed his information to prove lack of bias, but the debate raged on, "inevitably," she wrote, and drily introduced letters of rebuttal with: "Women … don't agree that custodial fathers make better 'mothers' than mothers." A letter signed "The Woman's Side in the Custodial Tug of War" expressed concern that a "snob and a snooper," so "critical of women," had custody of daughters and concluded that divorce reform contributed to increased numbers of custodial fathers, although "the agony of children being torn from their mothers is indescribable." Yet, owing to economics—and politics—a "good, competent mother" without economic resources could not win in the courts, "Woman's Side" wrote. Social workers supported the

---

25   IQG, "Challenged to Debate Custody Issue, She Says 'Thanks But No Thanks,'" *MJ*, January 6, 1982; IQG, "Dad with Custody of 3 Girls Says Some Fathers Are Best 'Mothers,'" *MJ*, November 21, 1981.

side of the parent with higher income, claiming "the best interests of the child" but acting in the interests of their employers, their counties averting costs of "welfare mothers," a popular epithet promulgated by politicians and repeated by media—and readers of the column.[26]

Debate on child custody raged for months, longer than most debates, back and forth in letters both from mothers and the "fathers movement" in the early 1980s, an era when a count of divorced readers among writers to the column rose to the highest level yet in letters sampled. Of the dozens in the 1980s who self-identified their marital or single status at all, almost 15 percent disclosed their divorced status—which is nearly triple the percentage of the divorced among the writers of letters sampled in the previous decade, which had almost tripled from a decade before. At the same time, a precipitous decrease in wedded bliss became evident, by comparison with data on letters sampled in previous decades. Fewer than half of the writers of letters sampled in the 1980s who self-identified their marital status also stated that they were married. Dating also declined among the divorced and widowed; some "singles" stated that, in the 1980s, they had given up on dating—and some had done so sooner. For example, "Where to From Here?" stated that she had not dated for a decade. Griggs, who had remained single to her forties, empathized—as she did with another non-dating widow in writing that "it's hard to lose a good husband."[27]

More often, however, her readers in the 1980s who were single again had opted to lose their spouses, as divorcees wrote to "Dear Mrs. Griggs" in droves, driving the agenda to discussions of issues of divorce and custody in the final decade of the column. Intriguing is that the increase in the number of divorced letter writers came with a concurrent increase in younger writers in letters sampled to almost two-thirds of contributors to the column who self-identified by age. The correlation was low, though, and was countered by the range of ages among the divorced. Many who self-identified as already in middle age and

---

26   IQG, "Dad with Custody"; IQG, "There Is No Substitute;" see also IQG, "Landlord Claims Bad Experience in Renting Flat to Welfare Mother," *MJ*, September 4, 1981.

27   IQG, "New Support Group Aims to Help Women Involved With Divorced Men," *MJ*, April 16, 1982; IQG, "Single Woman, 30, With Big Salary Is Dissatisfied and Full of Anxieties," *MJ*, January 13, 1981.

single still looked for love in the wrong places, as readers wrote who had met men in bars, and for the wrong reasons. "What's wrong with these men who say they're lonely, then proposition a woman on dates? They'll take you out and right away talk 'bed,'" wrote a reader. "Smooch a little, but go to bed on the first date? Never!" As she self-identified as in her sixties, her letter may have unsettled young readers but not the columnist, by then in her nineties. "In aspiring to a second chance at married life, stop using the word 'lonely,'" she replied. "I learned early in life never to think of myself as lonely, no matter what my personal situation might be." Worse, "the word suggests 'self-pity,'" not an attractive attribute on the dating scene. She also could not recommend meeting in bars—nor on her page. "Don't make a second mistake of trying to meet a wife-seeker through a newspaper column," wrote Griggs, again giving her "oft-repeated policy" against "matchmaking" for an older reader weary of dating a widower. He was not a "wife-seeker," wrote Griggs, but a "wife-mourner," and he did not merit yet more years of her life that could be spent happily single.[28]

The advice that "All Wives Should Be Prepared to Live On Their Own, Says Reader," a headline on one of several columns on late-life divorces and "displaced homemakers," continued as in decades before.[29] "Retirement/Divorce" wrote that only when their children had grown and gone did she realize that she repeatedly had given in to her husband and never had his respect.

> Instead of looking forward to a happy retirement ... I'm thinking of divorce. Divorce seems to be the only way I can salvage anything. Our children are grown and on their way.... Since the children have been gone for some time I thought a few years at least would be happily shared with my husband, and there would be no problems.
> Instead of being able to enjoy some things of interest to me, I have to do everything his way.... When our children were young, our [lives] revolved around them. We had fun. Now everything must revolve around him. He will make digs about my "dumb choices."[30]

---

28   IQG, "Widow Complains About Motive of Some of Those Lonely Widowers," *MJ*, November 19, 1981.

29   IQG, "All Wives Should Be Prepared to Live On Their Own, Says Reader," *MJ*, December 29, 1981.

30   IQG, "She Looked Forward to Retirement, But Only Divorce Looms in Future," *MJ*, October 13, 1981.

She now could see that his "sarcastic, negative attitudes" had "turned off the children, because any opinions they have are 'no good,'" and worried that staying with him could mean seeing less of her children, now almost her only companions, after his verbal abuse about her friendships.

> For a time I made a few outside friends and found a few activities, which I thought would give me some interests while still maintaining a home with him, but he found so much fault and nagged me so much that I gave them up.
>
> After all these years, I've had it. Marriage should be a shared and equal arrangement. I have never felt I wanted to run anything but I want to be a respected person who can take part in decisions and plans.[31]

She now had made a decision and had a plan of her own, Griggs' reader wrote. "As I look back, I can see he has controlled my life, but I am beginning to fight back. I'm beginning to use some of his own methods," such as surprising her with his decisions—buying their furniture, even their house—without her input. "I'm practically not a person in the eyes of my husband," she wrote, but he would have to notice her on an upcoming occasion, as she would surprise him with her decision: "I'm planning as his birthday present to tell him I am giving him a divorce."[32]

Amid other echoes of voices of earlier eras in letters about boyfriends behaving badly—as had girlfriends, teenagers, parents, siblings, neighbors, landlords, tenants, and other typical targets of readers' daily ire in Milwaukee for more than half a century—came concerns rarely raised before, although several letters in the 1980s about attitudes toward homosexuality did hark back to the 1950s era of a stigma of singleness for women. Now, single men could be suspect. "No one made anything of it" when "Sad Mother" had "bragged so much" about the success and self-sufficiency of her "bachelor son" a decade before, when he had been thirty years old.[33]

> But now they raise their eyebrows and look suspicious, as though there was something odd or wrong about him. Everything is

---

31   Ibid.

32   Ibid.

33   IQG, "Mom Asks Why 'Friends' Smirk When She Mentions Bachelor Son," *MJ*, November 24, 1981.

discussed so openly on TV these days that maybe they're reacting to something they've heard. The attitude I mention has distressed me so much, I find myself making excuses for my son's bachelorhood.... We give him opportunities to meet nice ladies, but he doesn't seem interested.... I'm getting nervous about this and wonder if I should question him. If I learned something unpleasant, like him being homosexual, I wouldn't stop loving him, but I would be hurt.[34]

No longer eager to assert her pride in her bachelor son, she now "dreaded to mention him for fear … of another knowing look" and pleaded for help in "how to handle this." Griggs advised that "eyebrow raisers and smirkers" were "ignorant persons," as the former "bachelor girl" knew.[35]

Griggs recalled for readers an era half a century earlier when, unwed until she was in her forties, she and her peers had witnessed the term "old maid" begin to fade from public discourse. They were "'bachelor girls' and proud of it," she wrote, "showing the world" that they did not "have to be married to be happy, successful and live normal lives." She supposed that some had been homosexual, but then and since, "there is no reason to look askance at the majority of unwed females and assume they exercise a lifestyle just because they haven't married.... I suggest you consider your unmarried son the same way," she wrote, as her reader had nothing to "fear" in a fine son. "Instead of assuming or 'fearing' he may be homosexual," Griggs wrote, "I suggest that you rise above the eyebrow raisers and retain your maternal pride." She encouraged other mothers, who wrote similar letters that they "wished that there was a supportive group" for parents of gays. A group soon would organize, with publicity in Griggs' column. However, others soon would school the columnist for wording that some read as "looking askance" at assumptions about unmarried women and men but not assumptions about a gay "lifestyle."[36]

That issues of gender orientation gained wider awareness in the early 1980s, little more than a decade after the "Stonewall Riots" gave rise to the gay movement, is evident in evolving terminology; the onetime slang term "gay" apparently had become acceptable as interchangeable

---

34   Ibid.
35   Ibid.
36   Ibid.

with "homosexual" to the newspaper's style committee. That the columnist had not also evolved, however, also became evident. Griggs' replies failed gay readers at times, if in a time when far younger journalists also looked askance at the emerging issue and failed to retain objectivity in reporting. Not that one of her readers understood, either, that he had not "been gay" only upon the onset of puberty or that attempting a heterosexual relationship would bring happiness.

> I never thought that I would be writing for advice, but I am so lonely and unhappy I can't think of anything else to do. I am 41 years old. I have been gay since I was 13 years old.
> I am not happy and would like to find me a girl, which I think would make me happier, but I am too shy to talk to one. Besides, if I met one I liked, I would be afraid to tell her that I've been gay most of my life and would like to change....
> Do you know of a club where I could meet a girl? I honestly want to change my life.[37]

Griggs opened her reply by admitting that "yours is the first request of the kind I have received," after more than half a century in the "advice industry," and raised a possibility of a hoax letter.[38]

"Very Lonely Milwaukee Man," however, asserted "this is not a fake letter," included his identifiers as a sign of sincerity, and Griggs discounted a hoax. She accepted its "authenticity," although she oddly veered off topic to recall other letters that she viewed as related, citing wives who "discovered their husbands had gay propensities" and realized "that instead of 'other women,' there were 'other men.'" She also referred to another reader's letter on cross-dressing, confusing transvestitism with homosexuality. Worse was to come from the columnist, confusing homosexuality with pedophilia.[39]

> It seems likely that you don't have a gay relationship and are not only remorseful but lonely. If your homosexual life started at age 13, it is probable that an adult gay took advantage of you. A psychiatrist might have a clearer insight into all this, but as you have contacted me....
> I don't consider it advisable to join a club in search of a girlfriend who might fill the void in your life.... You don't pinpoint other areas

---

37 IQG, "Man Who's Been 'Gay' Since Teens Seeks Heterosexual Relationship," *MJ*, January 21, 1983.

38 Ibid.

39 Ibid.

of your life—how you earn your living or your recreational interests or hobbies....

Concentrate on these areas to gain some measurable satisfaction in constructive accomplishments.... You may find friends who will keep you from being lonely.[40]

Reaction from the gay community came swiftly. Griggs acknowledged "a number of letters"—code for a sizeable, often outraged response—and gave another column to two letters, taking the unusual step of explaining her selection: Both included verifiable names and addresses, as many letters on the issue had not, and both had been vetted as representative of the gay community.[41]

The first writer demonstrated restraint, not attacking the columnist but aiming to educate her readers about gay life. "R.F.N." established his credentials; he headed a professional group of businessmen in "both the gay and the non-gay community" and opened by artfully appearing to ally with Griggs before asserting that she ought never have published the problematic letter.[42]

> My primary concern is that the letter was too vague on too many issues to respond in print. As you should appreciate, in dealing with an area as sensitive as homosexuality, more than extra precautions must be taken. Specifically, there is no such thing as a "gay relationship." If there were, it wouldn't mean what you said. There are "gay people" ... who fully reflect a balanced understanding of who they are as homosexuals.[43]

Her reply, he wrote, had lacked even a basic understanding that gays were born, not made—and that homosexuality hardly resulted from sexual assault, any more than did heterosexuality.

> Because one's homosexual life started in the teens, in no way does it "probably mean" (as you suggested) that an adult took advantage of the person's youth. That is bologna.... I had my first experience before age 13, and it wasn't with an adult....

---

40   Ibid.

41   IQG, "Homosexuals Criticize Advice to 'Gay' Man Seeking Girlfriend," *MJ*, February 4, 1983.

42   Ibid.

43   Ibid.

> The writer's letter suggests to me that he needs to go into in-
> depth counseling … with a psychologist, social worker or psychia-
> trist who has training on sexual identity.[44]

His list of professionals trained in the issue did not include advice
columnists, and Griggs agreed that it "it might have been better not
to presume the writer was taken advantage of by an adult," admitting
that she had made an "assumption"—a term laden with meaning in
journalism as characteristic of "cub reporters"—but claimed the best
intentions in her advice. However, the next writer asserted that she
lacked training and tolerance, a serious accusation against Griggs, as
well he knew as a longtime reader that she always advocated tolerance
at the core of her counsel. He also attacked her "assumption" and artic-
ulated a more probable cause of the writer's angst.[45]

> Although I have followed your column since I was very young,
> and I am familiar with your caring, albeit conservative advice, I was
> extremely dismayed by your answer.…
> Your reply was an awkward attempt to voice your own anxieties
> and, perhaps, subliminal intolerance toward homosexual people. I
> am particularly distressed by your statement that … it is probable
> that an adult took advantage. This is a very unsubstantiated assess-
> ment.… This man was explaining his entrance into puberty and the
> awareness that he was not heterosexual. This can be a painful, lone-
> ly, self-accusatory time for gay adolescents.…
> The social rejection gay adolescents feel and inability to commu-
> nicate with parents (who are often densely unaware and/or uncom-
> fortable with homosexuality) leads to a sense of social inferiority
> and eventually may trigger depression … in their adult lives.[46]

Griggs had attributed exotic causes to a case of clinical depression
caused by society, not by an imagined assault by an "adult gay"—when
the problem was actual assaults by media and others.

> Almost all can relate tales of cruel ridicule and social pressures.…
> He is suffering from a low self-esteem and perhaps blames himself
> or his sexuality for his depression. His shyness is probably a result
> of his bitter unacceptedness in growing up.

---

44   Ibid.
45   Ibid.
46   Ibid.

In 1983 a gay is still being assaulted by media and ... only a heterosexual can be happy.[47]

A chastened Griggs referred her reader to her previous apologia for poor research although she also argued that the writers were overly sensitive" and "defensive." Soon, she was on the defense with a local gay community newspaper, conducting a "media watch" to single out the columnist for criticism. The issue of gender orientation proved far different, if Griggs did not realize it, from her forte of issues of gender. Her forays into the topic became more cautious, as in a letter on a little girl co-sleeping with her mother. The letter writer wrote that she had "heard that's how lesbians start." Griggs' reply discounted the myth and was terse and dismissive of the letter.[48]

Readers realized more success in educating the columnist and community on other issues, as discussion of "the Pill" also continued in the column, but with an interesting twist by the 1980s, when "A Worried Mother" bemoaned that a daughter going away to college would not "bother" with birth control. A generation that had fought against bans on oral contraception for single women now had to fight with them to take "the Pill" and turned to the column.

> It was a shock a week ago to find my daughter is sexually active and has been for a year. On questioning [her], she said she wasn't protected in any way, wasn't taking "the pill," for instance, and didn't need to fear getting pregnant, because her boyfriend knows what to do that makes her safe. She doesn't want to take "the pill," she said....
>
> I almost hit the floor. On questioning my son, he said other girls feel the same way. Will you write something that will convince these young people that what they believe doesn't make them safe?[49]

Griggs, who had been a "bachelor girl" when federal law had banned even the distribution of information on birth control, agreed that, despite "accurate information on the 'facts of life' available, today's young people can still believe in myths," which she termed as a "tragic" situation, with "statistics showing the tremendous increase in

---

47   Ibid.

48   Ibid.; "In a Nutshell," *Out!*, May 1984; IQG, "Woman Writes to Salute 2 Teens Who Are Hard-working, Polite," *MJ*, June 7, 1985.

49   IQG, "Daughter, 17, Is Sexually Active, But Refuses to Bother with 'Pill,'" *MJ*, April 11, 1982.

pregnant teenagers." As that rate soared nationwide during the decade, Wisconsin was among the states with the highest rate of pregnancies among teenaged mothers in some demographic groups. Griggs repeatedly gave referrals to resources for parents and for "young people who think they are so ultra-smart!"[50]

Addictions from drugs to gambling to alcoholism, which had led to many letters for more than half a century, also continued as concerns in columns, if often complicated by more recent societal issues as the cause for readers' letters about their complex lives. "Non-Pot Smoking Mother" coped with court-ordered shared custody with an ex-husband who smoked pot in their children's presence, in his home, where his sister lived and also "let her boyfriend sleep over." Griggs' reader feared the influence of the "atmosphere" but also feared filing for a change in the father's visitation rights, if "the relationship between me and the children will be affected, and when they are older, they will hate me for not letting them visit with him." He also had not paid child support for several years. The columnist reminded her reader that "the priority … should be children's well-being" and recommended the court route, at least for child support—with no consideration of costly legal fees for a mother supporting children entirely on her own. Another mother already had faced alone the heartbreak of seeing her son's health suffer after a near-fatal escalation from "pot to LSD to cocaine," combined with alcohol. His father had given up on him. She could not do so, found help, and wrote Griggs to get other "parental heads out of the sand."[51]

Legalization of gambling in the 1970s, at least legalization of Wisconsin's beloved bingo games, may have led to a rise in letters about gambling addictions. The societal impact of the law was immeasurable in a state that long had held with pride to its state constitution's "absolute prohibition" on gambling for profit. A reader wrote that she had

---

50   Ibid.; Meg Kissinger, "Teen Birthrate Drops 16% in State," *MJS*, April 10, 2012; see also "U.S. Teenage Pregnancies, Births and Abortions: National and State Trends and Trends by Race and Ethnicity," Guttmacher Institute (January 2010, rev. February 2012), accessed July 9, 2012, at http://www.guttmacher.org/pubs/USTPtrends.pdf.

51   IQG, "Mother Worries That Her Husband Is a Bad Influence on the Children," *MJ*, March 21, 1984; IQG, "Teen Got Into Booze, Then Drugs, Now Making a Painful Recovery," *MJ*, August 19, 1985.

"come to terms with addiction to bingo" by "gaining self-control, and I might say respect, one day at a time. My horror days of losing money I couldn't afford are over, and I look back with wonder that I could have been so foolish." The sole woman in a Gamblers Anonymous chapter in Milwaukee, she sought to aid others addicted to bingo, "what may be called a 'ladies' form of gambling," as men more often became "addicts of sports betting, big card games, horse racing, and the stock market." The effects could be far-reaching and also hurt families and friends, Griggs agreed, if with hyperbole in recalling a case of murder by a compulsive gambler, allegedly owing to a raise in rent.[52]

Long limited to charitable purposes in church basements, bingo games and other forms of gambling soon would be legalized, with a state-sponsored lottery, to combine with the state's ubiquitous corner taverns and "bar culture" as well as local hunting culture. All also combined to cause many letters to Griggs, including one of the last letters to the column, which came from a group of wives writing about the annual season of infidelity that they called "dear hunting." As Griggs wrote in introducing the letter to other readers, "the thought of chillier weather" was not the only reason that the approach of autumn "drives some women to distraction" in Wisconsin.[53]

> We are six wives who have been friends for years…. Recently we got to talking about our husbands' fall behavior. One wife calls this the 'fall from grace.' Strangely, we all have fairly good husbands the rest of the year.
>
> It's this time when our husbands become dear hunters. That's what I mean, not deer hunters. So far as we know it's the only time they are unfaithful to us. Often, it lasts only a couple of months, then they get back into the steady domestic routine.[54]

To similar letters for decades from wives wondering about wandering husbands when away for fall rites, Griggs had counseled faith in men's faithfulness. These wives, however, had evidence.

---

52   IQG, "Gamblers Come in All Varieties, and There Are Ways to Help Them," *MJ*, April 11, 1985; see also State of Wisconsin Legislative Reference Bureau, "The Evolution of Legalized Gambling in Wisconsin," *Bulletins* (2000).

53   IQG, "6 Wives Are Worried That Their Husbands Are Doing Some Fall 'Dear Hunting,'" *MJ*, August 28, 1985.

54   Ibid.

We wives, after suspicions, pooled our money and hired a detective, who got proof....

Our husbands play cards at the same tavern, and the 'dears' either work there or come in for drinks. We want your opinion of ... what we might do about it.

We have all been married over 10 years and have children. We fear that [the men] might have sex with these women, with awful consequences.... We aren't out to oust or punish our husbands. We just want to keep them from getting in a dirty mess.[55]

Griggs suggested that the wives plan a vacation for the couples during deer season to a different destination "that would especially interest the husbands."[56] That the women inevitably would travel alone, had they heeded her less-than-satisfactory reply, reflected a lack of understanding of the depth of devotion to deer hunting—and other hunting grounds in Wisconsin woods: taverns.

As alcohol consumption began to wane elsewhere in the country by the 1980s, Wisconsin remained among the worst states for alcohol use and abuse, and few issues continued to resonate more in many readers' letters. Extrapolating from decades of letters sampled, Griggs may have read thousands of letters on desperate lengths to which alcoholics would go. That may have led to her reaction in another of her last columns about an abusive husband and father, who read her column "for laughs." Griggs unleashed her anger in introducing a letter in language unusually harsh for her, as the issue was no laughing matter: "What do you call a man who puts his liquor bottle before his baby's bottle? A souse? An alcoholic? An unloving, neglectful, despicable, abusive parent?" The answer was all of the above in the letter from "Frantic Wife and Mother."[57]

---

55   Ibid.

56   Ibid.

57   IQG, "Dad Puts His Bottle Before Baby's; Mom Doesn't Know What to Do," *MJ*, September 3, 1985; Thomas M. Nephew, Gerald D. Williams, Hsiao-ye Yi, Allison K. Hoy, Frederick S. Stinson, and Mary C. Dufour, *Apparent Per Capita Alcohol Consumption: National, State, and Regional Trends, 1977-2000* (Washington, D.C.: U.S. Department of Health and Human Services, 2003), 4-7; L.T. Midanik and T.K. Greenfield, "Trends in Social Consequences and Dependence Symptoms in the United States: The National Alcohol Surveys, 1984-1995," *American Journal of Public Health* 90:1 (January 2000), 53.

When I was pregnant with our child, who is now four months old, my husband wanted me to have an abortion. I refused. Since the baby arrived, he has never ... held him in his arms. He not only doesn't act like a father but is a souse.

I knew he liked his bottle, but I didn't realize how much until the baby came....

It is getting to the point we can hardly afford the cost of two bottles, his and our beautiful baby's.... This past weekend he was very drunk, and our baby wouldn't have had anything in his bottle, if I hadn't taken him to my mother's. She was appalled.... She said I should leave my husband. Strangely, I still love my husband. If only he would leave drink alone and have some feelings for the baby.

He reads your column, more for laughs than for anything else, but maybe some advice from you might sink in, when he is sober.[58]

Griggs gave her usual referrals, and then emphasized her reader's responsibility as a mother to "see that there is milk for the baby, whether or not there are groceries for the adults." If she could not get to a grocery store or had no money for food, Griggs recommended home delivery by a dairy and gave an additional referral to a family service agency for funding for food. The rest of the column addressed the husband, with her hope that, "instead of laughing," he would take her reply seriously. "A father who puts his bottle before his baby's bottle isn't a real man. He is not only a souse but a child abuser," she wrote. "Do you realize how many more there are like you in this country? Alcoholism is of great social concern, primarily because of the tragic mark on an alcoholic's family" and the family's "financial resources," in addition to the costs to society.[59]

Near the end of 1984, a recovering woman alcoholic wrote of looking forward for the first time in years to time with her family in upcoming holidays. She especially had missed an admired brother, from whom she had not "managed to hide my drinking," as in past. "He could see what was happening ... when he came home for the holidays and noticed I wasn't joining in the merriment.... I can still see the look of disgust on my brother's face," she wrote. "I couldn't forget his disgust after he left, but it was a long time before I could make myself look for help. I thought a drinking problem was too shameful," she wrote, but had benefitted from a "support group with other older women." Griggs

---

58   Ibid.
59   Ibid.

gladly endorsed her recommendation of "Women for Sobriety" groups in Milwaukee, which pioneered in emerging, "gender-responsive treatments" tailored to women as alternatives to Alcoholics Anonymous, after disaffected readers reported its resistance to adapting programs for men to the different needs and situations in lives of women.[60]

Griggs also gave a rare glimpse into her past, shared with readers who dreaded holidays. More than half a century after her husband's death, she recalled that his funeral had come at the end of the year. "I came to the Milwaukee Journal a few weeks later," she wrote. Not realizing that her own career neared its end, she wished readers "a joyous and blessed season" for what would be the last time. Griggs gave the rest of the column to referrals of groups seeking volunteers to visit hospitals, nursing homes, and other sites at "a lonely time of year."[61]

Personal recollections came more often in the 1980s, as the columnist neared her jubilee year with the Journal in 1984—and perhaps came more often owing to the occasion, as media attention from across the country meant constant reminders of her fiftieth anniversary in the "advice industry." Griggs gave an interview to the Associated Press, the largest news syndicate in the country. Asked whether issues in her column had changed in half a century, the woman who had seen it all saw little progress in readers' letters and lives: "There's still jealousy, in-laws, people having battles at the dinner table." With characteristic wit, the ageless columnist added that, while "people are more open now" on issues, many readers who had made attempts to shock her on issues of intimacy always had failed, as "after all, there's always been sex."[62]

If her readers had learned little, she had educated her editors in allowing an advice columnist more latitude in her replies to readers,

---

60   IQG, "Woman Who Beat Alcoholism Says Holidays Will Be a Joy Again," MJ, December 1, 1982; IQG, "Holiday Season Is Bittersweet for Those Who Lost a Loved One," MJ, December 6, 1984. On Milwaukee's pioneering programs for women, see Francine Feinberg, "Substance-abusing Mothers and Their Children: Treatment for the Family," pp. 228-247, in Lee Combrinck-Graham, ed., Children in Families at Risk: Maintaining the Connections (New York: Guilford Press, 1995).

61   IQG, "Holiday Season."

62   Alicia Armstrong, "Happy Retirement, I.Q.G.," MJ, September 22, 1985; "After 50 Years, Mrs. Griggs Still Gives Advice," NewsPrint, February 1984, 2; "Names & Faces," MJ, July 11, 1984.

Ione Quinby Griggs at her computer terminal at the *Milwaukee Journal* in the 1980s, near the end of her newspapering career of more than six decades, when she had been among the first in the newsroom to volunteer for computer training and to abandon typewriters—and in the city where a *Milwaukee Sentinel* editor, Christopher Latham Sholes, had invented the first practical typewriter in the 1860s, at a site across the street from the *Journal* building. Sholes also had created a new career field for women, the clerical workers then called "typewriters" who worked on "typing machines," and he said that he hoped that he had "done something for the women who always had to work so hard. This will enable them more easily to earn a living." Not long before Griggs had entered the field, also among the first to adapt to newsroom typewriters had been many women journalists, although editors still had accepted handwritten copy sent by mail by "female correspondents," when women were not welcome in many newsrooms, in the early decades of the twentieth century. (Copyright 2014 Journal Sentinel, Inc., reproduced with permission)

especially women. Griggs reiterated in another interview that "family problems haven't changed over the years," although her replies had
altered. She cited past controversies among editors when, "years ago,
you couldn't print the word 'pregnant.' Now you can print everything
except four-letter words." Of course, no editors still standing, and perhaps none still among the living, could recall that Griggs had eluded
that restriction from the first of her columns, half a century before,
when she had allowed a reader's use of "h___"—then herself repeating the "h___" in her reply, for her readers to fill in the blanks. As for
the future for the country's longest-lasting advice columnist, now in
her mid-nineties, she declared "no desire to retire." She planned "to stay
around a while" and to continue to conduct her column, and for the
full six days per week, she said, "unless I start writing backwards."[63]

Within months, however, she could not keep to her promise to keep
up the pace of six columns per week, but not by her choice. The company's internal marketing research revealed that the lowest readership
of the *Milwaukee Journal* came on Saturdays. A missive came from
the marketing department to the newsroom with a plan to reach new
publics. For reasons that passed all understanding of at least some editors implementing the experiment, and perhaps some readers, the plan
targeted the most successful section in the newspaper and altered its
formula. In 1985, Saturday's "Green Sheet" became a "Kids' Section,"
without the column that continued to attract a following of younger
readers. "Dear Mrs. Griggs" went to five days per week.[64]

To the end, the columnist continued to come daily to the office, to her
desk, whose placement in the newsroom had held significant meaning
for her since the start of her career. Then, in the 1920s, in a hilariously
self-deprecating "stunt story" on her psychoanalysis by an "alienist," she
had revealed to her Chicago readers that "it upsets me terribly to have
my desk moved" from the center of the newsroom, where front-page
reporters competed against the clock to meet deadlines and competed
against each other for bylines. As yet unborn then was one of her last
editors, in the 1980s, a comparative newcomer who was unaware of
newsroom lore on a previous instance of Griggs having to move her

---

63   "After 50 Years, Mrs. Griggs;" "Names and Faces."

64   The source on the internal marketing research, which is not cited as it is
      not in the public domain, was among the editors with access to the report
      and is a co-author of this study.

desk, when her protest to an editor had elicited a promise that never again would she have to do so. However, as ever was the wont of new editors, he envisioned a reconfiguration of the department that would require moving only a few desks—but including hers. He soon gained an education on the tenacity that had kept Griggs at her desk for five decades. Informed of his plan, she apprised him of his predecessor's promise. "The spineless editor," as he described himself in recalling the encounter, calculated their comparative value to the company. Wisely, he retreated to "reconfigure the reconfiguration again." In the end, he recalled, "everyone else in the department moved," with their desks, "but not Mrs. Griggs."[65]

To the end, just as Griggs had maintained placement of her desk in the *Journal* newsroom that so mattered to her, she also maintained her column as well as ever, according to the most crucial constituency: not her editors but her readers. "You really have your finger on the pulse of the community," as one wrote to Griggs in gratitude for publicity in the column on a parenting course that "received a large response from interested moms, dads, grandmothers, ministers, and social workers." Readers' gratitude remained her greatest reward, although she also continued to reap awards; a local Visiting Nurses Association inaugurated an award for community health education by giving the honor to Griggs and then naming the award for her. However, rather than publicity in brief announcements at the end of columns as before, some letters—essentially, press releases—came to comprise the entirety of columns in coming months. She especially continued to endorse readers' appeals for understanding of people with disabilities, long before campaigns for the laws that would protect them from discrimination. For example, and as in past, "A Concerned Mother" wrote of a son with epilepsy, and with his condition under control, but still repeatedly rejected by uninformed employers. Griggs gave her referrals to organizations of and for others with seizure disorders. Other readers also found each other in her column in the 1980s to form support groups for many more readers in need, from survivors of sexual assault

---

65   The source, the self-described "spineless editor," is a co-author of this study.

to survivors of divorce, whether divorced mothers or divorced women dating divorced fathers.[66]

Soon, if she was not "writing backwards," as she had feared, she often penned only a few sentences per column for introductions and replies, even only a one-word reply: "Noted." As her health slowly declined, "Dear Mrs. Griggs" also seemed to lose energy. Readers' discussions now rarely raged for days, when columns became as innocuous as one headlined "And Now, A Few Words from People Leading Peaceful, Pleasant Lives." The fewest words, however, were hers. On other days, perhaps as her health briefly improved, the column continued as of old and as evidence that the city and entire circulation area remained a maelstrom of messy marriages and other troubled relationships. Most striking in the letters, read *en masse*, was that all remained oblivious to the obvious ironies in their letters and in their lives that regaled other readers.[67]

Letters in one of the last weeks alone told of a wife too heavy for horseback riding that also would break a family budget; of a father remarried to "the other woman," while his ex-wife continued to mourn for a marriage that never had existed, except on her part; of one of the "other women," now a woman scorned, who mourned for a marriage that never happened; of a father who fought for custody of four children, won, and now was "going nuts" as he realized the realities of childrearing; of a retired, remarried octogenarian with a young wife who could only "gab and gripe," while he had to do the housework; of a housewife whose husband, a retiree and self-appointed "efficiency expert," could only criticize and "high-horse" her housework; of older neighbors gossiping to Griggs about younger neighbors who gossiped about older neighbors.[68]

---

66   Armstrong, "Happy Retirement, I.Q.G.;" see also IQG, "New Support Group;" IQG, "Divorced Mother;" IQG, "Group That Helps Elderly Women Seeks to Grow in Milwaukee Area," *MJ*, June 13, 1983.

67   IQG, "And Now, A Few Words from People Leading Peaceful, Pleasant Lives," *MJ*, August 15, 1985, a column that also signaled slippage in an uncommon gaffe, as Griggs assigned the same pseudonym—that of "Happy City Dweller"—to both of the letters published that day.

68   IQG, "275-pound Wife's Desire to Take up Horseback Riding Makes Him Angry," *MJ*, August 21, 1985; IQG, "Father Remarried Longtime Girlfriend After Children Grew Up and Moved," *MJ*, August 22, 1985;

Although her readers remained at no loss for words or reasons to write to Griggs, and they wrote their page in the newspaper more than ever before, inconsistency in the number of letters and length of a column's copy can be the bane of editors. Increasingly, Griggs' copy came so truncated that the feature desk readied more "filler" for her page, if she ran short. Colleagues could see—and worried that tour groups would see, to her embarrassment—visible signs that her health had declined. Many editors exchanged memoranda, as *Milwaukee Journal* management faced a situation without precedent and calling for delicacy, which is not the forte of those in the journalistic calling, and no employee handbook had advice on how to retire an iconic advice columnist. Management had at hand only recent internal research that continued to rate the revered columnist as readers' most popular feature in the newspaper. As the last of her greatest fans, her "Green Sheet" editors, wrote of Griggs: She had "counseled, consoled, and advised three generations of *Journal* readers." He offered a "wager that more people recognize her name than [those] of the mayor or governor." Apparently, no one put down money to take the bet—nor did anyone put the proposition to the test, lest the result only embarrass the mayor or governor.[69]

In the end, after an editor requested an audience with Griggs, she reluctantly but graciously agreed that the time had come to end her extraordinary career and had one request, that there be no "fanfare" for her retirement. With no advance notice, the news hit the newsroom, not prepared to pull together a traditional farewell fracas. Instead, two news clerks saved the day on her last day, indicative of Griggs' unfailing courtesy to all of her co-workers; as an ardently feminist reporter wrote in admiration, "one of the best ways to describe Mrs. Griggs is to say that she is a lady, through and through," to all whom she met. The low-paid news clerks, who least could afford a gift, got together to give Griggs a sendoff in style. To escort her from the office to her residential hotel only blocks away, the women hired a chauffeured limousine

---

IQG, "Father with Custody of 4 Children Is Going Bananas Handling Them," *MJ*, August 23, 1985; IQG, "Husband, 85, Takes Care of House, and All Younger Wife Does Is Gripe," *MJ*, August 26, 1985; IQG, "Vicious Gossip Can Hurt People, So Learn to Hold Your Tongues," *MJ*, August 27, 1985.

69   Chabot, "From All of Us, Goodby, Mrs. Griggs."

complete with champagne and glasses, uncorked a bottle, and gave Griggs a memorable last trip home from the office, which so delighted her that the trip turned into a longer tour of downtown Milwaukee.[70]

As Griggs also had requested no "fanfare" in print, in her final column, her faithful following of readers who turned to the back page of the newspaper on a Friday in September 1985 found a column much like more than fifteen thousand columns published before by their "Dear Mrs. Griggs." They also found a reassuring headline, that a "Husband and Wife Solved Problem" and now "Lived Happily." Whether they lived happily ever after, Milwaukeeans never would know, with no more columns of letters on the ongoing sagas of their neighbors' everyday lives. The topic that day concluded the last of readers' debates that had run for weeks, after an initial letter on marital conflict led to discussion of disparate metabolisms of "morning people" vs. "night people." The problem had been exacerbated by the recent introduction of all-night television networks—a new generation never would see signoffs at "the end of a broadcast day," a phrase that disappeared from discourse—and the writer detailed the marital distress for a "poor man who has to go to bed early," whose wife would "stay up and watch television." Griggs had counseled the wife to change her ways or "end up with a TV set instead of a husband," advice denounced as "silly" by a reader. She suggested, instead, that the husband "stop being grouchy about bedtimes," because he might find that his wife would join him "for the fun of it."[71]

The wifely half of the last column's problem-solving couple, however, agreed with Griggs and shared how she and her spouse had found marital happiness, despite disparate metabolisms. "Ready and Willing But Not Always Able" awoke early, while "only once in a while" did her husband "get up to cook his own breakfast." Yet they had "let the other partner have his or her own space"—or own time zone, as it were. Griggs complimented her "Ready and Willing" reader for realizing that "marriage is a partnership," her mantra for more than half a century. That had yet to help her reader who authored the last letter in the last column. "Bored" had wed for a companion in life, but "the life

---

70   Ibid.; Armstrong, "Happy Retirement, I.Q.G."

71   IQG, "Writer Backs Wife Who Chooses TV Over Husband's Early-to-Bed Wish," *MJ*, September 13, 1985; IQG, "Husband and Wife Solved Problem of Conflicting Hours, Lived Happily," *MJ*, September 20, 1985.

of the party" when dating had become a "boring dummy at breakfast," not willing to converse and hiding behind his morning newspaper before hurrying off to work, without a "kiss goodby," to leave her with a long day ahead of "dull duties of housework." Griggs replied that a downside of dating could be not experiencing "breakfast as a rule with your partner," implicitly counseling—and sanctioning—premarital cohabitation. As for "Bored," Griggs recommended taking the initiative to give a "goodby kiss" in mornings for her husband to be "eager to get home" at the end of the day. Griggs' concluding words in her last column comprised a fitting, final admonition of all-purpose advice for all of her readers, after her millions of words, and theirs, that had been expended in more than fifteen thousand columns for more than half a century: She advised the couple to "be more companionable."[72]

Two days later, most of her readers first found out about Griggs' retirement when she again made the front page, and in the Sunday edition. Another story followed the next day on the front page of the "Green Sheet." The coverage reviewed "one of the most colorful careers in American journalism," first "in wicked Chicago and later in relatively virtuous Milwaukee." The stories again reassured her readers that, in contrast to others in the "advice industry," Griggs had not employed a pseudonym or "a succession of people" but had singlehandedly conducted her column. Nor had she ever repeated columns, as had wicked Chicago's "Ann Landers," the latecomer widely criticized for doing so. Her counterpart could have avoided the contretemps with a letter to Griggs, who had commented at the time that "she should have written to me for some advice." Another glimpse of Griggs' wit came from one of her editors, about the dreaded "hoax" letters that had offended some journalistic sensibilities at the *Journal*. He recalled "challenging one of her columns one day, pointing out that the absurd letter she was answering obviously was spurious," from "some sniggering wag hoping to embarrass us." Imperturbable, his advice columnist had replied, "I can't see the harm in having a little fun, once in a while." Agreeing that "the world is grim enough," he recalled, he "let Ione go her own merry way."[73]

---

72   IQG, "Husband and Wife Solved Problem."

73   Armstrong, "Happy Retirement, I.Q.G.;" Mosby, "Heart of Milwaukee," 55; Wade Mosby, "Her Friends Are Legion," *MJ*, March 3, 1980;

Retellings of her witticisms contrasted with the retelling in some of the retirement stories of the reason that Griggs had so suddenly left Chicago, the site of her first successful career, for Milwaukee. The tragedies of her early years came as news to most readers; by then, few could recall coverage of the cause of her early widowhood, which had "scarred her for life," according to a colleague, and had turned a risk-taking, front-page Chicago reporter into a very private person in Milwaukee. Even few of Griggs' far younger co-workers could grasp the "extent of her efforts," he wrote, to "keep needless unhappiness out of the lives" of others and to prevent more heartbreak for thousands of readers, who had poured out their hearts to her from the Heartland.[74]

Other media also noted the end of an era, as Griggs remained newsworthy. Although her newspaper reported that she planned to "get up a little later in the mornings and take each day as it comes," a television reporter placed an early-morning call for comment on her "impending retirement." The former reporter issued a terse correction: "I have already retired. And you just woke me up." To media that got the story straight, however, Griggs continued to give gracious interviews for years to come. One update informed her former readers that, despite disparaging comments in her last column on television's impact, she appreciated the company's retirement gift: her first television set. However, she preferred to spend her time in reading mysteries.[75]

For her readers, not until Griggs again landed on the front page for the last time, would the mystery be solved that she had maintained throughout her career, the best-kept secret of the woman who knew more secrets of her city than anyone in the city: her age. She continued her practice of politely evading personal questions in interviews. Instead, their "Dear Mrs. Griggs" spoke of missing her readers and sent them a message: "I hope everyone I gave advice to has done well."[76]

"Wisconsin's Voice," 24; Janz, "Phil Osofer Says;" Conrad, Wilson, and Wilson, *Milwaukee Journal*, 117; "Names & Faces," *MJ*, July 11, 1984.

74   Schaleben, "Remarks at Theta Sigma Phi Dinner Honoring I.Q.G."

75   Armstrong, "Happy Retirement, I.Q.G.;" Loohauis, "Update: Looking In on a Green Sheet Legend," *MJ*, March 15, 1988; Chabot, "From All of Us, Goodby, Mrs. Griggs."

76   Loohauis, "Update: Looking In on a Green Sheet Legend;" Chabot, "From All of Us, Goodby, Mrs. Griggs."

8

Conclusions and Epilogue, 1985-1991

By the end of her career, the longevity of Ione Quinby Griggs had "become the story," journalism parlance conveying that the focus on her age came at a cost. Reporting focused on Griggs' long career resulted in lack of recognition of the remarkable collaboration that she had created with the other writers of her column—her readers and their role. More than Griggs' longevity accounted for the longevity of the column, and more than her readers' willingness to share their stories. Instead, this study argues, its popularity arose from Griggs' willingness to give agency to her readers in the advice-giving role and in setting the agenda of their column, from the start, when she had stated that topics would be guided by those most often mentioned in their letters.[1] That her success relied on the collaboration between the columnist and her readers became most evident near the end, as her role declined with her health. Although she continued to select the letters for publication, her role in researching and writing replies to their letters declined to only a few sentences per column. Yet "Dear Mrs. Griggs" continued to be the most popular feature in the newspaper—not the front page, nor the news sections, but the back page of the newspaper.

Readers came to the column not only for stories of other readers and for their advice but also for public discourse, especially to debate topics that rarely merited "news" elsewhere in the pages of newspapers, such as changing roles of women in the middle decades of the twentieth century. Earlier in the century, as historian Alice Fahs writes, "most newspaper women were hired" to write *for* women readers, as did Griggs, although she evolved to writing her column *with* her women

---

1 "After 50 Years, Mrs. Griggs," 2.

readers, pioneering in moving away from the prescriptive role of predecessors in the "advice industry" and their preachy "sermonettes."
Together, as Fahs writes of those women journalists, they and their
sources so often unheard, their women readers, left a legacy of "a lost
world of women's writings." The result "created a rich set of public conversations within the public spaces of the newspaper," if most often in
"women's pages," that proved "vital in shaping and disseminating ideas"
on "women's changing lives" in "the cultural politics of modern life."[2]

Together, too, Griggs and her readers collaborated to create a sort
of "sociable media" that presaged allegedly "modern" trends to "social
media" today. Scholars may find much to learn from this study about
a back page of a newspaper, where women readers could be heard in
their own words. While recent research such as Fahs' work contrib-
utes to overdue recognition of reportage by early women journalists,
even less studied are their advice columns. Widely read, front-page
"girl reporters" of their day, like Griggs at the start of her career, are
"little studied by historians," Fahs writes, and "might have been surprised by their invisibility today" in scholarly literature on women,
media, and mass culture. They might be more surprised that less attention is accorded those women journalists, again like Griggs later in
her career, who gained the widest readership. "Advice columns," writes
media historian David Gudelunas, "have been largely ignored by journalism scholars interested in 'objective' hard news'" as the only media
product worthy of study for meeting not only conventions of style but
also constraints and standards, as determined by a male-dominated
media industry that they claim to study with the objectivity and dis-
interestedness demanded of scholarship. In part, media scholars may
perpetuate the myths of the past, if they dismiss advice columnists as
"sob sisters" for allegedly writing only of and for the "lovelorn" rather than for authoring a record of many aspects of women's lives for
many women readers. That women readers collaborated in authoring
modern advice columns may have contributed to lack of respect for
the "advice industry" in an era of increasing professionalization in the
media industry. In sum, for the same reason stated by Fahs—for the
significant role of front-page women journalists in framing "public

2   Fahs, *Out on Assignment*, 2-3.

discourse"—Gudelunas also argues for advice columns "as a serious topic of study," despite their placement far from the front page.[3]

This study also argues that the "lost world of women's writings" in Griggs' column, the stories of her readers, gives insight into more than the misguided loves of women in a working-class city in the Midwest. Instead, women wrote in the column of many aspects of their lives, a contemporary record on the women, the working-class, and the Midwest, all too often missing from or mischaracterized in American history. That the range of topics in letters sampled went well beyond "sob stuff"—stories of "lovelorn" women scorned—is supported by both qualitative and quantitative analysis of the column in this study. Although Griggs also had anticipated that her column would attract only letters on "love problems," as she wrote in her invitation at its inception in 1934, she immediately adapted to a wider agenda set by her women readers.

Yet almost seven decades later, at her death—and almost at the end of a century, marked by momentous times in women's history that reframed the larger historical record—even her closest colleagues in the newsroom, like media scholars, could not grasp Griggs' contribution. The headline on an obituary on Griggs by one of her company's own newspapers continued to mischaracterize her career as advising the "lovelorn," as if love was the only issue in the lives of women readers. Another admirer among her Milwaukee colleagues wrote that year that Griggs was among those who exemplified the "genius" of Journal writers, but he did not grasp the reasons. She "may not have flourished in another place," he wrote, which ignored her successful career in a more competitive media workplace, Chicago, and in the cutthroat era of the 1920s. "But her half-century of homely advice about marriage, love, money, personal hygiene and decency," he wrote, "fit the good burghers of Milwaukee like a glove," neglecting mention of the majority of her readers: the good hausfrauen as well as another sort of women, whose letters to Griggs could provide even better copy for their column on the back page of the newspaper.[4]

This analysis of thousands of readers' letters from hundreds of her columns tells another story of Griggs—and, especially, of her readers

---

3   Ibid.; Gudelunas, Confidential to America, 3.

4   Herzog, "Ione Quinby Griggs Dies;" Paul G. Hayes, "These Writers We Remember Well," MJ, March 31, 1995.

and their stories. Mischaracterizations of her as well as her audience and their agenda were common, although most correctly identified the gender of most of her readers. Of letter writers who self-identified by gender, a total of 709 or almost 84 percent of all 847 letters sampled for this study, women readers comprised 613 letter writers, more than 86 percent of all letter writers. However, most hardly were "lovelorn." Indeed, less than a fourth—23.3 percent or 197 of letters sampled— of their letters concerned "love," which ranked as the second-highest of seven categories of their issues identified in this analysis. Of course, "love problems" surfaced in some letters in the third-highest-ranking category of readers' main concerns, "marriage," for 18.1 percent or 153 of all letters sampled. Yet almost half of letter writers who self-identified by their marital or single status—almost two-thirds of all writers, 65.9 percent or 559 writers in all letters sampled—were married, many happily so. In addition to writers who were wed—49.4 percent or 276 of the 559 writers—3.4 percent were widowed. Only one in twenty, 4.8 percent, self-identified as separated or divorced, although an increasing number of women did so in later decades of the column and this study. However, again, many formerly married readers also wrote to others of happiness in their "singleness."

No matter their marital or single status, readers' primary issue for more than fifty years was their families, the focus of more than a fourth—25.3 percent or 214 letters—of all letters sampled. The category of "family" passed "marriage" and surpassed "love" among concerns, although all three categories combined to total two-thirds—66.5 percent—of all letters sampled. Among the remaining third of readers' letters sampled, many covered a range of concerns in the category of "other" at 11.6 percent or 98 letters. "Self" was the focus of 7.0 percent or 59 letters, while "work" was the focus of only 3.9 percent, or 33 letters, the lowest of major categories of concerns for more than half a century, although working women comprised almost half of those letter writers who self-identified their employment status, at 45.3 percent or 77 letter writers. Of the total of 170 letter writers who self-identified their employment status, only 28.8 percent or 49 letter writers self-identified as non-working students. A fourth—25.9 percent or 44 letters—came from contributors to the column who self-identified as neither in the workforce nor in school.

That her readers ranged from working women to housewives working without pay, as well as students with their work lives still ahead of

The *Milwaukee Journal* "Green Sheet" feature section came last in the daily newspaper but first in the hearts of millions of readers in the Heartland. (Courtesy of Mel Kolstad, reproduced with permission)

them, suggests a reason for their range of concerns—and their curiosity to read about the lives of others, which gave Griggs' column its widespread appeal. Almost as numerous as writers with issues so varied as to come under the category labeled "other," however, were those writing with "no problem"—not "love problems" nor marital, family, or other problems. One in nine letters, 11.0 percent or 98 of all of the letters sampled, came to the column from writers sharing with other readers their general satisfaction in life, and in all walks of life, no matter their gender or gender orientation, marital status, or age. The age range of readers also suggests the widespread appeal of the column. Of 405 writers who self-identified their age or age group in general terms, most—53.6 percent or 217 writers—were teenagers or young adults. Almost a third—32.3 percent or 131 writers—self-identified as middle-aged. One in nine writers—11.6 percent or 47 writers—self-identified as an older adult.

Why did a wide range of readers return to Griggs' column, again and again, often doing so daily for decades? This analysis also categorized letters according to Maslow's "hierarchy of needs," attempting to identify the level of need in their lives that letter writers sought to satisfy. Of 758 writers of letters categorized according to Maslowian theory, one in five—20.3 percent or 154 writers—sought personal safety, a basic need. Almost one in three sought to fulfill higher-level needs; 15.4 percent or 117 writers sought means to self-esteem, and 15.4 percent or 117 writers sought means to self-actualization, the highest-level need for fulfillment in life. Almost half—47.6 percent or 361 writers—scored as seeking means only to the middle-level of needs, a sense of belonging in their lives, or perhaps at least in the community of readers of the column.

This analysis also argues for the columnist's ability to adapt and even to accede to readers' agenda, as almost all needs identified in their letters fluctuated from decade to decade. For example, the basic need for personal safety scored as a significant concern for a fourth of letter writers in the World War II decade of the 1940s and again for far more letter writers, four in every ten, in the law-and-order decade of the 1980s. Similarly, the highest-level need, self-actualization, was a focus for few letter writers during the Depression and World War II but soared to significance for a fourth of letter writers in the 1960s. Readers' need for a sense of belonging did steadily decline through the decades, according to this analysis, although a yen for community remained a focus even in the final year, as readers contributed most of the column-*cum*-community forum. That year, a reader reunited through the column with an adopted granddaughter said that she knew that she could rely on other readers, because "everybody reads Mrs. Griggs." Their yen for community consistently remained the focus for more contributors to the column in every decade than did any of the many other concerns revealed in their letters.[5]

While the column apparently provided a sense of community for her faithful readers, who returned again and again, whether they had a greater impact through the column on community-building in their city and beyond cannot be known. That is, beyond the undeniable boon of the column's popularity for the coffers of her company, the impact of the column on the newspaper's editors in defining "news" is not evident. Many agencies and organizations expressed gratitude to Griggs in letters and awards that attested to the impact of the column in providing publicity for their community services and causes that fulfilled the historic, basic, informational function of the media. Of more impact, however, is the media's role in setting the agenda on

---

5   Armstrong, "Happy Retirement, I.Q.G."

issues to be reported as "news," and her readers' agenda on the back page of the newspaper apparently had little influence on the agenda of her influential newspaper on the front page—perhaps to the detriment of the *Milwaukee Journal* and its community, in its city and across its circulation area. Historians of women's journalism suggest that male editors and publishers created "women's pages" only to increase advertising, so the men rarely read those pages, with the result that some women reporters engaged in "renegade reporting" on issues that otherwise would not have seen print.[6] Perhaps Milwaukeeans read Griggs' column more than did her editors, with similar result, although she shared her role and the "power of the press" to empower her readers as "renegade reporters" to write, in their own words, on their issues and on the realities of their lives.

In every decade of the column, readers wrote their stories that could have been front-page stories, even "scoops," as many issues that eventually emerged as major stories or at least earned more coverage in the newspaper first saw print in "Dear Mrs. Griggs." From its inception in the Great Depression, that the column elicited a range of readers' issues that went far beyond "love problems" indicated their interest in more coverage of community agencies and services during the Great Depression, and Griggs adapted the column to serve as a source for referrals. In World War II, the massive response by younger readers, when girls sent thousands of letters to Griggs in a single week to protest a threatened wartime curfew by city fathers, presaged postwar concern for an alleged rise in juvenile delinquency. However, that the "news" reportage was dismissive of girls' concerns presaged coverage to come of their serious issues as women in ensuing decades.

Had her editors read the letters and between the lines of Griggs' column in the 1950s, regarding readers' frustrations with their postwar role in peacetime, the men may have foreseen the rise of the modern women's movement to come in the 1960s—and especially in Wisconsin, which provided many national leaders of the movement whose names ought to have been known to more than women journalists and their readers of the "women's pages." The men also might have been better prepared for the societal impact of *The Feminine Mystique*, the best-seller by journalist Betty Friedan in the 1960s that surveyed college-educated women on the East Coast yet mirrored many letters

---

6   Fahs, "Newspaper Women and the Making of the Modern," 303-339.

years earlier by women in a Midwestern working-class city. Griggs' editors also might have had understanding of divisive debates within the
movement regarding differences due to class, which also arose in wom-
en's discussions in the columns in the 1960s and 1970s—as did their
discussion for decades of their desperate need for family planning.

Well before introduction of "the Pill" in 1960 and legislative debates
to end the state law limiting its availability only to married women until the 1970s, the widespread support for its wider availability among
women writing to Griggs gave warning, had editors and politicians
heeded her readers, that Wisconsin also would be in the forefront
of states in ratification of the Equal Rights Amendment in the early 1970s. Although the state became a battleground in the 1970s for
anti-ERA forces, a harbinger of the "conservative revolution" and backlash to come, the Wisconsin movement's campaign culminated in the
1980s with the community property act, the first in the country providing for full equality in property rights of women. Not until then did
the act become "news," after a campaign for a decade based on stories
of economic devastation wreaked by divorce—stories similar to those
told for decades by readers calling for change, prior to passage of the
landmark community property law in the closing months of Griggs'
column.[7]

Intriguingly, Griggs' column may have foreshadowed by decades a
more recent trend in media, "civic journalism," in advocating a community-building role. A leading proponent calls for "reframing stories to
make them more relevant to readers," "developing new listening posts
in the community," and "providing entry points to involve people and
encourage interaction" of journalists and their community—all aspects of Griggs' column that account for its success. This study suggests, however, that reframing media as "guide dogs" ought not replace
media roles of "attack dog" and "watch dog" nor entirely accede an
agenda-setting role to media audiences.[8]

In the case of the column, allowing readers to set the agenda for
the back page of the newspaper resulted in neglect of major concerns,

---

7   Ranney, "Anglicans, Merchants, and Feminists," 547-548.

8   Jan Schaffer, "Attack Dog, Watch Dog, or Guide Dog: The Role of the
    Media in Building Community," 1999, accessed July 1, 2013, at http://
    www.pewcenter.org/doingcj/speeches/s_batonrouge.html. Schaffer was
    executive director of the Pew Center for Civic Journalism.

notably racial issues, and especially in contrast to their prevalence on the front page. That few readers of color apparently were among letter writers is not sufficient explanation for lack of attention to racial relations, as recognized by the readers whose letters did raise racial issues to call for dialogue across the community. Of course, if the column reflects the agenda of letter writers, as Griggs claimed, then absence of interest in discussion of racial relations is instructive in itself in historical analysis of a city and region only recently meriting mention in the story of African Americans' civil rights movement nationwide—and then often only for the shortcomings of the movement in Milwaukee and the Midwest.

Despite the limitations of "Dear Mrs. Griggs"—whether of the columnist or her readers—the result of this analysis supports the argument that lack of recognition of the range of her body of work, in her column in Milwaukee as in her reportage in Chicago, has minimized the lessons that can be learned from tales of the two cities, as told by Griggs and by her readers. Her stories of women in her first city long have been lost from public memory, as historians of Chicago's press make no mention of her front-page career in its famed era of "Jazz Age" journalism. One historical account of that era in the city then called the "murder capital" of the country does mention her, but Douglas Perry presents a conflicted portrait that both praises her work and dismisses her as a "hack" and a "sob sister." Similarly dismissive views of advice columnists, and of advice columns as solely for the lovelorn, also have resulted in the loss from public memory of Griggs' stories of her women readers in her adopted city.

Griggs also is neglected in histories of Milwaukee, and if mentioned at all, often only as a nostalgic icon—and as if she wrote the column alone, with no recognition of the role of her column as a community forum also written by her readers. As a result, historians of both cities and of the region and beyond also miss the import of her work as a rich resource for research. Her wide range of reportage in Chicago gave voice to women of the city emerging in politics, business, and many sectors of the city in the 1920s. Historians of the region and the country also can find in her advice column a mother lode of primary resources, with women's self-reportage of their experiences in a more typical working-class city in the Midwest, and across many decades, from the mid-1930s into the mid-1980s, when the column ended.[9]

Readers' dear "Mrs. Griggs," however, continued to make front-page news in the 1990s.

Only well after her retirement, not long before her death, did co-workers discover Griggs' best-kept secret: her age. In an era prior to ready access to online census records and to a family genealogy, even hundreds of inquisitive journalists, her former colleagues, never unearthed the evidence of her birth year. Instead, the "scoop" came not from the newsroom but from the personnel office of the company, which provided Griggs' year of birth in processing her paperwork for retirement with the Social Security Administration. Word spread around the newspaper plant, if in violation of the law as well as the privacy of the woman who had prized the protection of others' privacy. In the newsroom, "flabbergasted *Journal* colleagues started doing the math," as one would recall. They calculated that the venerable columnist had learned to use a computer at eighty-five years old, had taught others how to do so at ninety years old, and then had continued to "work full-time solving her readers' problems" until she was almost ninety-five years old.[10]

To the end, former colleagues in contact with Griggs continued to courteously omit reference to her age in their updates for readers on the retiree. "Her fame lived on years after her retirement," read one report in the *Milwaukee Journal*, a story occasioned when "an impostor was uncovered, a woman in a local nursing home who claimed to be 'the real Mrs. Griggs.'" Long after her last column, the real Griggs again made news in the *Milwaukee Journal*. Noting another newspaper's use of the past tense in a mention of the former columnist, her newspaper sniffed: "That should come as a surprise to Mrs. Griggs, who is very much alive," although the story had omitted any reference to her age. The unsurprised Griggs then was ninety-eight years old,

---

9   Within a decade, the "Green Sheet" also met its demise in 1994, soon followed by the company's merger of the *Milwaukee Journal*, founded in 1882, with its even-older *Milwaukee Sentinel*, founded in 1836, into the *Milwaukee Journal Sentinel* in 1995.

10   Loohauis, "'Dear Mrs. Griggs.'"

Ione Quinby Griggs, at the age of ninety-five years, holding a plaque from the Milwaukee Press Club, the country's oldest press club, at her induction into its Hall of Fame in 1985, the club's centennial year and the year of her retirement—although even then, and to the end, she continued to claim to be a decade younger in conversation with colleagues, including *Milwaukee Journal* feature editor Beth Slocum (right), one of Griggs' many editors in her legendary career of fifty-one years at the newspaper and more than sixty-five years in newspapering. (Copyright 2014 Journal Sentinel, Inc., reproduced with permission)

yet sufficiently newsworthy to merit above-the-fold placement on page two.[11]

Only after she made the front page again, with an obituary upon her death in 1991—at one hundred years old—did readers discover that the iconic columnist, from an era when many a woman journalist did not disclose her age, had worked at her desk in the newsroom into her mid-nineties. Until her last months, she had continued to live close to the newspaper plant, at the residential hotel that had been her home for more than half a century. The staff of the Hotel Wisconsin was "very devoted to her" for decades, a companion recalled. The manager later memorialized Griggs in the lobby, in a gallery of historic photographs and newspaper clippings on the hotel, including several that enshrined its longtime resident. Many of her own historic photographs and other mementos of her career had accompanied Griggs to a nursing home in the last year of her life. There, as a former colleague wrote, "the woman who indeed was the real Mrs. Griggs was a reluctant celebrity," continuing to live up to Milwaukeeans' image of their longtime columnist. She left her room in the nursing home only when wearing—as ever—a hat.[12]

A year after Griggs' death, she again made news in both Chicago and Milwaukee, because she had ensured that her legacy would endure, not only in historical archives in her hometown but also in journalism schools of her adopted city. She had spent many hours in retirement in organizing her family papers for the Western Springs Historical Society in suburban Chicago, which also received a bequest from her estate of more than three-quarters of a million dollars. The "girl reporter" from Western Springs, who had commuted to night school and had completed only one college class before beginning her career in the 1920s, also had bequeathed major gifts to endow funding for "needy, talented" women studying journalism in her adopted hometown and state, at campuses in Milwaukee and elsewhere in Wisconsin, where

11   Ibid.; Meg Kissinger, "Taking Names," *MJ*, June 13, 1989.

12   Herzog, "Ione Quinby Griggs Dies;" Karen Herzog, "Hotel Wisconsin Opens Door on City History," *MJS*, December 17, 1995; Loohauis, "'Dear Mrs. Griggs.'"

Ione Quinby Griggs scholarships continue to assist aspiring student journalists today.[13]

Even before her death, Griggs already had made other, more unusual bequests. She had donated artifacts to the Milwaukee County Historical Society, near her newspaper plant, for an exhibit on her career: Her legendary collection of hats, worn at her desk daily for decades in Milwaukee, a carryover of the habit that she had attributed to her "brassy days" in Chicago. There, in an era when "career women" wore hats in public, she had learned that an ambitious "girl reporter" aiming for a front-page byline had to be ready to go "out on assignment" for the stories that her readers wanted to read, not only the stories of celebrities and royalty but also the stories that resonated most in readers' lives, the stories that could keep them reading through the news of the world all the way to the back page of a newspaper in Milwaukee. Indeed, there were found the stories to which they had learned to turn first, because Griggs knew her readers.

And in Milwaukee, she and her readers had left another legacy, in newspaper archives. On her page of the newspaper, which she had made their page as well, the women who had comprised most of her readers had looked daily for decades for the stories of others' lives, because everyone always wanted to know more about the neighbors next door. Even more, her women readers had written their own stories for others to read—the stories of their everyday lives that still resonate for readers today.

13   "WS Settler Leaves Gift;" Loohauis, "Looking In on a Legend;" Michael Zahn, "Will Leaves $200,000 for Scholarships," *MJ*, April 21, 1992. Journal Communications also continues to grant funding in Griggs' name for research on the field of journalism, including this study.

Bibliography

Abbreviations

In notes, newspapers frequently cited are identified by the following abbreviations:

CEP   *Chicago* (Ill.) *Evening Post*

MJ   *Milwaukee* (Wis.) *Journal*

MJS   *Milwaukee* (Wis.) *Journal Sentinel*

MS   *Milwaukee* (Wis.) *Sentinel*.

Full titles are provided for newspapers in this bibliography, which includes popular and scholarly sources about Ione Quinby Griggs and about her body of work, as well as her book and many of her magazine articles but not her newspaper articles, as too numerous to list herein.

Primary Sources

Arville Schaleben Papers. Wisconsin Historical Society Archives, Area Research Center, Golda Meir Library, University of Wisconsin-Milwaukee, Milwaukee, Wis.

Chicago (Ill.) *Evening Post*. Microforms Collections, Harold Washington Public Library, Chicago; Illinois State Historical Society, Springfield, Ill.

Chicago (Ill.) *Tribune*. Microforms Collection, Harold Washington Public Library, Chicago, Ill.

Milwaukee Press Club Records. University of Wisconsin-Milwaukee Archives, Golda Meir Library, University of Wisconsin-Milwaukee, Milwaukee, Wis.

Milwaukee (Wis.) *Journal*. Microforms Collection, Golda Meir Library, University of Wisconsin-Milwaukee, Milwaukee, Wis.

Milwaukee (Wis.) *Sentinel*. Microforms Collection, Golda Meir Library, University of Wisconsin-Milwaukee, Milwaukee, Wis.

Milwaukee (Wis.) *Journal Sentinel*. Microforms Collection, Golda Meir Library, University of Wisconsin-Milwaukee, Milwaukee, Wis.

Once a Year. Milwaukee Press Club Records, University of Wisconsin-Milwaukee Archives, Golda Meir Library, University of Wisconsin-Milwaukee, Milwaukee, Wis.

Out! Lesbian, Gay, Bisexual, and Transgender Studies Collection, University of Wisconsin-Milwaukee Special Collections, Golda Meir Library, University of Wisconsin-Milwaukee, Milwaukee, Wis.

Quinby Papers. Western Springs Historical Society, Western Springs, Ill.

University of Chicago Weekly. University of Chicago Archives, Chicago, Ill.

Secondary Sources

Books

Abramson, Phyllis Leslie. *Sob Sister Journalism.* Westport, Conn.: Greenwood Press, 1990.

Adler, Jeffrey S. *First in Violence, Deepest in Dirt: Homicide in Chicago, 1875–1920.* Cambridge, Mass.: Harvard University Press, 2006.

Asbury, Herbert. *Chicago: Gem of the Prairie.* Garden City, N.Y.: Garden City Publishing, 1940.

Barber, Lucy G. *Marching on Washington: The Forging of an American Political Tradition.* Berkeley: University of California Press, 2004.

Bayley, Edwin R. *Joe McCarthy and the Press.* Madison: University of Wisconsin Press, 1981.

Beetham, Margaret. *A Magazine of Her Own? Domesticity and Desire in the Women's Magazine, 1800-1914.* London: Routledge, 1996.

Bernstein, Arnie. *Hollywood on Lake Michigan: 100 Years of Chicago and the Movies.* Chicago: Lake Claremont Press, 1998.

Bordin, Ruth. *Frances Willard: A Biography.* Chapel Hill: University of North Carolina Press, 1986.

Brown, Victoria Bissell. *The Education of Jane Addams.* Philadelphia: University of Pennsylvania Press, 2004.

Brownmiller, Susan. *In Our Time: A Memoir of a Revolution.* New York: Dell, 1999.

Butcher, Fanny. *Many Lives, One Love.* New York: Harper & Row, 1972.

Chicago City Directory. Chicago: Chicago Directory Co., 1911.

Cohen, Marcia. *The Sisterhood: The Inside Story of the Women's Movement and the Leaders Who Made It Happen.* New York: Fawcett Columbine, 1988.

Conrad, Will, Kathleen Wilson, and Dale Wilson. *The Milwaukee Journal: The First Eighty Years.* Madison: University of Wisconsin Press, 1964.

Conzen, Kathleen Neils. *Immigrant Milwaukee: Accommodation and Community in a Frontier City.* Cambridge, Mass.: Harvard University Press, 1976.

Cummings, Kathleen S. *New Women of the Old Faith: Gender and American Catholicism in the Progressive Era.* Chapel Hill: University of North Carolina Press, 2009.

Dodge, L. Mara. *'Whores and Thieves of the Worst Kind': Women, Crime, and Punishment in Illinois, 1835-1973.* DeKalb: Northern Illinois University Press, 2002.

Doppler, George F. *America Needs Total Divorce Reform—Now!* New York: Vantage Press, 1973.

Douglas, Susan J. *Where the Girls Are: Growing Up Female with the Mass Media.* New York: Times Books, 1994.

Evans, Sara M. *Born for Liberty: A History of Women in America.* New York: Free Press, 1997.

Fahs, Alice. *Out on Assignment: Newspaper Women and the Making of Modern Public Space.* Chapel Hill: University of North Carolina Press, 2011.

Faludi, Susan. *Backlash: The Undeclared War Against American Women.* New York: Three Rivers Press, 1991; rev. ed., 2006.

Fielding, Raymond. *The American Newsreel, 1911-1967.* Norman: University of Oklahoma Press, 1972.

Flexner, Eleanor. *Century of Struggle: The Woman's Rights Movement in the United States.* Cambridge, Mass: Harvard University Press, 1959; rev. ed., 1975.

Friedan, Betty. *The Feminine Mystique.* New York: W.W. Norton, 1963.

Full Reversed Directory of the Elite of Chicago, 1883-4: Giving Names of Prominent Residents on the Most Fashionable Streets of the City and Principal Suburbs. Chicago: Elite Publishing Co., 1884. Lawrence J. Gutter Collection, University of Illinois at Chicago. Accessed September 22, 2011. http://www.archive.org/details/reverseddirector00lawr.

Fure-Slocum, Eric. *Contesting the Postwar City: Working-Class and Growth Politics in 1940s Milwaukee.* Cambridge, Mass.: Cambridge Press, 2013.

Gado, Mark. *Death Row Women: Murder, Justice, and the New York Press.* Westport, Conn.: Greenwood Press, 2008.

Gaylor, Annie Nicol. *Abortion Is a Blessing.* Madison, Wis.: Psychological Dimensions, 1976.

Giddings, Paula J. *Ida: A Sword Among Lions.* New York: Harper Collins, 2008.

Gilman, Mildred Evans. *Sob Sister.* New York: Cape & Smith, 1931.

Glad, Paul J. *History of Wisconsin, Vol. V: War, a New Era, and Depression, 1914-1940.* Madison: State Historical Society of Wisconsin, 1990.

Golembiewski, Dick. *Milwaukee Television History: The Analog Years.* Milwaukee, Wis.: Marquette University Press, 2008.

Griggs, Ione Quinby. *Growing Up with Jim and Jean....: Reprinted from the Columns of Ione Quinby Griggs.* Milwaukee, Wis.: Milwaukee Journal, 1947.

Grossvogel, David I. *Dear Ann Landers: Our Intimate and Changing Dialogue with America's Best-Loved Confidante.* New York: McGraw-Hill, 1989.

Gudelunas, David. *Confidential to America: Newspaper Advice Columns and Sexual Education.* New Brunswick, N.J.: Transaction Press, 2008.

Gurda, John. *The Making of Milwaukee.* Milwaukee, Wis.: Milwaukee County Historical Society, 2000.

Kane, Harnett. *Dear Dorothy Dix: The Story of a Compassionate Woman.* Garden City, N.Y.: Doubleday, 1952.

Kaplan, Laura. *The Story of Jane: The Legendary Underground Abortion Service.* Chicago: University of Chicago Press, 1995.

Kinsey, Alfred C., Wardell B. Pomeroy, Clyde E. Martin, and Paul H. Gebhard, *Sexual Behavior in the Human Female.* Philadelphia, Penn.: W. B. Saunders, 1953.

Klatt, Wayne. *Chicago Journalism: A History.* Jefferson, N.C.: McFarland, 2009.

Larsen, Sarah A., and Jennifer M. Miller. *Wisconsin Vietnam War Stories: Our Veterans Remember.* Madison: Wisconsin Historical Society, 2010.

Lesy, Michael. *Murder City: The Bloody History of Chicago in the Twenties.* New York: Norton, 2007.

Lutes, Jean Marie. *Front-Page Girls: Modern Journalists in American Culture and Fiction, 1880-1930.* Ithaca, N.Y.: Cornell University Press, 2006.

MacKellar, Landis. *The 'Double Indemnity' Murder: Ruth Snyder, Judd Gray, and New York's Crime of the Century.* Syracuse, N.Y.: Syracuse University Press, 2006.

Marzolf, Marian. *Up from the Footnote: A History of Women Journalists.* New York, N.Y. Hastings House, 1977.

May, Elaine Tyler. *America and the Pill: A History of Promise, Peril, and Liberation.* New York: Basic Books, 2010.

McBride, Genevieve G. *On Wisconsin Women: Working for Their Rights from Settlement to Suffrage.* Madison: University of Wisconsin Press, 1994.

_____, ed. *Women's Wisconsin: From Native Matriarchies to the New Millennium.* Madison: Wisconsin Historical Society Press, 2005.

McKernan, Maureen. *The Amazing Crime and Trial of Leopold and Loeb.* Chicago: Plymouth Court Press, 1924.

McPhaul, John J. *Deadlines & Monkeyshines: The Fabled World of Chicago Journalism.* New York: Prentice-Hall, 1962.

Meier, August, and Elliott Rudwick. *CORE, A Study in the Civil Rights Movement, 1942-1968.* Urbana: University of Illinois Press, 1975.

Miller, Kristie. *Ruth Hanna McCormick: A Life in Politics.* Albuquerque: University of New Mexico Press, 1992.

Mills, Kay. *A Place in the News: From the Women's Pages to the Front Pages.* New York: Columbia University Press, 1988.

Mitz, Rick. *The Great TV Sitcom Book.* New York: Richard Marek Publishers, 1980.

Moeller, Robert. *War Stories: The Search for a Usable Past in the Federal Republic of Germany.* Berkeley: University of California Press, 2003.

Moore, William T. *Dateline Chicago: A Veteran Newsman Recalls Its Heyday.* New York: Taplinger, 1973.

Nesbit, Robert C. *Wisconsin.* Madison: University of Wisconsin Press, 1989.

Nephew, Thomas M., Gerald D. Williams, Hsiao-ye Yi, Allison K. Hoy, Frederick S. Stinson, and Mary C. Dufour. *Apparent Per Capita Alcohol Consumption: National, State, and Regional Trends, 1977-2000.* Washington, D.C.: U.S. Department of Health and Human Services, 2003.

Noun, Louise. *Strong-Minded Women: The Emergence of the Woman-Suffrage Movement in Iowa.* Ames: Iowa State University Press, 1969.

Paulos, John Allen. *A Mathematician Reads the Newspaper.* New York: Anchor Books, 1995.

Perry, Douglas. *The Girls of Murder City: Fame, Lust, and the Beautiful Killers Who Inspired Chicago*. New York: Viking, 2010.

Pleck, Elizabeth H. *Not Just Roommates: Cohabitation After the Sexual Revolution*. Chicago: University of Chicago Press, 2012.

Pottker, Janice, and Bob Speziale. *Dear Ann, Dear Abby: The Unauthorized Biography of Ann Landers and Abigail Van Buren*. New York: Dodd, Mead, 1987.

Putnam, Robert D. *Bowling Alone: The Collapse and Revival of American Community*. New York: Simon and Schuster, 2000.

Quinby, Henry Cole. *Genealogical History of the Quinby (Quimby) Family in England and America*. Salem, Mass.: Higginston, 1993, rep. of Tuttle, 1915.

Quinby, Ione. *Murder for Love*. Chicago: Covici, Friede, 1931.

Ranney, Joseph A. *Trusting Nothing to Providence: A History of Wisconsin's Legal System*. Madison: University of Wisconsin Law School, 1999.

Rodriguez, Joseph, Sarah Filzen, Susan Hunter, Dana Nix, and Marc Rodriguez. *Nuestro Milwaukee: The Making of the United Community Center*. Milwaukee: United Community Center, 2000.

Ross, Ishbel. *Ladies of the Press: The Story of Women in Journalism by an Insider*. New York: Arno, 1974; rep. of 1936 ed.

Rotskoff, Lori. *Love on the Rocks: Men, Women, and Alcohol in Post-World War II America*. Chapel Hill: University of North Carolina Press, 2002.

Scanlon, Jennifer. *Inarticulate Longings: The Ladies' Home Journal, Gender, and the Promises of Consumer Culture*. New York: Routledge, 1995.

Schilpp, Madelon Golden, and Sharon M. Murphy. *Great Women of the Press*. Carbondale: Southern Illinois University Press, 1983.

Schmandt, Henry J., John C. Goldbach, and Donald B. Vogel. *Milwaukee: A Contemporary Urban Profile*. New York: Praeger, 1971.

Schmidt, Doug. *They Came to Bowl: How Milwaukee Became the Tenpin Capital*. Madison: Wisconsin Historical Society Press, 2007.

Spain, Daphne. *How Women Saved the City*. Minneapolis: University of Minnesota Press, 2001.

St. John, Robert. *This Was My World*. Garden City, N.Y.: Country Life Press, 1953.

Stevens, Michael E., and Ellen D. Goldlust, eds. *Voices of the Wisconsin Past: Women Remember the War, 1941-1945*. Madison: State Historical Society of Wisconsin, 1993.

Stevens, Michael E. *Voices from Vietnam*. Madison: State Historical Society of Wisconsin, 1996.

Strasser, Susan. *Never Done: A History of American Housework*, rev. ed. New York: Henry Holt, 2000.

Sugrue, Thomas J. *Sweet Land of Liberty: The Forgotten Struggle for Civil Rights in the North*. New York: Random House, 2009.

Swoboda, Marian J., and Audrey J. Roberts. *Wisconsin Women, Graduate School, and the Professions*. Madison: University of Wisconsin Board of Regents, 1980.

Thompson, William F. *History of Wisconsin, Vol. VI: Continuity and Change, 1940-1965*. Madison: State Historical Society of Wisconsin, 1988.

Trotter, Joe William, Jr. *Black Milwaukee: The Making of an Urban Proletariat, 1915-1945*. Urbana: University of Illinois Press, 1985.

Walters, Suzanna Danuta. *Lives Together/Worlds Apart: Mothers and Daughters in Popular Culture*. Berkeley: University of California Press, 1992.

Warshaw, Robin. *I Never Called It Rape*. New York: Harper and Row, 1988.

Wells, Robert W. *The Milwaukee Journal: An Informal Chronicle of Its First 100 Years*. Milwaukee, Wis.: Milwaukee Journal, 1981.

Articles, Chapters, Essays

Abelson, Elaine S. "'Women Who Have No Men to Work for Them': Gender and Homelessness in the Great Depression, 1930-1934." *Feminist Studies* 29:1 (Spring 2003), 104-127.

"A Dutch Treat for I.Q.G." *Milwaukee* (Wis.) *Journal*, October 28, 1954.

"After 50 Years, Mrs. Griggs Still Gives Advice." *NewsPrint*, February 1984, 2.

"Angel of the Green Sheet, That's the Journal's Ione Quinby Griggs." *Little Journal*, September 1953.

Apple, Rima D., and Judith Walzer. "Medical School Remembered: Women's Experiences at the University of Wisconsin." *Wisconsin Academy Review* 31:1 (December 1984), 14-17.

Armstrong, Alicia. "'Dear Mrs. Griggs': A Pioneer Among 'Sob Sisters,' I.Q.G. Has Helped Thousands." *Milwaukee* (Wis.) *Journal*, March 3, 1980.

_____. "'Dear Mrs. Griggs': In Chicago, Mrs. Griggs Met the Famous and Infamous." *Milwaukee* (Wis.) *Journal*, March 4, 1980.

_____. "'Dear Mrs. Griggs': Can You Imagine I.Q.G. Riding Atop an Elephant." *Milwaukee* (Wis.) *Journal*, March 5, 1980.

_____. "'Dear Mrs. Griggs': Mrs. Griggs Really Cares for Those Asking Her Help." *Milwaukee* (Wis.) *Journal*, March 6, 1980.

_____. "'Dear Mrs. Griggs': Issue on Teenage Morals Brought 7,000 Letters." *Milwaukee* (Wis.) *Journal*, March 7, 1980.

_____. "Happy Retirement, I.Q.G.: Mrs. Griggs, Longtime Green Sheet Advice Columnist, Caps Career." *Milwaukee* (Wis.) *Journal*, September 22, 1985.

Austin, Dorothy. "State Women Leaders Laud Bill Approval." *Milwaukee* (Wis.) *Sentinel*, March 23, 1971.

Baggaley, Andrew R. "Religious Influence on Wisconsin Voting, 1928-1960." *American Political Science Review* 56:1 (March 1962), 66-70.

Beasley, Maurine H. "Elizabeth M. Gilmer as Dorothy Dix: A Southern Journalist Rewrites the Myth of the Southern Lady." Paper presented at the Dorothy Dix Symposium, Trenton, Ky., September 27, 1991. Dorothy Dix Collection, F.G. Woodward Library Archives, Austin Peay State University, Clarksville, Tenn.

Bellais, Leslie. "'No Idle Hands': A Milwaukee WPA Handicraft Project," *Wisconsin Magazine of History* 84:2 (Winter 2000-01), 48-56.

Benedict, Helen. *Virgin or Vamp: How the Press Covers Sex Crimes.* New York: Oxford University Press, 1992.

Blinkhorn, Lois. "A New Day Dawns as Chapter Closes on Women's Rights." *Milwaukee* (Wis.) *Journal*, June 30, 1982.

Borden, Angela. "Local Personalities Have Fond Memories of Circus." *Milwaukee* (Wis.) *Journal*, July 7, 1985.

Bowman, Shayne, and Chris Willis. "We Media: How Audiences Are Shaping the Future of News and Information." American Press Institute Media Center, 2003. Accessed October 22, 2011. http://www.hypergene.net/wemedia/weblog.php.

Caizza, Amy B. *The Status of Women in Wisconsin.* Washington, D.C.: Institute for Women's Policy Research, 2002.

Carroll, Loren. "Ione Quinby Lays Bare 7 Souls in Exciting Murder Tales," *Chicago* (Ill.) *Evening Post*, February 18, 1931.

Casey, Janet Galligani. "Farm Women, Letters to the Editor, and the Limits of Autobiography Theory." *Journal of Modern Literature* 28:1 (Autumn 2004), 89-106.

Chabot, Dan. "From All of Us, Goodby Mrs. Griggs." *Milwaukee* (Wis.) *Journal*, September 23, 1985.

_____."A Tribute to Mrs. Griggs." *Milwaukee* (Wis.) *Journal*, August 20, 1991.

Chan, Chris. "Milwaukee's Local Color: The *Journal*, the Green Sheet, and Its Readers," *Wisconsin Magazine of History* 94:4 (Summer 2011), 14-27.

Cleary, Catherine B. "Marital Property Rights in Wisconsin, 1846-1872." *Wisconsin Magazine of History* 78:2 (Winter 1994-95), 110-137.

Clogston, John S. "Disability Coverage in American Newspapers." Pp. 45-58 in Jack A. Nelson, ed., *The Disabled, the Media and the Information Age.* Westport, Conn.: Greenwood Press, 1994.

Colbert, Ann. "Philanthropy in the Newsroom: Women's Editions of Newspapers, 1894-1896." *Journalism History* 22:3 (Autumn 1996), 90-99.

Cowan, Ruth Schwartz. "Two Washes in the Morning and a Bridge Party at Night: The American Housewife Between the Wars." *Women's Studies* 3:2 (1976), 147-172.

Cowles, May L., and Ruth P. Dietz. "Time Spent in Homemaking Activities by a Selected Group of Wisconsin Farm Homemakers." *Journal of Home Economics* 48 (January 1956), 29-35.

Cromie, Robert T. "Foreword." Pp. 7-10 in William Moore, *Dateline Chicago: A Veteran Newsman Recalls Its Heyday.* New York: Taplinger, 1973.

Davies, Jude, and Carol R. Smith. "Race, Gender, and the American Mother: Political Speech and the Maternity Episodes of *I Love Lucy* and *Murphy Brown.*" *American Studies* 39:2 (Summer 1988), 33-63.

"Demands Detailed by Women Strikers." *Milwaukee* (Wis.) *Journal*, August 26, 1970.

Dodge, L. Mara. "'Our Juvenile Court Has Become More like a Criminal Court': A Century of Reform at the Cook County Juvenile Court." *Michigan Historical Review* 26:2 (Fall 2000), 51-89.

Dornbrook, Don. "Wisconsin's Conscience." *Pageant*, March 1950, 11-22.

Doyle, Ruth B. "Women and the Law School: From a Trickle to a Flood." Pp. 65-73 in Marian J. Swoboda and Audrey J. Roberts, *Wisconsin Women, Graduate School, and the Professions.* Madison: University of Wisconsin Board of Regents, 1980.

"Eppie Lederer, 1918-2002: Ann Landers Was a Friend to Millions." *Chicago* (Ill.) *Tribune*, June 23, 2002.

Fahs, Alice. "Newspaper Women and the Making of the Modern, 1885-1910." *Prospects* 27 (2002), 303-339.

Fass, Paula S. "Making and Remaking an Event: The Leopold and Loeb Case in American Culture." *Journal of American History* 80:3 (December 1993), 919-951.

Feinberg, Francine. "Substance-abusing Mothers and Their Children: Treatment for the Family." Pp. 228-247 in Lee Combrinck-Graham, ed., *Children in Families at Risk: Maintaining the Connections*. New York: Guilford Press, 1995.

Forbes, Genevieve. "Tribune Woman Runs Gantlet of Ellis Island." *Chicago* (Ill.) *Tribune*, October 14, 1921.

————. "Ladies in Crime." *Chicago* (Ill.) *Tribune*, April 10, 1923.

————. "Death for 2 Women Slayers." *Chicago* (Ill.) *Tribune*, July 10, 1923.

————. "Dialect Jargon Makes 'Em Dizzy at Nitti Trial." *Chicago* (Ill.) *Tribune*, July 7, 1923.

————. "Hollywood Admires Chicago's Sky-Line." *Chicago* (Ill.) *Tribune*, June 12, 1927.

Fox, Margalit. "Ann Landers, Advice Giver to the Millions, Is Dead at 83." *New York Times*, June 23, 2002.

Frank, Stanley, and Paul Sann. "Paper Dolls." *Saturday Evening Post*, May 20, 1944, 20-23.

Galush, William J. "Purity and Power: Chicago Polonian Feminists, 1880-1914." *Journal of Polish American Studies* 47:1 (Spring 1990), 5-24.

Goldin, Claudia, Lawrence F. Katz, and Ilyana Kuziemko. "Homecoming of American College Women: The Reversal of the College Gender Gap." *Journal of Economic Perspectives* 20:4 (Fall 2006), 133-156.

Governor's Commission on Human Rights. "Negro Families in Rural Wisconsin: A Study of Their Community Life." Madison Wis.: Governor's Commission on Human Rights, 1959.

Griggs, Bruce E. "The Sacred Eye." *Winnipeg* (Man.) *Free Press*, November 26, 1932.

Griggs, Ione Quinby. "Dear Mrs. Griggs...." *Once a Year* (1984). Box 11, Folder 21, Milwaukee Press Club Records, University of Wisconsin-Milwaukee Archives, Golda Meir Library, University of Wisconsin-Milwaukee, Milwaukee, Wis.

————. "They Dance All Over Pop's Heaven." *Saturday Evening Post*, December 9, 1944, 24.

"Group Works to Help Ease Pain of Divorce." [Madison, Wis.] *Capital Times*, April 12, 1975.

Gutmacher Institute. "U.S. Teenage Pregnancies, Births and Abortions: National and State Trends and Trends by Race and Ethnicity." Accessed July 9, 2012. http://www.guttmacher.org/pubs/USTPtrends.pdf.

Hayes, Paul G. "These Writers We Remember Well." *Milwaukee* (Wis.) *Journal*, March 31, 1995.

Heard, Jacquelyn. "A 'Queen' of a Town Springs Up." *Chicago* (Ill.) *Tribune*, November 2, 1988.

Hentig, Hans von. "Pre-Murderous Kindness and Post-Murder Grief." *Journal of Criminal Law, Criminology, and Police Science* 48:4 (November-December 1957), 369-377.

Holmes, Joseph L. "Crime and the Press." *Journal of the American Institute of Criminal Law and Criminology* 20:2 (August 1929), 6-59.

"Ione Quinby Griggs Is Subject of Article in Pageant Magazine." *Milwaukee* (Wis.) *Journal*, February 13, 1950.

Jacobs, Herbert Austin. "The Wisconsin Milk Strikes." *Wisconsin Magazine of History* 35:1 (Autumn 1951), 30-35.

Janik, Erika. "Good Morning Homemakers!" *Wisconsin Magazine of History* 90:1 (Autumn 2006), 4-15.

Janz, William. "Phil Osofer Says He's Feeling Blue About Passing of the Green." *Milwaukee* (Wis.) *Sentinel*, March 18, 1994.

"Jobless Unattached Women Are Studied by Labor Board." *Milwaukee* (Wis.) *Journal*, July 26, 1938.

Kasparek, Jonathan. "A Day in the Life: The Beatles Descend on Milwaukee." *Wisconsin Magazine of History* 84:2 (Winter 2000-01), 14-29.

Kissinger, Meg. "Taking Names." *Milwaukee* (Wis.) *Journal*, June 13, 1989.

_____. "Teen Birthrate Drops 16% in State." *Milwaukee* (Wis.) *Journal Sentinel*, April 10, 2012.

Koss, M.P., K.E. Leonard, D.A. Beezley, and C.J. Oros. "Non-stranger Sexual Aggression: A Discriminant Analysis of the Psychological Characteristics of Undetected Offenders." *Sex Roles* 12 (1985), 981-992.

Koss, M.P., C.A Gidycz, and N. Wisniewski, "The Scope of Rape: Incidence and Prevalence of Sexual Victimization in a National Sample of Higher Education Students." *Journal of Consulting and Clinical Psychology* 55:2 (1987), 167-170.

Krause, Joy. "ERA Has Been on the US Agenda Since 1923." *Milwaukee* (*Wis.*) *Journal*, June 30, 1982.

"Letter to Paper Pops Up—to Change Tune of Wife." *Milwaukee* (Wis.) *Journal*, March 30, 1937.

Levine, Marc V., and Sandra J. Callaghan. *The Economic State of Milwaukee: The City and the Region.* Milwaukee, Wis.: UWM Center for Economic Development, 1998, 11-22.

"Library Exhibit Honors Mrs. Ione Q. Griggs." *Milwaukee* (Wis.) *Journal*, September 17, 1953.

Liguori, Eric W. "Nell Nelson and the *Chicago Times* 'City Slave Girls' Series: Beginning a National Crusade for Labor Reform in the Late 1800s." *Journal of Management History* 18:1 (2012), 61-81.

Loew, Patty. "The Back of the Homefront: Black and American Indian Women in Wisconsin During World War II." *Wisconsin Magazine of History* 82:2 (Winter 1998-99), 82-103.

Loohauis, Jackie. "A Love Story of Long Ago." *Milwaukee* (Wis.) *Journal*, February 14, 1983.

———. "Update: Looking in on a Green Sheet Legend." *Milwaukee* (Wis.) *Journal*, March 15, 1988.

———. "'Dear Mrs. Griggs': A Legend Dies." *Milwaukee* (Wis.) *Journal*, August 19, 1991.

———. "'Dear Mrs. Griggs'..." *Milwaukee* (Wis.) *Journal*, March 31, 1995.

Love, Jean C. "Twenty Questions on the Status of Women Students in Law School." *Wisconsin Women's Law Journal* (Summer 1997), 405-415.

Lutes, Jean Marie. "Sob Sisterhood Revisited." *American Literary History* 15:3 (Fall 2003), 504-532.

"Madison Woman Heads US Group." *Milwaukee* (Wis.) *Sentinel*, August 1, 1966.

"Magician Pulls Puppy from Hat, Makes a Young Lady Very Happy." *Milwaukee* (Wis.) *Journal*, December 30, 1959.

Martin, Douglas. "Robert St. John, 100, Globe-Trotting Reporter and Author." *New York Times*, February 8, 2003.

McBride, Genevieve G. "The Progress of 'Race Men' and 'Colored Women' in the Black Press in Wisconsin, 1892-1985." Pp. 325-348 in H. Lewis Suggs, ed., *The Black Press in the Middle West, 1865-1985.* Westport, Conn.: Greenwood Press, 1996.

_____. "'Forward' Women: Winning the Wisconsin Campaign for the Country's First ERA, 1921." Pp. 79-136 in Peter G. Watson Boone, ed., *The Quest for Social Justice III: Morris Fromkin Memorial Lectures, 1992-2002.* Milwaukee: University of Wisconsin-Milwaukee, 2005.

McBride, Marian. "Mothers Limited by Law." *Milwaukee* (Wis.) *Sentinel*, November 9, 1967.

McClellan, Michelle Lee. "'Lady Lushes': Women Alcoholics in American Society, 1880-1960." Ph.D. dissertation, Stanford University, 2000.

Midanik, L.T., and T.K. Greenfield. "Trends in Social Consequences and Dependence Symptoms in the United States: The National Alcohol Surveys, 1984-1995." *American Journal of Public Health* 90:1 (January 2000), 53-58.

"Miss Quinby Presents Seven Lady Slayers." *Chicago* (Ill.) *Evening Post,* March 20, 1931.

"Miss Wisconsin Goes On to Be Chief Judge." *Milwaukee* (Wis.) *Journal*, October 3, 1985.

Mosby, Wade H. "The Heart of Milwaukee." *American Mercury*, July 1957, 54.

_____. "Her Friends Are Legion." *Milwaukee* (Wis.) *Journal*, March 3, 1980.

"National Guardsmen Patrol Area Where Riot Erupted." *Milwaukee* (Wis.) *Journal*, July 31, 1967.

Nilsson, Jeff. "Then and Now: War, Work, and Women." *Saturday Evening Post.* Accessed July 1, 2012. http://www.saturdayeveningpost.com/2010/07/16/archives/then-and-now/war-work-women.html.

"Obituary: Ann Landers," *Chicago* (Ill.) *Tribune,* June 23, 2002.

Olszewski, Daryl J. "Statutory Rape in Wisconsin: History, Rationale, and the Need for Reform." *Marquette Law Review* 89 (2006), 693-719.

Otto, Jean. "Unwanted Pregnancy Forces Agonizing Decision." *Milwaukee* (Wis.) *Journal*, April 4, 1971.

_____. "Controversy Surrounds Birth Control, Abortion." *Milwaukee* (Wis.) *Journal*, April 6, 1971.

_____. "Girls in Trouble." *Milwaukee* (Wis.) *Journal*, September 26, 1971.

_____. "Girls in Trouble: Teens See No Way Out, So They Run Away." *Milwaukee* (Wis.) *Journal*, September 27, 1971.

_____. "Girls in Trouble: Parents of Runaways Ask Themselves, 'Why?'" *Milwaukee* (Wis.) *Journal*, September 28, 1971.

_____. "Girls in Trouble: Runaways Tell Their Story." *Milwaukee* (Wis.) *Journal*, September 29, 1971.

_____. "Girls in Trouble: Runaway Found, Authorities Seek Answers." *Milwaukee* (Wis.) *Journal*, September 30, 1971.

Park, Robert E. "The Natural History of the Newspaper," *American Journal of Sociology* 29:3 (November 1923), 273-289.

Potter, Claire Bond. "'I'll Go the Limit and Then Some': Gun Molls, Desire, and Danger in the 1930s." *Feminist Studies* 21:1 (Spring 1995), 41-66.

Quinby, Ione. "Vagabonds and Half-Baked Creeds." Pp. 134-135 in Franklin Rosemont, ed., *The Rise & Fall of the Dil Pickle: Jazz Age Chicago's Wildest and Most Outrageously Creative Hobohemian Nightspot*. Chicago: Kerr, 2003.

"Police and FBI Question Youths in Bombing at UW." *Milwaukee* (Wis.) *Journal*, August 26, 1970.

Ramey, Jessie. "The Bloody Blonde and the Marble Woman: Gender and Power in the Case of Ruth Snyder." *Journal of Social History* 37:3 (Spring 2004), 625-650.

Ranney, Joseph A. "Anglicans, Merchants, and Feminists: A Comparative Study of the Evolution of Married Women's Rights in Virginia, New York, and Wisconsin." *William & Mary Journal of Women and the Law* 6:3 (2000), 493-559.

Riback, William H. [Book review.] *American Literature* 5:2 (May 1933), 197.

Ross, J. R. "From First Female Lawmakers to Farrow, Times Have Changed." *Milwaukee* (Wis.) *Journal Sentinel*, April 27, 2001.

Rubin, Rita. "The Pill: 50 Years of Birth Control Changed Women's Lives." *USA Today*, May 8, 2010.

Sandin, Jo. "Women's Strike Day Gets Mixed Support." *Milwaukee* (Wis.) *Journal*, August 26, 1970.

Schaffer, Jan. "Attack Dog, Watch Dog, or Guide Dog: The Role of the Media in BuildingCommunity." Accessed July 1, 2013. http://www.pewcenter. org/doingcj/speeches/sbatonrouge.html.

Schwartz, Felice N. "Management Women and the New Facts of Life." *Harvard Business Review* (January-February 1980), 65-76.

Silvers, Amy Rabideau. "Defense Work Led Wilson to Calling as Union Activist." *Milwaukee*(Wis.) *Journal Sentinel*, January 31, 2008.

Skiba, Katherine. "2 Engaged Officers Spied Upon, Fired." *Milwaukee* (Wis.) *Journal,* September 14, 1978.

Smith, Russell E. "Hinterland Columnists: Heart to Heart Talks Help Human Relations." *Editor & Publisher,* November 27, 1953, n.p.

Steiner, Linda, and Susanne Gray. "Genevieve Forbes Herrick: A Front-Page Reporter'Pleased to Write About Women.'" *Journalism History* 11:1 (Spring 1985), 8-16.

Stevens, John D. "Social Utility of Sensational News: Murder and Divorce in the 1920s." *Journalism Quarterly* 62:1 (Spring 1985), 53-58.

Stingl, Jim. "Woman Literally Gave of Herself to Save Sick Infant." *Milwaukee* (Wis.) *Journal Sentinel,* November 17, 2009.

_____. "35 Years Ago, We Traded Typewriters for Terminals." *Milwaukee* (Wis.) *Journal Sentinel,* May 31, 2011.

Sweet, Ellen. "Date Rape: The Story of an Epidemic and Those Who Deny It." *Ms.* 14:4 (October 1985), 56-58.

Taylor, Leila. "Chamber of Horrors." *Saturday Review of Literature,* May 2, 1931, 798.

Thompson, Bill. "The Milwaukee Radio Market." *Broadcasting,* June 6, 1949, 3-8.

Unger, Nancy C. "The We Say What We Think Club." *Wisconsin Magazine of History* 90:1 (Autumn 2006), 16-27.

University of Wisconsin System Women's Studies Consortium. *Transforming Women's Education: The History of Women's Studies in the University of Wisconsin System.* Madison, Wis.: Office of University Publications, 1999.

Voss, Kimberly Wilmot, and Lance Speere. "Way Past Deadline: The Women's Fight to Integrate the Milwaukee Press Club." *Wisconsin Magazine of History* 92:1 (Autumn 2008), 28-43.

Walker, Juliet E.K. "The Promised Land: The *Chicago Defender* and the Black Press in Illinois, 1862-1970." Pp. 9-50 in H. Lewis Suggs, ed., *The Black Press of the Middle West, 1865-1985.* Westport, Conn.: Greenwood Press, 1996.

"What to Do With Ropes." *Saturday Evening Post,* December 9, 1944, 4.

Wisconsin, State of, Legislative Reference Bureau. "The Evolution of Legalized Gambling in Wisconsin." *Bulletins* (2000).

"Wisconsin's Voice of Conscience: I.Q.G." *Milwaukee* (May 1971), 25.

"Women Form Action Group." *Milwaukee* (Wis.) *Journal,* August 1, 1966.

"Women Lawyers on the Increase." *Gargoyle* 2:1 (Autumn 1970), 6.

Zahn, Michael. "Will Leaves $200,000 for Scholarships." *Milwaukee* (Wis.) *Journal*, April 21, 1992.

Acknowledgments

This work was many years in the making, and that the authors "made deadline" is due to the work of many others on the work in progress. Our research was made possible in part by grants from the Walter J. and Clara Charlotte Damm Fund of the Journal Foundation, through the Greater Milwaukee Foundation; the Office of the Provost and Graduate School of the University of Wisconsin-Milwaukee; and the Graduate Committee of the J. William and Mary Diederich College of Communication at Marquette University. Their grants made possible the contributions of our invaluable research assistants, former students, for whom we remain grateful for diligence in collating, coding, and more: John M. Caspari, Catherine S. Caspari, and Chelsey Pfiffner-Paschall, all of the University of Wisconsin-Milwaukee, and Jingyu Bao, Mandi Lindner, Molly Greenwood, David Kordus, Adam Loferski, and Ishwarya Shankar, all of Marquette University.

Our gratitude also goes to those affiliated with archives, including Betsy Brenner and Alan King of the *Milwaukee Journal Sentinel* for permissions for photographs from its files in the private domain as well as its photos now in the Wisconsin Historical Society's iconographic collection; Lisa R. Marine of the Wisconsin Historical Society; and many former and current members of the staff of the University of Wisconsin-Milwaukee Archives, who have preserved photographs and other records in the incomparable collection of the Milwaukee Press Club, the oldest press club in the country. Gratitude also goes to Mel Kolstad of Fond du Lac, Wisconsin, for her fascination with print artifacts as well as for her artistry in and permission for use of her "Green Sheets" montage from her blog, "Ephemeraology," at http://www.ephemeraology.com.

We are especially grateful to often-unsung volunteer archivists of local historical societies, whose efforts make possible so many historical studies. Alan Gornik of the Western Springs Historical Society opened its archives for us to peruse the Quinby Papers and answered many a call, and Vicki Lezon, Allyson Zak, and others of the society also proved as supportive and provided assistance. We also appreciate the expertise of Richard Roche of the Thomas Ford Memorial Library in Western Springs and other expert librarians on the staffs of the Walter Newberry Library and the Harold G. Washington Library in Chicago, the Illinois State Historical Society in Springfield, the Golda Meir Library of the University of Wisconsin-Milwaukee Libraries, the John P. Raynor Memorial Libraries of Marquette University, and the Central Library of the Milwaukee County Federated Libraries.

Many of our colleagues encouraged us in this project, and we are indebted to Dr. Bonnie S. Brennen of Marquette University, editor of the Diederich Studies in Communication and Media series of the Marquette University Press, Dr. Andrew Tallon, director of the Marquette University Press, and Maureen Kondrick, manager of the Press; Dr. Erik Ugland of Marquette University, and—as ever— Dr. Margo J. Anderson and Dr. Merry E. Wiesner-Hanks of the University of Wisconsin-Milwaukee. We also appreciate the encouragement of respondents to scholarly presentations of portions of this work in progress, notably Drs. Francesca Morgan and Joan Johnson of Northeastern Illinois University, organizers of the Newberry Seminar Series on Women and Gender of the Scholl Center for American History and Culture of the Newberry Library in Chicago. Nearby, Lewis University's Dr. Eileen M. McMahon, as editor, and her reader-referees also made useful recommendations on portions of the first chapter, previously published as "On the Front Page in the 'Jazz Age': Chicago's Ageless 'Girl Reporter,' Ione Quinby," *Journal of the Illinois State Historical Society* 106:1 (Spring 2013), 91-128.

Throughout, we have received encouragement from many former readers of "Dear Mrs. Griggs," including many of her former colleagues and ours in the newsrooms of the *Milwaukee Journal* and *Milwaukee Sentinel* at our irregular gatherings, where we regale each other with the stories behind the stories, the daily journalistic contributions to the historical record of our city, by great storytellers gone too soon. We note with sorrow that this work was so long in progress that it was not read by the late, great storyteller Jackie Loohauis-Bennett of the *Journal*, a close friend of Ione Quinby Griggs and faithful chronicler of her colleague's life, in Jackie's reportage referenced throughout these pages. We wish that Jackie had known that her friend finally would receive, herein, her due recognition, and we regret that we did not benefit from disagreement, no doubt lively as ever, on a few points of dispute between Jackie's record and ours. However, we can predict the result, as she would have agreed that any errors remain our own.

Genevieve G. McBride and Stephen R. Byers

Index

R

S